USED, ABUSED, AND SIDELINED

EDITED BY CHERYL GLENN AND STEPHEN BROWNE

THE PENNSYLVANIA STATE UNIVERSITY

Rhetoric and Democratic Deliberation focuses on the interplay of public discourse, politics, and democratic action. Engaging with diverse theoretical, cultural, and critical perspectives, books published in this series offer fresh perspectives on rhetoric as it relates to education, social movements, and governments throughout the world.

A complete list of books in this series is located at the back of this volume.

USED, ABUSED, AND SIDELINED

DEBATING THE DECLARATION

EDITED BY MARY E. STUCKEY

The Pennsylvania State University Press | University Park, Pennsylvania

This volume is published with the generous support of the Center for Democratic Deliberation at the Pennsylvania State University.

Library of Congress Cataloging-in-Publication Data

Names: Stuckey, Mary E. editor
Title: Used, abused, and sidelined : debating the Declaration / edited by Mary E. Stuckey.
Other titles: Debating the Declaration
Description: University Park, Pennsylvania : The Pennsylvania State University Press, [2025] | Series: Rhetoric and democratic deliberation series ; volume 36 | Collection of essays by Jelte Olthof and 15 others. | Includes bibliographical references and index.
Summary: "Examines the evolving significance of the US Declaration of Independence, analyzing its dual role as both a local and universal document used for liberatory purposes as well as a warrant for both regressive and progressive politics, while questioning its relevance as its 250th anniversary approaches"—Provided by publisher.
Identifiers: LCCN 2025010332 | ISBN 9780271099262 hardback | ISBN 9780271099279 paperback
Subjects: LCSH: United States. Declaration of Independence—Criticism, Textual | Rhetoric—Political aspects—United States | Equality—United States | United States—Politics and government
Classification: LCC E221 .U88 2025 | DDC 973.3/13—dcundefined
LC record available at https://lccn.loc.gov/2025010332

Printed in the United States
Published by The Pennsylvania State University Press, University Park, PA 16802-1003

The Pennsylvania State University Press is a member of the Association of University Presses.

It is the policy of The Pennsylvania State University Press to use acid-free paper. Publications on uncoated stock satisfy the minimum requirements of American National Standard for Information Sciences—Permanence of Paper for Printed Library Material, ANSI Z39.48-1992.

CONTENTS

ACKNOWLEDGMENTS

First and foremost, I have to thank the various authors who contributed their expertise, insight, and acumen to this project; I am in awe of all of them. I also want to thank the series editors, editors, and staff at Penn State University Press: Cheryl Glenn and Steve Browne, Archna Patel, Josie DiKerby, Emily Lovett, and the marketing team have all been great; as well as Gretchen Otto from Motto Publishing Services. The reviewers provided careful, thoughtful, and helpful feedback, and we are all appreciative of their efforts to improve our work. I am immensely grateful to and for my colleagues in the College of the Liberal Arts at Penn State University, and especially those in the Department of Communication Arts & Sciences. There is nothing better than getting to work with great people and smart scholars, and my life here is full of both. Both the Department of Communication Arts & and Sciences and the Graduate School at Penn State provided financial support for this volume, which I deeply appreciate. This project was part of a sabbatical leave and was also supported by my Sparks professorship; I'm truly thankful for these and the many other opportunities I am afforded at Penn State.

Through the Declaration's long history, there have been many people who were excluded by it and damaged by the nation's explicit claims that the United States was a model of democratic inclusion. Many of these people and their allies chose (and choose) to believe in the Declaration's promise and fought (and fight) to bring the nation closer to the ideals so eloquently presented therein. The nation still has a long way to go; that it has come as far as it has is a testament to the suffering, efforts, and achievements of these people. This book is gratefully dedicated to them.

THE DECLARATION OF INDEPENDENCE

In Congress, July 4, 1776.

The unanimous Declaration of the thirteen united States of America,

When in the Course of human events, it becomes necessary for one people to dissolve the political bands which have connected them with another, and to assume among the powers of the earth, the separate and equal station to which the Laws of Nature and of Nature's God entitle them, a decent respect to the opinions of mankind requires that they should declare the causes which impel them to the separation.

We hold these truths to be self-evident, that all men are created equal, that they are endowed by their Creator with certain unalienable Rights, that among these are Life, Liberty and the pursuit of Happiness. — That to secure these rights, Governments are instituted among Men, deriving their just powers from the consent of the governed, — That whenever any Form of Government becomes destructive of these ends, it is the Right of the People to alter or to abolish it, and to institute new Government, laying its foundation on such principles and organizing its powers in such form, as to them shall seem most likely to effect their Safety and Happiness. Prudence, indeed, will dictate that Governments long established should not be changed for light and transient causes; and accordingly all experience hath shewn, that mankind are more disposed to suffer, while evils are sufferable, than to right themselves by abolishing the forms to which they are accustomed. But when a long train of abuses and usurpations, pursuing invariably the same Object evinces a design to reduce them under absolute Despotism, it is their right, it is their duty, to throw off such Government, and to provide new Guards for their future security. — Such has been the patient sufferance of these Colonies; and such is now the necessity which constrains them to alter their former Systems of Government. The history of the present King of Great Britain is a history of repeated injuries and usurpations, all having in direct object the establishment of an absolute Tyranny over these States. To prove this, let Facts be submitted to a candid world.

He has refused his Assent to Laws, the most wholesome and necessary for the public good.

He has forbidden his Governors to pass Laws of immediate and pressing importance, unless suspended in their operation till his Assent should be obtained; and when so suspended, he has utterly neglected to attend to them.

He has refused to pass other Laws for the accommodation of large districts of people, unless those people would relinquish the right of Representation in the Legislature, a right inestimable to them and formidable to tyrants only.

He has called together legislative bodies at places unusual, uncomfortable, and distant from the depository of their public Records, for the sole purpose of fatiguing them into compliance with his measures.

He has dissolved Representative Houses repeatedly, for opposing with manly firmness his invasions on the rights of the people.

He has refused for a long time, after such dissolutions, to cause others to be elected; whereby the Legislative powers, incapable of Annihilation, have returned to the People at large for their exercise; the State remaining in the mean time exposed to all the dangers of invasion from without, and convulsions within.

He has endeavoured to prevent the population of these States; for that purpose obstructing the Laws for Naturalization of Foreigners; refusing to pass others to encourage their migrations hither, and raising the conditions of new Appropriations of Lands.

He has obstructed the Administration of Justice, by refusing his Assent to Laws for establishing Judiciary powers.

He has made Judges dependent on his Will alone, for the tenure of their offices, and the amount and payment of their salaries.

He has erected a multitude of New Offices, and sent hither swarms of Officers to harrass our people, and eat out their substance.

He has kept among us, in times of peace, Standing Armies without the Consent of our legislatures.

He has affected to render the Military independent of and superior to the Civil power.

He has combined with others to subject us to a jurisdiction foreign to our constitution, and unacknowledged by our laws; giving his Assent to their Acts of pretended Legislation:

For Quartering large bodies of armed troops among us:

For protecting them, by a mock Trial, from punishment for any Murders which they should commit on the Inhabitants of these States:

For cutting off our Trade with all parts of the world:

For imposing Taxes on us without our Consent:

For depriving us in many cases, of the benefits of Trial by Jury:

For transporting us beyond Seas to be tried for pretended offences:

For abolishing the free System of English Laws in a neighbouring Province, establishing therein an Arbitrary government, and enlarging its Boundaries so as to render it at once an example and fit instrument for introducing the same absolute rule into these Colonies:

For taking away our Charters, abolishing our most valuable Laws, and altering fundamentally the Forms of our Governments:

For suspending our own Legislatures, and declaring themselves invested with power to legislate for us in all cases whatsoever.

He has abdicated Government here, by declaring us out of his Protection and waging War against us.

He has plundered our seas, ravaged our Coasts, burnt our towns, and destroyed the lives of our people.

He is at this time transporting large Armies of foreign Mercenaries to compleat the works of death, desolation and tyranny, already begun with circumstances of Cruelty & perfidy scarcely paralleled in the most barbarous ages, and totally unworthy the Head of a civilized nation.

He has constrained our fellow Citizens taken Captive on the high Seas to bear Arms against their Country, to become the executioners of their friends and Brethren, or to fall themselves by their Hands.

He has excited domestic insurrections amongst us, and has endeavoured to bring on the inhabitants of our frontiers, the merciless Indian Savages, whose known rule of warfare, is an undistinguished destruction of all ages, sexes and conditions.

In every stage of these Oppressions We have Petitioned for Redress in the most humble terms: Our repeated Petitions have been answered only by repeated injury. A Prince whose character is thus marked by every act which may define a Tyrant, is unfit to be the ruler of a free people.

Nor have We been wanting in attentions to our Brittish brethren. We have warned them from time to time of attempts by their legislature to extend an unwarrantable jurisdiction over us. We have reminded them of the circumstances of our emigration and settlement here. We have appealed to their native justice and magnanimity, and we have conjured them by the ties of our common kindred to disavow these usurpations, which, would inevitably interrupt our connections and correspondence. They too have been deaf to the voice of justice and of consanguinity. We must, therefore, acquiesce in the necessity, which denounces our Separation, and hold them, as we hold the rest of mankind, Enemies in War, in Peace Friends.

We, therefore, the Representatives of the united States of America, in General Congress, Assembled, appealing to the Supreme Judge of the world for the rectitude of our intentions, do, in the Name, and by Authority of the good People of these Colonies, solemnly publish and declare, That these United Colonies are, and of Right ought to be Free and Independent States; that they are Absolved from all Allegiance to the British Crown, and that all political connection between them and the State of Great Britain, is and ought to be totally dissolved; and that as Free and Independent States, they have full Power to levy War, conclude Peace, contract Alliances, establish Commerce, and to do all other Acts and Things which Independent States may of right do. And for the support of this Declaration, with a firm reliance on the protection of divine Providence, we mutually pledge to each other our Lives, our Fortunes and our sacred Honor.

Georgia
Button Gwinnett
Lyman Hall
George Walton

North Carolina
William Hooper
Joseph Hewes
John Penn

South Carolina
Edward Rutledge
Thomas Heyward, Jr.
Thomas Lynch, Jr.
Arthur Middleton

Massachusetts
John Hancock

Maryland
Samuel Chase
William Paca
Thomas Stone
Charles Carroll of Carrollton

Virginia
George Wythe
Richard Henry Lee
Thomas Jefferson
Benjamin Harrison
Thomas Nelson, Jr.
Francis Lightfoot Lee
Carter Braxton

Pennsylvania
Robert Morris
Benjamin Rush
Benjamin Franklin
John Morton
George Clymer
James Smith
George Taylor
James Wilson
George Ross

Delaware
Caesar Rodney
George Read
Thomas McKean

New York
William Floyd
Philip Livingston
Francis Lewis
Lewis Morris

New Jersey
Richard Stockton
John Witherspoon
Francis Hopkinson
John Hart
Abraham Clark

New Hampshire
Josiah Bartlett
William Whipple

Massachusetts
Samuel Adams
John Adams
Robert Treat Paine
Elbridge Gerry

Rhode Island
Stephen Hopkins
William Ellery

Connecticut
Roger Sherman
Samuel Huntington
William Williams
Oliver Wolcott

New Hampshire
Matthew Thornton

INTRODUCTION

Mary E. Stuckey

The US Declaration of Independence was both radically local and determinedly universal.[1] Over its history, the Declaration has served as a warrant for arguments both in the United States and globally; it has been used to advocate for social justice and as a justification for the maintenance of inequitable social hierarchies, and has served as a model for justifying revolutions in other nations and to declare independence from the US federal union. As it turns 250 years old, there are important questions about its history and its continuing relevance. Thinking about its history, we might ask if the Declaration has mostly been used in the cause of freedom or if it has a murkier past, also legitimating injustice.[2] We might also ask if it is still relevant or if the complicated history of US democracy as it has been practiced both at home and overseas has led to a lessening of its rhetorical power. This book addresses these questions while leaving room for readers to answer them for themselves.

The easy version of the role of the Declaration in US political history begins with claims about its importance as the North American British colonies united around a set of universal ideological principles, including natural rights, political equality, and a specific view of republicanism.[3] But it is also true that the nation was built around a set of important exclusions, which are either announced in the Declaration (as in its treatment of Indigenous people) or avoided (as in its treatment of slavery).[4] As Nikole Hannah-Jones writes, "The United States was founded on both an ideal and a lie."[5] Like the Declaration, the US revolution was complicated, and these complexities have continued throughout the history of the nation.

Even after 250 years, the Declaration of Independence remains important. For better or worse, it has long pervaded political discourse in the United States. Not especially important in the immediate aftermath of the revolution, the Declaration gained currency in later years as a definitive statement of US national values. When it is used as a warrant for political belief and a justification for political action, it is also reimagined. While most speakers argue that they (and sometimes they alone) are revealing the "true" meaning and the "original" purpose of the Declaration, this commitment to originalism is often a disguise for relying on specific (and sometimes absurd) renditions of "what the founders really meant." As with many other elements of the nation's founding, people tend to read into that moment what they most want to see. The Declaration is thus an important but not a particularly stable source of political legitimacy.

As the following chapters show, the Declaration is a remarkably flexible document, combining as it does justifications for conflicting and even contradictory arguments about liberty and equality.[6] It was used to justify Southern secession and civil war. It was used to authorize arguments for women's suffrage. It was used during the long civil rights movement to support claims for political equality. It is one of the inspirations for the United Nations' Universal Declaration of Human Rights, passed in 1948. It has been used to legitimate both liberatory and repressive policies.[7] Its signal importance within the United States is reflected in the ways it is mobilized for overtly political purposes such as these but also in its centrality as an icon in popular culture.

The Declaration also has a long global history.[8] It influenced the French Declaration of the Rights of Man in 1789, for example. It was used as a model for early independence movements in places such as Haiti (1804) and Venezuela (1811), as well as other nations. It has been used by Indigenous and other colonized peoples to declare their independence from colonizers (New Zealand, 1835; Vietnam, 1945; Liberia, 1947). It has been an exemplar for those declaring new states on ancient homelands (Israel, 1948; Palestine, 1988). And it has served white minorities seeking independence to maintain their power (Southern Rhodesia, 1965). More recently, the Declaration has provided a generic template for those declaring their independence from the Soviet Union (Ukraine and Belarus, 1991) and was referenced in the Tunisian Constitution (2014).

The gaps in this long history are also important. While in the Western Hemisphere the Declaration's reach has been long and deep, it is less clear that it has had the same impact in other regions, such as Asia, Africa, and the Middle East. Demands for both liberty and equality are increasingly made in terms that center local and Indigenous rhetorical histories, on the one hand, and emphasize global and transnational ideas, on the other. It is not clear, in other words, that the universals that have often been considered reasons for the Declaration's staying power are as universal as its advocates have argued.

Finally, there are questions about whether the Declaration continues to have the power it once enjoyed. As the institutions associated with US democracy are increasingly threatened and appear increasingly fragile, it is possible that new institutions and processes, with different kinds of ideological and rhetorical justifications, will arise. It is also possible that new institutions and processes will require a reinvigorated Declaration. The authors of the following chapters have their own perspectives on these important questions; we invite you to think along with us as you read the various chapters. Before we get to that, however, I want first to offer a bit of history and a quick reading of the meaning of the Declaration, setting the table, so to speak, for the feast to follow.

Declaring Independence

The actual writing of the Declaration has been the subject of significant scholarly discussion and debate—questions about its primary authorship, its editing, and its production have all been well researched and explained.[9] While there were many different documents that authorized, demanded, or discussed independence prior to 1776, the one that emerged then spoke for what would become the entire nation.[10] The actual crafting of the document that would become the Declaration of Independence began in June 1776, when Richard Henry Lee, a delegate to the Second Continental Congress from the colony of Virginia, proposed that the colonies actively declare their independence from Great Britain. The Lee Resolution forced a commitment on the question of independence, asking Congress to make a final and irrevocable decision on the matter. Congress responded by endorsing the proposal and appointed a "Committee of Five" to draft such a document.

The Committee of Five, which included John Adams, Benjamin Franklin, Thomas Jefferson, Robert Livingston, and Robert Sherman, delegated the drafting to Jefferson, known even then for his eloquent pen. Jefferson spent the next weeks, in consultation with his committee, on the draft, which was presented to Congress for debate and discussion on June 28, 1776.[11] It is notable that Jefferson, generally credited as the Declaration's primary author, was accompanied to Philadelphia and attended there by one of those he enslaved, Robert Hemings. The person who penned the words declaring universal human equality was himself a slaver, whose labor on the document was eased by Hemings's invisible work.[12]

Between them, the committee and the Continental Congress made eighty-six total changes to Jefferson's initial draft.[13] The most important of these was the deletion of a 168-word condemnation of the slave trade, which the original draft blamed on King George. This was the first, but by no means the last, time that the tension between the ideals justifying the Revolution and the necessity of protecting slavery in order to preserve unity among the colonies and states would be decided in favor of unity rather than principle.

Practical action was increasingly urgent, as the British fleet sailed into New York harbor on July 2, 1776. Congress responded by adopting the Declaration on July 4, 1776; only John Hancock and Charles Thomson, president and secretary of the Continental Congress, signed it on that day. The Declaration was printed and publicly distributed over the next two days.[14] George Washington ordered it read to the troops on July 9, 1776, and ten days later, Congress ordered it signed by all members of the Continental Congress. It was sent to King George III and to Parliament, arriving in Great Britain in August, and was reprinted and circulated around Europe.[15] It was also circulated throughout the several states of which the United States was now comprised.

Since independence, the original Declaration has wandered around the nation, finding temporary homes in the State, War, and Navy Building, and then the Library of Congress, until it was housed in the National Archives Building in 1952, where more than a million people visit it every year.[16] Considered one of the nation's most sacred texts, it is one of the most read and most quoted documents in US history.

Reading the Declaration

As many scholars have noted, the Declaration has several important elements: it justifies separation from England to the world; it claims that there are self-evident truths; it offers a list of injuries and usurpations; it provides an argument that these have gone unredressed; and it declares independence.[17] My understanding of the document is a little more granular than this, as I want to explain here for your consideration as you engage with the chapters to come.

The Declaration begins with the words "When in the course of human events," an opening that reflects the Enlightenment belief that history is neither given nor inevitable but depends on the actions of those who participate in it. This claim is immediately followed by an assertion that political bonds are dissolvable—and that it is sometimes necessary to do so. This means that politics, unlike "peoplehood," is artificial: political communities are made by humans and can be constructed, destroyed, or reconstructed, as humans deem necessary. Peoplehood, however, the sense of community that underlies these political communities, is not artificial and therefore temporary but is somehow more natural and potentially, at least, more enduring.

Political communities are fictions, human constructions, and as such they are separate and equal. They share something like a station, a place in a hierarchy; which, regardless of the realities of political, economic, and military power, requires that they be equally respected. National rights to equality and respect are in some ways analogous to individual rights, which the Declaration claims are divinely ordained. The "Laws of Nature and Nature's God" provide rights as well as, importantly, the wherewithal to defend them. This equality in turn requires a "decent respect for the opinions of mankind," which also requires that independence be both openly declared and publicly justified, actions that had not been thought necessary in any previous revolution or rebellion but would be, as we shall see throughout this volume, frequently repeated.

Having given human action considerable power, the Declaration then claims that this power is also divinely ordained: "all men are created equal," it states, with equal and unalienable rights. These rights exist prior to government and, because they are God given, are more important than loyalty to government, a human creation. Indeed, governments are legitimate only to the extent that they protect these rights. This passage, is, of course, the most quoted and also the most contentious part of the Declaration. There have been and will continue to be arguments over who, exactly, is included in the phrase "all men." Manifestly, if that term is interpreted in the most expansive way, there is an enormous gap between the theory expressed here and its application in the colonies, where many people were enslaved, where women's rights were severely restricted, and where Indigenous peoples were enmeshed in a variety of complicated sets of relationships, very few of which admitted of even the possibility of equality. If, however, the phrase was meant to refer only to white men above a certain age who owned sufficient property, those admitted to full membership in the polity, then the power of the claim is as restricted as its application—a conundrum indeed.

Equally problematic is the list of rights provided. Undoubtedly it is meant to be illustrative rather than complete, yet only some rights were thought worth mentioning—namely, life, liberty, and the pursuit of happiness. Governments, then, were charged with protecting the lives, the liberty, and the opportunity for material success (which is what the signers understood the pursuit of happiness to mean) and were legitimate only to the extent that they did so. That legitimacy rested on the popular will: the people alone had the right to determine whether governments so constituted were doing their duty. And if they failed in that duty, the people were obligated to take action—even violent action—to protect those rights.

Then, follows a long list of misdeeds perpetrated by the British king (notably, by the king, not the British people). The details of this list are less important here than the fact of the list: it constitutes a claim that even though political communities are temporary, they shouldn't be changed on a whim but only for good and sufficient reasons.

The appeal of this document is easy to see. It sets forth, in eloquent language, claims that allowed for various understandings of divinely ordained human rights. It gave agency to that mysterious entity, "the people," and it provided them with rights as well as both the capacity and the obligation to defend them. In theory, this seems so very simple; in practice, it has proven to be anything but.

The Complicated Declaration

The Declaration of Independence is fraught with a number of notable tensions, many of which have animated political debates throughout US national history. First and most obviously, the Declaration, endorsed by a collection of slaveholders and those willing to allow the continuation of slavery, announces as a self-evident truth the fact of human equality. This most famous element of the document has been used to justify appeals for policies and practices that bring the nation closer to the ideal, as we see in the eloquent prose of speakers such as Abraham Lincoln and Martin Luther King Jr. It has also been used to opposite ends, of course, as in the language of secessionists and the contemporary Alt-Right, those who advocate white supremacy and oppose gender, religious, and racial equality. But it is not clear who exactly is included in the phrase "all men." Certainly, if we read the document in terms of its immediate context, the exclusions of the enslaved, women, many immigrants, and Indigenous peoples is stark. We can read the document, as Lincoln and King chose to, as offering what the latter called a "promissory note," of more equality to come, or we can read it as secessionists did, as offering intended and eternal exclusions. Its prose proved to be something of a bind for members of Indigenous nations, for example, who sought to maintain their sovereignty within an increasingly colonized context. The Declaration has proven to be unevenly useful in arguments for more equal treatment among American citizens made by workers, women, and African Americans, and to claims for human rights in places like Eastern Europe.

Other tensions appear when we move between the general and the specific. There is a question about whether and how these universals apply to members of the international community, especially to non-European nations. Many of those who signed the Declaration governed a nation with imperial ambitions. And while other nations, such as the French and the Haitians, took inspiration from the document, and it helped inspire revolutions in Latin America, it is not necessarily clear that the signers would have endorsed all of these causes with equal fervor. And it is not clear, as the case of Syria indicates, that these universal claims have power in all cultural and political contexts.

This points to yet another tension, one that mediates between claims to unity and justifications for division and separation. It is not clear what exactly makes a group of humans "a people." Nor is it obvious how long "peoplehood" endures or exactly how these transient political bonds are to be maintained. Some of these ambiguities are clear in the rhetorical contortions that characterized arguments for southern secession; others are apparent at other moments and in other contexts, including both Indigenous and Alt-Right claims to sovereignty.

There is also a tension between how the Declaration might have been understood in its own time and across time. It is not clear if contemporary citizens are obligated to the document's original meaning and context, and if so, what the nature of that obligation might be. Knowing the original meaning is complicated enough; translating it into a contemporary context is even more so. Viewing its meaning through the lens of popular culture, examining it in light of how it is fragmented, reconstructed, and repurposed as a matter of cultural practice and public policy, illuminates this tension. The signers tend to be treated as whoever various advocates need them to be.

And finally, there is a tension between the needs that were reflected in the original document and the needs of the contemporary political world. Specifically, the notions of grievance and injustice that motivated the Declaration may now be echoed in ways that harm rather than nurture the nation and the world. It is possible that reorienting ourselves to the Declaration, aiming at an ethical politics of care, would help ease some of the political tensions in the nation and point toward more ethical global possibilities.

The chapters that follow tease out these tensions by presenting a set of overlapping conversations about the Declaration. We begin with the document's early history, with chapters from Jelte Olthof, Stephen Howard Browne, and Anna Young. Olthof starts us off by discussing the immediate audiences and reception of the document. Then Browne details the intrinsic tensions within the Declaration, which both caused consternation and conflict in the immediate moment and allowed for various interpretations of it over time. Young adds to those observations by putting the Declaration in conversation with the Constitution, focusing on questions of style and pointing toward ways that the Declaration, as an example of masculine style, has contoured national politics, not always in beneficial ways.

The second section focuses on how the Declaration influences interpretations of appropriate civic action, especially regarding relations between the states and the federal government. Mary Stuckey begins that conversation by attending to the arguments used by antebellum Americans to justify their very different views on slavery and its abolition, secession, and war. This chapter marks secession as justified in the service of protecting slavery and thus antithetical to the Declaration's values. Jason Edward Black complicates this view by focusing his attention on the question of sovereignty and Indigenous nations in the United States. Stephen Heidt makes a similar move, attending to the use of the Declaration in Latin America. Scott Varda contributes to this conversation through a discussion of how claims to national sovereignty are used to justify individual claims to sovereignty.

The third section concentrates on some of the ways the Declaration is used to argue for imperative moral action, especially in terms of human rights. Mary Anne Trasciatti begins this section by examining how the Declaration was used to justify radical arguments in the early twentieth century. Davis Houck adds to that discussion with attention to the arguments used throughout the long civil rights movement. The focus then shifts to the international arena, as Noor Ghazal Aswad casts some doubt on the international power of the Declaration, arguing that contemporary Syrians find more leverage in other sources, and Rebecca Oliver analyzes the Velvet Revolution in Czechoslovakia, which centered the Declaration.

The final section brings the conversation back to where it began, focusing again on questions of the tensions and contradictions the document has always contained. Christopher Wernecke and Ann Burnette underline the contemporary relevance of the Declaration by analyzing its prevalence and meaning in popular culture. Leslie Hahner shows how the Declaration has been fragmented and repurposed to serve specific ideological ends, and Mark Hlavacik notes its usefulness in arguments about public education and the "culture wars." Brandon Inabinet concludes by focusing on the question of what kinds of "abuses and usurpations" the Declaration prepares us to tolerate and what kinds to resist, as well as how we might rely on the Declaration to create a different kind of politics in the future.

All of these chapters are motivated by efforts to understand the Declaration, both in its time and in ours. They unite to illustrate its continuing power and the limits on that power. It is easy to celebrate the Declaration as fundamental to individual human rights. It is worth remembering, however, that it is also open to deliberation, to contention, and to interpretations that serve undemocratic ends. Like the United States, it has a rich, textured, and complicated history.

NOTES

1. A number of books address the processes of writing and signing the Declaration. See, for example, Becker, *Declaration of Independence*; Grafton, *Declaration of Independence*; Maier, *American Scripture*; Skousen, *How to Read the Constitution*.

2. The Constitution is equally complicated and equally pliable. See Goldstein, *Real Americans*.

3. For an insightful analysis of the document's political, historical, and rhetorical antecedents, see Lucas, "Rhetorical Ancestry."

4. For a discussion of these exclusions, see Parkinson, *Thirteen Clocks*.

5. Hannah-Jones, "America Was Not a Democracy," 11.

6. Allen, *Our Declaration*.

7. And sometimes even liberatory efforts have dangerous contradictions. See, for example, Greene, "Social Argumentation."

8. See, for example, Armitage, *Declaration of Independence*.

9. Becker, *Declaration of Independence*; Grafton, *Declaration of Independence*; Maier, *American Scripture*.

10. Pauline Maier found over eighty such documents; see Maier, *American Scripture*.

11. A fragment of the original draft was discovered in 1947, indicating that Jefferson worked and reworked the prose. That fragment is now held by the Library of Congress.

12. Hannah-Jones, "America Was Not a Democracy."

13. See the Library of Congress's timeline: https://www.loc.gov/exhibits/jefferson/jeffdec.html.

14. These versions were printed by John Dunlap and are now known as the "Dunlap Broadsides"; fewer than thirty of them exist today.

15. This circulation was somewhat limited, as the Declaration was written in English and the language of diplomacy at the time was French.

16. Ritzenthaler and Nicholson, "Declaration of Independence."

17. Scholars differ on the number of parts; I've chosen these as the most extensive. See Armitage, *Declaration of Independence*, 26–28.

BIBLIOGRAPHY

Allen, Danielle. *Our Declaration: A Reading of the Declaration of Independence in Defense of Equality*. New York: W. W. Norton, 2014.

Armitage, David. *The Declaration of Independence: A Global History*. Cambridge, MA: Harvard University Press, 2007.

Becker, Carl Lotus. *The Declaration of Independence: A Study in the History of Political Ideas.* New York: Harcourt, Brace, 1922.

Goldstein, Jared A. *Real Americans: National Identity, Violence, and the Constitution.* Lawrence: University Press of Kansas, 2022.

Grafton, J., ed. *The Declaration of Independence and Other Great Documents of American History: 1775–1865.* New York: Dover, 2000.

Greene, Ronald Walter. "Social Argumentation and the Aporias of State Formation: The Palestinian Declaration of Independence." *Argumentation and Advocacy* 29, no. 3 (1993): 124–36.

Hannah-Jones, Nikole. "America Wasn't a Democracy, until Black Americans Made It One." *New York Times Magazine* 14 (2019).

Lucas, Stephen E. "The Rhetorical Artistry of the Declaration of Independence." *Rhetoric and Public Affairs* 1, no. 2 (1998): 143–84.

Maier, Pauline. *American Scripture: Making the Declaration of Independence.* New York: Vintage, 2012.

Parkinson, Robert G. *Thirteen Clocks: How Race United the Colonies and Made the Declaration of Independence.* Charlottesville: University of North Carolina Press, 2021.

Ritzenthaler, Mary Lynn, and Catherine Nicholson. "The Declaration of Independence and the Hand of Time." *Prologue Magazine* (National Archives) 48, no. 3 (Fall 2016). https://www.archives.gov/publications/prologue/2016/fall/declaration.

Skousen, Paul B. *How to Read the Constitution and the Declaration of Independence.* Salt Lake City, UT: Izzard Ink, 2017.

PART I

THE DECLARATION IN ITS TIME

1

AN APPEAL TO THE TRIBUNAL OF THE WORLD: THE RECEPTION OF THE TIMELY AND TIMELESS MESSAGES OF THE DECLARATION IN 1776 AND BEYOND

Jelte Olthof

Who was the Declaration of Independence written for? The answer to this simple question is as complicated as the supposed self-evident truths proclaimed by it. This difficulty stems from the fact that, as Philip Detweiler points out, "the Declaration has had a different message at different times for different persons."[1] This, of course, is true for most texts, but what makes the Declaration particularly interesting—or difficult—is that it contains at least two such messages—one universal, the other particular to the world in 1776—that fell in and out of favor with the two main audiences—foreign and domestic—at different times over its 250-year career.

The authors of the Declaration, as Jack Rakove notes, faced a "perplexing cluster" of considerations and had to "calculate what effect a formal declaration would have on US American public opinion, on the British government and public, at the courts of potential European allies, and upon the authority and influence of Congress itself."[2] To make matters even more complicated, Thomas Jefferson—its principal author—lived to the ripe old age of eighty-three and offered varying statements later in life on the aims of his most famous piece of writing. As I will explain below, Jefferson witnessed and was actively involved in changing the reputation of the Declaration from its immediate purpose of justifying revolution and rallying support for independence to a sacred testament of the universal rights of man. Especially later in life, Jefferson claimed not just to have written for his fellow colonists or even the European courts but for all mankind.

Today, this latter view of the Declaration dominates. Stephen Lucas notes the "enormous gulf" between the contemporary reverence for the Declaration and its original purpose. "Posterity has made the Declaration a *timeless* document," he writes, "but Jefferson and Congress were satisfied in 1776 that it be *timely*. Indeed, had it failed to be timely, chances are it would never have become timeless."[3] That the timeless message of the Declaration was indeed timely becomes clear when we realize the paradoxical nature of self-evidence, as Lynn Hunt argues. After all, she writes, "if equality of rights is so self-evident, then why did this assertion have to be made" in a declaration in the first place? Can these rights be said to be self-evident, she asks, "when scholars have argued for more than two hundred years about what Jefferson meant by his phrase?"[4]

In this chapter, I want to start answering the question of who the audience of the Declaration was, and continues to be, by studying both its timely and timeless messages. In doing so, I will treat the Declaration as a rhetorical intervention that persuaded audiences across time and space. While its immediate message was clearly designed to convince those living at the time—on both sides of the Atlantic—the rhetoric of the Declaration is also universal in its appeal and reaches across the time and place that gave birth to it. Jefferson's words have touched readers who may never have heard of him and only had a faint notion of the republic to which they gave birth.

In the following sections, I shall begin by looking at the timely Declaration's audience and then proceed to the timeless one. In both cases, this audience must be understood to be twofold:[5] one was and is "domestic"—that is, the US American colonists and posterity—and the other global—namely, the world that first took notice of the Declaration and has responded to it since. After looking more closely at whom Thomas Jefferson (claimed he) had in mind when drafting the Declaration, I shall discuss the immediate reception of the Declaration in the colonies and the three main European powers that it addressed: Britain, France, and the Netherlands. The final topic will be the timeless audience to whom Jefferson claimed to speak and how the universal message of the Declaration took hold in the United States and abroad.

The Timely Declaration

We are accustomed and encouraged today to view the Declaration as a sacred document whose timeless principles supposedly form the essence of the US

American political creed. One of the best-selling books on the history of the drafting, ratification, and reception of the document bears the telling title *American Scripture*. In this book, Pauline Maier shows that Jefferson himself played a crucial role in this sacralization of the Declaration by, among other things, suggesting it as a theme to John Trumbull for one of his epic paintings and even supplying a sketch for him.[6] Tellingly, the original words he chose for the most famous phrase in the Declaration was "We hold these truths to be sacred and undeniable."

This view, of the Declaration as sacred scripture, would have astonished many of those who actually adopted and signed it in 1776. Jefferson was acutely aware of this and, in a letter written in 1825, points out that the Declaration's main aim was to make "an appeal to the *tribunal of the world* . . . for our justification, this was the object of the Declaration of Independence. Not to find out new principles, or new arguments, never before thought of, not merely to say things which had never been said before; but to place before *mankind* the common sense of the subject, in terms so plain and firm as to command their assent, and to justify ourselves in the independent stand we are compelled to take."[7] In Jefferson's telling, the main aim of the Declaration was, in other words, to persuade those outside the Continental Congress that the colonies were justified in declaring themselves an independent nation. This view of the Declaration as justifying to the world the Resolution for Independence, adopted by Congress two days earlier, was directed at those living during the summer of 1776. This immediate audience, "the tribunal of the world," was the one Jefferson and his coauthors could picture in their minds and that they intended to persuade of the righteousness of their cause.

Jefferson's letter brings into focus an often-overlooked aspect of the Declaration—namely, that it was meant as much for foreign as domestic consumption. Its main audience today—apart from students of history—may be US American, but it was clearly written as a public document, meant to reach the coffeehouses and coffee tables of the Old World in particular. Jefferson's notes of the debate in the Continental Congress over the summer of 1776 show that this foreign audience was constantly in the minds of the American revolutionaries. In fact, the proponents and opponents of the Declaration quarreled vigorously over how European powers would respond to independence. Those reluctant to declare independence feared that European powers would ally with Britain to prevent the fever of independence from spreading to their possessions in the Americas. Proponents of independence, on the other hand, claimed that it was crucial for obtaining foreign support, since only by declaring independence would trade and diplomatic relations with European powers become possible. France and Spain, they argued, would realize that their best option was to side with the colonies against Britain, but "should they refuse, we shall be but where we are; whereas without trying we shall never know whether they will aid us or not."[8]

As this debate shows, delegates of the Congress were acutely aware of the global ripples their decision would make in the Atlantic world. As the quotation illustrates, many at the time viewed declaring independence as a political Hail Mary pass. As we will see, their fear that the self-proclaimed friends of the colonies' cause in Europe might not back up their words with action were not unfounded. International diplomacy clearly played an important role in the decision to declare independence and, as the debate illustrates, Congress's ambition went beyond simply notifying the inhabitants of the thirteen colonies of the birth of this new republic called the United States.

In short, the "tribunal"—to stay with Jefferson's metaphor—that the Declaration appealed to was both domestic and foreign; it extended all the way from ordinary colonists to the king of France. In order to persuade this vast and varied audience, the language of the Declaration aimed to address both particular grievances suffered by US American colonists—the "long train of abuses"—as well as universal principles and rights that would resonate beyond the thirteen colonies. While the reception of the Declaration in the thirteen colonies has received a lot of scholarly attention, the study of its global reception has only become more serious in recent decades. It is on these two contemporary audiences in 1776 that I will focus before moving on to the Declaration's timeless appeal to global posterity.

Domestic Audiences

Jefferson's letter quoted above was written from the comfortable certainty that, by the mid-1820s, the Declaration had succeeded in its aim of establishing the United States as an independent republic on the world stage. Even though the recent conflict over Missouri's admission had shocked Jefferson and laid bare the shaky foundations of the union, his mind was mostly set on securing his position in history.[9] In old age, Jefferson seemed greatly concerned with making sure posterity would remember him as the author of the Declaration and resigned to leaving the fate of the union it had created in the hands of the next generation.[10]

It is important to keep in mind what the political situation in the early summer of 1776 looked like. With war raging in Massachusetts and spreading across the colonies, it was not at all clear that independence could be secured. Moreover, it was clear to everyone involved that simply declaring independence did not automatically make it so. For the United States to truly function as an independent state, this independence had to be recognized: first by the inhabitants of the colonies themselves, who were sharply divided between Tories and patriots, and then by the international community—Great Britain among them—as well.

The immediate goal of the Declaration in 1776, in other words, was for the US American colonists to adhere to and support their claim to independence and for the rest of the world to accept it and, in the case of France, the Netherlands, and other rivals of Great Britain, to ally themselves with the United States and aid it in making independence real. As a result of this dependence on foreign approval, both George Billias and David Armitage have noted that the proper title for the document should be "declaration of *inter*dependence." As Billias points out, the colonies left the "relative insularity imposed by being a part of the British Empire" and tried to become "a member of the international community."[11] The same holds true, of course, for the local audience. Without strong popular support, as Rakove notes, the decision to declare independence would ring hollow and fail to lend credence to the American cause.[12]

Interestingly, scholars disagree about who among these two—local or global—was the *primary* audience of the Declaration back in 1776. For David Armitage, this audience was global. "Americans," he writes, "were not the audience to which the text implicitly directed its argument. That was instead the 'Opinions of Mankind,' the collective public opinion of the powers of the earth."[13] He points to the concerns in Congress about being taken seriously internationally without a public claim to independence and the fear of being partitioned by the European powers.[14] As stated earlier, this certainly loomed large in the minds of many delegates. For a long time, however, most scholars treated the Declaration as intended primarily for the inhabitants of the thirteen colonies.[15] Stephen Lucas makes this case most explicitly; for him, the "rhetorical brilliance" of the Declaration lies in its ability to persuade colonists from all walks of life and with different points of view. To be sure, Lucas does not deny that the Declaration was meant for a foreign audience or even posterity, but he writes that "they were not the readers for whom the Declaration was *primarily* intended. . . . The key audience for the Declaration was not humanity in general but the people of America."[16]

In the end, the debate over who constituted the primary audience of the Declaration forces an unnecessary issue. Clearly, the document aimed to address both, as the opening paragraph illustrates by connecting the local ("one people") with the global ("the opinions of mankind") audience. For some members of Congress—including the delegates from embattled Massachusetts—obtaining the support of their sister colonies was probably more important than international support. For various reasons, many colonists were less than enthusiastic about independence.[17] Those who relied on Great Britain for their livelihood, including merchants and administrators but also planters, farmers, and artisans whose products were shipped to Britain, viewed independence as potential economic ruin. It is no coincidence that the colonies of Pennsylvania and New York—home to bustling commercial ports—were slow to come around to the idea. Apart from economic interest, there was also tradition. Many colonists were proud to call themselves Britons and feared giving up their guaranteed rights as English subjects—however damaged of late—and replacing these with the uncertain title of "American."[18]

A sizable share of those who opposed independence can even be said to have been beyond persuasion. These so-called loyalists took the side of Britain in the conflict, and most initially welcomed the redcoats as restorers of order. Estimates about their size vary greatly among scholars—from one-fifth of the population to half—since many who sympathized with Britain chose to hide their true loyalties out of fear for their livelihood, family, and safety.[19] In addition, the Revolutionaries painted the loyalist group as fringe to make it seem as if the colonists were united in their opposition to Britain.[20] The rhetoric of the Declaration, with its emphasis on "one people" separating from another, is a good case in point: Jefferson carefully chose his words to make it seem as if the colonies spoke with one voice, even though many were fearful and even opposed independence outright.[21]

The public reading of the Declaration across the thirteen colonies, often followed by public celebrations, may have been a response to this hesitation.[22] As Jay Fliegelman has shown, Jefferson intended this public role for the Declaration and that it be read out loud.[23] In other words, independence was quite literally declared publicly to the colonial audience. Whether this helped sway public opinion in favor of independence is hard to say, but if the aim was to make it appear as if the colonies were united in their struggle, these public celebrations certainly helped make it seem so. The international response to the Declaration, however, would not turn out to be as encouraging.

International Audiences

As Carl Becker points out in his classic study of the political ideas underpinning the Declaration, its primary purpose was "to convince a candid world that the colonies had a moral and legal right to separate from Great Britain."[24] Becker's view of the aim of the Declaration is amply supported by the concluding paragraph of the Declaration, which famously states, "We, therefore, the Representatives of the united States of America, . . . do, in the Name, and by Authority of the good People of these Colonies, solemnly publish and declare, That these United Colonies are, and of Right ought to be Free and Independent States . . . and that as Free and Independent States, they have full Power to levy War, conclude Peace, contract Alliances, establish Commerce, and to do all other Acts and Things which Independent States may of right do." War and alliances, in short, were the reasons why Congress wanted to declare independence to the international community. For both these purposes, the colonies had to cease their reliance on Great Britain as colonies and form an independent state. The Declaration served to achieve the former—independence—while the political union was the work of a separate commission altogether.[25]

As the Declaration was making its way across the ocean to Britain and the European continent, many delegates no doubt waited impatiently for reactions from Europe. The Declaration was published in full in London newspapers in early August. From there it spread across the British Isles and to the continent. An important step along the way was its publication on August 30, in French translation, in the widely read Dutch newspaper *Gazette de Leyde*.[26] As Armitage points out, French was still the leading language in diplomatic circles, and publication in the *Gazette de Leyde* made the text available to a larger audience than the original could reach.[27] By September it had reached Copenhagen, Florence, and Warsaw.[28]

Now let's take a closer look at the immediate reception in the three places most prominently in the minds of the drafters of the Declaration, namely, Britain, France, and the Netherlands. Though few expected positive reviews, the reactions in Britain were of particular interest to Congress. By the time the Declaration appeared in London newspapers, four copies had separately reached the desk of the British prime minister. Few reactions were favorable. "A more impudent, false, and atrocious Proclamation was never fabricated by the Hands of Man," one British official noted before dispatching the Declaration to his superiors.[29] The significance of the Declaration was not lost on the British government, of course, but nevertheless no official reply was issued from Westminster. The British government *could not* officially respond to the Declaration, one pamphleteer argued, since this would mean that they "recognized that equality and independence, to which subjects, persisting in revolt, cannot fail to pretend."[30] The danger of this went beyond the colonists themselves: recognition—even in denial—of the Declaration of Independence could be invoked by hostile foreign powers (most notably France) to claim that the war in North America was one between separate states, in which they could interfere, rather than an internal affair, in which they could not.

The overseas audience that Congress hoped to persuade with the Declaration did not live in London but in places such as Paris and The Hague. Congress hoped the Declaration would convince the French and Spanish governments that the colonies' bid for independence was serious. Four days after the Declaration was adopted, Congress sent a copy to Silas Deane, their agent in France, with the instruction to "immediately communicate the piece to the Court of France."[31] Unfortunately for Congress, this copy was lost, and Deane did not get his hands on an official copy of the Declaration before November 1776. When the French government eventually did react, their response was similar to that of Britain. Although sympathetic, the French government declined to act immediately out of fear of betting on a losing horse. Instead of an alliance, Deane received a polite but resolute "Merci." It would take the better part of two years, after the American victory against the British at Saratoga in 1778, before the French government agreed to an official alliance.

In the Dutch Republic, the official response to the Declaration was similar. The Declaration first appeared in print in the abovementioned *Gazette de Leyde* in late August 1776. Congress had hoped that the news would give them access to the fabled wealth of the Dutch bankers in the form of loans necessary to wage an all-out war against the British. The Dutch Republic of the late eighteenth century was no longer a great military power, but its financial assistance and the arms and munition it could smuggle through the island of St. Eustatius were just as important.[32] For the famously parsimonious Dutch bankers, however, the young United States seemed too risky an investment at the time, and to the great chagrin of the first American envoy to the Netherlands, John Adams, they refused to put their money where their mouth was. As Dutch historian Jan Willem Schulte Nordholt notes, "It was for money that John Adams came to Holland, but it took him two years to obtain it."[33] Only in 1782, long after the French had entered the war, did the Dutch Republic sign the much-coveted treaty with the United States.

While the official response in Great Britain and Europe was one of diplomatic silence, public reactions to the Declaration were much more outspoken. In Britain, the liberal opposition to Prime Minister North saw independence as vindication of his disastrous North American policy. Few supported independence outright, but many wrote glowingly of the Revolution as a model for domestic reform. One example is the prominent minister and writer Richard Price, who stopped short of endorsing independence but celebrated the United States as mankind's best hope for the future.[34]

In France, public enthusiasm to the news of independence was, in no small part, fueled by schadenfreude over its long-standing rival and enemy Great Britain.[35] The marquis de Condorcet aptly captured this sentiment when he wrote, "America had hardly declared its independence when political leaders clearly understood that this happy revolution would necessarily result in the ruin of England and the prosperity of France."[36] As in Britain, it was initially not so much the words of the Declaration that enthused people but the blow to the British Empire that it symbolized. At the same time, the Declaration's message of resistance to oppression provided a model for many reform-minded Europeans and doubled their efforts at home as well.[37] For yet others, the events in America held little significance and were viewed mostly as specific to the colonies and having limited applicability outside of it. During the debates on the French counterpart to the Declaration, the comte de Lally-Tollendal noted the "enormous difference" between the "recently born . . . colonial people breaking away from a distant government" and the "ancient" French people.[38]

In the Netherlands, finally, public reaction to the Declaration among the reform-minded Patriotten Party was also elated. One of the leaders of this movement, Joan Derk van der Capellen tot den Pol, was an early enthusiast of all things American and provided a Dutch translation of the Declaration.[39] Radical leaders in the northern province of Friesland even went as far as to urge the Estates General—the central governing assembly of the Dutch Republic—to recognize American independence straight away, much to the chagrin of the more cautious patricians.[40]

In sum, even where the Declaration was greeted with great enthusiasm—as was the case among the French and Dutch elites, for whom America was thought to be entirely *en vogue*—the official declaration of their independence did not immediately bring Congress the alliances and support they had hoped for. Both the French and Dutch governments refused to aid the US cause until it became clear that the former colonists stood a chance against the British army. Independence—it is a cliché—was won on the battlefield, though the eventual contributions of the French navy in particular proved crucial for that victory.

The Timeless Declaration

After the signing of the Peace of Paris of 1783, in which Great Britain formally acknowledged US independence, the first phase or life cycle of the Declaration ended. With independence recognized at home and abroad, the primary and immediate persuasive goal of the Declaration was achieved. President Woodrow Wilson famously voiced this understanding of the Declaration in his Fourth of July address of 1914 when he called it "a mere historic document" that had served its original purpose and, in this sense, had lost "its national significance." For Wilson and his generation, independence was completely self-evident; the real question was how the United States should comport itself in the future. "It is one thing to be independent," Wilson told the crowd gathered at Independence Square, "and it is another thing to know what to do with your independence." Here, as Wilson himself emphasized, the "spirit" of the Declaration and "the immortal voices" that proclaimed it served as a beacon for "all generations" of Americans yet to come.[41]

Wilson's speech evinces the transition from the immediate aim—and audience—of the Declaration to its timeless quality and appeal. This latter aim can be called universal in the sense that it transcends time and place, and it is most clearly articulated, of course, in the self-evident truths by way of which the revolt against the British Empire was justified. While this universal quality of the Declaration was recognized from the start, it became the focal point of the document in the decades after independence was achieved. Over time, it gave the Declaration the sacred status that it still enjoys in US political life and served as a source of inspiration and blueprint for countless activists in and outside the United States seeking their own version of independence. I shall first look at how the Declaration assumed its sacred status in the United States and continues, for better or worse, to inspire reverence there today and then turn briefly to the global reception of the Declaration's universal message.

The Declaration as a Sacred Domestic Document

As Pauline Maier demonstrates, the sacralization of the Declaration really picked up steam after the conclusion of the War of 1812 with the Peace of Ghent (1815). This so-called Second War of Independence inspired a renewed interest in the people and events of the Revolution that led, among others, to Trumbull's famous painting depicting the committee presenting their draft to Congress, which he finished in 1818.[42] This process of "domestication" of the Declaration, as Armitage calls it, meant that the document had to be detached from its world-historical context and "made into something specifically American." In the process, the modern understanding of the Declaration as extending a promise of equality to posterity took hold. "It was in the light of this renewed interest that the second paragraph of the Declaration began its progress towards becoming the heart of the Declaration's meaning in the United States," Armitage writes. "When peace had been restored with Britain, and the precise incidents that lay behind the grievances in the main body of the Declaration had been forgotten, all of substance that remained to be revered was the second paragraph."[43]

In Fourth of July speeches and celebrations, emphasis shifted more and more from the story of independence to the self-evident truths proclaimed in the Declaration. Especially after Jefferson's and Adams's coinciding deaths on July 4, 1826, the growing distance from the actual events of the Revolution allowed for an increased emphasis on the timelessness of the Declaration. Maier quotes Lincoln, who praises Jefferson's foresight in "introduc[ing] into a merely revolutionary document, an abstract truth, applicable to all men and all times."[44] As she points out, not everyone bought into this new narrative of reverence, of course. Both slave-owners and Abolitionists resisted this version of the Declaration. John Calhoun, the South's stalwart defender of states' rights, claimed that Jefferson's words referred to men in the state of nature and in no way called into question the inferiority of slaves to their masters. For him, the Declaration was a historical document aimed at establishing independence and contained no universal message of political principles beyond that.[45] Frederick Douglass, on the contrary, exposed the Fourth of July as a "hollow mockery," and in doing so, he and other opponents of slavery turned the Declaration into a promise of equality that needed to be made real.[46] The fusing of the two functions—revolution and self-evident truths—was completed most prominently by Martin Luther King Jr. in his famous "I Have A Dream" speech.[47]

Global Reception

From the start, the timeless message of the Declaration was aimed to convince audiences abroad as well. Congress had originally claimed the right to resist Parliament's taxes *as Britons* in a number of official statements, but these failed to resonate with the British government. As the conflict worsened, however, some colonists started to consider other sources for their claim to autonomy.[48] By the spring of 1776, it dawned on Congress that claiming the right to resist oppression as mere Britons would never convince the outside world, while building their case on universal rights would. As Scott Gerber notes, the Declaration "became the act that turned what had begun as a colonial struggle for the rights of Englishmen into a struggle for the rights of man."[49] In line with the Enlightenment thinking of the time, this gave the Declaration a timeless and universal character, as Becker explains, since "the rights and laws which, being suited to man in general, were most likely to be suited to particular men, everywhere and always."[50]

There is, however, a fascinating debate over the extent to which this timeless message was intended and understood at the time. On the one hand is the universal message that any government abusive to its people should be overthrown, while, on the other, there is the particular case for the legitimacy of the colonies to do just this in light of British despotism. US Americans have since debated which of the two should dominate our understanding of the Declaration. In the wake of the French Revolution, prominent Federalists hastened to distance "their" revolution from the bloody conflict that they witnessed across the Atlantic in France.[51] Following in their footsteps, some scholars have also denied the revolutionary character of the Revolution in general and the Declaration in particular. David Armitage, for example, claims that the authors of the Declaration were "decidedly *un*revolutionary" and wanted to "conform as far as possible to the regulatory norms of contemporary politics. Least of all would it [the Declaration] be an incitement to rebellion or revolution elsewhere in the world, rather than an inducement to reform."[52] Richard Morris, on the other hand, points out that the American Revolution contained a "subversive message" and a "new mystique of world revolution," and argues that "Americans were by no means innocent of responsibility for launching it."[53]

As far as the reception in Europe is concerned, the oft-quoted favorable response to the Declaration reported by Franklin—"all Europe is now on our side of the question"—concerned the former message, not the latter. Billias claims that the Declaration was "viewed as America's specific response to British tyranny," not tyranny in general. He points out that the Continental Congress could not hope to secure French military assistance while simultaneously questioning the foundations of its absolute monarchy.[54] While it may be true that most delegates to the Congress were more concerned with establishing independence than spreading republicanism beyond their shores in 1776, it is clear they never had control over how their words would be interpreted and by whom. In this light, it is hard to maintain, as Gordon Wood does, that "no one in his right mind dared suggest deposing kings and replacing them with republican governments. That was dangerous, seditious, and treasonous."[55] Billias seems to recognize this when he writes that "America had given them [those hoping to reform France] a living example."[56]

This view of the Declaration as spreading the gospel of liberty is one endorsed by Jefferson's letter quoted at the beginning of this chapter. The Declaration, he claims, was written "for mankind," not just those living in 1776, and in this reading the "tribunal of the world" included all future generations of the world. This universal view of the Declaration also prevails in one of the last letters Jefferson wrote on June 24, 1826, ten days before his passing. In that letter, Jefferson explained that he hoped the Declaration would serve as a beacon of liberty for the world. "May it be to the world what I believe it will be . . . the signal of arousing men to burst the chains, under which Monkish ignorance and superstition had persuaded them to bind themselves, and to assume the blessings & security of self-government." The Declaration would serve as a source of inspiration for this new age of self-government: "All eyes are opened, or opening to the rights of man. The general spread of the light of science has already laid open to every view the palpable truth that the mass of mankind has not been born, with saddles on their backs, nor a favored few booted and spurred, ready to ride them legitimately, by the grace of God." In the United States itself, its purpose was to remind the public of the principles that underlay the republic: "For ourselves let the annual return of this day, forever refresh our recollections of these rights and an undiminished devotion to them."[57]

Conclusion

The audience that the Declaration of Independence reached is vast, both in time and space. The historical or timely audience included supporters and discontents at home as well as sympathetic and antagonistic readers across Europe, and its timeless message continues to inspire people in and outside of the United States. The continued public interest in the Declaration across time and space is testimony to its successful fusing of the specific grievances of 1776 with the universal claim to opposition to tyranny and appeal to the rights of man. As I have tried to make clear, however, successive generations each adapted the Declaration to their needs and found things in it to praise.

Initially, those living in 1776 viewed the Declaration's significance as announcing and justifying the bid for independence and were in some cases more concerned with finding support and allies than with the political philosophy underlying this bid. Within the colonies, the Declaration had to appeal to those committed to the cause as well as those reluctant or fearful of independence, while simultaneously making it seem as if both were united as one people. Abroad, its potentially subversive message of overthrowing oppressive regimes had to be cloaked to appeal to the equally oppressive governments of France and across the continent.

Over time, as the independence of the United States became officially recognized and self-evident in its own right, the meaning of the Declaration shifted. Domestically, it was increasingly viewed as the sacred birth certificate of the new nation and all but stripped of its original foreign outreach purpose. Interestingly, the Declaration served as a text that both advocates and opponents of slavery cited in support and that subsequent generations of Americans emulated in the cause of segregation as well as civil rights, gender equality, and worker's rights.[58] Internationally, the Declaration inspired many movements seeking to break away from the old regime and establish political independence, from Haiti (1804) and Venezuela (1811) to Liberia (1847) and Vietnam (1945). In fact, the Declaration can be said to have established a normative *rite de passage*: declaring independence is seen as a necessity by new regimes even though, as one scholar points out, it does not "effectuate 'real' statehood."[59]

That the Declaration was and continues to be able to reach so many generations across so many different parts of the world is in no small part due to its timeless rhetoric. While the authors of the Declaration sweated over what grievances to include in the "long train of abuses" that makes up the bulk of the text, few contemporary readers take notice of this part today; if they read the Declaration at all, they focus on the first two paragraphs. There, for time immemorial, they are reminded that "it is their right, it is their duty, to throw off [despotic] government, and to provide new guards for their future security."

NOTES

1. Detweiler, "Changing Reputation," 557.
2. Rakove, *Beginnings of National Politics*, 88.
3. Lucas, "Justifying America," 68, 120; my emphasis.
4. Hunt, *Inventing Human Rights*, 19, 20.
5. I am deliberately leaving out a fascinating third dimension, namely, that the Declaration actually created the American audience it addressed in the first place. I plan to discuss this in a forthcoming publication.
6. Maier, *American Scripture*, 181–82.

7. Thomas Jefferson to Henry Lee, May 8, 1825, Founders Online, https://founders.archives.gov/documents/Jefferson/98-01-02-5212; my emphasis.

8. Boyd, *Papers of Thomas Jefferson*, 1:313.

9. For more on this, see Olthof, "Sowing the Seeds of War," 81–95.

10. Olthof, "Sowing the Seeds of War," 81–95.

11. Billias, *American Constitutionalism*, 30.

12. Rakove, *Beginnings of National Politics*, 88.

13. Armitage, *Declaration of Independence*, 30.

14. Armitage, *Declaration of Independence*, 44–45.

15. See, in particular, Deshler, "How the Declaration Was Received," 165–87; Detweiler, "Changing Reputation."

16. Lucas, "Justifying America," 85, 79, 81; my emphasis.

17. Rakove, *Beginnings of National Politics*, 75.

18. See Greene, "Empire and Identity."

19. Larkin, "Loyalism," 292.

20. Larkin, "Loyalism," 292.

21. Becker, *Declaration of Independence*, 9.

22. See Washington reading before the troops in Loyalist New York, in McCullough, *1776*, 137; see also Deshler, "How the Declaration Was Received" for an overview of public readings.

23. Fliegelman, *Declaring Independence*, 25.

24. Becker, *Declaration of Independence*, 203.

25. On June 7, the same day that Congress ordered the Declaration to be drafted, it passed a resolution stating "that a plan of confederation be prepared and transmitted to the respective colonies." This plan would become the Articles of Confederation. See Ford et al., *Journals of the Continental Congress*, 5:425.

26. The issue of the *Gazette* can be found online at https://www.gazettes18e.fr/Gazette_leyde_du_30_08_1776, pp. 2 and 3. For an in-depth discussion of the French translations of the Declaration, see Marienstras and Wulf, "French Translations and Reception," 1299–1324.

27. Armitage, *Declaration of Independence*, 71.

28. Armitage, "Declaration of Independence," 51.

29. Quoted in Armitage, *Declaration of Independence*, 73.

30. Lind, "Answer to the Declaration," 5.

31. Smith, *Letters of Delegates to Congress*, 4:405.

32. Schulte Nordholt, "Recognition of the United States," 38.

33. Schulte Nordholt, "Recognition of the United States," 44.

34. Macleod, "Proper Manner," 286; Morris, *Emerging Nations*, 79.

35. Billias, *American Constitutionalism*, 67.

36. Quoted in Marienstras and Wulf, "French Translations," 1302.

37. Billias, *American Constitutionalism*, 68.

38. Quoted in Marienstras and Wulf, "French Translations," 1309.

39. Schama, *Patriots and Liberators*, 61.

40. Kuiper, "Friese Staten," 19–29.

41. Link, *Papers of Woodrow Wilson*, 30:250, 253, 254–55.

42. Maier, *American Scripture*, 175.

43. Armitage, *Declaration of Independence*, 64, 93.

44. Maier, *American Scripture*, 206.

45. Maier, *American Scripture*, 200.

46. Blassingame, *Frederick Douglass Papers*, 2:371.

47. Sundquist, *King's Dream*, 26.
48. See Richard Henry Lee's speech, in Smith, *Letters of Delegates to Congress*, 1:46.
49. Thelen, "Reception," 191–212.
50. Becker, *Declaration of Independence*, 62.
51. Detweiler, "Changing Reputation," 566.
52. Armitage, *Declaration of Independence*, 65.
53. Morris, *Emerging Nations*, 40, 41.
54. Billias, *American Constitutionalism*, 66–67.
55. Wood, *Radicalism of the American Revolution*, 96.
56. Billias, *American Constitutionalism*, 68.
57. Thomas Jefferson to Roger Chew Weightman, June 24, 1826, Founders Online, https://founders.archives.gov/documents/Jefferson/98-01-02-6179.
58. Foner, *We, the Other People*.
59. Knotter, "Why Declare Independence?," 253.

BIBLIOGRAPHY

Armitage, David. *The Declaration of Independence: A Global History*. Cambridge, MA: Harvard University Press, 2007.

———. "The Declaration of Independence and International Law." *William and Mary Quarterly* 59, no. 1 (2002): 39–64.

Becker, Carl L. *The Declaration of Independence: A Study in the History of Political Ideas*. New York: Harcourt, Brace, 1922.

Billias, George Athan. *American Constitutionalism Heard Round the World, 1776–1989: A Global Perspective*. New York: NYU Press, 2009.

Blassingame, John W., ed. *The Frederick Douglass Papers*, vol. 2: *1847–54*. Series One: Speeches, Debates, Interviews. New Haven, CT: Yale University Press, 1982.

Boyd, Julian P., ed. *The Papers of Thomas Jefferson*. Vol. 1. Princeton, NJ: Princeton University Press, 1950.

Deshler, Charles D. "How the Declaration Was Received in the Old Thirteen." *Harper's New Monthly Magazine* 85, no. 506 (1892): 165–87.

Detweiler, Philip F. "The Changing Reputation of the Declaration of Independence: The First Fifty Years." *William and Mary Quarterly* 19, no. 4 (1962): 557–74.

Fliegelman, Jay. *Declaring Independence: Jefferson, Natural Language and the Culture of Performance*. Stanford, CA: Stanford University Press, 1993.

Foner, Philip S., ed. *We, the Other People: Alternative Declarations of Independence by Labor Groups, Farmers, Woman's Rights Advocates, Socialists, and Blacks, 1829–1975*. Urbana: University of Illinois Press, 1976.

Ford, Worthington C., Hunt Gaillard, John Clement Fitzpatrick, Roscoe R. Hill, Kenneth Harris, and Steven D. Tilley, eds. *Journals of the Continental Congress 1774–1789*. Vol. 5. Washington, DC: Government Printing Office, 1906.

Greene, Jack P. "Empire and Identity from the Glorious Revolution to the American Revolution." In *The Oxford History of the British Empire*, edited by P. J. Marshall, 208–30. Oxford: Oxford University Press, 1998.

Hunt, Lynn. *Inventing Human Rights: A History*. New York: W. W. Norton, 2007.

Knotter, Lucas. "Why Declare Independence? Observing, Believing, and Performing the Ritual." *Review of International Studies* 47, no. 2 (April 2021): 252–71.

Kuiper, Yme. "Friese Staten: Trendsetter Bij Erkenning VS." In *Gevierde Friezen in Amerika*, edited by Peter De Haan and Kerst Huisman, 19–29. Leeuwarden, Netherlands: Friese Pers, 2009.

Larkin, Edward. "Loyalism." In *The Oxford Handbook of the American Revolution*, edited by Jane Kamensky and Edward G. Gray, 291–310. Oxford: Oxford University Press, 2012.

Lind, John. "An Answer to the Declaration of the American Congress." London, 1776.

Link, Arthur S., ed. *The Papers of Woodrow Wilson*. Vol. 30. Princeton, NJ: Princeton University Press, 1979.

Lucas, Stephen E. "Justifying America: The Declaration of Independence as a Rhetorical Document." In *American Rhetoric: Context and Criticism*, edited by Thomas W. Benson, 67–130. Carbondale: Southern Illinois University Press, 1989.

Macleod, Emma. "A Proper Manner of Carrying on Controversies: Richard Price and the American Revolution." *Huntington Library Quarterly* 82, no. 2 (2019): 277–302.

Maier, Pauline. *American Scripture: Making the Declaration of Independence*. New York: Alfred A. Knopf, 1997.

Marienstras, Elise, and Naomi Wulf. "French Translations and Reception of the Declaration of Independence." *Journal of American History* 85, no. 4 (1999): 1299–1324.

McCullough, David. *1776: America and Britain at War*. New York: Simon and Schuster, 2005.

Morris, Richard B. *The Emerging Nations and the American Revolution*. New York: Harper and Row, 1970.

Olthof, Jelte. "Sowing the Seeds of War: Conflict, Conciliatory Rhetoric, and the Legacy of Jefferson's Empire of Liberty in the Missouri Compromise Debate." In *America: Justice, Conflict, War*, edited by Amanda Gilroy and Marietta Messmer, 81–95. Heidelberg: Winter, 2014.

Rakove, Jack N. *The Beginnings of National Politics: An Interpretive History of the Continental Congress*. New York: Alfred A. Knopf, 1979.

Schama, Simon. *Patriots and Liberators: Revolution in the Netherlands 1780–1813*. 2nd ed. London: Harper Perennial, 2005.

Schulte Nordholt, J. W. "The Recognition of the United States by the Dutch Republic." *Proceedings of the Massachusetts Historical Society* 94 (1982): 37–48.

Smith, Paul H., ed. *Letters of Delegates to Congress, 1774–1789*. Vol. 1. Washington, DC: Library of Congress, 1976.

———, ed. *Letters of Delegates to Congress, 1774–1789*. Vol. 4. Washington, DC: Library of Congress, 1979.

Sundquist, Eric J. *King's Dream*. New Haven, CT: Yale University Press, 2009.

Thelen, David. "Reception of the Declaration of Independence." In *The Declaration of Independence: Origins and Impact*, edited by Scott Douglas Gerber, 191–212. Landmark Events in U.S. History Series. Washington, DC: CQ Press, 2002.

Wood, Gordon S. *The Radicalism of the American Revolution*. New York: Alfred A. Knopf, 1992.

2

"AN IMPUDENT, FALSE, AND ATROCIOUS PROCLAMATION": LOYALIST CRITIQUE AND THE LIMITS OF DISSENT IN COLONIAL AMERICA

Stephen Howard Browne

In the spring of 1825 Henry Lee prompted his friend and fellow Virginian to reflect on his role in the composition of the Declaration of Independence. Thomas Jefferson, now eighty-three, struggled to recall some of the details, but of this he was certain: the aim was not "to find out new principles, or new arguments, never before thought of, nor merely to say things which had never been said before." No. He sought rather to make it "an expression of the American mind, and to give to that expression the proper tone and spirit called for by the occasion." History will record that Jefferson succeeded. The Declaration has secured its status, in Pauline Maier's phrasing, as "American Scripture," at once so singular and so expressive of "the American mind" that it has become a secular version of Holy Writ. It took a few years, but soon enough even the day of its proclamation had become sanctified. Philadelphians, reliably festive, could now toast: "May the Fourth of July, that glorious and ever memorable day, be celebrated throughout America . . . from age to age till time shall be no more. Amen, and amen."[1]

So much is familiar to most US Americans, and this quite by design. Nation-states, if they hope to remain in being, need to tell stories about themselves. Some of course are more worthy than others: some endure, others do not, but they are yet stories. This means that certain elements of the past will be included, some perhaps highlighted, others omitted; that is how narratives work. The story of the Declaration is no exception; indeed, it exemplifies the dynamics of remembering and forgetting like few other texts in the national lore. Students of rhetoric are keen to ask how this process of narrative identity and difference works; in the following, I offer one such account. It is predicated on the assumption that the Declaration works rhetorically by occluding its own status as a rhetorical text. To the extent that we can situate the text within its immediate argumentative field, there to see it contested and wrangled over, we afford ourselves a much more interesting and instructive view of the subject. A second reflection will help define my particular approach to the subject; here we can rely on one Jacob Dunham, a local worthy of New Brunswick, New Jersey, as he remembered a public reading of the Declaration: "There was great excitement in the town over the news, most of the people rejoicing that we were free and independent, but a few looking very sour over it."[2]

In the event, those sour-looking people had rather a lot to say. And in giving expression to their frustrations, their anger, and their anxieties, they in effect exposed and reconstituted the rhetorical work of the Declaration. In the process, these Loyalists positioned the text as an appropriate object of dissent. Such a statement may appear—plausibly—truistic. But we might well ask: How—really—does one argue with a declaration, much less *the* Declaration? Like its cousin the manifesto, the genre announces in its very form that the debate is over, period; that's the point. Declarations function not to argue the case but to leverage principles beyond argument: the "necessary, the self-evident," the "inalienable," the "laws of nature and of nature's god." Thus the very terms defining the realm of the rhetorical—persuasion, deliberation, contingency, probability, and so forth—are conspicuously exported from the scene. In their stead: the absolute rectitude of truth. It is but a posture, of course, though sometimes a very powerful one indeed. We know, in any case, that there were more than "a few looking very sour over it" all, and we have available to us a number of quite striking statements contesting the assumptions and implication of the Declaration at its moment of appearance in the world.

Three such counterarguments ground the following analysis. No pretense of being comprehensive is made here, but they do provide suggestive resources for filling out the picture of the Declaration and the rhetorical landscape from which it emerged. They are John Dickinson's speech against independence on the threshold of the final vote on July 4, Thomas Hutchinson's *Strictures upon the Declaration of the Congress at Philadelphia*, and John Lind's *An Answer to the Declaration of the American Congress*. After a bit of scene-setting, we will treat each of these in turn.[3]

What, exactly, did it mean to be a "Loyalist"? The question itself is misleading because there was—and remains—no exact definition of this term.

For starters, virtually *all* Anglo-colonial subjects—very much including "Patriots"—professed fealty to the Crown until the eve of the revolution. Loyalism is thus best conceived of as designating a genus, the species of which ranged from obdurate ministers in Whitehall to opposition critics, from London radicals to Boston hell-raisers, from Quakers to Anglicans, from New Hampshire farmers to Charleston enslavers. We are thus immediately put on notice that facile generalizations about the meaning of Loyalism, though tempting, are to be avoided. We may ask, then, whether there are certain geographical determinants at work in creating these species. Up to a point, the answer is yes, but again caution is in order. Demographically, we know that the more stubborn varieties of colonial Loyalism tended to cluster in the coastal mid-Atlantic region and Charleston, South Carolina, and along the north-south axis of the Appalachian and southern outback. If anything can be inferred from these locations, historians suggest, it is that those who had reason to fear change were most likely to resist the call of patriotism. No surprise there, but those reasons were not ill-founded: the coastal carrying trade depended heavily on British maritime protections; expansionists worried, with cause, that their relentless movement west would be checked; and who knew what "liberty" might mean in the slave-holding South?[4]

What, then, did our Tories hold in common? Not much, perhaps, but a few things for sure. To a person they felt themselves to be *English*, and proud of it. Whether through kinship and blood affinity or folkways and traditions of faith, and certainly through shared identity with good King George, Loyalists understood themselves to be exactly that: loyal. For them, patriots, so-called, were in truth precisely the opposite of what real patriotism meant: they were, in the richly colored language of the day, "a race of unnatural and ungrateful bastards." Real patriots knew how good they had it and reaffirmed that knowledge through rituals of gratitude, love, and trust that defined a true subject of the empire. To this obligation was added a second, starkly utilitarian logic of relative advantage—that is, such fealty to Crown and Country yielded demonstrable gains in the form of military protection against the enslaved and Indigenous peoples, Spanish adventuring, French colonial interests, and all manner of dangers on the high seas. At minimal cost and for remarkably low rates of taxation, American colonists enjoyed a level of collective prosperity unknown elsewhere on the entire globe. It beggared the imagination to believe that such protection might be ceded for the sake of a false and utterly precarious claim to sovereignty.[5]

These convictions were borne by a people proud of their English heritage, proud therefore of their own, genuine Revolution of 1688. It was then that

Parliament secured its true birthright, vesting now Commons, Lords, and king into a single, coherent constitution widely thought the greatest political achievement of humankind. A third commonplace accordingly asserts itself with the advent of the Continental Congress in 1774. Many loyalists—not all—insisted that such a body had no legitimate claim to legitimacy, no rationale, and certainly no mandate. Who or what was this "Congress"? It had no standing in the imperial order; indeed, it was outside the law as such. Did it claim to be representative of the people? Fifty-six "insolent vermin" gathered to foment rebellion? And delegated by whom, exactly? The questions clustered around a common set of assumptions about power, about its alleged sources, and ultimately, about the capacity of "the people" to act rationally in their own best interests. Hector St. John de Crèvecoeur spoke for many when he recalled that "no European can possibly conceive the secret ways" instigated by this faux body" and insisted that "the great combination of poison and subtle sophisms which have from one end of the continent to the other allured the minds, removed every ancient prejudice, and in short, prepared the way for the exhibition of this astonishing Revolution."[6]

The British ministry and its supporters routinely mobilized similar language on the basis of such commonplaces. There are more, but here it is enough to note that they subtended, implicitly or in more obvious ways, the Loyalist countercampaign against the revolting colonies. Because they are designed specifically for the purposes of attack, such rhetorical measures are necessarily reductive; the motives of patriots are at once flattened out and depicted in the most extreme and lurid colors. We know, however, that Loyalism spoke in many voices, expressed in tones ranging from outright denunciation to the much more subtle and often quite compelling arguments of Dickinson, Hutchinson, and Lind. On the US American strand, these voices spoke more often in the cadences of moderation, of conciliation, and even at times of sympathy and pained regret.

John Dickinson and the Politics of Prudence

The American colonies had been at war with their own government for more than a year when Congress undertook debate on independence. Initial engagements at Lexington and Concord in April 1775 and at Bunker Hill in June had shown promise of a kind; more recently, the ill-fated effort to invade Quebec late in the year cast the prospects of success in a rather different light. While the ink was still drying on the Declaration, Britain would advance on New

York with the largest armada in its distinguished maritime history. Worse, much worse, was to come. Under the circumstances, could any reasonable person seriously entertain Richard Henry Lee's June 7 resolution "that these united colonies are and of right ought to be free and independent states"? Certainly not Charles Inglis, the New York clergyman, who stood "aghast at the prospect." "My blood runs chill," he wrote, "when I think of the calamities, the complicated evils that must ensue." He was not alone, and the upshot of the July debates only made his blood the more chill. "By a Declaration of Independency," Inglis warned, "every avenue to an accommodation with Great-Britain would be closed; the sword only could then decide the quarrel; and the sword would not be sheathed till one had conquered the other."[7]

The timing was just terrible, and no one was more certain of this than the political insider John Dickinson. Three days before the final vote on the Declaration, the wealthy Philadelphian stood before Congress and delivered a powerful, apparently quite moving address countermanding the growing sentiment for independence. Less famous than his "Farmer" letters—indeed, scarcely known to most historians until the twentieth century—Dickinson's speech was judged even by his critic John Adams to be the result of "great labor and ardent zeal" and delivered "with great ingenuity and eloquence." The text comes to us in the form of speaker's notes and is often cryptic; fortunately, the labors of J. H. Powell allow for a plausible interpretation of its primary thrust. For the purposes of this analysis, Dickinson's speech on that day provides a rich opportunity to identify a key argument in the arsenal of moderate opinion generally and against the Declaration in particular.[8]

At the heart of this critique was the matter of foreign policy, or properly, the lack of such a policy appropriate to the exigencies at play. This perception—the moderates' view that the Declaration would prove disastrous in aligning support "among the powers of the Earth" may seem on its face ridiculous. No less a historian of foreign policy than George C. Herring reminds us, after all, that "whatever place the Declaration has since assumed in the folklore of US nationhood, its immediate and urgent purpose was to make clear to Europeans, and especially the French, the colonies' commitment to independence." So much is true; but it leaves unnoted an equally "immediate and urgent" concern among many that the Declaration could only be provocative; that its timing was so premature, so likely to dissuade potential allies, that it must only produce more harm than good. It was for precisely this reason, recalled Robert Morris, that "I have uniformly voted against and opposed the Declaration of Independence." His reason: "Because, in my poor opinion, it was an improper time, and will neither promote the interest nor redound to the honor of America."[9]

Dickinson knew exactly what his friend and fellow Pennsylvanian meant. This famous advocate of colonial rights, this "Penman of the Revolution," author of the Articles of Confederation, president of his state, signer of the Constitution, and namesake of Dickinson College and regional high schools, would not and did not sign the Declaration of Independence. Neither did the distinguished New Yorkers George Clinton and Robert Livingston, along with several others. They each had their distinctive reasons, no doubt, but behind them was a shared though hardly unique conviction that the Declaration would in fact prove calamitous. The reasons, as noted above, were not mysterious: anyone who cared to look could see that dangers lurked on all sides. And the only way to ensure the survival of the colonies was not to "dissolve the political bands" that kept the Americans and their English defenders together in a pact of mutual advantage but to strengthen them. Here is the heart of Dickinson's case, and to it we now turn.

"I must speak, tho I should lost my life, tho I should lost the Affections of my Country," Dickinson began. But he must "offer to this Honorable Assembly in a full and clear Manner, those Reasons, that have so invariably fixed my own Opinion." The modern reader may be inclined, understandably, to chalk up such talk to the protocols of eighteenth-century oratory. The history of revolutions, on the other hand, teaches us that it is the moderates, not the radicals, who stand the best chance of losing their heads.[10]

Dickinson would not lose his head, but his reputation took a mighty hit. After a brief appeal to Divine Goodness, the speaker launches directly into the matter of the Lee Resolution and the Declaration that will formally announce colonial intentions. We are on the very threshold here; a little patience in reviewing the arguments will pay off with a clearer picture of moderate critique. At its heart is the conviction that the Declaration represented not a triumph but a failure of political reasoning. And the basis of this failure was the willful distortion of American foreign policy. When that document concludes by announcing "that the united colonies" have "full power to levy war, conclude peace, contract alliances, establish commerce," in what sense are we being asked to take such a claim seriously? Such powers are the province of political entities understood by other nations to be treaty-worthy. The historian Eliga Gould puts the issue just right: "What we sometimes forget—though people at the time knew it—is that the United States could not become the nation that Americans imagined without the consent of other nations and people. . . . Because Americans were founding a nation among nations, they were doing so, at least in part, on someone else's terms."[11]

No wonder Inglis stood "aghast at the prospect": given the truly formidable face of European empire-building, what reasonable person could with any confidence entertain such prospects? Not John Dickinson. Those naïve or impassioned enough to support the resolution for independence, he argues, claim that it will "Convince foreign Powers of our Strength and Unanimity and we would receive their aid in consequence thereof." US Americans, he counters, may declare their worthiness all they want; in the end, "foreign Powers will not rely on Words." Thus the gentle farmer asserts a realpolitik notably missing from the operators before him. It was inconceivable, Dickinson maintains, that France or any other nation would be so foolhardy as to cast their own fortunes on behalf of a people who chose *this* moment, when the greatest military power on earth was invading their shores, to proclaim their independence.[12]

It was all a question of timing. Dickinson and the moderates he represented were *not* in principle dead set against independence; if anything, they thought themselves the greater patriots by searching for the better, the more realistic, means to that end. "Prudence": that is what Congress needed, and prudence required patience. The colonies were at war—let us register a few victories; establish cordial diplomatic relations with France, perhaps Spain; stroke their pride a bit. That's how you do it. Let us first find out how they "would regard this Stranger in the States of the World"; then we make the move. "People are fond of what they have attained," Dickinson astutely observes of the French. "A Cement of Affection exists between them. Let us Allow them the Glory of appearing the Vindicators of Liberty. It will please them." Benjamin Franklin could not have said it better.[13]

Dickinson concludes with a glance upon the offing and sees only disaster ahead: "When our Enemies are pressing Us so vigorously, When We are in so wretched a State of Preparation, When the Sentiment and Designs of our expected Friends are so unknown to Us, I am alarmed at this Declaration being so vehemently presented." In retrospect, of course, we can see what Dickinson could not: that "Deliberation, Wisdom, Caution, and Unanimity" were, truly, virtues of a kind; but they were not and never have been the virtues of revolution.

Hutchinson's Strictures: Counterconspiracy

Four decades after the publication of the Declaration of Independence, John Adams marveled at the time when "thirteen clocks had been made to strike together—a perfect mechanism, which no artist had ever before effected." As is frequently the case, Adams's reflection may be viewed as both on the mark and quite wrong. Yes, that the colonies—so different, so localized—did in fact come together and thereby launch a collective war of independence is a breathtaking act of unanimity. But we must not let the ringing of those bells drown out more discordant sounds of dissent and disappointment. Among the most forceful of these voices was the beleaguered ex-governor, Adams's old nemesis and fellow Bay Stater Thomas Hutchinson. Self-exiled to England now, Hutchinson was provoked by the Declaration to compose and circulate his own *Strictures upon the Declaration of Independence*, a thirty-one-page takedown of the assumptions, arguments, and implications of the American manifesto.[14]

For the purposes of this essay, the *Strictures* may usefully be cited for its resolute claim that the colonists' problem was the result of pernicious design by unscrupulous men, a rank and deeply cynical effort on the part of the few to dupe the many: the consequence, that is, of *conspiracy*. Owing to the groundwork laid by Bernard Bailyn, Pauline Maier, and Gordon Wood, we are now quite aware of the role and function—the sheer ubiquity—of conspiracy rhetoric during the period. "Everywhere people sensed designs within designs," Wood notes; cabals within cabals. There were court conspiracies, backstairs conspiracies, ministerial conspiracies, factional conspiracies, aristocratic conspiracies, and by the latter half of the eighteenth century, even conspiracies of gigantic secret societies that cut across national boundaries and spanned the Atlantic. Whether or not everyone believed such things, no one, then or now, could doubt the utility of such language—it just seemed to explain so much, so well and so very efficiently.[15]

Scholars across a number of disciplines continue to seek answers to the question of why these people—perhaps people in general—found conspiracy appeals so attractive. Here we may rely on Hutchinson to illustrate a more specific but productive way into the question. Conspiracy talk is essentially a form of the exposé. Those leveling the charge hope to bring designs heretofore hidden to light; such allegations work best when they can plausibly account for a given phenomenon by inscribing its greater narrative. This narrative in turn functions as the prime medium of disclosure; it provides sources, characters, conflict—and resolution if we can only see the forces now revealed. For all their documented absurdities, then, we might accept the point begrudgingly that conspiracy appeals work, when they work, because they make sense of what seems otherwise inexplicable.

If anyone had just cause to doubt the patriots' grasp on reality, surely it was the author of the *Strictures*. Or so he was convinced. For decades he had been fighting a combination of truly formidable opponents, chief among them no less than John and Sam Adams, James Otis, and John Hancock—Bay Staters all. These were leaders, as an anonymous London pamphleteer charged, "for the most part necessitous men, turbulent, seditious Spirits . . . fond of promoting Anarchy and Confusion." Their most maddening trait, Hutchinson thought, was the inability to see that he was in fact deeply committed to colonial rights; that he had publicly disapproved the Stamp Act, for example, lamented the Boston Massacre and the punitive resolves of 1774. The rebels' claims to government designs on their liberty simply made no sense—unless those claims were themselves the product not of ministerial designs but of colonial conspiracy. Hutchinson's *Strictures* was accordingly offered as a counterargument, the point of which was to expose this conspiracy and so to make the Declaration intelligible—not in and of itself, of course, but as the product of concerted and fallacious design, the absurdity of which was itself proof of its authors' twisted and tenuous grasp on reality. There was no other way to account for the Declaration except as the result of conspiratorial forces.[16]

The *Strictures* is presented as a public epistle "to a Noble Lord." It thus avails itself of a familiar genre in eighteenth-century Anglo-American discourse and works by addressing at once an individual and the reading public. Its thirty-two pages are disposed into a general case against the rebels and their English supporters, turning to the Declaration itself by taking on its famous first paragraphs and then subjecting that text's list of grievances to a seriatim rebuttal. No effort here will be made toward a comprehensive treatment of its many features, nor is is there any need for extensive paraphrase. A finite set of arguments may nevertheless be identified that conveys something of its rhetorical nature and function.

Hutchinson is eager above all to establish the facts—the reality—of the matter. This means first that all the talk about taxes and duties, standing armies and Parliamentary overreach, and so forth was just that—talk—and talk, he stresses early in the text, designed specifically to camouflage the fact that the rebels had been scheming for independence ever since the conclusion of the British-French wars of the 1750s–1760s. To those who had naïvely urged treating the colonists as favored sons, letting them flourish under conditions of "salutary neglect," Hutchinson insists that such a policy would not have mattered. The exercise of this or that policy simply "was not the object from the beginning." Once alerted to this truth, the reader could now see the "many irrefragable proofs of this determined design." The rebels, crying justice, were in reality crying freedom.[17]

With that much made clear, the author must now explain how it all came about: how, that is, the movement for independence so cloaked was able to advance its insidious ends. The blame lay not on the good, if gullible, people themselves. Rather, the crisis was brought to this point by the concerted efforts of "despots" throughout the provinces; it was they who determined to "irritate and inflame the minds of the people, and dispose them to revolt. Dissensions and commotions in any Colony, were cherished and increased." These local demagogues proved adept in the arts of what today we might call fake news. Fictitious letters had been circulated; perfectly legal measures had been misconstrued and made grievous; powerful individuals in London had been "courted and deceived, by false professions, and the real intentions of the revolters were concealed." And so it was that finally "many thousands of people who were before good and loyal subjects, have been deluded, and by degrees induced to rebel against the best of Princes, and the mildest of Governments."

A century and a half later, Progressive Era historians began to scrutinize the rhetoric of revolution as masking elite ambitions for power. Hutchinson believed that he knew very well what was going in his own day and saw the same thing. Who exactly stood to benefit from independence—"the people"? Hardly; according to Hutchinson, "fifty or sixty Despots" as always, who had managed to arrogate to themselves "a supreme authority over the whole." A product of these very despots, the Declaration could only be understood as cover for the base intentions of the rebel elite; none of it made any sense otherwise. Indeed, Hutchinson notes, it begins with a nonsensical appeal to a coherent, unified "one People." There was "one distinct people," Hutchinson quite reasonably argues: namely, colonies governed by a sovereign center to whom obeisance was required by law. One people: *What* one people? *What* "We"? And that language about all men being created equal? "I could wish to ask the Delegates of Maryland, Virginia, and the Carolinas, how their Constituents justify the depriving [of] more than a hundred thousand Africans of their rights to liberty, and *the pursuit of happiness.*"

This is a fair question, or it was thought so by many at home and abroad. The *Strictures* spoke for a significant part of the population who simply could not grasp the rationale for independence as given. All sides prided themselves on being reasonable, and indeed one is hard put to locate another revolutionary movement so invested in the power of language to secure or thwart its ends. Hutchinson's effort was bent toward exposing the essentially "fallacious" arguments of the rebels, whose rhetoric of justification could now be seen as a cynical and deeply reckless attempt to mobilize popular opinion on behalf of heretofore hidden ambitions. The "professed reason for publishing the Declaration," he concludes, "was a decent respect to the opinions of mankind." This was absurd: "the real design was to reconcile the people of America to that Independence, which always before, they had been made to believe was not intended. This design has too well succeeded." As a result, "no man may, by writing or speaking, contradict any part of the Declaration, without being deemed an enemy to his country, and exposed to the rage and fury of the populace." Of this tendency in the rhetoric of revolution Thomas Hutchinson, Loyalist critic and erstwhile governor of Massachusetts, now exiled to the land of his ancestors, knew to be at least one true fact.

John Lind's Answer to the Declaration and the Politics of Principle

By October 1775, George William Frederick, king of Great Britain and Ireland, "Farmer George," better known as George III, had had quite enough of his rebellious subjects in America. Since his assumption to the throne in 1760, they had proved an unending source of exasperation, expense, and indeed embarrassment to the Crown and Cabinet. It was time—past time—to put them in their place. The king thus dedicated his speech to Parliament to letting his sentiments be known. "I have acted with the Same Temper, anxious to prevent, if it had been possible, the Effusion of the Blood of My Subjects," he explained, but to no avail. Still the American rebels refused to understand "that to be a Subject of Great Britain, with all its Consequences, is to be the freest Member of any Civil Society in the known World." Military operations and alliances were thus being readied; if it was war the Americans wanted, war they shall have. Still, George concluded in the faint tones of scripture, "when the unhappy and deluded multitude, against whom this force will be directed, shall become sensible of their error, I shall be ready to receive the misled with tenderness and mercy."[18]

The rebels did not become sensible of their errors, and tenderness and mercy were not at the top of any ministerial list of priorities thereafter. The Crown's policy toward the colonies was fraught by ministerial tensions, flummoxed leadership on the battlefield, and a deeply ambivalent prime minister. But the bottom line never changed; sovereignty could only rest with Parliament, including both houses and the monarchy, and the colonies could only and forever be just that: territorial adjuncts serving at the pleasure of the home government. At stake was the very coherence, the essential *dignity*, of the empire. That much was absolutely nonnegotiable, and so war it must be. This matter of imperial dignity reminds us as well of a related truism in the eighteenth-century world of European affairs: it was one thing to be challenged by a rival nation-state, quite another by one's own children.[19]

It is in this context of Crown dignity that John Lind's *Answer to the Declaration* may be read with profit. The 132-page pamphlet was written at the behest of Lord North and with the assistance of the author's friend Jeremy Bentham shortly after the circulation of the Declaration in London. The fact that it was composed by a political "ministerial hack," as Maier calls Lind, and published anonymously is telling. As a die-hard Tory, recently admitted lawyer, and itinerant hireling for ministerial needs, Lind was perfect for the job. It would have been undignified for the prime minister to respond in public and inconceivable for the king himself to so: "Ill would it become the dignity of an insulted Sovereign," Lind begins, "to descend to altercation with revolted subjects." And yet *something* must be said, some sort of rebuttal representing Crown interests without evident ties to the throne. The result is a scathing attack on the Declaration as a whole and on the individual charges in particular. In this the *Answer* bears comparison with Hutchinson's *Strictures*. Here we will focus on Lind's treatment of the rebel appeal to the principles, the vaunted rights and "self-evident" truths, so favored by these deluded colonists.[20]

The very idea that principles may be considered plausible goads to revolutionary action is not itself a given; indeed, historians continue to debate the question. That the ideas invoked in the Declaration might themselves be taken seriously strikes Lind as ludicrous. Jefferson and his friends seemed to Lind to have been under the delusion that they were actually establishing "a theory of Government[,] a theory," he asserts, "as absurd and visionary, as the system of conduct in defence of which it is established, is nefarious." How so? The *Answer* can be scurrilous, no question, but its author was not without insight; in his own way, he grasped the radical implications of the Declaration as perhaps few others did. He saw that its purported theory of government was inherently a contradiction, at least within established terms of what was meant by "government." Such premises upon which the Declaration depends were by their very nature "repugnant to the British Constitution," in effect "subversive of every actual or imaginable kind of Government."

The Declaration of Independence, again, just made no sense. Dickinson thought the same thing and revealed its profound misconstruction of international realities; Hutchinson thought so as well and so exposed the twisted conspiracies that were warping rebel perceptions. Lind's position is similarly situated, in this case by simply asking whether any of the Declaration's assumptions could possibly square with the common sense of things. They could not. All men are created equal? So "a child at the moment of his birth, has the same quantity of natural power as the parent, the same political power as the magistrate." Long-established governments should not be changed for light or transient reasons? That is precisely what these so-called patriots seek to do. A people justified in overturning their government when unhappy with its policies? There "is not that subject in the world, but who has, ever has had, and ever must have, reason sufficient to rebel." In that case, Lind concludes, "there never was nor never can be, established any government upon earth." The list goes on, the indictment of a hired lawyer, dogged, sarcastic, self-consciously out of patience, but determined to wrestle each and every precept to the soiled mat. The *Answer* does not make for inspired reading, but credit must be extended: Lind pays attention to the details, implications, and alleged inconsistencies.

There is a hypocrisy, sighs Lind in conclusion, that "pervades the whole of the Declaration," its faults so pernicious, its "principles" so bereft of common sense. And yet the very absurdity of that text may itself prove productive of good. So glaring are its contradictions that it will quiet the factional noise; perhaps "the eyes of those who saw not, or would not see, that the Americans were long since aspiring at independence, will be opened; the nation will unite as one man, and teach this rebellious people . . . that to accomplish their independence is not quite so easy as to declare it."

The *Answer* will not go down as one of the age's great literary or philosophical productions; it was designed to be neither. The aim was rather to issue, quickly, a sturdy blast against the pretensions of the rebels and their supporters among the opposition. To this end five hundred copies were hurried off to the colonies, and the pamphlet created enough demand at home for at least six reprints within the year. So staid a publication as the *London Magazine* reported its author to be a "very able disputant," though a bit evasive," "more plausible than convincing." To Lind's dismissal of colonial complaints, it slyly concludes, the author might want to recall that such grievances were similarly voiced as a cause of the English Revolution. And so it would, again. Lind did not live to see this war's end, but his rough and ready pamphlet may be viewed as a genuine contribution to the record. It took on the Declaration's claims to fact, as did many of its critics. But the author also subjected its very assumptions to a withering critique. Appealing to the reader's common sense, Lind asked bluntly how such audacious language could be taken seriously. It was not an outlandish question after all and invites us still to pause over the text, this US American Scripture.[21]

Conclusion

The banners of revolution are carried in the name of freedom. Those who would dissent thereby declare themselves enemies not only of their fellow subjects but of liberty itself. Little surprise, then, that the historiography of the US American Revolution in general and of the Declaration in particular has been less than accommodating to the Loyalist legacy. There are exceptions: in the twentieth century, Lawrence Labaree, William Nelson, and especially Craig Calhoun did much to bring Loyalists back into the picture; more recently, Maya Jasanoff, Kathleen Duval, and Holger Hock have dramatically expanded our perspective on the subject. Here it is enough to briefly remind ourselves of certain features of the Loyalist cause. These reminders are perhaps obvious to contemporary scholars, but they warn against pitfalls that remain surprisingly persistent in conventional treatments of the period.

Our three spokesmen were scarcely abject apologists for the government; indeed, they had proven themselves to be deeply committed to the welfare of the colonies. They were accomplished figures, cultural and economic elites, learned and keenly attuned to the historical stakes of the moment. In the end, they held to a faith that rational argument, as they understood it, would so alter the terms of engagement as to restore the empire to its original promises. Dickinson, Hutchinson, and Lind were wrong but arguably not wrong-headed. The Declaration of Independence in any case offered itself up as a perfect target for Loyalist critique. That text proved a very formidable target indeed, because by its very form and function it announced that the time for rhetoric, at least of a deliberative kind, was quite over. Its ancestry in English tradition traces back to Magna Carta, if one wishes to push it that far, and may include the numerous petitions, remonstrances, and appeals to the Crown thereafter. More obviously, the text's most immediate relation is the 1689 Declaration of Right, enshrined, as it was meant to be, as the cornerstone of constitutional government—England's own Holy Writ. Many Americans were thus primed to hear and act on the most famous Declaration of them all. But were they ready to hear those who thought it nothing more than an "impudent, false, and atrocious Proclamation"?[22]

NOTES

1. Thomas Jefferson to Henry Lee, May 8, 1825, in Peterson, *Thomas Jefferson: Writings*; *Pennsylvania Evening Post*, July 5, 1777.

2. The standard account of the Declaration's rhetorical functions remains Lucas, "Justifying America." The best general treatment of its composition is Maier, *American Scripture*. Dunham quoted in Hoock, *Scars of Independence*, 103.

3. Dickinson, "Arguments Against the Independence of These Colonies," in Powell, "Speech of John Dickinson"; Hutchinson, *Strictures*; Lind, *Answer*.

4. On moderate opinion in the colonies, see especially Rakove, *Revolutionaries*. A fresh perspective is provided by Duval, *Independence Lost*.

5. *Morning Post* (New York), March 10, 1778. Still useful for a general treatment is Nelson, *American Tory*.

6. Moore, *Songs and Ballads*, 128; de Crèvecoeur, *Sketches*, 426.

7. Inglis, *True Interest of America*, 3.

8. Powell, "Speech of John Dickinson," 469; Adams quoted in Powell, "Speech of John Dickinson," 461. For biography and analysis of Dickinson's thought, see Calvert, *Quaker Constitutionalism*.

9. Herring, *From Colony to Superpower*, 15; Morris quoted in Reed, *Life and Correspondence of Joseph Reed*, 202.

10. Powell, "Speech of John Dickinson," 469. All subsequent quotes are from this edition.

11. Gould, *Among the Powers*, 2.

12. Powell, "Speech of John Dickinson," 471.

13. Powell, "Speech of John Dickinson," 472.

14. John Adams, Letter to Hezekiah Niles, February 12, 1818, https://founders.archives.gov/documents/Adams/06-04-02-0130.

15. Wood, "Conspiracy and the Paranoid Style," 407.

16. *Independency the Object*, 113.

17. Hutchinson, *Strictures*, 6; all subsequent citations are to this text.

18. As published in New York circular *His Majesty's Most Gracious Speech to Both Houses of Parliament*.

19. For context, see O'Shaughnessy, *Men Who Lost America*, esp. pp. 47–82.

20. Maier, *Scripture*, 122; Lind, *Answer*, 3; all successive citations are to this text. Neil York provides an instructive treatment of Lind's work in "Natural Rights Dissected and Rejected."

21. *London Magazine* 4 (1776): 663.

22. Ambrose Serle, personal secretary to General Howe, as quoted in Gould, *Among the Powers*, 114.

BIBLIOGRAPHY

Calvert, Jane E. *Quaker Constitutionalism and the Political Thought of John Dickinson*. New York: Cambridge University Press, 2009.

de Crèvecoeur, Hector St. John. *Sketches of Eighteenth-Century America*. Edited by Albert E. Stone. New York: Penguin, 1981.

Duval, Kathleen. *Independence Lost: Lives on the Edge of the American Revolution*. New York: Random House, 2015.

Gould, Elijah H. *Among the Powers of the Earth: The American Revolution and the Making of a New World Empire*. Cambridge, MA: Harvard University Press, 2012.

Herring, George. *From Colony to Superpower: US Foreign Policy Since 1776*. New York: Oxford University Press, 2008.

His Majesty's Most Gracious Speech to Both Houses of Parliament. New York, 1776.

Hoock, Holger. *Scars of Independence: America's Violent Birth*. New York: Crown, 2017.

Hutchinson, Thomas. *Strictures upon the Declaration of Congress at Philadelphia in a Letter to a Noble Lord*. London, 1776.

Independency the Object of Congress in America. London: Rivington, 1776.

Inglis, Charles. *True Interest of America, Impartially Stated.* Philadelphia: Humphreys, 1776.

Lind, John. *An Answer to the Declaration of the American Congress.* London, 1776.

Lucas, Stephen E. "Justifying America: The Declaration of Independence as a Rhetorical Document." In *American Rhetoric: Contexts and Criticism,* edited by Thomas W. Benson, 67–130. Carbondale: Southern Illinois University Press, 1989.

Maier, Pauline. *American Scripture: Making the Declaration of Independence.* New York: Vintage, 1998.

Moore, Frank, ed. *Songs and Ballads of the American Revolution.* New York: Applegate, 1856.

Nelson, William. *The American Tory.* Boston: Beacon Press, 1964.

O'Shaughnessy, Andrew Jackson. *The Men Who Lost America: British Leadership, the American Revolution, and the Fate of Empire.* New Haven, CT: Yale University Press, 2013.

Peterson, Merrill D., ed. *Thomas Jefferson: Writings.* New York: Library of America, 1984.

Powell, J. H. "Speech of John Dickinson Opposing the Declaration of Independence." *Pennsylvania Magazine of History and Biography* 65, no. 4 (1941): 458–81.

Rakove, Jack. *Revolutionaries: A New History of the Invention of America.* New York: Mariner, 2011.

Reed, William, ed. *Life and Correspondence of Joseph Reed.* Philadelphia: Lindsey and Blackiston, 1847.

Wood, Gordon S. "Conspiracy and the Paranoid Style: Causality and Deceit in the Eighteenth Century." *William and Mary Quarterly* 39, no. 3 (1982): 401–41.

York, Neil. "Natural Rights Dissected and Rejected: John Lind's Counter to the Declaration of Independence." *Law and History Review* 35, no. 3 (2017): 563–93.

3

A DECLARATION OF STYLE: MASCULINITY'S ENDURING RESONANCE

Anna M. Young

A quick online search on "masculine style" yields a link to life coaching to help people identify and develop the way they enact their personal brand of masculinity in the world, several posts from menswear experts on tailoring and bespoke clothing, and a quiz to help people find their masculine "archetype." The style this chapter is concerned with, however, is rhetorical style, the ways in which the authors of the Declaration of Independence articulated a US American masculinity that permeates and saturates our cultural fabric even today. Both in style and in content, the Declaration of Independence is often read by rhetorical scholars of US American political discourse and history in relationship to the Constitution. The Declaration is masculine; the Constitution, feminine. The Declaration is unyielding; the Constitution, malleable. The Declaration is an end; the Constitution, the means. Our scholarship on the Declaration in rhetorical studies is largely absent a consideration of style aside from limited attention to its prose.[1] I argue in this essay that the stylistically gendered nature of the Declaration instantiates a kind of US American masculinity that persists in our national rhetorical constructions, self-image, and media ecology, and that, while a masculine style in general and the Declaration's masculine style in particular make the Declaration strategically effective and contextually resonant, there are also germinations in the document of a kind of US American masculinity that is more troubling and requires our attention.

Style is a *logos*, an aesthetic logic that each of us constructs materially, affectively, and performatively. Style is a way of "understanding the dynamics of our social experience or the relationship between rhetorical appeals and political decisions."[2] Considering the Declaration, there is a logic to the way the text itself interacts with the medium, the context of its writing in history, and the political feelings of the signatories in speaking for a nascent country. That is, the rhetorical style of the Declaration is a bricolage of particular social meanings that centers masculinity as a fundamentally US American *topos*. This chapter ends with a consideration of how stylistically masculine politics both compel and constrain us in the current moment, and how we might counter dangerous versions of US American masculinity rhetorically.

A broad note on style before we get into the literature and the document itself. Contemporary audiences will read the Declaration and likely see a document of polite majesty. Aside from someone practicing recitation as part of a poetry seminar, we can scarcely imagine writing or speaking in the way Jefferson and the signatories do in the Declaration. But we need to be mindful of its eighteenth-century context. Throughout this chapter, I shall attribute the language and meaning of the Declaration to the stylistic "vibration" of the time. It is a product of an era. We must keep in mind that this document was not, as we think of it, a polite declination. Consider the following analogy, when former president Trump was bringing sixty borderline-catastrophic legal challenges to the 2020 election. At one point, the Third Circuit court ruled unanimously that Rudy Giuliani, representing the Trump team, had brought a case challenging the election results in Pennsylvania citing "massive fraud."[3] They unanimously ruled against the Trump team, and the decision, written by Trump appointee Steven Bibas, was described by Reuters law and justice reporter Brad Heath as having "nuked [Trump] from orbit."[4] Similarly, while we might be inclined to believe the Declaration was the height of polite civility, in its day it would have nuked George III from orbit.

Theorizing Rhetorical Style

Style has always been a part of the rhetorical canon, but quite a lot of our disciplinary history with the subject relegates style to concerns about delivery or genre and not to a broader aesthetic politics that requires an exchange between author and audience. In the last few decades, scholars in rhetorical studies have taken up theorizing style in ways that better situate style as a hub with many spokes, a *topos* of feelings, media artifacts, politics, history, culture, genre, and so forth. Stuart Ewen has noted the ubiquity of style (it's in magazines, on TV, in architecture, and so on) and suggests it is the "key to understanding the contours of contemporary culture."[5] Robert

Hariman posits that style is a "means for modulating perception and shaping response."[6] Barry Brummett articulates a more forward-thinking, publicly engaged definition, writing that style is a "socially held sign system that [is] used to accomplish rhetorical purposes across the cultural spectrum."[7] Style, in other words, is critical to understanding rhetoric and the moment in which it occurs.

Other recent treatments of style underscore the social performativity of style and even its constitutive effect—that meaning is created not by the speaker or audience discretely but by their social interaction. Andrea Olinger defines style as "the dynamic co-construction of typified indexical meanings (types of people, practices, situations, texts) perceived in a single sign or a cluster of signs and influenced by participants' language ideologies."[8] By "indexical meanings," Olinger means how genres operate as cultural markers that audiences socialized in a culture would understand as a coalescing of signs. In Brummett's understanding, communities come together around a stylistic core. While he investigates gun culture, we could say this principle operates across any group: marathon runners, Swifties, the PTA. If you start distance running with the goal of finishing a marathon, that alone does not make you a "marathon runner" stylistically. For that, you will likely be professionally fitted for running shoes, so you become a Brooks person or an ASICS person or a HOKA One One person. And then you'll start subscribing to *Runner's World*. You'll follow several trainers' personal blogs online to learn how to map out your training. You'll buy electrolyte tablets and goo, and start carb loading. You'll talk with others about your long run, tapering, your PR. All of these signs are part of the genre "distance runner style." It is the way that you perform membership in a community and that others will recognize you as authentically one of them—or "one of those," depending on their attitude toward obsessed athletes.

In terms of style, each of us acts as a bricoleur, pulling together a way of being in the world that is "read" by those around us as an identifiable persona. Reimagining Pierre Bourdieu's concept of habitus, one might think of style as having three interrelated and overlapping parts. First, it is physiological: we perform "expressive forms and rituals" on our bodies, ranging from what we wear to how we stand, from how much conversational space we occupy to what we eat.[9] Second, it is psychological: we are said to "have style" when there is a kind of consistency between who we say we are and how we act in the world; it means others can identify something as "on brand" for us. And third, it is sociological—that is, we cannot do style in a vacuum; it is a social performance. Style is relational, a way of being with others; it is how we understand the dynamics of relationships and the power structures that undergird our politics.[10]

This particular kind of US American masculinity in the Declaration is consistent with how we typically understand masculinity in popular and political culture today. But it also gives us a point in time to trace stylistic features that are more antidemocratic, violent, and problematic. We might also consider how that point in time, the separation of what would become the United States away from its parent kingdom and the messy, tumultuous birth of this nation, also had social and political features we might connect to this point in time, a moment of threat to the very democracy that the Declaration's signers hoped to create. Let us turn now to the Declaration, where we see the nascence of these masculine throughlines.

All Men Are Created Equal

We begin by noting that the Declaration is, well, a declaration. A declaration is a formal announcement and an explicit statement marking the beginning of something, in this case the beginning of the United States of America. The Declaration, in other words, was written by Thomas Jefferson (and others) and signed by the fifty-six delegates to the Continental Congress to announce formally our country's independence. It is critical to start here because this document was not an opening to a conversation, nor was it something like the founders' version of an op-ed, nor was it a negotiation. The historical record makes clear that the colonists did, indeed, try to petition King George III and his Parliament, and did, to the extent possible, try to negotiate with him and with them. They were not successful, at least to the degree they deemed rightful. And so they *declared* themselves independent of Britain and of its king and of its laws. By contrast, the Constitution was meant to shape the governance of a still-young nation and is quite literally a list of compromises, some deeply democratic, some contested, others inhumane, to achieve that end. In general, given women's socialization and enculturation toward flexibility, cooperation, and affability, it would be nearly impossible to imagine a group of women at that time, even very powerful ones, literally declaring themselves done with the rule of an entire monarchy's; even now, feminine styles encourage hedging, disclaimers, and room for feedback. The Declaration's masculinity begins with the fact that these men felt they were endowed with divine rights of self-governance, that as I tell my kids about setting boundaries, "No is a complete sentence." This is the original documentation of what the kids call a hard pass.

The Declaration is also a remarkably succinct document. It is both blunt and direct. Many scholars across multiple disciplines have charted whether brain differences in men and women determine differences in communication, but most concur that instead socialization is responsible for the lion's share of the patterns of difference.[11] As Katherine Baxter notes, men's communication marks them as agents, as the ones with both power and authority to shape their paths.[12] In an interview, scholar Lise Elliot explains that "women tend to be more tentative in their speech, less declarative and more likely to engage in 'uptalk,' which is ending sentences in what sounds like a question, conveying less confidence in their assertions."[13] Men, on the other hand, tend to use a "reporting" style, eschewing personal anecdotes in favor of data and avoiding pathos-heavy descriptions. The fact that the Declaration is a report of twenty-seven transgressions by Britain and its king and still, in its original form, took one large page of real estate reinforces a masculine frame.

The text of the Declaration itself is divided into five sections: introduction, preamble, the case against George III, the case against the British people, and a conclusion. The introduction does not bury the lede: "When in the Course of human events, it becomes necessary for one people to dissolve the political bands which have connected them with another, and to assume among the powers of the earth, the separate and equal station to which the Laws of Nature and of Nature's God entitle them, a decent respect to the opinions of mankind requires that they should declare the causes which impel them to the separation." Contemporary audiences who read this opening will probably think it does not seem like a provocation. Contextualizing the choices, though, reveals urgency and force. Perhaps the most significant rhetorical move Jefferson makes is the word "necessary." As Stephen Lucas unpacks in his line-by-line explication of the Declaration, the word "necessary" implies that it is impelled by fate or determined by the operation of inextricable natural laws and thus beyond the control of human agents. Chambers's Cyclopaedia defines "necessary" as "that which cannot but be, or cannot be otherwise."[14] The author and signatories, then, establish the colonies' independence as divinely ordained by Nature's God, supported by the Laws of Nature, and impermeable to critique. It "cannot be otherwise." Confidence, and most certainly overconfidence, is a hallmark of arguing online with men especially on the site formerly known as Twitter, but that assuredness and imperviousness to challenge is centuries old.

The preamble, especially its lead sentence, is arguably the most famous portion of the Declaration: "We hold these truths to be self-evident, that all men are created equal, that they are endowed by their Creator with certain unalienable Rights, that among these are Life, Liberty and the pursuit of Happiness." Of course, prior to our more recent focus on inclusive language, including language around sex and gender, most US Americans would have read "all men" as "all people," but it is worthy of note that the authors and signatories limited citizenship to white men, the clear heirs of the divine rights of Nature's Laws. Indeed, Elizabeth Cady Stanton wrote in the Declaration of Sentiments at Seneca Falls in 1848 a parallel, "All men and women are created equal," clearly considering the amplification necessary.[15] The original preamble continues: "But when a long train of abuses and usurpations, pursuing invariably the same Object evinces a design to reduce them under absolute Despotism, it is their right, it is their duty, to throw off such Government, and to provide new Guards for their future security. Such has been the patient sufferance of these Colonies; and such is now the necessity which constrains them to alter their former Systems of Government." Scottish minister and rhetorical theorist Hugh Blair refers to the writing style of the preamble as "Style Periodique," which is "pompous and musical" and "gives an air of gravity and dignity to composition."[16] The masculine ethos embraces duty, honor, and service.[17] The signers and the colonists they represent in this Continental Congress have borne the burden and obligation of loyalty to their former empire like the allegiant men they imagine themselves to be, but men are too proud and too strong to obey a despot, and men are bound by duty and honor to provide for women and children by dissolving this abusive union.

Masculine style also champions rationality. While the idea that men are the arbiters of rationality is problematic and incoherent in many ways, when we think about our language use, "women are semantically associated with emotion and feeling and men are semantically associated with reason and thinking."[18] The preamble is syllogistic, rather than enthymematic—meaning the audience fills in a commonly held assumption—in form, that is, it takes us through four separate, interrelated claims and arrives at a concluding claim: (1) all men are created equal; (2) they are endowed by their creator with certain unalienable rights; (3) among these are life, liberty, and the pursuit of happiness; (4) to secure these rights, governments are instituted among men; and (5) whenever any government becomes destructive of those unalienable rights, it is men's duty to change or to eliminate it. The reliance here on formal syllogistic logic rather than inviting enthymematic interpretation again communicates a statement and not an invitation to feedback. It is a closed case and precludes polysemy. It is also noteworthy that this country's founders call out the scale to which they have been victimized in the preamble and then specify the methods bringing about their aggrievement in the rest of the document, foreshadowing how victimhood becomes a significant trope of contemporary toxic masculinity. But more on that later.

The preamble ends with, "Let Facts be submitted to a candid world." While shorter than Martin Luther's treatises nailed to a door, the Declaration lists twenty-seven statements of fact that a "candid world" will surely understand are egregious wrongs deserving of this forceful a response. Typically, we would anticipate that a colony trying to separate from its colonizer would provide a rationale for this move, but the key word here is "Facts." Eighteenth-century lawyers would take "Facts" here to mean that this is a case a lawyer could and would make in court before a judge. This is the sort of writing that someone would bet their professional reputation on. Several of these statements of grievance are particularly useful for understanding the Declaration not only as the start of a nation but also as a rhetorical blueprint for American masculinity. The first part of this list is aimed at George III, then monarch of Britain, the second at the British Parliament acting with George III. Some of the grievances against the king include:

> He has refused his Assent to Laws, the most wholesome and necessary for the public good.
>
> He has forbidden his Governors to pass Laws of immediate and pressing importance, unless suspended in their operation till his Assent should be obtained; and when so suspended, he has utterly neglected to attend to them.
>
> He has erected a multitude of New Offices, and sent hither swarms of Officers to harass our people, and eat out their substance.
>
> He has kept among us, in times of peace, Standing Armies without the Consent of our legislatures.

We see the word "necessary" again in the first example, which we recall is part of the colonists' divine right to self-determination. In this first part of the list, note the consistent parallel structure: each sentence begins with "He has." Anaphora is a rhetorical device in which the writer or speaker uses the same words or phrases at the beginning of successive sentences. In lay terms, anaphora creates a sort of drumbeat. Most of us can hear words in our heads as we read silently, so even when reading the Declaration to ourselves, we still find this percussive. In his work on the Marjorie Stoneman Douglas survivors of a mass school shooting, Justin Eckstein ties the repetitive sounds of gunfire to a broader conception of rhetoric as a sensorium, a place where sensory experiences meet and interact.[19] Certain sounds are "stitched to masculinity,"[20] including the sound of gunfire, and while a drumbeat provides a far less dangerous version of that sensory experience, it belongs in the same category of masculinity. In addition, "He has" exhibits amplification—that is, "a sonic trope used to intensify a position or standpoint."[21] Through anaphora and amplification, the Declaration manifests an experiential quality that we would code as masculine: forceful, nonnegotiable, relentless, and loud.

The second half of the list of grievances in the Declaration is aimed at both George III *and* his parliament as co-conspirators against the colonists. Again, every grievance needn't be included to prove this point, but they include such injuries as:

> For Quartering large bodies of armed troops among us:
> For protecting them, by a mock Trial, from punishment for any Murders which they should commit on the Inhabitants of these States:
> For cutting off our Trade with all parts of the world:
> For imposing Taxes on us without our Consent:
> For depriving us in many cases, of the benefits of Trial by Jury:

We see the same combination of the rhetorical tropes anaphora and amplification as in the first half of the list, in this case starting every sentence with "For" and then articulating an injury to the colonists. This kind of pulsing rhythm of the writing outlining the facts of the case against George III and his parliament hits an affective register. If we were to read these statements aloud, one after the other, there would be a clear beat, a sonic masculinity. Deborah Tannen calls masculine professional communication "report talk," in relation to to feminine professional communication, which she calls "rapport talk."[22] The emphasis in masculine communication is on "declarative statements" that are "objective and 'to the point,'" focused on "facts more than feelings." Masculine rhetorical style is "forceful" in that it "sounds confident, competent and authoritative," and maybe most significantly, it communicates status.[23] We see all these characteristics throughout this section of the Declaration. Despite the list of injuries, this is not a documentation of feelings but a document that *manufactures* feelings of anger and righteous indignation, feelings more likely to be associated with masculine styles than feminine ones. It accomplishes this generative work by vibrating on an affective register that we would also characterize, as like Eckstein notes, as "stitched to masculinity."

The final section of the Declaration is the conclusion, which comprises three short paragraphs. The first paragraph ends by saying, "A Prince whose character is thus marked by every act which may define a Tyrant, is unfit to be the ruler of a free people." In contemporary parlance, we would note that Jefferson is publicly trashing George III—that is, Jefferson and the signatories are essentially saying, "We tried being reasonable and we tried using typical channels of communication, but you are an insufferable, incompetent despot and we are washing our hands of you."

The second paragraph trashes the British people: "We have appealed to their native justice and magnanimity, and we have conjured them by the ties of our common kindred to disavow these usurpations, which, would inevitably interrupt our connections and correspondence. They too have been deaf to the voice of justice and consanguinity. We must, therefore, acquiesce in the necessity, which denounces our Separation, and hold them, as we hold the rest of mankind, Enemies in War, in Peace Friends." This paragraph typifies an appeal to brotherhood, man to man. The implication here is that the colonists have tried reasoning with their "common kindred," but those men have chosen to maintain loyalty not to the brotherhood of which they are a part but to the Crown, of which they are not.

The final clause, "Enemies in War, in Peace Friends," is an instance of chiasmus, the rhetorical figure in which words or phrases are repeated in reverse order, using the same phrases or being modified as we see in this example. The flourish here is designed to hit the ear rather than the eye in the same way that anaphora and amplification work in the previous section. And despite the poetry, the energy of the chiasmus delivers the penultimate blow of this Declaration.

The final paragraph of the conclusion and the Declaration itself shows the entire document to be a series of shorter syllogisms within an overarching syllogism. Here we reach the deductive end:

> We, therefore, the Representatives of the united States of America, in General Congress, Assembled, appealing to the Supreme Judge of the world for the rectitude of our intentions, do, in the Name, and by

> Authority of the good People of these Colonies, solemnly publish and declare, That these United Colonies are, and of Right ought to be Free and Independent States; that they are Absolved from all Allegiance to the British Crown, and that all political connection between them and the State of Great Britain, is and ought to be totally dissolved; and that as Free and Independent States, they have full power to levy War, conclude Peace, contract Alliances, establish Commerce, and to do all other Acts and Things which Independent States may of right do. And for the support of this Declaration, with a firm reliance on the protection of divine Providence, we mutually pledge to each other our Lives, our Fortunes and our sacred Honor.

This is the single most agentive move the colonists make. Masculine styles center agency; indeed, "Facts" in this document are not only pieces of evidence as part of a larger claim but are also active. To an eighteenth-century audience, facts were also "things you do"; they are active. Agency is active, not passive. Throughout this paragraph, what we see is a group of men taking what they believe is rightfully and divinely granted: their freedom. In the eighteenth century, it was only white men who could possibly dare not only to demand freedom from a significantly stronger colonizing nation but also to do so by staking a claim to providence. This "freedom from" and "freedom to" language, of course, is adopted in the Constitution, but here, too, adopted as a dynamic, ongoing draft. Syllogistic logic, by its nature, ends the inquiry. This, this, this, and therefore that. This is not a document that had to be amended simply to be ratified; this is a declaration. It is *the* Declaration.

Masculinity Then, Masculinity Now

It is not surprising that the Declaration can be argued to be a masculine document stylistically. It was written by men; it was written for men. And we can recognize the benefits of this masculinity: direct, curt, forceful, and supremely confident. While that may not be what the signers felt in writing and releasing this document to England, a much more established, far stronger, militarily successful kingdom, writing as if the signers were deeply committed to and confident in their declaration emphasized a kind of muscularity that was politically necessary. A masculine style is, on its own, neither good nor bad: it can be either and it can be both. We ought to be able to celebrate the success of the Declaration and the strengths of the

US American masculinity it authors while at the same time considering the ways it also establishes some of what we see today as dangerous and antidemocratic masculinities that are also very commonly, but not uniquely, US American.

The Declaration is an appeal to rationality and a list of grievances. And it is angry. There are many manifestations of these features in our culture today that are largely neutral or even good. A "Captain America" movie has all of these features, and I don't stay up at night worrying that Steve Rogers is poisoning the body politic. But there is a growing undercurrent of toxicity in masculinity, especially in our politics, that we may trace to these same features. And that rhetorical style is worth making more visible and seeking an antidote.

Certainly, good critics will note that the near poetry of the Declaration and, for instance, the discursive practices of more reactionary masculine creators online are different in important ways. The tone, the lexicon, the literacy level, the mediums, and the particular (as opposed to universal in the Aristotelian sense) audiences are starkly different. And yet, both that moment in time and this one may share a kind of political and social vibration that invites more-problematic masculinities as a stylistic response. If we think in terms of tectonic plates, periods of relative stability in this country are marked by stillness, by a lack of fracture and tension in the plates. By contrast, the lead-up to the Declaration was hardly placid. Students of US American history will know that tensions had been rising in the colonies and that colonists were increasingly angry about their treatment by Britain in general and by its king, George III, in particular. And while that anti-British and anti-monarchical sentiment was not universal, it was pronounced enough that it led the Continental Congress to vote in favor of independent rule. That was, in many ways, our democracy's birth. Our current moment is characterized by increasing fears of that same democracy's impermanence and even death. So we ought not be entirely surprised that features of the Declaration that were never intended to be weaponized to end our democratic experiment might still be stylistically resonant in another era of tectonic shift. A number of scholars in rhetoric have taken up this question of the current state of masculinity, often centering Donald Trump as its archetype, and we shall weave some of those threads together here.

Casey Ryan Kelly has written extensively about the toxicity of certain branches of white masculinity and of patriarchal structures more generally. Kelly argues that "Trump's appeals to rage, malice, and revenge" are part of an "underlying emotional-moral framework in which victimization, resentment, and revenge are civic virtues."[24] One of his key examples is Trump's June 27, 2017, rally in Youngstown, Ohio, where, as in all of his rallies, he made a number of unsubstantiated claims and freewheeled through a list of complaints:

> We have tough people. Our people are tougher than their people. Our people are tougher and stronger and meaner and smarter than the gangs. One by one we are finding the illegal gang members, drug dealers, thieves, robbers, criminals and killers. And we are sending them the hell back home where they came from. And once they are gone, we will never let them back in. Believe me. The predators and criminal aliens who poison our communities with drugs and prey on innocent young people, these beautiful, beautiful, innocent young people will, will find no safe haven anywhere in our country.[25]

The prose does not sing like the anaphoric rhythm of "He has" in the Declaration, but one of the key features of Trump's rhetoric and the rhetoric of toxic masculinity in general is grievance. Here the grievance is emphatically racialized, and one of the key findings from the crosstabs on data on the 2016 election is that people who expressed high levels of anxiety about Brown and Black people "cutting the line" in Arlie Hochschild's terms (see Hochschild's examination of Trump supporters in *Strangers in Their Own Land*) and having what they considered too much power were the strongest supporters of Trump.[26] But as Denise Bostdorff contends, Trump's sexism and misogyny was an even bigger draw with his rallygoers and voters.[27] Kimberle Crenshaw has established a significant link between racism and patriarchy, so we would expect a near-perfect circle in this Venn diagram overlap.[28] In his October 14, 2016, address in Greensboro, North Carolina, Trump "harkened to a pre-feminist time when white men's status was secure. He depicted a nation in crisis due to a feminized establishment where men—especially the Black man at its helm—did not act manly, while women malevolently pursued selfish, conspiratorial motives."[29] Trump's rhetoric is crude, but it pulls the thread of masculine grievance and anger toward "the Other" in a similar way to the Declaration's pulling no punches with George III and his parliament.

Intimately connected to grievance is victimhood. In Kenneth Burke's guilt-purification-redemption cycle, he explains that we are all sinners because we all break our covenants with a higher power—God, America, democracy—and so we feel guilt.[30] Feeling the need to purify ourselves of this guilt, we can do this either by mortification or self-blame or by scapegoating the Other. Because many of us are not interested in blaming ourselves, we typically purify ourselves by scapegoating. Our feeling of joy in this purification is never permanent, however, because we sin again and the cycle begins anew. In the Declaration, the authors scapegoated George III, his enablers in Parliament, and the British people as a whole. Trump scapegoats specific politicians—Hillary Clinton, Barack Obama, Nancy Pelosi, Joe Biden—and the coalitions of citizens they tend to represent: women; ethnic, racial, and religious minorities; LGBTQ+ people; immigrants. Paul Johnson contends that "Trump's rhetorical form functions through a toxic, paradoxically abject masculine style" that "helps [his adherents] imagine themselves as victims of a political tragedy centered around the displacement of 'real America' from the political center by a feminized political establishment."[31] Victimhood is an odd trope in toxic masculinity, since masculinity would seem to leave no oxygen for weakness. But victimhood functions in toxic masculinity not as weakness but as a marker of the alienation of the elite, the establishment, and the institutions of the elite establishment, particularly universities and mainstream media. That is, if you can claim that you *feel* victimized, you stake a claim to membership in a group that is ready to fight the establishment. The Declaration does not amplify victimhood the way Trump does, but it certainly nods a number of times in that direction and for the same reason: the colonists had every right, in fact the God-given right, to fight the establishment because they had been victims of a despotic ruler.

Conclusion

The Declaration's rhetorical style in context, form, and content centers masculinity. That thread of masculinity is woven into our cultural fabric such that it is ubiquitous in politics and culture. Style is important not only for what it is but also for what it does. The Declaration's success offers a set of features of American masculinity that have served our politics well. As a culture, our ethos is optimistic and forward-thinking, confident in our ethics and values and committed to self-governance. But we are not in typical times. And when we consider our lurches toward authoritarianism and our dalliances with antidemocratic rhetorics and practices, we ought to think about how to respond more effectively. There is no simple answer; if there were, we would not be dealing with this iteration of US American masculinity—and yet we are: because we are, we are surrounded by guns and violence, by anti-trans and anti-LGBTQ+ rhetoric and policies, and by hatred of and violence toward so many marginalized Others. While it is an important contribution for rhetorical scholars to think about the Declaration, it is an even more critical project to take seriously its longitudinal influence both good and bad. I hope that this chapter will serve as a beginning to that project.

NOTES

1. Lucas, "Stylistic Artistry."
2. Hariman, *Political Style*, 8.
3. Jenna Ellis (@realJennaEllis), "Rudy Giuliani and me on Third Circuit's opinion," Twitter, November 27, 2020, 9:46am, https://x.com/realJennaEllis/status/1332380180065738754.
4. Brad Heath (@bradheath), "The Third Cir. was required to take this case," Twitter, November 27, 2020, 10:34am, https://x.com/bradheath/status/1332392306490679296.
5. Ewen, *All Consuming Images*, 2.
6. Hariman, *Political Style*, 2.
7. Brummett, *Rhetoric of Style*, 3.
8. Olinger, "Sociocultural Approach to Style."
9. Hebdige, *Subculture*, 3.
10. Adapted from Young, *Prophets, Gurus, Pundits*, 6–8.
11. These are far too numerous to be inclusive, but, for example, see Ariyani and Hadiani, "Gender Differences"; Carli, "Gender, Interpersonal Power, and Social Influence"; Dousti and Rasekh, "ELT Students' Gender Differences."
12. Baxter, "Masculine Men."
13. Valenzuela, "Do Men and Women."
14. Lucas, "Stylistic Artistry."
15. "Elizabeth Cady Stanton."
16. Blair, *Lectures on Rhetoric and Belles Lettres*, 25–29.
17. Matthews et al., "Duty and Honour."
18. Pavco-Giaccia et al., "Rationality Is Gendered."
19. Eckstein, "The (Parkland) Kids Are Alright."
20. Eckstein, "Conversation."
21. Eckstein, "Conversation."
22. Tannen, *Talking from 9 to 5*.
23. Turner, "Masculine Feminine Difference."
24. Kelly, "Donald J. Trump," 4.
25. Merica, "Trump Makes 'Presidential' Pitch."
26. McElwee and McDaniel, "Economic Anxiety."
27. Bostdorff, "Donald Trump, *Access Hollywood*," 217.
28. Crenshaw, "Mapping the Margins."
29. Bostdorff, "Donald Trump, *Access Hollywood*," 216.
30. Burke, *Permanence and Change*, 190.
31. Johnson, "Art of Masculine Victimhood," 230.

BIBLIOGRAPHY

Ariyani, Emma, and Dini Hadiani. "Gender Differences in Students' Interpersonal Communication." *Responsible Education, Learning and Teaching in Emerging Economies* 1, no. 2 (December 2019).

Baxter, Katherine. "Masculine Men Do Not Like Feminine Wording: The Effectiveness of Gendered Wording in Health Promotion Leaflets in the UK." *National Library of Medicine Online* (October 2022). https://www.ncbi.nlm.nih.gov/pmc/articles/PMC9612536/.

Blair, Hugh. "Lectures on Rhetoric and Belles Lettres." Vol. 3. In *Eighteenth Century Collections Online*. https://name.umdl.umich.edu/004786433.0001.001. University of Michigan Library Digital Collections.

Bostdorff, Denise. "Donald Trump, *Access Hollywood*, and the Rhetorical Performance of Aggrieved White Masculinity." *Western Journal of Communication* 87, no. 2 (April 2023). https://doi.org/10.1080/10570314.2022.2118549.

Brummett, Barry. *A Rhetoric of Style*. Carbondale: Southern Illinois University Press, 2008.

Burke, Kenneth. *Permanence and Change: An Anatomy of Purpose*. 3rd ed. Berkeley: University of California Press, 1984.

Carli, Linda L. "Gender, Interpersonal Power, and Social Influence." *Journal of Social Issues* 55, no. 1 (December 2012). https://doi.org/10.1111/0022-4537.00106.

Crenshaw, Kimberle. "Mapping the Margins: Intersectionality, Identity Politics, and Violence Against Women of Color." *Stanford Law Review* 43, no. 6 (July 1991). http://www.jstor.org/stable/1229039.

Declaration of Independence: A Transcription. America's Founding Documents, U.S. National Archives and Records Administration. https://www.archives.gov/founding-docs/declaration-transcript; last modified June 8, 2022.

Dousti, Masoumeh, and Abbass Eslami Rasekh. "ELT Students' Gender Differences in the Use of Hedges in Interpersonal Interaction: A Mixed Method Approach Applied." *Journal of Applied Linguistics and Language Research* 3, no. 1 (2016). http://jallr.com/index.php/JALLR/article/view/248.

Eckstein, Justin. Conversation with Anna M. Young, September 2023.

———. "The (Parkland) Kids Are Alright." *Communication and the Public* 5, no. 2 (2020). https://doi.org/10.1177/2057047320950630.

"Elizabeth Cady Stanton." Library of Congress Research Guides. https://guides.loc.gov/chronicling-america-elizabeth-cady-stanton.

Ewen, Stuart. *All Consuming Images: The Politics of Style in Contemporary Culture*. San Francisco: Harper, 1999.

Hariman, Robert. *Political Style: The Artistry of Power*. Chicago: University of Chicago Press, 1995.

Hebdige, Dick. *Subculture: The Meaning of Style*. London: Methuen, 1979.

Johnson, Paul E. "The Art of Masculine Victimhood: Donald Trump's Demagoguery." *Women's Studies in Communication* 40, no. 3 (2017): 229–50. https://doi.org/10.1080/07491409.2017.1346533.

Kelly, Casey Ryan. "Donald J. Trump and the Rhetoric of Ressentiment." *Quarterly Journal of Speech* 106, no. 1 (2020): 2–24. https://doi.org/10.1080/00335630.2019.1698756.

Lucas, Stephen E. "The Stylistic Artistry of the Declaration of Independence." National Archives. https://www.archives.gov/founding-docs/stylistic-artistry-of-the-declaration.

Matthews, Gethin, Ben Rees, Sean Kenny, and Alys Rosser. "Duty and Honour: The Important Notions of Masculinity During the First World War."

McElwee, Sean, and Jason McDaniel. "Economic Anxiety Didn't Make People Vote for Trump, Racism Did." *The Nation*, May 8, 2017. https://www.thenation.com/article/economic-anxiety-didnt-make-people-vote-trump-racism-did/.

Merica, Dan. "Trump Makes 'Presidential' Pitch at Ohio Rally." CNN, July 26, 2017. https://www.cnn.com/2017/07/25/politics/trump-youngstown-ohio-campaign-rally/index.html.

Olinger, Andrea. "A Sociocultural Approach to Style." *Rhetoric Review* 35, no. 2 (Spring 2016): 121–34. http://dx.doi.org/10.1080/07350198.2016.1142930.

Pavco-Giaccia, Olivia, Martha Fitch Little, Jason Stanely, and Yarrow Dunham. "Rationality Is Gendered." *Collabra: Psychology* 5, no. 1 (2019). https://doi.org/10.1525/collabra.274.

Tannen, Deborah. *Talking from 9 to 5: Women and Men at Work*. New York: William Morrow, 2001.

Turner, Caroline. "Masculine Feminine Difference: How We Talk." Huffpost.com, July 2014. https://www.huffpost.com/entry/masculinefeminine-differe_b_5559127.

Valenzuela, Diana. "Do Men and Women Actually Communicate Differently? Experts Weigh In." Katie Couric Media, September 23, 2022. https://katiecouric.com/lifestyle/relationships/gender-differences-in-communication-style/.

Young, Anna M. *Prophets, Gurus, Pundits: Rhetorical Styles and Public Engagement*. Carbondale: Southern Illinois University Press, 2014.

PART 2

THE SOVEREIGN DECLARATION

4
THE ANTEBELLUM DECLARATION: ABOLITION, SECESSION, AND REVOLUTION

Mary E. Stuckey

The Declaration of Independence is a dangerous document. Most obviously, in 1776 it incited a war and put the signers' lives in imminent peril. But its dangers are not confined to the moment of its creation. The Declaration serves as something of a rhetorical template for political division; the argument that any "one people," however understood, has the right to their "separate and equal station" has been used to authorize various kinds of political disunion ranging from the peaceful to the violent.[1] Michael J. Lee and R. Jarrod Atchison argue that the Declaration is a useful warrant for secession for at least three reasons: it sets up a rationale, arguing that denial of human rights is sufficient cause for separation; it claims the right of a people to "alter or abolish" a government; and it argues that separation can be justified based on racial or cultural difference.[2] Combining claims of human equality with arguments that those claims justify distinct political identities, the Declaration offered a clear justification for many kinds of political separation. Yet the Declaration is not clear about what may constitute "a people," how we might objectively know when one has been created, or at what cost separation might be authorized, enabling individuals and groups to determine these matters for themselves. Consequently, in the United States, threats of secession are nearly as old as the union itself, and they cut across partisan lines, material interests, and geographic regions.[3]

The pliability inherent in the Declaration reveals other hazards as well. Most prominent among these is the contradiction inherent in a collection of slaveholders declaiming that "all men are created equal."[4] There are at least two ways to resolve this contradiction: to acknowledge it and dedicate the nation to policies that more closely approximate those values, or to reinterpret those values in light of unequal practices and policies. In the antebellum period, abolitionists tended to take the first approach, a tendency that has left a legacy that requires both the rectification of past injustice and its erasure in favor of the narrative of an ever-improving nation. Many slavers argued that the claim of human equality was never intended to be a universal, applying to all people, but was limited to white men. Widely argued among those declaring and defending the Confederacy, this understanding interpreted the Declaration as a document that authorized Southern secession and the racial hierarchies that Confederates were dedicated to protecting. This interpretation did not die with the Confederacy but remains an integral part of the Lost Cause ideology and has mutated and developed along with that ideology as it is wielded by contemporary white supremacists.

From a contemporary perspective, the Civil War looks like the inevitable result of decades of increasing sectional conflict, all of which was concentrated on the issue of slavery. But as David M. Potter points out, from the perspectives of those who experienced those decades, war was not necessarily inevitable, and many people on both sides sought to prevent it.[5] Still, arguments for Southern secession date to at least the 1820s.[6] The secession crisis of the 1850s that culminated in the Civil War was a product of increasing tensions over slavery, exacerbated by questions of national expansion, brewing since the 1840s and escalating as the nation moved west.[7] These changes increased sectional animosities and damaged the ability of the party system to manage them.[8] Slave states, dedicated to the belief that since the original Constitution protected slavery and aware that ratification depended on that protection, argued that continued protection was required to preserve the Union. Northerners, equally aware of the Constitution's commitment to slavery, took a variety of positions, ranging from the view that the Union was guilty of original sin in endorsing slavery in the Constitution and that participation in a political system legitimated by the Constitution was morally wrong, to a belief that the Constitution and the Union could be redeemed by purging slavery from both, or to a belief that slavery would die a natural death if left alone. And, of course, there were those in the North who did not object to slavery as an institution, and many more who preferred to see the end of slavery but not of its associated racial hierarchies.[9] Advocates for all these positions found support for their stances in the Declaration of Independence. This chapter focuses on some of these uses of the Declaration, beginning with a brief discussion of the abolitionist understanding of the Declaration and then moving to an analysis of how Confederates relied upon the form and content of the Declaration, using each for different purposes.

The chapter closes with a brief look at the legacies of these interpretations, which are covered in more detail in other chapters of this volume.

Declaring the Necessity of Abolition

While the Declaration wasn't widely used as a warrant for political action immediately following the revolution, by the early 1800s it had increasingly gained heft as legitimating a range of political beliefs. Abolitionists in particular found the Declaration to be a powerful touchstone for their arguments concerning slavery. Probably the most famous such use is Frederick Douglass's "What to the Slave Is the Fourth of July?," an oration delivered in Rochester, New York, on July 5, 1852. Douglass begins the address with a series of rhetorical questions: "Pardon me, and allow me to ask, why am I called upon to speak here today? What have I, or those I represent, to do with your national independence? Are the great principles of political freedom and of natural justice, embodied in that Declaration of Independence, extended to us?"[10] He continued in the same vein, excoriating the hypocrisy evident in a nation that celebrated its independence and dedication to universal values while supporting slavery. This claim to inconsistency and hypocrisy was a bulwark of abolitionist argumentation.

Douglass may be the most famous exemplar of this argumentation, but he was not the first. As early as 1829, abolitionists such as David Walker were pointing to the nation's hypocrisy:

> See your Declaration Americans!!! Do you understand your own language? Hear your language, proclaimed to the world, July 4th, 1776—"We hold these truths to be self evident—that ALL MEN ARE CREATED EQUAL!! that they *are endowed by their Creator with certain unalienable rights*; that among these are life, *liberty*, and the pursuit of happiness!! Compare your own language above, extracted from your Declaration of Independence, with your cruelties and murders inflicted by your cruel and unmerciful fathers and yourselves on our fathers and on us—men who have never given your fathers or you the least provocation!!!!!![11]

Walker thus exemplifies a standard trope in abolitionist discourse: calling out the explicit contradiction between the principles outlined in the Declaration, which authorized rebellion, independence, and the new nation, and the material practices of that new nation.

The Declaration served other comparative purposes as well. Like Douglass, William Lloyd Garrison used both the Declaration and the holiday dedicated to its commemoration to argue for abolition. In a speech delivered at Boston's Park Street Church in 1829, he noted that the list of wrongs enumerated in the Declaration were "pitiful" when compared to the wrongs suffered by enslaved persons.[12] Similarly, the Constitution of the American Antislavery Society, founded in 1833, quoted both the biblical injunction to love one's neighbor and the Declaration's claim that "all men are created equal," specifically connecting the two sources to one another: "The Most High God 'hath made of one blood all nations of men to dwell on all the face of the earth,' and hath commanded them to love their neighbors as themselves; and . . . our National Existence is based upon this principle, as recognized in the Declaration of Independence, 'that all mankind are created equal, and that they are endowed by their Creator with certain inalienable rights, among which are life, liberty, and the pursuit of happiness.'"[13] The natural conclusion was that abolition was both a political and a moral necessity. As Ralph Waldo Emerson put it as he encouraged opposition to the Fugitive Slave Law, "You must all be Declarations of Independence,"[14] an exhortation that required listeners to internalize the precepts of the Declaration and then act upon them.

This connection of the political and the moral was critical to abolitionist discourse, and abolitionists frequently joined the Declaration and the Bible to one another. Supporters of slavery often argued that the institution was authorized by the Bible and therefore did not run afoul of either the founding principles or its Christian antecedents. Abolitionists thus needed to counter that argument, and so rhetors like Angelina Grimké argued that the practices of chattel slavery were directly opposed to the nation's founding principles and to Christianity as well, thus associating the practices of good Christians, good citizens, and abolitionists. Grimké wrote, "We must come back to the good old doctrine of our forefathers who declared to the world this self-evident truth that *all* men are created equal, and that they have certain *inalienable* rights, among which are life, *liberty*, and the pursuit of happiness. . . . If a self-evident truth that *all* men everywhere and of every color are born equal, and have an *inalienable right to liberty*, then it is equally true that *no* man can be born a slave, and no man can ever *rightfully* be reduced to *involuntary* bondage and held as a slave, however fair may be the claim of his master or mistress through wills and titles."[15] Grimké does not deny that slavery is legal, protected by "wills and titles." But she does deny its legitimacy, arguing that it violates the higher law that the Declaration was based upon. Others went even further, arguing that the failure to live up to the principles of the Declaration undermined free institutions across the nation.[16]

Of course, no one was more likely to rely on the Declaration in debates about slavery than Abraham Lincoln, who often endowed that document with "scriptural authority."[17] Lincoln saw in the Declaration two documents: one that "merely" authorized independence and one that enunciated universal truths.[18] Lincoln argued that the signers

> meant to set up a standard maxim for free society, which should be familiar to all, and revered by all; constantly looked to, constantly labored for, and even though never perfectly attained, constantly approximated, and thereby constantly spreading and deepening its influence, and augmenting the happiness and value of life to all people of all colors everywhere. The assertion that "all men are created equal" was of no practical use in effecting our separation from Great Britain; and it was placed in the Declaration not for that, but for future use. Its authors meant it to be—as, thank God, it is now proving itself—a stumbling-block to all those who in after times might seek to turn a free people back into the hateful paths of despotism.[19]

In that second document, Lincoln saw a uniquely US American identity, one that was dedicated, as he would later argue, "to the proposition that all men were created equal."[20]

In the antebellum period, abolitionists relied on the content of the Declaration and generally limited themselves to the claims of universal rights stemming from divinely ordained universal human equality. Those advocating slavery and secession had a different set of tasks. While form and content are not easily or reliably separated, it is analytically useful to consider those tasks in light of how secessionists relied on the form of the Declaration when they justified secession and how they dealt with its content when it came to asserting the right to revolution.

The Declaration as a Warrant for Secession and War

One of the important differences during the antebellum period involved opinions concerning the nature of the union itself. Many in the North, but also some in the slave states, argued that the states had "fused their sovereign identities" to form a unitary nation. Others, almost entirely in the South, argued that the states retained their sovereignty within a union best understood as a confederacy.[21] The other primary justification derives from the right of revolution as proclaimed in the Declaration of Independence.[22] In general, when secessionists argued from a claim that the federal union was a compact, they found utility in echoing the form of the Declaration. When they treated secession as implicit in the right of revolution, they found utility in its content. Here, when I refer to form, I intend to draw attention to the generic qualities of the Declaration—its formulaic attributes; when I refer to content, I am addressing its internal arguments in favor of the right to revolution.

The Confederate Theory of Union: Arguments from Form

When secessionists relied on the theory of the union as a confederation of sovereign states rather than proclaiming the right of revolution, they modeled their claims on the Declaration. As a template, the Declaration has five constituent elements: the requirement to justify separation to the world; a claim to truths that are held to be self-evident; a list of injuries and usurpations; an argument that these have gone unredressed; and an explicit declaration of independence.[23] In relying on this form, secessionists authorized their actions by making the argument that their situation was analogous to that of the colonists in 1776 and hoped to accrue to themselves the moral authority of that moment.[24]

Of the eleven states that seceded from the Union, four (South Carolina, Mississippi, Georgia, Texas) issued statements declaring their reasons for doing so. Thirteen states drafted ordinances of secession (South Carolina, Mississippi, Florida, Alabama, Georgia, Louisiana, Texas, Virginia, Arkansas, Tennessee, North Carolina, Missouri, and Kentucky).[25] In this, they obviously were following the pattern set by the Declaration, making a public statement about the causes for their separation. South Carolina, for example, declared in 1852 that although it was not currently exercising it, the state had the right to secede. In so doing, South Carolina also stated its version of what appeared in the Declaration as a "long train of abuses and usurpations," noting "frequent violations of the Constitution of the United States by the Federal Government, and its encroachments upon the reserved rights of the sovereign states of the Union, especially in relation to slavery."[26] Moreover, South Carolinians noted in this ordinance that "it is her right, without let, hindrance, or molestation from any power whatsoever, to secede from the said Federal Union; and that for the sufficiency of the causes which may impel her to such separation, she is responsible alone, under God, to the tribunal of public opinion among the nations of the earth."[27] Here, South Carolina explicitly nodded to the Declaration's statement that public announcements of independence were signs of "decent respect for the opinions of mankind," while also seemingly sharing that document's assumption that this show of respect would assist in the cause of independence. This argument appears in many contexts regarding secession. In his inaugural address, for example, Confederate president Jefferson Davis declaimed against the "wanton aggression" of the North and argued, "The impartial and enlightened verdict of mankind will vindicate the rectitude of our conduct, and He who knows the hearts of men will judge on the sincerity with which we labored to preserve the Government of our fathers in its spirit."[28] Hoping during the moment of his inauguration to accrue to himself the symbolic power of the founding presidents, like them, he relied on the power of public opinion.

Echoes of the Declaration run throughout secessionist discourse. Take, for example, South Carolina's "Declaration of the Immediate Causes Which Induce and Justify the Secession of South Carolina from the Federal Union."[29] It begins by announcing the action taken by "the people of South Carolina in Convention assembled on the 26th day of April, AD, 1852, declared that the frequent violations of the Constitution of the United States, by the Federal Government, and its encroachments upon the reserved rights of the States, fully justified this State in withdrawing from the Federal Union, but in deference to the opinions and wishes of the other slaveholding States, she forbore at that time to exercise this right. Since that time, these encroachments have continued to increase, and further forbearance ceases to be a virtue." In this single paragraph, the document declares peoplehood ("the people of South Carolina"), claims a "long train of abuses," and acknowledges the importance of public opinion, which occasioned the publication of the document itself. South Carolina's declaration thus relies on the language of the Declaration of 1776. It continues: "And now the State of South Carolina having resumed her separate and equal place among nations, deems it due to herself, to the remaining United States of America, and to the nations of the world, that she should declare the immediate causes which have led her to this act." Note here especially the claim that the state has resumed its status as an independent entity; unlike the original Declaration, this document was not announcing a new status but the resumption of an old one. Louisiana and Virginia made similar stipulations, and many states declared their status as independent and sovereign states, although they did not necessarily mark this as the resumption of a previously held status.[30]

Texas, having more justification for an argument that it was resuming sovereign status, noted that the state had "abandoned her separate national existence and consented to become one of the confederated Union" and was "received into a Commonwealth,"[31] a term that surely would have astounded the framers of the Constitution. Texas's list of complaints was colorful, extensive, and informative: "By the disloyalty of the Northern States and their citizens and the imbecility of the Federal Government, infamous combinations of incendiaries and outlaws have been permitted in those States and the common territory of Kansas to trample upon the federal laws, to war upon the lives and property of Southern citizens in that territory, and finally, by violence and mob law, to usurp the possession of the same as exclusively the property of the Northern States."[32] Texas was outraged by the actions of the federal government in the territories and even more outraged by its lack of action in Texas, which had been subjected to the depredations of "Indian savages" and "murderous forays of banditti." Texans here echoed the racist claims made in the Declaration, accusing King George of fomenting attacks by Indigenous nations upon the colonies.

There were other ways the Texas ordinance borrowed from the Declaration: it argued that these abuses had been long and patiently tolerated, for example ("These and other wrongs we have patiently borne in the vain hope that a returning sense of justice and humanity would induce a different course of administration"). And it offered its own version of self-evident truth: "We hold as undeniable truths that the governments of the various States, and of the confederacy itself, were established exclusively by the white race, for themselves and their posterity; that the African race had no agency in their establishment; that they were rightfully held and regarded as an inferior and dependent race, and in that condition only could their existence in this country be rendered beneficial or tolerable." The argument that the Declaration had been intended to announce the rights of white men was a common one among secessionists. They relied on the fact that most of the signers were slaveowners and declared that as such, they could not possibly have meant that slaves were "men" within the meaning of the document. Because the states were sovereign, because the federal government had no right to legislate slavery in the states, and because enslaved persons could not be considered "men," slave states collectively argued that the federal union required protection of slavery as a system. Denying that protection invalidated the union itself.[33]

Jefferson Davis, for example, noted in a speech bidding "Farewell to the US Senate," that secession differed from nullification in that secession "is to be justified on the basis that the states are sovereign."[34] Under this theory, the federal government had no right to legislate (specifically, to restrict slavery) in the states or territories. Thus, "slavery exists in the United States independent of the Constitution, in a three-fold aspect, first as property, second as a domestic relation of service of labor under the law of a state, and lastly as a basis of political power. And viewed in any or all of these lights, Congress has no power under the Constitution to create or destroy it anywhere."[35] That is, whether one understood enslaved persons as property, slavery as a system of labor, or slavery as a fundamental aspect of the organization of the nation's political affairs, it was authorized and protected, and if the federal government refused to recognize that elemental fact, the union itself was perforce dissolved. "We maintain that in every compact between two or more parties," said Davis, "the obligation is mutual; that the failure of one of the contracting parties to perform a material part of the agreement, entirely releases the obligation of the other; and that where no arbiter is provided, each party is remitted to his own judgment to determine the fact of failure, with all its consequences."[36] This is a peculiar rendition of how contracts work and is but one example of the kinds of contortions necessitated by the secessionist commitment to slavery.

It is thus notable that secessionists, so intent on the rights of the states to maintain slavery, were equally intent on objecting to states' rights when it was a matter of the rights of non–slave states. Southerners were, for example, outraged at the efforts of some Northern states to avoid, nullify, or otherwise subvert the noxious Fugitive Slave Law, which required them to return escaped enslaved persons to their former masters. Southerners likewise resented the efforts of those who resided in the territories to restrict slavery in those territories. States' rights were applied in the South only in defense of slavery, never in favor of those who opposed it or its expansion.

Some Southerners, it should be said, were strongly opposed both to the act of secession and to the theory of state supremacy that justified it. Andrew Johnson, for example, in 1860 a senator representing the border state of Tennessee, declared, "You have entered into the compact; it was mutual; it was reciprocal; and you of your own volition have no right to withdraw and break the compact, without the consent of the other parties. What remedy, then, has a state? It has a remedy that remains and abides with every people upon the face of the earth. When grievances are without a remedy, or without redress, when oppression becomes intolerable, they have the great, the inherent right of revolution."[37] Some secessionists agreed with Johnson's understanding of the Constitution, if not with his refusal to secede, and they enjoined their compatriots to act upon their right of revolution. In doing so, they based their claims on the content of the Declaration.

The Right of Revolution: Arguments from Content

Some secessionists did not rely on the idea that the states were sovereign but argued that they found themselves in the same position as the colonists of 1776: having become a distinct people, they were necessarily exercising their right to separate. If that right was denied by their fellow states, they, like the colonists before them, were compelled to rebel. In this context, both individual interlocutors and the states speaking as collectives referred to the founding and echoed much of the content of the Declaration. South Carolina, for example, noted that the signers "solemnly declared that whenever any 'form of government becomes destructive of the ends for which it was established, it is the right of the people to alter or abolish it, and to institute a new government,'"[38] relying on the Declaration as a warrant for secession. In another example, Jefferson Davis argued in his inaugural address that "our present condition, achieved in a manner unprecedented in the history of nations, illustrates the American idea that that governments rest upon the consent of the governed, and that it is the right of the people to alter or abolish governments whenever they become destructive of the ends for which they were established."[39] He continued by claiming that when the Southern states seceded, "in this they merely asserted a right which the Declaration of Independence of 1776 had defined to be inalienable: of the time and occasion of for its exercise, they, as sovereigns, were the final judges, each for itself."[40] He thus argued that the Declaration authorized the people, as sovereigns, to determine when independence was necessary to defend their rights. Similarly, in his "Cornerstone Speech," an address most often referenced for its explicit claim that slavery was the primary cause of secession, Confederate vice president Alexander Stephens refers to secession as "one of the greatest revolutions in the annals of the world."[41] These secessionists all argued from analogy in making the claim that their actions mirrored those of the founders. In doing so, they were making the case that they were not traitors to the union but patriots, defending the same principles that motivated the US American Revolution.

Other echoes of the Revolutionary Era abounded. In 1860, for example, the *Charleston Mercury* stated that "the tea has been thrown overboard, the revolution of 1860 has been initiated."[42] Likening South Carolina's secession to the Boston Tea Party, the newspaper implicitly argued that the nobility of the two causes was also analogous. Knowing that secession, especially given its inescapable connection to the protection of slavery, was a difficult cause to champion on the world stage, secessionists found in analogies to the American Revolution a source of justification. In making this argument, they had to contend with the content of the original Declaration, which entailed several key contradictions for them. For example, they argued that the slave-owning states, which enjoyed different cultural predispositions and political sentiments from non–slave states, were constituted therefore as "one people." Enslaved persons, however, were not able to similarly constitute themselves. This, of course, required secessionists, as we saw in Davis's speech, to deny the personhood of those they enslaved and to interpret the meaning of the word "men" as it appeared in the Declaration as applying only to "white men." Mississippi, for instance, included in its list of abuses perpetrated by the federal government's advocacy of "negro [*sic*] equality" and its opposition to slavery, which they viewed as meaning that "utter subjugation awaits us in the Union."[43] Slavery, Mississippi declared, was more important to its identity and its freedom than union.

As in this example, having declared themselves to be a distinct people and having announced that their communal identity was based on the system of chattel slavery, secessionists also then had to reinterpret the meaning of "freedom." Recall that abolitionist rhetoric depended in part on highlighting the contradiction between the declaration of universal human equality, which authorized universal human rights, and slavery. Abolitionists argued that national values and national practices had to be brought into alignment. Secessionists, on the other hand, resolved the dilemma by restricting, rather than broadening, the meaning of "freedom." For them, the freedom of the Declaration applied to their ability to own humans as property but not to the right of enslaved humans to their own freedom. Freedom and mastery over others were equated.[44]

Davis argued, for example, that his home state of Mississippi

> has heard proclaimed the theory that all men are created free and equal and this made the basis for an attack upon her social institutions; and the sacred Declaration of Independence has been invoked to maintain the position of equality of the races. The Declaration is to be construed by the circumstances and purposes for which it was made. The communities were declaring their independence; the people of those communities were asserting that no man was born—to use the language of Mr. Jefferson—booted and spurred to ride over the rest of mankind; that men were created equal—meaning the men of the political community.[45]

He went on to argue that since the Declaration "has no reference to the slave," the universal principles outlined in that document could have no relevance to the status of enslaved persons.[46] Davis, like many secessionists, was also quick to note that the Constitution itself authorized slavery, and that, far from making them persons and thus at least eligible for inclusion in the universal rights claimed in the Declaration, the Constitution assigned to them only partial personhood, amounting to three-fifths of that status.[47] Secessionists thus depended on reducing the applicability of the universal claim to human freedom in order to protect chattel slavery. They similarly had to limit the meaning of "equality."[48] In his Cornerstone Speech, for example, Stephens argues that, despite the language of the founding, the "assumption of the equality of races" was "an error." Like freedom, equality was limited only to some people; others were denied human status and access to human rights.

Secessionists, willing to initiate war rather than eliminate slavery, were badly in need of justifications for that willingness. They found one powerful warrant in the Constitution, which explicitly protected slavery. The Constitution presented a difficulty, however, in that it delineates mechanisms for change. The founders themselves, in fact, assumed that future generations would find a way out of the dilemma posed by slavery, a solution they were unable to locate. But the Declaration of Independence is timeless in a way that the Constitution is not. It articulates universal principles based on self-evident truths. They echoed it and offered what they argued was a more legitimate interpretation of its fundamental doctrines. Although the South lost the war and the question of the legitimacy of secession has apparently been resolved, the arguments made about the Declaration continue to echo in the rhetoric of contemporary political actors.

Legacies of the Antebellum Declaration

There is no question but that the root cause of the Civil War was slavery. Also important is the connection between slavery and white supremacy. Having lost the Civil War, former Confederates—and much of the North—remained committed to the latter.[49] The arguments made in 1860 have had an extended life since 1865,[50] and so we shall look briefly at some of the ways they remain with us.

The abolitionists argued that the nation was founded upon a set of universal principles and that it was obliged to keep re-creating itself to better align its practices with those principles. This claim, of course, finds its most eloquent articulations in the Gettysburg Address and Martin Luther King Jr.'s "I Have a Dream" speech. But the idea that the nation is coming ever closer to realizing the ideals of the Declaration has its own troubled history. On the one hand, this claim has motivated arguments in favor of rights for women, African American civil rights, LGBTQ+ rights, and more. But this laudable legacy is complicated. The nation has waged war in defense of its definition of democracy and has engaged in any number of questionable practices related to that ostensible aim, invading other nations in the name of democracy and sometimes engaging in repressive practices to "preserve" it at home. Equally worrying are the ways in which belief in this legacy of an ever-evolving, ever more just nation compels narratives that misread the national history, eliding the treatment of Indigenous people and other systemic and systematic acts of violence. National narratives tend to celebrate increasing justice without really dealing with past injustices or their continuance into contemporary moments.

The secessionist legacy is less subtle and far more dangerous. That legacy begins immediately after the war, with the inception of the "Lost Cause," a term usually dated to Edward A. Pollard's book of the same name, first published in 1866 and followed by a second book in 1868.[51] Pollard was the first but by no means the last person to argue in print that the Civil War was fought not in defense of slavery, as contemporary interlocutors consistently argued, but for manifold other reasons, including defense of states' rights and the right of secession. Important during Reconstruction, the myth of the Lost Cause, and especially the central claim that slavery was not a cause of the war, became even more central to southern identity in the 1940s as major institutions (such as baseball and the US military) were desegregated and the long civil rights movement delivered legal and social successes, especially in the aftermath of the landmark *Brown v. Topeka Board of Education* decision in 1954.

Opposition to civil rights has always been closely connected to claims to "states' rights." Take, for example, the 1956 "Southern Manifesto," drafted in response to "the unwarranted decision of the Supreme Court in the public school cases," which signers characterized as the substitution of "naked power for established law."[52] Preferring the Court's ruling in *Plessy v. Ferguson*, which established the "principle" of "separate but equal," to that of *Brown*, which declared that separate could never be truly equal, the manifesto's signatories relied on the Constitution rather than the Declaration but made essentially the same claim as their progenitors: the states were sovereign entities that should not be subject to the will of the federal government in the management of their own affairs. Notably, the manifesto's formal title is "Declaration of Constitutional Principles." Its nickname references the original Southern Manifesto, a document published in 1860 and signed by a number of Southerners. That document announced, in December of 1860, that "the argument is now exhausted" and "that the sole and primary aim of each slaveholding State ought to be its speedy and absolute separation from an unnatural and hostile union."[53] Both manifestos argued for the primacy of states' rights in defense of racial hierarchies. Both thus depend on arguments that derived from the supposed content of the Declaration.

These noxious legacies continue into our moment. Echoing Alexander Stephens's argument that the Declaration's claim to universal human equality was "in error," Alt-Right forefather Samuel Francis, for example, argued that the Declaration's assertion that "all men are created equal" must "be considered one of the most arcane—and one of the most dangerous—sentences ever written, one of the major blunders of American history."[54] Like secessionists, members of the contemporary Alt-Right argue that what was articulated as universal and self-evident truths are better understood as limited and restricted partial truths, rendering timeless values contingent claims. In so doing, they limit the Declaration's grandeur as well as its rhetorical and political power.

We find in the Declaration what we look for in it. It is, therefore, as was noted at the beginning of this chapter, a dangerous document. It makes sweeping claims to universal truths. US Americans have never quite managed to live up to those claims, a fact that creates both inspiration and despair. Because it can be read in ways that authorize gross injustice and oppression, in the United States, at least, it leaves a legacy with which we must contend.

NOTES

1. See Armitage, *Declaration of Independence*; Bush, *American Declarations*; Lee and Atchison, *We Are Not One People*, 42; Pavkovič and Radan, *Ashgate Research Companion to Secession*.

2. Lee and Atchison, *We Are Not One People*, 39–44.

3. By the early 1800s, for example, the New England states were threatening secession over the Assumption Act, and the South made similar threats over the tariff of 1828. On the prevalence of secessionism in the United States, see Lee and Atchison, *We Are Not One People*.

4. See, among many others, Foner, *Story of American Freedom*, 3; Condit and Lucaites, *Crafting Equality*.

5. Potter, *Impending Crisis*, 8.

6. See especially arguments made by Robert Barnwell Rhett and Louis Wigfall, cited in Lee and Atchison, *We Are Not One People*, 75–76.

7. Foner, *Story of American Freedom*, 77.

8. For details, see Potter, *Impending Crisis*.

9. For a detailed analysis of the complicated views on slavery and race in the North, see among many others, Potter, *Impending Crisis*, 52–60.

10. Frederick Douglass, "What to the Slave Is the Fourth of July?," July 5, 1852, https://www.owleyes.org/text/what-to-the-slave-is-the-fourth-of-july/read/text-of-douglasss-speech.

11. David Walker, *An Appeal in Four Articles, Together with a Preamble, to the Colored Citizens of the World, but in Particular, and Very Expressly, to Those of the United States of America, Written in Boston, State of Massachusetts, on September 28, 1829*. University of North Carolina, https://docsouth.unc.edu/nc/walker/walker.html.

12. William Lloyd Garrison, "First Anti-slavery Address," Boston, July 4, 1829, https://archive.org/details/garrisonsfirstanoogarr.

13. Anti-slavery Society, Constitution, 1833, https://teachingamericanhistory.org/document/constitution-of-the-american-anti-slavery-society/.

14. Bush, *American Declarations*, 118.

15. Grimké, *Appeal to Christian Women*. For a discussion of Grimké's rhetoric, see Browne, *Angelina Grimké*.

16. Zaeske, *Signatures of Citizenship*, 88–89.

17. Bush, *American Declarations*, 93.

18. As Ralph Lerner notes, "That 'merely' is designed to make you pause and catch your breath." See Lerner "Lincoln's Declaration—and Ours."

19. Abraham Lincoln, "Springfield Speech," June 26, 1857, http://www.mrlincolnandfreedom.org/pre-civil-war/dred-sc.tt/speech-at-springfield-june-26-1857/.

20. Abraham Lincoln, "Address at the Dedication of the National Cemetery at Gettysburg, Pennsylvania" [Gettysburg Address], November 19, 1863. Online by Gerhard Peters and John T. Woolley, The American Presidency Project, https://www.presidency.ucsb.edu/node/201980.

21. Potter, *Impending Crisis*, 479.

22. Potter, *Impending Crisis*, 483.

23. Scholars differ on the number of parts; I've chosen these as the most extensive. See Armitage, *Declaration of Independence*, 26–28.

24. In its secession ordnance, for example, Mississippi declared, "For less cause than this, our fathers separated from the Crown of England"; see State of Mississippi, "Secession Ordinance," February 8, 1861, http://civildiscourse-historyblog.com/blog/2018/7/1/secession-documents-mississippi. On the ways both sides of the abolition debate sought to mobilize the Revolution, see Sheppard-Wolf, *Race and Liberty*, 193.

25. Missouri and Kentucky did not secede, but the politics of union/disunion were complicated in both states.

26. "Journal Resolution and Ordinance," State Convention of South Carolina, April 26–30, 1852, 60–61, in Loewen and Sebesta, *Confederate and Neo-confederate Reader*, 61.

27. "Journal Resolution and Ordinance," State Convention of South Carolina, 61.

28. Jefferson Davis, "First Inaugural Address," Montgomery, Alabama, February 18, 1961, https://jeffersondavis.rice.edu/archives/documents/jefferson-davis-first-inaugural-address.

29. Confederate States of America, "Declaration of Immediate Causes Which Induce and Justify the Secession of South Carolina from the Federal Union," December 24, 1860, https://avalon.law.yale.edu/19th_century/csa_scarsec.asp. All subsequent quotations are from this source.

30. State of Louisiana, "Secession Ordinance," January 1, 1861, https://content.wisconsinhistory.org/digital/collection/quiner/id/23321; State of Virginia, "Secession

Ordinance," April 17, 1861, https://encyclopediavirginia.org/entries/virginia-ordinance-of-secession-april-17-1861/. States that declared themselves sovereign include Florida, Georgia, and Tennessee; their secession ordinances are all available here: https://civildiscourse-historyblog.com/blog/2018/7/1/secession-documents-florida-louisiana-virginia-north-carolina-and-tennessee.

31. Confederate States of America, "Declaration of Immediate Causes Which Induce and Justify the Secession of South Carolina from the Federal Union," December 24, 1860, https://avalon.law.yale.edu/19th_century/csa_scarsec.asp.

32. State of Texas, "Secession Ordinance," February 2, 1861, https://digital.sfasu.edu/digital/collection/EastTexRC/id/3849/#:~:text=%22A%20Declaration%20of%20the%20Causes,February%2C%20A.D.%2C%201861.%22. All subsequent quotations are from this source.

33. See Sheppard-Wolf, *Race and Liberty*, 31.

34. Jefferson Davis, "Farewell to the US Senate," January 21, 1861, 170–74, in Loewen and Sebesta, *Confederate and Neo-confederate Reader*, 171. It is notable that the Confederate Constitution was premised on the consent of "We, the people of the Confederate States, each State acting in its sovereign and independent character." See Confederate States of America, "Constitution," March 11, 1861, https://avalon.law.yale.edu/19th_century/csa_csa.asp.

35. "Resolves of the Southern Convention at Nashville," June 10–11, 1859, 55–59, in Loewen and Sebesta, *Confederate and Neo-confederate Reader*, 58.

36. The first state to secede, South Carolina made similar arguments in its "Ordinance of Secession." See State of South Carolina, "Ordinance of Secession," December 20, 1860, https://www.americanyawp.com/reader/the-sectional-crisis/south-carolina-declaration-of-secession-1860/.

37. Andrew Johnson, "The Constitutionality and Rightness of Secession," December 18 and 19, 1860, https://www.loc.gov/item/11004421/.

38. "Journal Resolution and Ordinance," State Convention of South Carolina.

39. Davis, "Inaugural."

40. Davis, "Inaugural."

41. Alexander Stephens, "Cornerstone Speech," Savannah, Georgia, March 21, 1861, https://www.battlefields.org/learn/primary-sources/cornerstone-speech. See also Hébert, *Cornerstone of the Confederacy*.

42. Quoted in Dew, *Apostles of Disunion*, 25.

43. State of Mississippi, "Secession Ordinance."

44. For a discussion of this point, see Foner, *Story of American Freedom*, 64.

45. Davis, "Farewell to the US Senate," 172.

46. Davis, "Farewell to the US Senate," 173.

47. Davis, "Farewell to the US Senate," 173.

48. See Lee and Atchison, *We Are Not One People*, 91.

49. On the connections between slavery and white supremacy and the continuing commitment to the latter, see, among many others, Dew, *Apostles of Disunion*; Kendi, *Stamped from the Beginning*; Lee and Atchison, *We Are Not One People*, 81; and James W. Loewen, "Introduction," 3–21, in Loewen and Sebesta, *Confederate and Neo-confederate Reader*, 11–12.

50. Harwell, *Confederate Reader*, xxii; Lee and Atchison, *We Are Not One People*, 100–101; Main, *Rise of the Alt-Right*; Murantonio, *Confederate Exceptionalism*.

51. Pollard, *Lost Cause* and *Lost Cause Regained*.

52. Signed by nineteen senators and seventy representatives, all from the South, the Manifesto asserted states' rights over federal control of education. See the 1956 "Southern Manifesto." Southern Manifesto, 1956, https://content.csbs.utah.edu/~dlevin/federalism/southern_manifesto.html.

53. See the 1860 "Southern Manifesto," https://tarheelcivilwarleaders.wordpress.com/2012/08/06/1860-the-southern-manifesto/.

54. Main, *Rise of the Alt-Right*, 128–29.

BIBLIOGRAPHY

Armitage, David. *The Declaration of Independence: A Global History*. Cambridge, MA: Harvard University Press, 2007.

Browne, Stephen Howard. *Angelina Grimké: Rhetoric, Identity, and the Radical Imagination*. East Lansing: Michigan State University Press, 1999.

Bush, Harold K., Jr. *American Declarations: Rebellion and Resistance in American Cultural History*. Urbana: University of Illinois Press, 1999.

Condit, Celeste Michelle, and John Louis Lucaites. *Crafting Equality: America's Anglo-African Word*. Chicago: University of Chicago Press, 2012.

Dew, Charles B. *Apostles of Disunion: Southern Secession Commissioners and the Causes of the Civil War*. 15th anniversary ed. Charlottesville: University Press of Virginia, 2001.

Foner, Eric. *Story of American Freedom*. New York: W. W. Norton, 1999.

Grimké, Angelina. *Appeal to Christian Women of the South*. In *The American Yawp Reader*. https://www.americanyawp.com/reader/religion-and-reform/angelina-grimke-appeal-to-christian-women-of-the-south-1836.

Harwell, Richard B., ed. *The Confederate Reader: How the South Saw the War*. New York: Dover, 1989.

Hébert, Keith S. *Cornerstone of the Confederacy: Alexander Stephens and the Speech That Defined the Lost Cause*. Knoxville: University of Tennessee Press, 2021.

Kendi, Ibram X. *Stamped from the Beginning: The Definitive History of Racist Ideas in America*. London: Hachette, 2016.

Loewen, James W., and Edward W. Sebesta, eds. *The Confederate and Neo-confederate Reader: The "Great Truth" About the "Lost Cause."* Jackson: University Press of Mississippi, 2010.

Main, Thomas J. *The Rise of the Alt-Right*. Washington, DC: Brookings, 2018.

Maurantonio, Nicole, *Confederate Exceptionalism: Civil War Myth and Memory in the Twenty-First Century*. Lawrence: University Press of Kansas, 2019.

Pavkovič, Aleksandar A., and Peter Radan, eds. *The Ashgate Research Companion to Secession*. Burlington, VT: Ashgate, 2011.

Pollard, Edward Alfred. *The Lost Cause: A New Southern History of the War of the Confederates; Comprising a Full and Authentic Account of the Rise and Progress of the Late Southern Confederacy—the Campaigns, Battles, Incidents, and Adventures of the Most Gigantic Struggle of the World's History*. Baltimore: EB Treat, 1866.

———. *The Lost Cause Regained*. 1868. Reprint, Freeport, NY: Books for Libraries, 1970.

Potter, David M. *The Impending Crisis: 1848–1861*. Completed and edited by Don E. Fehrenbacher. New York: Harper and Row, 1976.

Sheppard-Wolf, Eva. *Race and Liberty in the New Nation: Emancipation in Virginia from the Revolution to Nat Turner's Rebellion*. Baton Rouge: LSU Press, 2006.

Walker, David. *An Appeal in Four Articles, Together with a Preamble, to the Colored Citizens of the World, but in Particular, and Very Expressly, to Those of the United States of America, Written in Boston, State of Massachusetts, on September 28, 1829*. University of North Carolina, https://docsouth.unc.edu/nc/walker/walker.html.

Zaeske, Susan. *Signatures of Citizenship: Petitioning, Antislavery, and Women's Political Identity*. Chapel Hill: University of North Carolina Press, 2003.

5

FROM DECLARATION TO SELF-DETERMINATION: DECOLONIAL SHIFTS IN INDIGENOUS RHETORICAL AUTHORITY

Jason Edward Black

In October 1829, as US public support for the Indian Removal Act (1830) churned into a frenzy, Chief John Ross (Tsalagi/Cherokee) delivered a speech to the Cherokee Nation announcing his resistance to the policy. The Cherokee Nation was unique among Indigenous nations during this era, having based nearly all their civic ideologies and constitutional structures on the US model.[1] To the colonial charge that Indigenous nations ought to "introduce among themselves the habits and arts of civilization," a sizeable number of Cherokee communities in the nineteenth century within what is now Georgia and North Carolina responded by assimilating to US cultural practices.[2] Thus, it made sense that in his objections to the impending removal policy Ross would write, "The preservation and happiness of the Cherokee people are at stake and . . . we can only look with confidence to the good faith and magnanimity of the General Government, whose precepts and profession inculcate principles of liberty and republicanism, and whose obligation[s] are solemnly pledged to give us justice and protection."[3] At first glance, argues Maureen Konkle, Indigenous rhetors like Ross invoking republican rhetoric "looks like a capitulation" to colonial ideals. However, Indigenous nations' strategic deployment of such language in the nineteenth century served "as a means for Indigenous peoples to disrupt U.S. political authority" by exposing its contradictions.[4] Typically relying on the precepts embedded in the Declaration of Independence as authority, such Indigenous rhetoric sought to decolonize foundational documents, to lay them bare for their failed promises, while also centering Indigenous agency or the capacity, license, and power to act.[5]

Almost two hundred years later, in 2016, hip-hop artist Nataanii Means (Očhéthi Šakówiŋ / Oglala Lakota), son of the late American Indian Movement leader Russell Means (Očhéthi Šakówiŋ / Oglala Lakota), gathered with fellow activists at Standing Rock Reservation to resist construction of the Dakota Access Pipeline.[6] The pipeline's path through the Great Sioux Nation's ancestral homelands was another US governmental contrivance, this one paired with corporatized colonial forces to displace Indigenous peoples while simultaneously desecrating spiritual ground.[7] Unlike his forebears, though, Means and his fellow activists did not launch a republican resistance inspired by the Declaration's ideals. Rather, he relied on a Native understanding that "enlivens, embodies, fortifies, and Indigenizes memory of land, peoples, and nonhumans."[8] Inspired by the Standing Rock moment, Means rapped, "I'm a warrior, the last of the dying breed with dreams of being free / Hooked up to the tree to breathe // . . . Fed lies from the school system / Misinterpretin' Thanksgiving, teachin' history like it's fiction / What's written ain't fact / We take down these flags and raise the eagle staff / . . . Creator got my back, but Crazy Horse is my savior / . . . I'm a warrior, the last of a dying breed, with dreams of being free . . . / Till I'm with my people up in the sky."[9] Missing from Means's resistive rhetoric is any sense of turning around the principles of "liberty and republicanism" as Ross had. Instead, an epistemology of self-determination becomes centered: linking Indigenous lifeways to the living land, denouncing colonial history, replacing US symbols with the ceremonial eagle staff, anchoring authority in Indigenous heroes, and establishing pride with the help of ancestors. The arc of shifting authority in Indigenous resistance—emblematic in the time between Ross's reliance on the Declaration's principles and Means's inward gaze of self-determination—is this chapter's focus.

The Declaration codified aspirational goals for the (white) US nation but also afforded generations the grounds for material governance and useful liberties. While such ideals have overwhelmingly benefited a colonizing nation—one fortified by the forced labor of and violence against enslaved Black people on land held by Indigenous nations for generations and with the aid of exploitative immigrant toil—the Declaration has also been a prototype for colonized peoples' resistance to the very nation the document purported to sustain and from which colonized peoples were roundly excised.[10]

For nearly two centuries, most (but not all) Indigenous activists used the Declaration's republican ideals as a warrant to resist policies such as Indian removal, the allotment of reservation land, assimilation of Indigenous communities, the reservation system, and tribal termination.[11] They also used progressive rhetoric regarding the return of land via honoring treaties, the protection of natural resources, and control of Bureau of Indian Affairs trusts.[12] Indigenous nations have channeled the Declaration mostly through a rhetorical tactic of *détournement*. Colloquially known as "the turnaround," this form of decolonial resistance exposed the inconsistencies of the Declaration as they applied to Indigenous people and dually served as spaces of dissension and invention to demand Indigenous sovereignty.[13] While "turning around" the Declaration yielded some success in frustrating colonial plans, in the main, Indigenous nations, particularly following the height of the Red Power Movement years (1968–1978), have distanced themselves from the document, as its ideals have proven to do little more than fortify colonialism through sustained control of Indigenous peoples' land, labor, bodies, symbols, and cultural lifeways.[14] As a result, contemporary Indigenous activists have turned instead to Indigenous epistemologies of self-determination to fight for liberties and material changes.[15]

This chapter begins with a description of Indigenous activism in the 19th century, a time when the Declaration's republican values were centered as the *sine qua non* authority for resistance, relying on brief representative cases of decolonization from southeastern nations' resistance. Next I show how the Red Power Movement served as a bridge to contemporary Indigenous communities, relying partially on the Declaration as an authoritative resource for decolonization while also leaning inward to Indigenous cultures themselves. As examples of Indigenous rhetoric in this vein I examine the *20-Point Position Paper* (1972) and a Day of Mourning protest speech (1970). I conclude by describing contemporary self-determination with aid from Red Nation organizer Nick Estes's (Sičhą̧ğu Oyáte / Lower Brule Sioux) treatise on liberation.[16] Ultimately, this chapter argues that Indigenous rhetoric over time has shifted from centering the Declaration as a foundational resource to elevating Indigenous knowledge as the primary standard of authority.

The Declaration as Indigenous Decolonial Authority

Nineteenth-century Indigenous resistive rhetoric, a corpus that has been discussed as a template for successive Indigenous discourses, found drawing from the Declaration's principles to be useful.[17] Ironically, the Declaration deemed Indigenous nations "merciless Indian savages" (as in the Crown exposing colonists to so-called hostile tribes).[18] Still, as decades of the government's Indian policies demanding Indigenous assimilation unfolded, the foundational document became a fertile space for pushing back against the government. Using the language and policies of the US government against itself demonstrated the inconsistencies of principles such as justice and equality, particularly when these principles did not apply to Indigenous people. Such a rhetorical move, in turn, became a crucial piece of authority.[19]

Indigenous rhetoric that centered the Declaration as an authority and yet called out its colonial logics as empty might be labeled a type of decolonization. Colonization largely involves the control of land, labor, bodies, and symbols by an imperial power.[20] Much of colonization occurs in material ways, but of course rhetorical and material means exist in a Möbius loop. Decolonization through language challenges both the ideology of colonization and the material havoc this ideology permits.[21] Though decolonization began to be theorized beginning in the twentieth century, the spirit of decolonization was very much materializing in nineteenth-century Indigenous rhetoric.

Relying on the Declaration worked through *détournement*. This process effectively (re)possesses the arguments of powerful entities by "cutting the vocal cords" of their colonial narratives.[22] The point here is to be able to demystify how powerful rhetoric presents problems, inaccuracies, distortions, and inconsistencies. Arnold Krupat puts this rhetorical tactic best: "To take possession of the master's books is to obtain some important part of the master's power—which then, to be sure, may be turned to one's own purposes."[23] We find a key example of "detourning" the Declaration in the rhetoric of southeastern nations resisting "Indian removal."

The Choctaw, Muscogee Creek, Chickasaw, and Seminole nations reworked principles from the Declaration as a way to expose the hypocrisies of removal. Decolonial rhetoric here demonstrates that Indigenous communities were not voiceless, and in fact a great deal of scholarship focuses on how their "talking back" ruptured the government's discourse.[24] The tenacity of antiremoval rhetoric challenges the myth that Indigenous people disappeared or only engaged in warfare as a response to colonization. We ought to remember that Indigenous rhetoric is a vital part of US rhetorical history; it must be centered not as additive but rather as transformative.

The Indian Removal Act commenced through a series of treaties with Indigenous nations. The southeastern nations became the first litmus tests of President Andrew Jackson's removal policy. According to the Indian Removal Act, Indigenous nations could opt to either remove or remain on their lands in the East. But these removal treaties were negotiated under a ton of physical, political, and economic duress from 1830 to 1835; they were unquestionably compulsory. Still, that the Indian Removal Act allowed for Indigenous agency to engage in treaties conferred prima facie an important sense of power to Indigenous communities. After all, treaties are, by definition, formal agreements between two or more fully sovereign and recognized states.[25]

The most robust decolonial tactic of this time involved Indigenous nations asserting their sovereignty through republican memories shared between themselves and the US government. Often, Indigenous rhetors rewrote the script concerning key figures of US civic history such as the Declaration's primary author Thomas Jefferson and regarding foundational documents like the Declaration, rooting Indigenous sovereignty in these memories.

An example of this tactic includes how anti-removal activist Ames (Chahta/Choctaw) employed the Declaration and its republicanism to demonstrate the Choctaw Nation's sovereignty. While governmental officials contended the Constitution provided for interference into Indigenous affairs—Congress was emboldened "to regulate commerce with foreign nations . . . and with the Indian tribes"—Ames insinuated that the Choctaw Nation being paired with "foreign nations" nodded toward sovereignty.[26] To this effect, Ames remarked that the "right to sovereignty and liberty" was first recorded "by the Declaration" and was secured by the Constitution: "Congress cannot impose conditions . . . for the right of admission was absolute, and could not be restricted or clogged by any law of Congress."[27] Here, Ames roots authority for Choctaw agency in an interpretation of foundational documents that warrants his nation's liberty.

Similarly, Pushmataha (Chahta/Choctaw) and Puckshunnubbee (Chahta/Choctaw) crafted a memory of the "friendly" Jefferson administration to counter the territoriality of the US government and to hearken back to independence. These rhetors decolonized the Declaration's concepts of liberty and property in the face of the removal policy: "It is said we have no claim to the land here. . . . How different is this from the language of the illustrious Jefferson,—'go home,' said this great and good man to our fathers, 'build your houses, clear your fields, and cultivate the earth.' Said he, 'as you live in peace with me and mine . . . you shall live upon your lands undisturbed.'"[28] Pushmataha and Puckshunnubbee employed the memory of Jefferson as authority to remain on their homelands. As early as 1803, Jefferson asked Indigenous nations to remain in the East in order to "improve." He saw this as part of assimilation to the Declaration's ideals.[29] The Choctaw Nation had taken his advice. Thus, Pushmataha and Puckshunnubbee averred, "If ever the Choctaw character is renovated, here is the place to do it—if we are ever to experience the blessings of civilization, here is the place."[30]

When the Muscogee Creek Nation was forced to remove, leaders Yoholo (Este Mvskokvlke / Muscogee Creek), Tuckaubatchie Hajo (Este Mvskokvlke /

Muscogee Creek), Tustenuggee (Este Mvskokvlke / Muscogee Creek), and Smut Eye (Este Mvskokvlke / Muscogee Creek) sent a memorial to Congress illustrating their reliance on republican notions of natural rights, property, and divine protection—all superstructural to the Declaration—to justify the Muscogee Creek Nation's right to its homeland. The group claimed that, "as far back as their tradition is disposed to tell, long before they saw the ancestors of this Great Council fire . . . we were a free people, in the undisturbed enjoyment of those rights held sacred among men, derived from the Great Master of Breath, who created mankind equal and in possession of an unmolested enjoyment of life, and the blessings of self-government."[31] Here, the Muscogee Creek argument to remain on its Alabama territory was positioned not in European contact and "doctrines of discovery" but rather in a spirit for "all time eternal."[32] Moreover, the "Great Master of Breath" endowed them with the natural rights of equality, freedom, the "enjoyment of life," and the "blessings of self-government." That members of the Muscogee Creek Nation rooted their sovereignty in republican rights to property seemed homologically similar to the Declaration. Consider the Declaration's famous line—"All men are created equal, that they are endowed by their Creator with certain unalienable rights, that among these are life, liberty and the pursuit of happiness"—alongside the passage above.[33] Overall, the Muscogee Creek Nation tended to decolonize by pointing to the inconsistencies of the Declaration's sacred republicanism in the face of a rights-denying policy such as removal.

A final decolonial tactic involved deploying the savage/survivor dichotomy used in the Declaration's grievances against Great Britain. In the same fashion that the Declaration's framers constituted the Crown as "savage," so too did Seminole Nation respondents resituate the label of "savage" to reflect US governmental identities.[34] No rhetor demonstrated this tactic more than Coacoochee (Seminole), who spoke to a group of US Indian agents to rebuke Jackson's removal policy. Combating the false promises involved in the Seminole removal treaties of Payne's Landing and Fort Gibson, Coacoochee constructed the government as evil and wild: "Still [the US government] gave me his hand in friendship; we took it. . . . He had a snake in the other; his tongue was forked; he lied and stung us."[35] An untrustworthy character, the US government, said Coacoochee, extended friendship, perhaps even paternalism, on the one hand and "stung" on the other.[36] The "forked tongue" with which US Indian agents negotiated the treaties confirmed for the Seminole Nation the dishonesty in removal rhetoric. We catch a glimpse here of reliance on the Declaration's pre-grievance salvo: "The history of the present

King of Great Britain is a history of repeated injuries and usurpations, all having in direct object the establishment of an absolute Tyranny over these States. To prove this, let Facts be submitted to a candid world."[37] Locating decolonial authority by turning the republican mirror on the US government was Coacoochee's signature tactic. Calling out colonial oppressors is closely related to the tone in the Declaration's grievance section.

This small sample of southeastern nations' decolonial responses to removal indicate a savvy tactic of detourning dominant language. But in the course of Indigenous-US affairs, reliance on the Declaration became less and less important. When those republican principles fell flat as Indigenous nations faced allotment, relocation, assimilation, and termination from the fin de siècle years through the first third of the twentieth century, a turn inward seemed necessary for Indigenous knowledge to survive. This internal move encouraged Indigenous communities by way of pride and agency, shifting their ethos away from sentiments tucked into documents such as the Declaration to their cultural lifeways, ancestors, and—vitally—the living land itself. In the mid-twentieth century, the Red Power Movement (RPM)—mostly led by the American Indian Movement (AIM)—began to resituate agency in an Indigenous-centered authority. At the same time, though, the RPM still brokered in a reliance on the Declaration. In many ways, RPM rhetoric was a bridge from "Declaration to Self-Determination."

The Red Power Movement and Hybrid Decolonization

The RPM of the 1960s and 1970s followed from inner-nationalist movements in the United States, such as Black Power, that located esteem less in US ideals and more in community traditions, languages, domestic life, economies, and values of the cultural community outside the bounds of US mores. The RPM's main task was to balance material changes in Indigenous-US policy such as resource rights, the fulfillment of land treaties (hundreds of which had been "canceled" in 1871), and the sovereign control over funds held by the government along with a revitalization of Indigenous heritage, much of which had been criminalized by the US government and excised from US civic culture. Scholars have argued that the RPM mostly directed its rhetoric inward in the hopes of supporting Indigenous identity and attaining material change by "adopting a ritual *self-address*."[38] But at the same time, as Casey Ryan Kelly has pointed out, RPM leaders "emphasized the importance of collectively reading the key texts [e.g., the Declaration] used in defense of colonialism to expose their contradictions. . . . Their rhetoric commandeered authoritative Euro-American texts and redirected them to make an argument against colonialism."[39] The RPM's hybrid "Declaration" and "Self-Determination" approach paved the way for authority rooted in Indigenous ways of knowing.

The RPM era of the last third of the twentieth century involved a significant move toward Indigenous communities suturing the wounds of colonial policies deployed by the US government. Coming up through and out from destructive policies such as assimilationist education and the termination of tribal sovereignty, leaders and activists started to look internally for a recuperation of Indigenous traditions and for the purpose of inspiring a new Indigenist politics both on and off reservations.[40] Yet, as did their forebears, the RPM leaders still often clung to the republican language and rhetorical forms inspired by the Declaration.[41] Deliberative and republican aims still wielded influence in Indigenous rhetoric during the Red Power years.

The *20-Point Position Paper* was drafted in St. Paul, Minnesota, in 1972 at the pinnacle of the movement's activist work, much of which involved the self-labeled "takeover" as a tactic. By occupying traditionally sacred Indigenous sites such as Alcatraz Island, Wounded Knee (the location of the cataclysmic murder of three hundred members of the Miniconjou Band of the Lakota Sioux in 1890), and Plymouth Rock, the RPM staked a material and symbolic claim to space, thus decolonizing by way of a bond between body and land.[42] During the "Longest Walk" along the "Trail of Broken Treaties," members of the American Indian Movement and the Pan Native Quest for Justice—both part of the larger RPM—organized a four-mile-long caravan of Indigenous people and traveled from Minnesota to Washington, DC, to deliver to President Richard Nixon their *20-Point Position Paper*. When they arrived and found no executive audience, the group occupied the Bureau of Indian Affairs building for seven days before Nixon finally agreed to read the document.[43]

The RPM's manifesto functioned through republican language. For instance, it modeled the form of the Declaration right from its opening. The document begins, "We seek a new American majority—a majority that is not content merely to confirm itself by superiority in numbers, but which by conscience is committed toward prevailing upon the public will in ceasing wrongs and in doing right. For our part, in words and deeds of coming days, we propose to produce a rational, reasoned manifesto for construction of an Indian future in America. If America has maintained faith with its original spirit, or may recognize it now, we should not be denied."[44] Rooting ethos in an originating contract of past treaty-making and involving issues of both justice and oppression, the RPM confirms that the manifesto's policy points are predicated on the US government's "original spirit," trusting that its principles will be realized in the present. Similar to the Declaration, the 20-Point manifesto appeals to the colonizing power's conscience and good faith in fulfilling its own principles and in the "construction of an Indian future." Moreover, the RPM situates the manifesto in the written word (a Western logic) and concomitantly in republican principles of "rational, reasoned" argument. Homologically, the 20-Point manifesto's preamble echoes the Declaration's in content and form.

Republican overtones continue throughout the remainder of the document's twenty paragraphs, each representing a different policy goal, from creating a treaty review board and an Indigenous seat in Congress to reorganizing the Bureau of Indian Affairs and all Indigenous trusts. None of the goals are demands so much as they are suggestions, framed as "should" and "shall" rather than "must" and "will." It was clear that the US government wielded the most agency in the policy "asks" of the manifesto. This is found in the constant grounding of governmental branches as subjects of the policies. One point notes, "The President should impanel and the Congress establish, with [*sic*] next year, a Treaty Commission. . . . Authority should be granted to allow tribes to contract by separate and individual treaty"; another suggests that "Congress should direct the reports to be concluded upon the disposition of land rights and land title."[45] The government authority permits, "grants," "direct[s]," "allows," and "establishes." Given the power ascribed to the US government through these verbs, the status quo colonial authority seemingly becomes the subject of the reform rather than colonized people themselves.[46]

The 20-Point manifesto is still a mechanism of decolonization. After all, it does progressively attempt to "recognize the building of effective Indigenous political structure" within republican bounds.[47] However, RPM rhetoric during this time also extended decolonization into Indigenous-centered epistemologies outside of the Declaration's principles and framework, a move that has motivated the larger body of Indigenous self-determination politics today.

One place we find RPM activists stepping into self-determinist decolonization is through the retelling of history. The critique of history was not new to Indigenous people during the RPM era. For decades the use of memory and the recall of Indigenous-US events had been leveraged for changes to colonial policies. But during the RPM years, history became a living, breathing body of meaning itself rather than an ancillary warrant for change within a republican structure. As Linda Tuhiwai Smith (Ngāti Awa / Ngāti Porou iwi) writes, "Contested stories and multiple discourses about the past, by different communities, is closely linked to the politics of everyday contemporary indigenous life. It is very much a part of the fabric of communities that value oral *ways of knowing*."[48] The focus on Indigenous epistemologies ("ways of knowing") as the apogee of decolonial history served to anchor Indigenous authority.

An example is the famous "Suppressed Speech" of Wamsutta Frank B. James (Wôpanâak/Wampanoag) in 1970, a decolonial response to the Town of Plymouth's (Massachusetts) 350th anniversary of the landing at Plymouth Rock.[49] James was asked to speak at a town celebration to extol the virtues of Indigenous-settler relations. But settler organizers, having reviewed his scathing speech to the contrary, disinvited him. James and members of the United American Indians of New England (UAINE)—an RPM organization—gathered outside Pilgrim Hall, where they surrounded Plymouth Rock, shared stories, and listened to James's speech. In subsequent years UAINE publicized their annual events, and soon activists from RPM began journeying to Plymouth each year to protest the colonizing Pilgrim mythology celebrated each Thanksgiving.[50] Over fifty years later, this National Day of Mourning event continues to thrive.

James's "Suppressed Speech" dwells not in republican language but in Indigenous experience, where Indigenous people themselves are agents. Such emphasis on decolonization through narrative "models a greater consciousness of the effects of colonization on culture, thought, and institutions" and provides a sense of self-determination of Indigenous pasts, presents, and futures.[51] In the speech, James admits that "we now have 350 years of experience living amongst the white man. We can now speak his language. We can now think as a white man thinks." However, he reminds his people that "we are [also] now being listened to."[52] This flip from object to subject is a *ne plus ultra* watermark of decolonization. (Notice how different the 20-Point manifesto was concerning agency.) He continues with a narrativized version of Thanksgiving-era events from his Wampanoag perspective, digging into stories passed down about Sachem Massassoit (Wôpanâak/Wampanoag), who befriended the settlers (what James concludes was "perhaps our biggest mistake"), as well as outlining events that prompt him to say, "It is with heavy heart that I look back upon what happened to my People."[53]

James decolonizes the Thanksgiving story, and thus the larger epochs of US colonization that followed, by centering Indigenous fortitude. As the

Town of Plymouth was extolling settlers such as William Bradford next door in Pilgrim Hall, James was recounting how "down through the years there is record after record of Indian lands taken and, in token, reservations set up. . . . Stripped of power [we] could only stand by and watch while the white man took his land for personal gain. This the Indian could not understand . . . land was survival, to farm, to hunt, to be enjoyed. It was not to be abused."[54] But survivance became his decolonial watchword. James insisted that, despite the historical amnesia afflicting contemporary US Americans and the lived atrocities that befell Indigenous people historically, the RPM was helping folks reject colonization and turn toward Indigenous ways of knowing and being: "The important point is that along with these necessities of everyday living, we still have the spirit, we still have the unique culture, we still have the will and, most important of all, the determination to remain as Indians. We are determined, and our presence here this evening is living testimony that this is only the beginning of the American Indian . . . to regain the position in this country that is rightfully ours."[55] Such strength works outside republican language and Western epistemologies. It reclaims both stories and land ("country that is rightfully ours"). It demands that Indigenous people persist with "presence" rather than merely being present. Decolonization in this iteration illustrates a "means of [Indigenous people] explaining to themselves and others their reclamation of Indigenous knowledge rooted in land and history."[56] Spirit, culture, will, living testimony—all imprints of the self-determination that followed.

Contemporary Self-Determination as Decolonization

The more self-determined timbre of the RPM's rhetoric has likely helped shift to near absence the Declaration and its republican principles as being authoritative in contemporary Indigenous decolonial rhetoric. As Indigenous lifeways—first sharpened in the days of Red Power—have energized a renaissance of Indigenous knowledge, traditions, connections to the earth, and ideological sovereignty, reliance on Western logics has dwindled.[57] Thus, earlier Indigenous tactics of decolonizing from within colonial epistemologies, though foundational to an Indigenist rhetorical tradition, are thought by some Indigenous public intellectuals to reify "colonizing values secreted by masters."[58] Instead, strategies of "epistemic disobedience" that emphasize Indigenous lifeways and rhetorical pathways are front and center. In denying Western-centric patterns of thought, epistemic disobedience provides Indigenous people with the agency to prevail over colonization.[59]

One tactic of self-determination involves delinking from Western systems as much as possible. A group that advocates for this is The Red Nation (TRN), the moral inheritors of the RPM. According to founding leader Nick Estes (Sičhąǧu Oyáte / Lower Brule Sioux), the group formed in 2014 "out of a collective desire to create a platform for revolutionary Native organizing and to fight back against this settler colonial system that seeks our annihilation."[60] Estes's treatise, "Native Liberation," has become a veritable guidepost for contemporary protest efforts, from the water protectors' labor at Standing Rock (2016) and the preservation of Bears Ears National Monument (2017) to securing the Indian Child Welfare Act (2023) and demanding accountability for boarding school atrocities (2020–present).

Delinking can mean many things, but for TRN and other Indigenous public intellectuals, it primarily centers the connection of people to the earth and the repudiation of viewing land in particular as commodity. Estes roots colonization in late capitalism, "the enemy of life." He argues that "as Native people, our kinship with human and nonhuman relatives is fundamental to our being. . . . It is a revolutionary love . . . but the land can no longer sustain us if capitalism continues to stalk the earth. . . . For life to live on this planet, capitalism must die."[61] We see in Estes's words a focus on shifting the terrain of the colonial project.[62] Enough, he seems to intimate, with profiteering negotiation: "We can't fundraise or lobby our way out of" the desecration of land. What if, he asks, "we transcend these power structures"?[63]

Land has always been interwoven with Indigenous culture. Harm to any one fiber of Indigenous lifeways is a harm to all. As Dina Gilio-Whitaker (Enselxcin / Colville Confederated Tribes) puts it, our "cultures and identities are linked to their original places in ways that define [us]: they are reflected in language, place names, and cosmology. . . . There is no separation between people and land, between people and other life forms, or between people and their ancient ancestors whose bones are infused in the land they inhabit."[64] It would seem anathema to rely on Western republican principles that broker in individual liberties and civic production when Indigenous epistemologies require communal respect. Instead, Estes urges self-determination by way of repudiation: "We have to refuse the false promise of capitalistic development—which is commonly disguised as tribal economic self-determination and state-sponsored colonial reconciliation. . . . You cannot heal from a system that continues to violate and kill the land."[65]

Delinking, though, requires a relinking. If, as Taiaiake Alfred (Kahnawà:ke/ Mohawk) notes, decolonization demands "disengagement from direct state control" and if, as Gerald Vizenor (Anishinaabe / White Earth Band of the Chippewa Nation) reminds us, "Indigenous knowledge comes into the present with new life," what does that mean for self-determination?[66] First, for Estes, relinking means moving away from *past* US principles coded in the Declaration and more toward an international framework of sovereignty. He writes, "Treaties are evidence of our sovereignty. After all, you do not enter treaty negotiations with 'domestic' or 'dominated' peoples. Treaty-making is one of the oldest and [most] diplomatic traditions between and among sovereign nations."[67] One might argue that Estes is calling for a relinking with another governing body (e.g., the United Nations [UN]). But, he counters, it is treaties with the US government that have been feigned mechanisms of paternalism and control. By relinking with a body such as the UN that shares diplomatic philosophies across the East and West—and certainly well beyond the United States—Indigenous people might be able to look forward. Estes urges TRN members to forget treaties of the past, to delink from all the US values of republicanism instantiated there. Instead, self-determination can only be had in recognizing that treaties "are future-oriented documents" with "promises of fundamental human rights."[68] Ostensibly, we see here a turn away from the Declaration of Independence and more toward the UN Declaration of Human Rights. Self-determination, therefore, involves the move from US civil rights to international human rights and a temporal shift from past US treaties to future treaties brokered by larger authorities.

Second, relinking also involves an internal commitment, an affirmation of Indigenous agency. Leanne Betasamosake Simpson (Misi-zaagiing / Mississauga Nishnaabeg) writes that "nationhood doesn't just radiate outwards, it also radiates inwards. It is my physical body, my mind, and my spirit. It is our families . . . big, beautiful, diverse."[69] Indeed, according to Estes, Indigenous "primary concerns [are] to address the common experience of Natives."[70] Thus, relinking, too, means Indigenous communities privileging their own epistemologies and lifeways above all else. Or, as Estes writes, "[we should] take the struggle back where it belongs: in the hands of the people" instead of negotiating with colonial agents and their founding documents (as perhaps the 20-Points authors would have it).

TRN hints at a sense of familial strength, of cultural survivance, in the idea of relinking with immemorial pasts and sacred presents. To visual artist and poet Quill Christie-Peters (Anishinaabe), such relinking celebrates Indigenous authority steeped in self-determination, beyond the binds/bounds of colonial power found in republican documents. She writes, "Body, the whispers of ancestors tending to a lodge, the smell of rain on the mossy bog the ability to feel loved and held, the smile of my grandmother as she holds my child, the chuckle of my father as he paints futures with me, all that we are, all that we will be forever flickering. *Sovereign in our complexity; we are everything they can never reach.*"[71] Such complexity is to be celebrated as epistemology, even if it appears inscrutable to colonizing systems and settler logics. Christie-Peters's inwardly directed words demonstrate Indigenous rhetoric's powerful turn away from the Declaration and toward self-determination.

NOTES

Reflexively, I am mindful of my privilege writing in the cultural spaces of Indigeneity and my limitations in participating in decolonial work as a settler-colonial. Nonetheless, I follow Emma LaRocque's (Cree/Métis) lead: "The onus to deconstruct and to rebuild cannot fall solely [upon] the colonized. The responsibility to clean up colonial debris lies [also] with the colonizer to dismantle their colonial constructs" (LaRocque, *When the Other Is Me*, 163). I am committed to labor that centers Indigenous cultures, spotlights Indigenous agency, and seeks to unsettle colonialism. This chapter is part of these efforts.

1. Within Turtle Island (North America) I use the word "Indigenous" to refer to Native Americans / American Indians living in the present-day United States and the three major groups of Native Canadians / First Peoples in Canada (First Nations, Inuit, and Métis). The identifier "refers to separate nations that occupied territory before the arrival of Europeans" (Younging, *Elements of Indigenous Style*, 63). Moreover, "Indigenous" as an identifier is used in the United Nations Declaration of Indigenous Human Rights and marks subject-positions of political power and sovereign agency versus categories of anthropological taxonomy. "Indigenous" is an antidote to the colonial term "Indian" or "Aboriginal" that has been used to classify Indigenous people as inferior. See Mihesuah, *So You Want to Write*; Tuhiwai Smith, *Decolonizing Methodologies*; and Vowel, *Indigenous Writes*.

2. Civilization Fund Act, March 3, 1819, U.S. Statutes at Large, 3:516–17.

3. John Ross, "Annual Message," *Cherokee Phoenix*, October 14, 1829, 4–5; also found in *Niles' Weekly Register*, 189–90.

4. Konkle, *Writing Indian Nations*, 45, 49.

5. Black, *American Indians*, 12.

6. Nataanii Means, "Warrior."

7. Presley, "Between a Rock and a Hard Place," 285–86.

8. Cordes, "Place Is Everything," 193.

9. Nataanii Means, "Warrior."

10. See Parkinson, *Thirteen Clocks*.

11. For more on the termination policy, see Kelly, "Orwellian Language," 351–71.

12. See Black, "Chief John Ross," 24–26; Na'puti, "Rhetorical Contexts," 12–21; Kelly and Black, introduction to *Decolonizing Native American Rhetoric*, 1–23; and Black, *American Indians*.

13. Black, "Native Resistive Rhetoric," 82–83.

14. Na'puti, "Archipelagic Rhetoric," 4–25.

15. Indigenous epistemologies should be discussed within a particular Indigenous nation's traditions. In the service of tracing larger decolonial patterns, though, I am engaging in what postcolonial scholar Gyatri Spivak calls "strategic essentialism" or condensing into a macro-unified unit numerous groups "in order to disrupt or subvert

the dominance that oppresses or marginalizes it." Eide, "Strategic Essentialism and Ethnification," 76. Future treatments of rhetorical authority might examine singular Indigenous cases.

16. Nick Estes, "Native Liberation: The Way Forward," Red Nation, http://therednation.org/native-liberation-the-way-forward/; last accessed April 14, 2023.

17. Maddox, *Citizen Indians*, 16.

18. "Declaration of Independence," 12.

19. Pulley Hudson, "Forked Justice," 51.

20. Buescher and Ono, "Civilized Colonialism," 131.

21. Black, *American Indians*, 11.

22. Cited in McCloud, *Making the American Religious Fringe*, 74–75.

23. Krupat, *Ethnocentrism*, 156.

24. Hoxie, *Talking Back to Civilization*, 21.

25. Prucha, *American Indian Treaties*, 2.

26. "Constitution of the United States," 22–23.

27. Ames, "The Choctaws," *Cherokee Phoenix*, December 23, 1830, 22.

28. Pushmataha and Puckshunnubbee, "For the Cherokee Phoenix," *Cherokee Phoenix*, September 22, 1829, 2.

29. For instance, Jefferson declared to Congress his desire to assimilate Indigenous nations by leading them "to civilization . . . and preparing them ultimately to participate in the benefits of our Government." Jefferson, "Letter on Indian Trading Houses," 341.

30. Jefferson, "Letter on Indian Trading Houses," 341.

31. Yoholo et al. "Memorial of the Creek Nation of Indians," *Cherokee Phoenix*, March 17, 1830, 4.

32. Yoholo et al., "Memorial of the Creek Nation of Indians," 4.

33. "Declaration of Independence," 9.

34. Pearce, *Savagism and Civilization*, 53–56.

35. Coacoochee, "Speech to Removal Council."

36. Coacoochee, "Speech to Removal Council."

37. "Declaration of Independence," 9.

38. Lake, "Enacting Red Power," 142.

39. Kelly, "Detournement," 169.

40. For a fuller history of these policies, see Kelly, "Orwellian Language," 351–71; and Hoxie, *Final Promise*, xviii.

41. Sanchez and Stuckey, "Rhetoric of American Indian Activism," 126.

42. See Smith and Warrior, *Like a Hurricane*.

43. Kelly, "Detournement," 168.

44. *Trail of Broken Treaties 20-Point Position Paper*, American Indian Movement, http://www.aimovement.org/archives/; last accessed October 1, 2023.

45. *Trail of Broken Treaties 20-Point Position Paper*.

46. Derek Wanzer-Serrano calls such ascension of governmental agency as here "the West's claim to epistemic privilege." Wanzer-Serrano, *New York Young Lords*, 14.

47. Parham, *Pan-tribal Activism in the Pacific Northwest*, 73.

48. Tuhiwai Smith, *Decolonizing Methodologies*, 33.

49. Wamsutta Frank B. James, "The Suppressed Speech to Have Been Delivered at Plymouth, Massachusetts, 1970," United American Indians of New England, http://www.uaine.org/suppressed_speech.htm; last accessed November 4, 2022.

50. Black, "Performing Native America," 5.

51. Champagne, "In Search of Theory and Method," 362.

52. James, "Suppressed Speech."

53. James, "Suppressed Speech."
54. James, "Suppressed Speech."
55. James, "Suppressed Speech."
56. Kicummah Teuton, *Red Land, Red Power*, 234.
57. Belanger, *Rhetoric and Settler Inertia*, 22.
58. Coulthard, *Red Skin, White Masks*, 39.
59. Mack and Na'puti, "Our Bodies Are Not Terra Nullius," 347–70.
60. Estes, "Native Liberation."
61. Estes, "Native Liberation."
62. Na'puti, "Rhetorical Contexts," 22.
63. Estes, "Native Liberation."
64. Gilio-Whitaker, *As Long as the Grass Grows*, 27.
65. Estes, "Native Liberation."
66. Alfred, "Sovereignty," 467; Vizenor, *Native Liberty*, 85.
67. Estes, "Native Liberation," n.p.
68. Estes, "Native Liberation."
69. Betasamosake Simpson, *As We Have Always Done*, 9.
70. Estes, "Native Liberation."
71. Christie-Peters, "Body: An Acknowledgement"; emphasis mine.

BIBLIOGRAPHY

Belanger, Patrick. *Rhetoric and Settler Inertia: Strategies of Canadian Decolonization*. Lanham, MD: Lexington Books, 2019.

Betasamosake Simpson, Leanne. *As We Have Always Done: Indigenous Freedom Through Radical Resistance*. Minneapolis: University of Minnesota Press, 2017.

Black, Jason Edward. *American Indians and the Rhetoric of Removal and Allotment*. Jackson: University Press of Mississippi, 2015.

———. "Chief John Ross and Indigenous Anti-removal Rhetoric in the Jacksonian Age." In *A Rhetorical History of the United States*, edited by Paul Stob, 3:34–45. East Lansing: Michigan State University Press, 2025.

———. "Native Resistive Rhetoric and the Decolonization of American Indian Removal Discourse." *Quarterly Journal of Speech* 95, no. 1 (2009): 66–88.

———. "Performing Native America: Image Events in the Thanksgiving Day of Mourning Protests." *Enculturation: A Journal of Rhetoric, Writing and Culture* 6, no. 2 (2010): 1–23.

Buescher, Derek, and Kent Ono. "Civilized Colonialism: Pocahontas as a Neocolonial Rhetoric." *Women's Studies in Communication* 19, no. 2 (1996): 127–53.

Chaat Smith, Paul, and Robert Allen Warrior. *Like a Hurricane: The Indian Movement from Alcatraz to Wounded Knee*. New York: New Press, 1996.

Champagne, Duane. "In Search of Theory and Method in American Indian Studies." *American Indian Quarterly* 31, no. 2 (2007): 353–72.

Christie-Peters, Quille. "Body: An Acknowledgement." *Canadian Art* (December 2020). https://canadianart.ca/features/body-an-acknowledgement/; last accessed September 5, 2023.

Coacoochee. "Speech to Removal Council." In *The Origin, Progress and Conclusion of the Florida War*, edited by John T. Sprague, 6. New York, 1848.

"The Constitution of the United States." In *A Documentary History of the United States*, edited by Richard D. Heffner, 22–27. New York: Signet, 2002.

Cordes, Ashley. "Place Is Everything: Remembering Responsibilities Between and Beyond Land Acknowledgements." *Communication and Critical/Cultural Studies* 20, no. 2 (2023): 191–99.

Coulthard, Glen Sean. *Red Skin, White Masks: Rejecting the Colonial Politics of Recognition*. Minneapolis: University of Minnesota Press, 2014.

"Declaration of Independence." In *A Documentary History of the United States*, edited by Richard D. Heffner, 12–15. New York: Signet, 2002.

Eide, Elisabeth. "Strategic Essentialism and Ethnification: Hand in Glove?" *Nordicom Review* 31, no. 2 (2010): 63–78.

Gilio-Whitaker, Dina. *As Long as the Grass Grows: The Indigenous Fight for Environmental Justice from Colonization to Standing Rock*. Boston: Beacon Press, 2019.

Hoxie, Frederick. *A Final Promise: The Campaign to Assimilate the Indians, 1880–1920*. Lincoln: University of Nebraska Press, 1984.

———. *Talking Back to Civilization: Indian Voices from the Progressive Era*. Boston: Bedford / St. Martin's, 2001.

Jefferson, Thomas. "Letter on Indian Trading Houses, January 18, 1803." In *A Compilation of the Messages and Papers of the Presidents*, vol. 1, edited by James D. Richardson, 341. Washington, DC: Bureau of National Literature and Art, 1937.

Kelly, Casey Ryan. "Detournement, Decolonization, and the American Indian Occupation of Alcatraz Island (1969–1971)." *Rhetoric Society Quarterly* 44, no. 2 (2014): 168–90.

———. "Orwellian Language and the Politics of Tribal Termination (1953–1960)." *Western Journal of Communication* 74, no. 4 (2010): 351–71.

Kelly, Casey Ryan, and Jason Edward Black. Introduction to *Decolonizing Native American Rhetoric: Communicating Self-Determination*, edited by Casey Ryan Kelly and Jason Edward Black, 1–23. New York: Peter Lang, 2018.

Kicummah Teuton, Dean. *Red Land, Red Power: Grounding Knowledge in the American Indian Novel*. Durham, NC: Duke University Press, 2008.

Konkle, Maureen. *Writing Indian Nations: Indigenous Intellectuals and Politics of Historiography, 1827–1863*. Chapel Hill: University of North Carolina Press, 2004.

Krupat, Arnold. *Ethnocentrism: Ethnography, History, Literature*. Berkeley: University of California Press, 1991.

Lake, Randall. "Enacting Red Power: The Consummatory Function in Native American Protest Rhetoric." *Quarterly Journal of Speech* 69, no. 2 (1983): 127–42.

LaRocque, Emma. *When the Other Is Me: Indigenous Resistance Discourse, 1850–1990*. Winnipeg: University of Manitoba Press, 2010.

Mack, Ashley N., and Tiara Na'puti. "Our Bodies Are Not Terra Nullius: Building a Decolonial Feminist Resistance to Gendered Violence." *Women's Studies in Communication* 42, no. 3 (2019): 347–70.

Maddox, Lucy. *Citizen Indians: Native American Intellectuals, Race and Reform*. Ithaca, NY: Cornell University Press, 2005.

McCloud, Sean. *Making the American Religious Fringe: Exotics, Subversives, and Journalists, 1955–1993*. Chapel Hill: University of North Carolina Press, 2004.

Mihesuah, Devon. *So You Want to Write About American Indians? A Guide for Writers, Students, and Scholars*. Lincoln: University of Nebraska Press, 2005.

Na'puti, Tiara. "Archipelagic Rhetoric: Remapping the Marianas and Challenging Militarization from 'A Stirring Place.'" *Communication and Critical/Cultural Studies* 16, no. 1 (2019): 4–25.

———. "Rhetorical Contexts of Colonization and Decolonization." In *Oxford Research Encyclopedia of Communication*, edited by Matthew Powers, 12–21. New York: Oxford University Press, 2020.

Nataanii Means. "Warrior." SoundCloud. 2017. Digital file; last accessed April 14, 2023.

Parham, Vera. *Pan-tribal Activism in the Pacific Northwest: The Power of Indigenous Protest and the Birth of Daybreak Star Cultural Center.* Lanham, MD: Lexington Books, 2018.

Parkinson, Robert G. *Thirteen Clocks: How Race United the Colonies and Made the Declaration of Independence.* Chapel Hill: University of North Carolina Press, 2021.

Pearce, Roy Harvey. *Savagism and Civilization: A Study of the Indian and the American Mind.* Baltimore: Johns Hopkins University Press, 1967.

Presley, Rachel. "Between a Rock and a Hard Place: Rhetorical Strategies for Environmental Protection and Tribal Resistance in the Dakota Access Pipeline Movement." In *Decolonizing Native American Rhetoric: Communicating Self-Determination*, edited by Casey Ryan Kelly and Jason Edward Black, 285–86. New York: Peter Lang, 2018.

Prucha, Francis Paul. *American Indian Treaties: The History of a Political Anomaly.* Berkeley: University of California Press, 1997.

Pulley Hudson, Angela. "Forked Justice: Elias Boudinot, the U.S. Constitution and the Cherokee Removal." In *American Indian Rhetorics of Survivance: Word Medicine, Word Magic*, edited by Ernest Stromberg, 50–66. Pittsburgh: University of Pittsburgh Press, 2006.

Sanchez, John, and Mary E. Stuckey. "The Rhetoric of American Indian Activism in the 1960s and 1970s." *Communication Quarterly* 48, no. 2 (2000): 120–36.

Taiaiake Alfred. "Sovereignty." In *A Companion to American Indian History*, edited by Philip Deloria and Neal Salisbury, 460–74. New York: Blackwell, 2002.

Tuhiwai Smith, Linda. *Decolonizing Methodologies: Research and Indigenous Peoples.* London: Zed Books, 2012.

Vizenor, Gerald. *Native Liberty: Natural Reason and Cultural Survivance.* Lincoln: University of Nebraska Press, 2009.

Vowel, Chelsea. *Indigenous Writes: A Guide to First Nations, Métis, and Inuit Issues in Canada.* Winnipeg: Portage and Main Press, 2016.

Wanzer-Serrano, Darrel. *The New York Young Lords and the Struggle for Liberation.* Philadelphia: Temple University Press, 2015.

Younging, Gregory. *Elements of Indigenous Style: A Guide for Writing By and About Indigenous People.* Ottawa: Brush, 2018.

6

DECLARING ECONOMIC INDEPENDENCE: ARGENTINA, JUAN DOMINGO PERÓN, AND POLITICAL TIME

Stephen J. Heidt

On July 9, 1947, President Juan Domingo Perón, along with his cabinet, provincial authorities, President González Videla of Chile, and thousands of citizens, commemorated Argentina's Independence Day. From his vantage point in the city of Tucumán, where Argentina had declared independence from Spain 131 years earlier and the hub of annual celebrations remembering the nation's birth, Perón gazed upon thousands of patriotic citizens and announced that he was declaring economic independence. Vowing that the struggle for freedom had not concluded with nationhood, Perón argued that true political sovereignty could never be achieved if the nation remained economically dependent on and subservient to foreign powers. Thus, he marked his "Declaration of Economic Independence" as the first step for uniting the people and the government in a collective struggle to fend off the forces of imperialism and neocolonialism.

Perón's Declaration spooked foreign interests, especially after he renationalized several large commercial enterprises and resisted the call for Argentina to join the postwar economic order organized at Bretton Woods, New Hampshire.[1] Resonating across national and international contexts, as Monica Rein explains, Perón's Declaration bound together "political sovereignty and economic independence," implying that only meaningful economic independence from foreign interests "would accord the country true political sovereignty."[2]

Perón followed up on the Declaration by nationalizing the railroad, an act that generated "mistrust and hostility" on the part of the United Kingdom, irreparably damaging relations between the two nations.[3] Relations with the

United States also suffered, as Perón's sovereignty rhetoric generated fears that he would resort to "anti-US sentiment" to "strengthen his political position."[4] For example, a report by the CIA concluded that the United States needed to leverage Argentina's need for "dollars from the US," to restrain Perón's economic program, unironically proving the Argentine president's point.[5]

Scholarly histories of Perón's Declaration remain unsatisfying because they focus on how the Argentine, British, and US governments responded to his desire for independence from the postwar economic order, how his policies destabilized Argentina's economy, and how his mandate connected to fears of communist incursion in South America. Missing from these stories is an account of the Declaration as a unique rhetorical and political artifact. In this chapter, I argue that Perón's Declaration of Economic Independence drew on the US Declaration of Independence as a source of inspiration. By offering a familiar form and structure, Perón's Declaration became the vehicle by which he could connect past struggles for political independence with midcentury economic challenges, contextualize the gravity of the contemporary challenge, and understand the significance of his policy program.

As a formative document used by independence movements around the globe, but especially in the Western Hemisphere, the US Declaration of Independence bundled inspiration and aspiration such that by 1826 it had emboldened similar acts of political resistance across the region. Circulating more than just an idea, it circulated a language, structure, and form for expressing the importance and necessity of political sovereignty. Political movements across the region often employed text from the US Declaration, rendering the document into a platform for liberation from colonial rule anywhere it existed. Sometimes listing grievances to justify independence, consolidate unity and identity, and demand recognition abroad, as was the case with the original thirteen colonies, these declarations employed "us versus them" discourse to establish new national identities and blame colonial masters for political, economic, and social problems.[6] As with the United States, these declarations also sought to have other nations recognize them as a state, one that would join the world of nations rather than disrupt it.[7]

Perón's Declaration renewed and updated this rhetorical model by invoking temporal connections between the United States and Argentina to push against the neocolonial aspects of the postwar order. Relying on the US Declaration as a model foregrounded his own political project by enacting a form of chronopolitics—the politics of time—to connect the present and past in a collective and continuous narrative about Argentina's political order.

Distinguishing the prior struggle as the triumph of democracy over colonial rule, he used the United States' founding document to expose the ways the capitalist economic system endangered the political system. By recalling the past to contextualize the present, Perón placed political and economic progress in a linear, temporal continuum that depicted economic sovereignty as a logical progression of political development.

The significance of political time in international and domestic contexts takes three forms. Some scholars view time as exerting influence and power on the political world—as a force of change.[8] Others recognize how politicians grapple with the rapid speed of the contemporary world, rendering time into something to be governed.[9] Both approaches offer insights into how policymakers make decisions and how institutions change. A third approach treats time as a rhetorical force. This option has existed since at least the time of the ancient Greeks, who articulated the concept of *kairos*, the idea that persuasive success depends on making an appropriate rhetorical intervention at the appropriate moment.[10] In a contemporary context, the term "chronopolitics" explains how rhetoric about time punctuates political movements, impacting public feelings about issues and events.[11] As a rhetorical technique, time serves political elites by authorizing their leadership in the present, directing audiences to their preferred path forward, and explaining the consequences of failing to act, all of which enables them to exert influence.[12] Political discourse about time—usually in narratives that elaborate national stories over different eras—give meaning and context to present challenges by connecting them to enduring cultural memories related to prior struggles.[13] For example, presidents draw attention to political issues and stress the urgency of action via narratives that work back through the past to explain the present and offer insight into the future.[14] In other words, when speakers emphasize time, they compress complex social realities into a temporal dimension that situates audiences within ongoing stories and memories related to national heritage, directing them to act in ways consistent with the historical chronology.[15]

Reading Perón's Declaration of Economic Independence as an act of chronopolitics and political time isolates the rhetorical technology that enabled one of Latin America's most significant political leaders to justify and legitimize his economic project. Following the form and, in part, content of the US Declaration, Perón's proclamation connected Argentina's contemporary economic challenges to collective memories related to the historic struggle for independence, memories revitalized in schools and celebrated annually. In making this argument, the following chapter first turns to Perón's rhetoric prior to the Declaration, including his publication of a Bill of Rights of the Workers of Argentina, before assessing the Declaration of Economic Independence. Examining Perón's broader rhetorical enterprise demonstrates how the US American revolutionary experience served as a source of inspiration for resisting the postwar economic system and its undemocratic nature, a feature that continues to live on in hemispheric memory. It concludes by assessing the resistant potential of the US Declaration of Independence in the contemporary era.

The US Declaration of Independence and Argentina

The US Declaration of Independence marked a titanic shift in modern political discourse. While many of the themes and political values mentioned in the document had been discussed by political philosophers such as Thomas Paine and Emer de Vattel, whose work *The Law of Nations* influenced the writing of the Declaration, no colonial territory at that point had sought to separate itself from its parent state via a high-minded political discourse that connected independence to fundamental political themes such as democracy, self-rule, and freedom since the Dutch revolt from Spain in 1581. Revolts in Corsica (1765) and Poland (1772), violently suppressed by the French, Prussians, Russians, and Austrians, signaled the growing desire for self-rule but had not included any formal justification. Indeed, the partition of Poland served as a cautionary tale for the colonists. Daniel Leonard, Richard Henry Lee, and Thomas Paine all explicitly warned of the potential for revolt to lead to partitioning of the colonies. Rather than halt the quest for independence, however, those warnings drove colonial unity and bolstered the case for a Declaration of Independence as a document that would force European powers to negotiate with the new country.[16] A product of extensive debates about how to separate from England, the final document provides "an assertion of statehood."[17] Its opening statement announces the existence of "the thirteen united States of America," a subtle, but important departure from the previous status of colonies. Next, it claims that "the political bands" connecting England and the United States have been "dissolve[d]," signaling that the remainder of the document would provide an explanation and rationale for this development. After detailing an extensive list of "injuries and usurpations," the document concludes that the colonies are now "Free and Independent States," establishing their sovereignty over the land and demanding recognition of that status by other states.[18]

With sovereignty established as the major premise justifying revolt and separation, the US Declaration inspired colonial territories around the world seeking greater degrees of autonomy and self-rule.[19] These declarations drew directly from the US document and became more than justifications or rationalizations for revolt. Beginning with Haiti in 1804 and spreading across the Western Hemisphere in the decades that followed, they signaled the rise of new political entities and the collapse of colonial empires. Assertions of sovereignty and the battles for independence that followed fundamentally altered the political landscape of the hemisphere and its relationship to European nations but rarely elaborated individual rights or provided for the protection of those rights. As with the US experience, post-independence constitutions addressed (or not) the question of who could enjoy the benefits of sovereignty and how, frequently resorting to political compromises that omitted political and economic rights for many. Implying that those omissions could be addressed down the road, political independence movements enacted a modern form of chronopolitics that rendered political change into an ongoing project requiring continual actions by members of the polity.

Argentina adopted its own Declaration of Independence on July 9, 1816, six years after it launched its bid to separate itself from Spain. Employing the hyperbolic language that typified the US version, Argentina asserted itself as "a nation free and independent of King Ferdinand VII, his successors, and the mother country." While the document did not provide an elaborate list of grievances, it decried the "despotic power of the Kings of Spain," while asserting the "justice" of the "sacred object of independence."[20] And, as with the United States, Argentina's Declaration only demanded independence from Spain, leaving the ultimate "political system" that would govern that land "uncertain."[21] In the aftermath of independence, Argentina's founders produced a "hastily written constitution" that "everyone ignored," leaving the new country with regional "authoritarian leaders" (*caudillos*) who ruled without much concern or oversight from the national government.[22] The weak constitutional system combined with authoritarian rule meant that, unlike the United States, only Argentina's Declaration of Independence lived on in public memory as a foundational and inspirational text.

By the twentieth century, Argentina had consolidated into a weak modern state, beset by underdevelopment, political infighting, and vast inequality. After undergoing rapid modernization in the 1920s, the Great Depression shattered the "economic dynamism" that had typified Argentina's economic rise.[23] The economic collapse fueled populist and nationalist impulses, leading to political instability over the next two decades. In 1930, at the start of what became known as the "Infamous Decade," the military deposed the democratically elected president and installed a repressive military regime.[24] Inspired by the workers' revolution in Russia in 1917, Argentine communists clashed with military rule by "foster[ing] a political culture aimed at the dissemination of Marxism and the achievements of the Soviet experience," and centered on anti-imperialism and anti-fascism.[25] The military government cracked down on the communists but failed to rescue the nation from economic and social strife.

Domestic strife deepened with the outbreak of war in Europe. As an export-dependent country, the dried-up demand for Argentine agricultural products exacerbated the economic crisis. Weakening foreign markets sparked an era of domestic industrialization, contributing to "economic nationalism" that challenged British-owned companies (the railroad in particular) while expanding and deepening the power of labor unions across the country, most of which railed against the government's conservative policies.[26] Economic disruption and political instability, along with rising "working-class expectations for social reform," came to a head on October 17, 1943, when the military once again deposed the sitting president. This mostly bloodless coup left Colonel Juan Domingo Perón as the labor minister of the new government. As labor minister, he initiated significant reforms intent on addressing income inequality, but, perhaps most important, he spoke at "factories and . . . [in] working class neighborhoods," employing "a language particular to Argentina's lower classes, enhanc[ing] his popular appeals."[27] His outreach and rhetorical appeals fostered identification between him and the middle classes, elevating his political power beyond that of his station. Concerns about his national profile and rising popular support led the military junta to arrest and imprison him in October 1945. But the move backfired. After massive protests that "shook the social and political foundations of the country," he was released on October 17. Four months later, on February 24, 1946, he was elected president.[28]

Perón's anti-imperialist, populist rhetoric played a central role in his rise to power by establishing his popular persona with the middle and lower classes. While historians typically attribute his rise to a nexus of material factors like urbanization, industrialization, economic disruption, and the rise of labor unions, domestic and international disputes fomented the conditions for Perón's unique form of rhetorical leadership. US accusations that Argentina was "pro-Nazi," for example, fueled nationalist sentiments, while the fractured relationship with Britain energized calls for economic independence and the public ownership of public goods.[29] These factors, combined with economic stagnation and international antagonism, created fertile conditions for populist leadership. Perón stepped into the void with a populist, anti-imperialist rhetorical enterprise that isolated national and international interests constraining Argentina's economic development. Sowing the seeds of political change, this rhetoric established his personal credibility as a leader by scapegoating domestic and international forces while presenting his leadership as necessary.

As president, Perón's discourse favored populist themes intended to energize the lower and middle classes.[30] His populism, known as *justicialismo*, emerged as "a multiclass political alliance formed by middle-class and military leadership that incorporated the growing working class into national affairs." Principally, Perón's policy priorities focused on "economic nationalism, national industrialization," establishing better relations between civilian and military leadership, and negotiating with organized labor, but they also "hinted strongly of antiforeign sentiment," if not outright anti-imperialism.[31] For example, in the lead-up to his election, the US ambassador to Argentina publicly painted Perón as a Nazi sympathizer. This move backfired by making "his opponent [appear] . . . beholden to . . . foreign interests," energizing Perón's nationalist appeals. Once he was inaugurated, the president of the International Monetary Fund (IMF) was one of Perón's first visitors. The meeting did not go well: referring to the IMF as a "dangerous monster," Perón warned that Argentina was "dealing with a new putative deformed spawn of imperialism."[32] This focus on imperialism typified Perón's writing and speeches. One analysis found a repetitive line across Perón's discourse: "the history of the people, since the Phoenicians till today, has been of its struggle against imperialism."[33]

Perón's commitment to anti-imperialist, populist, and nationalist themes underscored his central political challenge: he came to power in an era of extreme political instability, under dubious conditions, and with a weak hold on power. His rhetorical enterprise had launched him into the center of the Argentine political universe, but cleavages across Argentine society created by nationalist, communist, cosmopolitan, and fascist political movements made it difficult to establish legitimacy.[34] Routinely speaking about the perils of economic colonialism became an important rhetorical device for establishing his mandate and justifying his policy program. For example, in 1946, when announcing his first five-year plan, he claimed, "We aspire to absolute liberation from all economic colonialism, which rescues us from dependence on foreign finances."[35] Harking back to the colonial era, Perón implied that Argentina continued to live in the same political time period as when they were ruled by Spain. He implied that while political structures might have changed, the essential elements of domination continued. This rhetoric deepened the notion that political sovereignty meant little in a postwar, globalized world in which foreign nations could use economic power to direct or coerce domestic policy decisions.

The US revolution and its significance often appeared in this rhetorical repertoire. Perón's *Blue and White Book,* published in 1946, responded to accusations from the US ambassador that he was a fascist by quoting George Washington's Farewell Address:

> Nothing is more essential than that permanent, inveterate antipathies against particular nations, and passionate attachments for others, should be excluded; and that, in place of them, just and amicable feelings towards all should be cultivated. The nation which indulges towards another a habitual hatred or a habitual fondness is in some degree a slave. It is a slave to its animosity or to its affection. . . . Antipathy in one nation against another disposes each more readily to offer insult and injury, to lay hold of slight causes of umbrage, and to be haughty and intractable, when accidental or trifling occasions of dispute occur.[36]

Shaming the US ambassador for behavior while invoking one of the greatest of democratic heroes, Perón also analogized Argentine subservience to British and US American interests as a modern form of slavery. Acknowledging that Argentina was "jealous of the US's liberties and rights," he sought to "establish a balanced form of agreement and interests between the two nations" and urged the United States to recognize that the two nations have "parallel destinies."[37] Once again, the politics of time served as an essential rhetorical fulcrum for Perón's argument. Drawing from the great hero of the US revolution to remind present leaders that nations should strive for harmony and equality, he concluded that doing so would push both nations toward a better, more equitable future. Utilizing time in this way acknowledged a trajectory for Argentina's political development and the power differentials between the two countries.

As president, Perón continued to draw on US revolutionary-era discourse. For example, the publication of a Bill of Rights of the Workers of Argentina on February 24, 1947, connected the present to the past by following the form and format of the US Bill of Rights. It listed ten essential freedoms workers should enjoy. These "individual liberties," the document explained, "constitute the natural, inalienable and imprescriptable attributes of human beings." Listing things such as the right to work, with a fair wage, in safe conditions, the ninth clause also specified that workers had "the right to better economic conditions." While not explicitly elaborating the factors impinging upon those "economic conditions," when taken as part of a broader rhetoric of economic nationalism, specifying these "rights" fit the spirit of anti-imperialism that dominated Perón's political discourse.[38] Moreover, the elaboration of these rights spoke to the continuing necessity of economic independence mimicking that of Argentina's North American neighbors. This rhetoric identified a constitutional gap in the elaboration of individual rights. Expounding on this theme at Teatro Colon, he explained that workers' rights "had rested on unstable and indeterminate bases and foundations." This left workers vulnerable to political will. Thus, his Bill of Rights would "establish, once and for all . . . the right of individuals recognized by the State." Filling the constitutional void by following the model elaborated by the authors of the US Constitution but with a more modernist inflection focused on the plight of workers in the global capitalist system led to the inclusion of those ten rights in Argentina's constitution in 1949.[39]

Declaring Economic Independence

Four months after presenting the Bill of Rights, Perón published his Declaration of Economic Independence. This document provided continuity for the temporal elements of his anti-imperialist, anticolonial rhetoric by once again linking the past with the present. Drawing on the US model, several things stand out. First, the look and feel of the document sought to establish it as a timeless proclamation—one that exists in the past, present, and future. Toward that end, Perón had the document printed on yellowed parchment, making it appear as if it dated to a prior era. Engineering the document to resemble an old manuscript rendered it into a cultural object that could be read by audiences in a specific, historical way. Reflecting a rhetorical effect Cara Finnegan called "image vernaculars," aging the document encouraged audiences to connect the contemporary document to Argentina's revolutionary past.[40] The frayed edges and small tears strategically placed around the border as well as the folds and wrinkles add to its aged look. Harking back to the colonial era and Argentina's Declaration of Independence from Spain, only the typed text disrupts the parchment's likeness. But even that disruption is modest, since most audiences would not easily distinguish between modern printing presses and those used in the early nineteenth century. Perón's signature in its grand, flowing script completes the image. Reminiscent of John Hancock's famous signature on the US Declaration of Independence, albeit without the risk of reprisal that hung over the colonial leader's head in 1776, the signature is the first of many, elevating Perón as leader while granting credibility to the document and its intentions.

Beyond the look and feel of the document, the Declaration echoes the style and form of its North American ancestor. Laying out foundational principles of democracy and sovereignty in the preamble, the script adopts the high-minded, eternal language of declarations past. As with the US Declaration, the document addresses Argentina while incorporating a universal language which implies that the principles and rights proposed apply to all. It establishes the declaration as a "solemn act," advanced on "behalf of the people," that "invoke[s] Divine Providence" to declare economic independence, "in defense of human solidarity."[41] Like the US Declaration, this strategy suspends political time—the themes described are not contingent upon a specific set of temporal problems; rather, they are unbound by circumstances. They are principles that guide and direct political order itself and thus should be acted upon with haste. The absence of a detailed list of grievances—a notable departure from the US Declaration—underscores the timeless nature of the rights elaborated. It implies that no one entity can be faulted for the economic challenges facing Argentina because those challenges derive from a systemic disequilibrium disconnected from current political factors.

Beyond its visual and stylistic elements, the ceremonial and deliberative features of the document and its presentation to the Argentine people also advanced its own chronopolitics. Perón signed the Declaration in the city of San Miguel de Tucumán on July 9, 1947, in the same place where 131 years prior Argentina had declared its independence from Spain. Located in northwest Argentina, on the slopes of the Aconquija Mountains, Tucumán has served as a governing city since the mid-sixteenth century. During the struggle for independence, which began in 1810, it became the hub of Argentina's move to political sovereignty. The Congress of Tucumán wrote Argentina's founding document, its Declaration of Independence, at the Casa de Tucumán. In 1941, the government declared the site a National Historic Monument of Argentina, completing repair and reconstruction work in 1943, when it reopened to the public as a museum.[42] As a space of "shared values, memories, and ideals," harking back to the political process that established independence from Spain, Tucumán occupies a place of specific cultural significance in Argentina.[43]

When Perón arrived in Tucumán, he marched through the principal plaza, accompanied by political and military leaders, climbed the steps of the Casa de Tucumán, and delivered a radio and television address introducing his Declaration before an audience of thousands.[44] By virtue of their position as national icon, presidents who travel "in and through space to a designated place or location" drive "attention" to their issues and agendas.[45] For Perón, selecting Tucumán as the site for the Declaration evoked connections between the economic challenges of the 1940s and the political challenges of 1816. His traveling to Tucumán and the movement of his body through that sacred space connected the geographical spot and its historical significance to contemporary political time. Using the historic space as a sort of symbolic currency, his presence amplified the nationalistic and patriotic fervor that typifies Independence Day celebrations while connecting his Declaration to the one that made Argentine sovereignty possible.

Timing his Declaration to coincide with national Independence Day celebrations via a trip to the center of Argentina's political universe drew attention to his proclamation and its themes. At Tucumán, he presented the Declaration with a prepared speech to the assembled crowd. The document and his remarks gave new weight to his warnings about the dangers of economic colonialism, foreign debt, and economic dependency. The text of the Declaration began by establishing connections between the exploitative capitalist economic system and political sovereignty. In the opening paragraph, it declared its "purpose . . . to consummate [the Argentine people's] economic emancipation from the foreign capitalist powers and those in the country linked to them that have exercised tutelage, control, and domination via reprehensible forms of economic hegemony."[46] Speaking in the people's voice, the document subtly scapegoated undefined foreign interests—implicitly referring to the British, who retained ownership of most of the railways in the country—for Argentina's economic challenges. Grappling with inflation, a consequence of having embarked on a campaign to renationalize much of the economy and redistribute wealth, the Declaration helped absolve Perón from responsibility for postwar stagnation while also offering a clear path forward for the nation. But it also underscored a central point. For Perón, sovereignty—the essential political value celebrated on Independence Day—could not be truly achieved as long as the nation made concessions to foreign businesses over resource extraction, transportation networks, and more interests.

The Declaration's extension of political time facilitated Perón's desire to absolve his administration of blame and chart a path forward for the nation. Narrating the present as a continuation of the past's political revolution, the document's second paragraph invoked the people's will as part of a discussion about international economics—what we might now call neoliberalism—before "affirm[ing]" the people's "will to be economically free, just like, one hundred and thirty-one years ago, the founders proclaimed themselves to be politically independent."[47] Recalling the collective nature of the struggle for political sovereignty and the bloody conflict with Spain, it invoked the past to signal the need for continuous struggle against contemporary international economic policy. Indeed, Perón presented that struggle as part of the same era of political time. Economic and political freedom became two sides of the same coin, and Argentina could not have one without the other. The preamble made this clear. Political freedom, it exhorted, required "break[ing] the ties of foreign capitalism and domination embedded in the country and recover[ing] the rights to self-government of national economic sources." Given that political and economic freedom are linked, the document continued, "the nation achieves its economic freedom by retaining, consequently, in fact and in law, the broad and full power to act in ways required for universal justice and economy."[48] In short, by extending political time from 1816 to 1947, the Declaration renewed efforts in the struggle for true political freedom via economic sovereignty, something only achieved by dispelling foreign creditors and reasserting autonomous control over the entirety of Argentina's economy.

Perón's speech announcing the Declaration reinforced the connection across political time, urging continuity in the revolutionary spirit. He established the connection between political and economic freedom by narrating the story of Argentina's political development. Yet in his version, the spirit of 1810 had been disrupted by the forces of capitalism and greed. As he recalled, "In 1810 we were politically free thanks to those heroes we always remember, [but] we cannot affirm the same about those who succeeded them who . . . have wasted our time and have delivered us to a situation of true colonialism like never before."[49] This language implied that the journey toward true sovereignty remained incomplete because of dickering profit seekers beholden to foreign interests. It also established economic freedom as a political value on par with the political values advanced by revolutionary heroes. In referencing his heroic predecessors, Perón sought "to associate [his] policy choices with similar tough choices faced by iconic leaders . . . to highlight 'an ideal behavior to be imitated' . . . to signal the kind of leadership [he sought] to provide . . . [and] to signal a broader 'way of reading [Argentine] political culture.'"[50] This rhetorical form, what Donald Rice called the rhetoric of the "authorizing figure," appropriates and redeploys the memory of iconic leaders in service of political and policy goals.[51] US presidents frequently employ these figures as a source of authority.[52] Similarly, Perón's authorizing figures established an understanding of political time that drew attention to his agenda while supporting his legitimacy as president and political leader.

The fusion of time and place played a crucial role in Perón's appeal. Vowing that economic independence would forever protect the nation from the recurrence of "national or international oppression or slavery," the speech hinted at the "historical range of political possibilities"[53] by explicitly linking his cause to the city of Tucumán and its "sacred altar for the cause of freedom."[54] Referring to his return to Tucumán, "the capital city of this province," Perón noted its "proud . . . history and its destinies." Tucumán, he vowed, would, "for all times [be] the Mecca of our independence." For that reason, he had chosen the city as the site for signing the Declaration, "pages [that] contain the very essence of nationality . . . [and] a creed of independence." The city, in this rhetoric, served as the temporal bridge connecting past struggles for freedom to contemporary ones. It established the city's continuing importance to Argentine sovereignty and explicitly linked economic independence to political freedom.

With Tucumán established as a beacon of freedom shining across time, Perón's expression of political time reflected both Argentina's continuing struggle for freedom and the continuity of colonial forces. As Perón put it, "economic dispossession" had become "the path to modern colonialism." For this reason, he claimed that "when we declare economic independence, we are dismembering an empire, even if we do not realize it."[55] This rhetoric elaborated the Declaration as not just a set of principles but as policy. Demarcating a new beginning in an active and ongoing historical struggle, the Declaration embodied Perón's chronopolitics by linking this new policy with the heroism of Argentina's revolutionary heroes. While heroes long past had struggled for political sovereignty by articulating their emancipation from Spanish rule, the Declaration, he vowed, would lead to a "socially just, economically free and politically sovereign Argentina."[56] Looking forward in time, he concluded the speech by pledging "that no Argentine, no matter how miserable they feel, will ever be able to expose the blessing of its sovereignty and independence before any power on earth."[57] While he could not keep these promises, attaching them to a sacred political space—Tucumán, a city that contained a host of nationalist and patriotic meanings—offered continuing significance to Argentina's contemporary economic challenges by moving back and forward in political time. Invoking the city in this way on this day drew attention to Perón's declaration and elevated its significance beyond that of a single act of commemoration.

When the Ministry of Finance published the Declaration, the connection between place and past became more obvious as it circulated across Argentine culture. At the top of the page, under the title "Argentine Independence," the document drew direct connections between the contemporary and historical struggles for sovereignty. Characterizing the present effort as essentially "similar to how our heroes declared political independence," the document noted that "we declare our economic independence" at Tucumán, "the same place" where Argentina declared independence from Spain. This language connected past to present in a singular arc of political time and struggle. The page then split into two columns: the left-hand column led with "1816 Political Independence Act" and contained an excerpt from Argentina's Declaration of Independence from Spain; the right-hand column copied the form, leading with "1947 Economic Independence Act." Side by side, the text of the new Declaration appears similar to that of the old one, sprinkling familiar phrases across the lead paragraph, including "We, the representatives of [the people] . . . invoke Divine Providence . . . solemnly declare to the face of the earth," and so on. While there are differences in the content offered, the form of that content evokes a historical sensibility that bases the contemporary declaration in the revolutionary context. The reader is led to see the twin Declarations as essentially similar, as connected, and as part of an ongoing project for freedom. Below the excerpts, the page concludes with "Why have we declared it? Because we have already been conquered!"[58] Speaking to the anti-imperialist nature of Perón's rhetoric and its place as the rhetorical fulcrum for his political platform in 1947, this language indicates how Perón wanted audiences to understand his Declaration—as a diagnosis, a call to action, and an expression of timeless political values.

The Legacy of Perón's Declaration

Perón's Declaration may have helped establish his legitimacy as president, but it did not produce the desired economic benefits. He followed up the Declaration by renationalizing railroad, telephone, and gas companies. These policies may have made matters worse. Under the government's management, all three major industries faced crises, service interruptions, and scandals that undermined public trust in Perón's leadership. Similarly, his agricultural and land reforms produced dissensus and unrest. After winning reelection in 1952, opposition to his policies began to grow across the country, some of it violent. His wife, Evita, had been a unifying figure, but her death from cancer in 1952 exacerbated those tensions. With Argentina becoming increasingly polarized, beset by economic challenges, and Perón pushing an agenda that antagonized large sections of the country, including the Catholic Church, the military ultimately ousted the president in a coup in 1955. He barely escaped to exile.[59]

While his Declaration might not have fundamentally altered Argentina's economic political structure, it did alter the political language and context under which economics can be understood in the country. Beyond the Declaration's circulation across television, radio, and print media in 1947, presenting it on Argentina's Independence Day forever linked the concept of economic freedom to Argentina's quest for national sovereignty. Year after year, national and local governments, public radio stations, and more celebrate Perón's Declaration on July 9th.[60] By 1952, the Ministry of Education had approved the proclamation for inclusion in elementary school curricula.[61] And as late as 2015, Argentina's Ministry of Education lists Perón's Declaration as one of the preferred materials for high school history students.[62]

Ultimately, Perón's narrative of political time—his chronopolitics—demonstrate the resistant potential of the US Declaration of Independence in the contemporary era. By drawing on the world's most inspirational and resonant statement of national sovereignty, a document that sparked revolutionary movements around the globe, Perón connected Argentina's past and present, while at the same time extending its content to criticize the nature of the postwar economic order. This critique provided him legitimacy as president, drew attention to his agenda, and shielded him from certain forms of international criticism. It also demonstrated the rhetorical power of historic memory in populist times, something of continuing significance in Argentina, a country that continues to grapple with political challenges, economic problems, and Perón's lasting imprint upon Argentine political culture.

NOTES

All translations are by the author.

1. Skidmore, *Case Study*, 7.
2. Rein, *Politics and Education in Argentina*, 24.
3. Howkins, "Formal End to Informal Imperialism," 237.
4. Skidmore, *Case Study*, 23; CIA, *Probable Argentine Policy*, 8.
5. CIA, *Probable Argentine Policy*, 13–14.
6. Armitage, *Declaration of Independence*, 66–67.

7. Armitage, *Declaration of Independence*, 64–65.
8. Hom, *International Relations*, 13.
9. See Innerarity, *Future and Its Enemies*, 77; and Stahl, "Clockwork War," 76.
10. Lynch, "Generational Chronotopes," 285.
11. Corrigan, *Black Feelings*, xiv.
12. Skowronek, *Presidential Leadership*, 78.
13. Lynch, "Generational Chronotopes," 286.
14. Skowronek, *Presidential Leadership*, 18.
15. Mills, "Chronopolitics of Racial Time," 300.
16. Armitage, *Declaration of Independence*, 42–43, 47–48.
17. Armitage, *Declaration of Independence*, 18.
18. Declaration of Independence (July 4, 1776), https://www.archives.gov/founding-docs/declaration-transcript.
19. Armitage, *Declaration of Independence*, 109.
20. Declaration of Independence, Argentina (July 9, 1816), https://declarationproject.org/?p=383.
21. J. Brown, *Brief History of Argentina*, 98.
22. J. Brown, *Brief History of Argentina*, 105.
23. J. Brown, *Brief History of Argentina*, 191.
24. Spruk, "Rise and Fall," 8.
25. Petra, *Intellectuals and Communist Culture*, 38–39.
26. J. Brown, *Brief History of Argentina*, 198.
27. J. Brown, *Brief History of Argentina*, 203.
28. J. Brown, *Brief History of Argentina*, 206.
29. J. Brown, *Brief History of Argentina*, 193.
30. Goebel, *Argentina's Partisan Past*, 65.
31. J. Brown, *Brief History of Argentina*, 207–8.
32. Perón, *La hora de los pueblos*, 173. Despite this rhetoric, Perón sought entry into the Bretton Woods institutions. See Kedar, "Chronicle of an Inconclusive Negotiation," 637–68.
33. Oscar Castelluci, editorial Introduction to Perón, *La hora de los pueblos*, 10.
34. Goebel, *Argentina's Partisan Past*, 73–75.
35. Perón quoted in "9 de julio de 1947 Declaración de la Independencia Económica," *VisiónPaís Argentina*, July 9, 2020, https://visionpais.com.ar/9-de-julio-de-1947-declaracion-de-la-independencia-economica/.
36. Perón, *Libro azul y blanco*, 3.
37. Perón, *Libro azul y blanco*, 127.
38. Juan Domingo Perón, Bill of Rights of the Workers of Argentina, February 24, 1947, https://faculty.chass.ncsu.edu/slatta/hi216/documents/peronbill.htm.
39. "El Decálogo de los Derechos del Trabajador de 1947," Ministerio de Cultura Argentina, February 22, 2021, https://www.cultura.gob.ar/el-decalogo-de-los-derechos-de-los-trabajadores-de-1947-10159/.
40. Finnegan, "Recognizing Lincoln," 34.
41. "Declaración de la Independencia Económica," July 9, 1947, https://www.labaldrich.com.ar/wp-content/uploads/2014/07/Acta-de-declaraci%C3%B3n-de-la-Independencia-Econ%C3%B3mica-1947.pdf.
42. Blasco, "Productos culturales conmemorativos," 60.
43. Prasch, *World Is Our Stage*, 30.
44. This march through the square can be seen, in part, at https://www.youtube.com/watch?v=10z04rDv44g&t=39s.
45. Prasch, *World Is Our Stage*, 29.

46. Perón, "Declaración de la Independencia Económica."

47. Perón, "Declaración de la Independencia Económica."

48. Perón, "Declaración de la Independencia Económica."

49. Perón quoted in "La Independencia que la historia nos oculta: La Declaración de la Independencia Económica de 1947," La Baldrich, July 9, 2023, https://www.labaldrich.com.ar/declaracion-de-la-independencia-economica-2/.

50. Finnegan, "Picturing the Presidents," 212.

51. Rice, *Rhetorical Uses of the Authorizing Figure*, xiv.

52. L. Brown, "Greats and the Great Debate," 125; Murphy, "Inventing Authority," 71; Edwards and Smith, "Myth and Anti-myth," 17–25; Strate, "Heroes and/as Communication," 20.

53. Skowronek, *Presidential Leadership*, xi.

54. Perón, *Discursos, mensajes, correspondencia y escritos*, 400–402.

55. Perón quoted in Pignatelli, "El otro Congreso de Tucumán."

56. Perón, *Discursos, mensajes, correspondencia y escritos*, 400–402.

57. Perón, quoted in Pignatelli, "El otro Congreso de Tucumán."

58. Ministry of Finances of the Nation, "Independence Argentina," n.d., https://www.labaldrich.com.ar/declaracion-de-la-independencia-economica-2/.

59. "Perón Deposed in Argentina," History, February 9, 2010, https://www.history.com/this-day-in-history/peron-deposed-in-argentina.

60. See, e.g., "A 76 años de la Declaración de la Independencia Económica," *La Radio Publica*, July 9, 2023, https://admin.radionacional.com.ar/a-76-anos-de-la-declaracion-de-la-independencia-economica/.

61. Girbal-Blacha, "Historical Time."

62. Ministerio de Educación, *El diseño curricular*, 36.

BIBLIOGRAPHY

Armitage, David. *The Declaration of Independence: A Global History*. Cambridge, MA: Harvard University Press, 2007.

Blasco, María Élida. "Productos culturales conmemorativos: La Azarosa Constitución de la Casa Histórica de la Independencia durante la década de 1940." *Anuario* 32, no. 1 (2017): 60. http://anuarioiehs.unicen.edu.ar/Files/2017%201/04%20Anuario%20IEHS%2032(1)%20a.Blasco.pdf.

Brown, Jonathan C. *A Brief History of Argentina*. New York: Facts on File, 2003.

Brown, Lara M. "The Greats and the Great Debate: President William J. Clinton's Use of Presidential Exemplars." *Presidential Studies Quarterly* 37 (2007): 124–38.

CIA. *Probable Argentine Policy Toward the US to 1952 and Its Effects on US Interests*. Washington, DC: Government Printing Office, 1949. https://www.cia.gov/readingroom/docs/DOC_0000258559.pdf.

Corrigan, Lisa. *Black Feelings: Race and Affect in the Long Sixties*. Jackson: University Press of Mississippi, 2020.

Drucker, Susan, and Gary Gumpert, eds. *Heroes in a Global World*. Cresskill, NJ: Hampton Press, 2008.

Finnegan, Cara. "Picturing the Presidents: Obama and the Visual Politics of White House Art." In *The Rhetoric of Heroic Expectations: Establishing the Obama Presidency*, edited by Justin S. Vaughn and Jennifer R. Mercieca, 209–34. College Station: Texas A&M University Press, 2014.

———. "Recognizing Lincoln: Image Vernaculars in Nineteenth-Century Visual Culture." *Rhetoric and Public Affairs* 8, no. 1 (2005): 31–57.

Girbal-Blacha, Noemi M. "Historical Time and the Political Uses of the Past: The Power of the Word in Peronist Argentina (1946–1955)." *Revista Pilquen* 21, no. 1 (2018), http://www.scielo.org.ar/scielo.php?script=sci_arttext&pid=S1851-31232018000100004.

Goebel, Michael. *Argentina's Partisan Past: Nationalism and the Politics of History.* Liverpool, UK: Liverpool University Press, 2011.

Hom, Andrew R. *International Relations and the Problem of Time.* Oxford: Oxford University Press, 2020.

Howkins, Adrian. "A Formal End to Informal Imperialism: Environmental Nationalism, Sovereignty Disputes, and the Decline of British Interests in Argentina, 1933–1955." *British Scholar* 3, no. 2 (2010): 235–62.

Innerarity, Daniel. *The Future and Its Enemies: In Defense of Political Hope.* Stanford, CA: Stanford University Press, 2012.

Kaid, Linda Lee, ed. *The Millennium Edition: Communication in the 2000 Campaign.* Lanham, MD: Rowman & Littlefield, 2003.

Kedar, Claudia. "Chronicle of an Inconclusive Negotiation: Perón, the International Monetary Fund, and the World Bank (1946–1955)." *Hispanic American Historical Review* 92, no. 4 (2012): 637–68.

Lynch, John. "Generational Chronotopes and Accounting for Unethical Medicine: Bill Clinton's Apologies for Radiation Research and the Tuskegee Syphilis Study." *Quarterly Journal of Speech* 107, no. 3 (2021): 284–304.

Mills, Charles W. "The Chronopolitics of Racial Time." *Time and Society* 29, no. 2 (2020): 297–317.

Ministerio de Educación, *El diseño curricular para la Nueva Escuela Secundaria, Ciclo Orientado del Bachillerato, Economía y Administración.* Buenos Aires: Gobierno de la Ciudad de Buenos Aires, 2015.

Murphy, John M. "Inventing Authority: Bill Clinton, Martin Luther King, Jr., and the Orchestration of Rhetorical Traditions." *Quarterly Journal of Speech* 83 (1997): 71–89.

Perón, Juan Domingo. *Discursos, mensajes, correspondencia y escritos.* Buenos Aires: Biblioteca del Congreso de la Nación, 1949.

———. *La hora de los pueblos.* Buenos Aires: Biblioteca del Congreso de la Nación, 2017.

———. *Libro azul y blanco.* Buenos Aires: Editorial Azul y Blanco, 1946.

Petra, Adriana. *Intellectuals and Communist Culture: Itineraries, Problems, and Debates in Post-war Argentina.* Translated by Rebecca Wolpin. Buenos Aires: Palgrave Macmillan, 2022.

Pignatelli, Adrián. "El otro Congreso de Tucumán: El día que Perón declaró la independencia económica y auguró 60 años sin crisis." Infobae, July 8, 2023. https://www.infobae.com/sociedad/2023/07/09/el-otro-congreso-de-tucuman-el-dia-que-peron-declaro-la-independencia-economica-y-auguro-60-anos-sin-crisis/.

Prasch, Allison M. *The World Is Our Stage: The Global Rhetorical Presidency and the Cold War.* Chicago: University of Chicago Press, 2023.

Rein, Monica. *Politics and Education in Argentina, 1946–1962.* Translated by Martha Grenzeback. New York: M. E. Sharpe, 1998.

Rice, Donald E. *The Rhetorical Uses of the Authorizing Figure: Fidel Castro and Jose Marti.* New York: Praeger, 1992.

Skidmore, Thomas E. *A Case Study in Comparative Public Policy: The Economic Dimensions of Populism in Argentina and Brazil.* Washington, DC: Wilson Center, 1978. https://www.wilsoncenter.org/sites/default/files/media/documents/publication/wp3_the_economic_dimensions_of_populism_in_argentina_and_brazil.pdf.

Skowronek, Stephen. *Presidential Leadership in Political Time.* 2nd ed., rev. and exp. Lawrence: University Press of Kansas, 2011.

Spruk, Rok. "The Rise and Fall of Argentina." *Latin American Economic Review* 28, no. 16 (2019): 1–40.

Stahl, Roger. "A Clockwork War: Rhetorics of Time in a Time of Terror." *Quarterly Journal of Speech* 94, no. 1 (2008): 73–99.

Strate, Lance. "Heroes and/as Communication." In *Heroes in a Global World,* edited by Susan Drucker and Gary Gumpert, 19–46. Cresskill, NJ: Hampton Press, 2008.

7

SOVEREIGNTY REIMAGINED: TROPES, SOVEREIGN CITIZEN DISCOURSES, AND THE DECLARATION OF INDEPENDENCE

Scott J. Varda

Just after 9 a.m., on April 19, 1995, a powerful explosion ripped through Oklahoma City, killing 168 people, injuring another 680, and damaging more than three hundred buildings. The explosion came from the back of a Ryder truck parked in front of the Alfred P. Murrah Federal Building.[1] At the time, it was the deadliest terrorist attack in United States history, and to this day it remains the worst domestic terror attack in United States history. This attack was perpetrated by Timothy McVeigh, a white supremacist who "considered himself part of the [militia] movement," and Terry Nichols, a self-described "sovereign citizen."[2] When law enforcement found the bombers' getaway car, they discovered a collection of anti-government and white supremacist reading materials, as well as a hand-written message that read, "Obey the Constitution, and we won't shoot you." The message had been scrawled on a copy of the US Declaration of Independence.[3]

This chapter examines the use and misuse of the Declaration of Independence as a source, inspiration, and rhetorical justification for historical terrorist violence and contemporary sovereign citizen actions. Sovereign citizens, a heterogenous collection of discourses and practices from overlapping anti-government groups, express belief in the illegitimacy of established governments. These discourses, most often expressed by self-identified sovereign citizens, are also interwoven throughout a network of other anti-government extremist rhetorics, including those of the Proud Boys, Oath Keepers, and increasingly, QAnon. This chapter considers the rhetorical significance of those discourses and pays special attention to use of the Declaration of

Independence as justification for anti-government violence as wielded by sovereign citizens. I begin by briefly describing the sovereign citizen movement and explain its importance as a site where anti-government views can justify violence. In so doing, I also briefly consider the system of legal language—pseudolaw sovereigns employ both in courtrooms and publicly to convey their understandings of "secret knowledge." Then I turn to a consideration of how the sovereign citizen movement appropriates the Declaration to justify not only their anti-government views but also violence as a legitimate extension of those views, explaining how the use of figures of speech—the tropes of metonymy and synecdoche—helps mobilize support for anti-government protest. I conclude with the suggestion that the use of the Declaration's aesthetic appeal not only facilitates these figures of speech but helps speed the digital transmission of these views to other extremist groups.

Identity and the Sovereign Citizen Movement

Over the previous half century, scholars have used seemingly endless space debating the definition of social movements. Scholars from (at least) sociology, political science, history, religion, psychology, and communication have all made substantial contributions to this debate. Here, social movements will be understood as "networks of informal interaction between a plurality of individuals, groups and/or organisations, engaged in a political and/or cultural conflict, on the basis of a shared collective identity."[4] This definition informs social movement research in the field of rhetoric, which has gained prominence since the late 1940s.[5]

Rhetorical attention to social movements continues today with good reason. Social movements are inherently rhetorical in that they "organize symbols to persuasive ends."[6] While many scholars of rhetoric study social movements in various ways, the field collectively analyzes social movement discourse to understand the persuasive power of those movements, from recruitment to retention to messaging with the wider public. The rhetorical study of social movements is organized around attention to "how symbols . . . shape our perception of reality and invite us to act accordingly."[7] However we define "social movements," rhetorical scholars insist it is productive to approach the study of these collectives by analyzing the symbols and discourses they produce. This chapter uses rhetorical analysis to study sovereign citizens.

The Sovereign Citizen Movement (SCM) is a loose confederation of overlapping groups, individuals, and discourses, largely centered around the idea of the illegitimacy of the federal government. Like the movement itself, debate over how to define the movement or its "members" is complex. Those who might be considered sovereign citizens (also referred to as sov-cits, sovereigns, or "Freemen on the land") include far-right conspiracy theorists, tax protestors, white supremacists, religious identity adherents, militia movement activists, and anti-federalists, to name a few.[8] Definitions from the Federal Bureau of Investigation and the Department of Homeland Security include threats of violence (real, threatened, or justified) as a necessary precondition for referring to sovereign citizen extremists. Christine Sarteschi, one of the foremost experts on the SCM, prefers a more elegant formulation approximating as "any individual who believes they are immune from U.S. law because of the illegitimacy of the U. S. federal government."[9]

As many as half a million US Americans likely subscribe to some version of SCM rhetoric, believing taxation is unconstitutional, traffic laws are unenforceable, and financial debts can be incurred without ever having to pay them back. Accurate estimates of the number of such sovereign citizens are difficult to ascertain, as governmental counts are either classified or nonexistent.[10] Best estimates of sovereign citizen numbers suggest between 300,000 and 500,000 people in the United States,[11] and the Southern Poverty Law Center reports for 2021 saw more than 75 active groups in the United States.[12] Numbers are growing, however, with recent increases being largely attributable to introductions through QAnon discourses.[13] But belief in conspiracy theories is not a new phenomenon,[14] nor is it illegal, so why should we be interested in SCM discourses?

SCM discourses collectively reject the governance of nearly any democratic assembly whatsoever. The premise of SCM arguments is that the government cannot make any attempt to regulate behavior to which an *individual* did not personally agree beforehand. In other words, SCM rhetorics suggest adherents are "above the law" and may act without regard for others.[15] For instance, breaking into someone's house, changing the locks, and declaring the property your own is an allowable action within the logic of sovereign citizens. Proclaiming one's right as if the right of affirmation conquered all may seem criminal to nonbelievers, but for those invested in SCM ideologies, it is foundational. For instance, in a case that went viral on TikTok, Hubert John allegedly broke into a New Jersey woman's home, changed the locks, and presumed ownership in 2021.[16] While this case was well publicized, it was not, unfortunately, an isolated event.[17]

Some SCM discourses are conveyed through a system of pseudolaw. SCM discourses are encountered on websites, pamphlets, social media, and self-help books. In legal documents and courtrooms, scholars describe these discourses as existing through a "doctrine of pseudolaw" or "a collection of legal-sounding but false rules that purport to be law."[18] Pseudolaw is most often employed to delay official proceedings, harass government officials, and justify extralegal behavior; slowing the entire legal system, draining community resources, and inconveniencing citizens, law enforcement, and court officials. While some pseudolaw rhetorics merely attempt to avoid traffic citations or protest systems of taxation, others unofficially "charge" prosecutors with treason or demand recognition of an individual's autonomy from actual laws. These acts of "paper terrorism," a tactic employing frivolous lawsuits, liens, and official-sounding but fraudulent pronouncements often cost huge sums of money, slow down the legal system, cost citizens time and financial resources to combat, and render governance of our country much more difficult.[19]

Self-help books and hundreds of websites contribute to constructing an invented vision of reality where "secret knowledge" conveys the tricks to navigate modern life and build a community of ideological adherents. In books such as *Title 4 Flag Says You're Schwag: The Sovereign Citizen's Handbook*, readers are offered "all the background knowledge and information you'll need to understand the principles of Sovereignty and common law."[20] And on websites, audiences are invited to participate in alternate versions of "US American" and "United States" history. For instance, the website USA the Republic asserts, "The real start of America was with the Declaration of Independence on July 4, 1776. The real start of the United States was on September 17, 1787, with the ratification of the Constitution. YES! There is a difference! It will be explained as we go."[21] These discourses purport to teach audiences how "America" began with the Declaration of Independence and its citizens had their sovereignty stripped from them when the US Constitution was ratified. Whether these discourses are actually believed by their authors or are simply efforts to sell conspiracy-laden beliefs about the law interspersed with lengthy stories about the author touring with the Grateful Dead is irrelevant to audiences' belief in the legitimacy of these views.[22] These discourses allege themselves to convey "secret knowledge" that practitioners can use to legitimate their otherwise unsupported beliefs and illegal acts.[23] While not premised in a reality anyone else acknowledges, these expressions of "secret knowledge" do help build community with other sovereigns and are reflective of many other conspiracy-laden ideological systems.[24]

While paper terrorism and psuedolaw simply cost money and inconvenience thousands, it would be a mistake to understand SCM adherents as merely nonviolent nuisances. In the just over a quarter century since the Oklahoma City bombing, hundreds of acts of violence have been directly attributed to SCM.[25] The most likely risk of violence posed by SCM adherents is generally against law enforcement, usually following traffic stops.[26] There have, however, been isolated instances of ambush-style attacks on law enforcement,[27] as well as acts of arson, attempted kidnapping, and mass shooting. And, of course, numerous sovereign citizens participated in the January 6th attack on the US Capitol.[28]

As with many modern-day extremist groups, these collectives exist both in gatherings of people and in circulated language. Social movements exist in two related but distinct ways—as an assembly of people who identify with that movement's central tenets but also as the collection of meanings manifest within the symbolic language indexing the ideologies of that group.[29] For the SCM, this means that the "movement" consists of both the actual individuals who declare the federal government's illegitimacy and the discourses and symbols announcing, often through conspiratorial thinking, justifications for their beliefs. Documents central to these beliefs include the Magna Carta, the Bible, and the Declaration of Independence. In the remainder of this chapter, we consider how SCM discourses leverage the idea of the Declaration, as well as the aesthetic symbolism of the Declaration, to create a nostalgic rhetoric to attract new adherents and offer rhetorical resources for other like-minded anti-government groups.

The Declaration as Metonym

The Declaration of Independence is an example of rhetorical artistry and represents perhaps the "the best-known document of the American founding."[30] Rhetorical scholars have justly praised the text as "perhaps the most masterfully written state paper of Western civilization."[31] Its rhetorical significance lies not simply in its stylistic brilliance but in its capacity to serve as a model. In chapter 4 of this volume, Mary Stuckey rightly explains that the Declaration offers a "rhetorical template for political division." To wit, in the first half century after its signing, at least twenty other countries had announced the establishment of a new state with documents modeled after the US Declaration, and today nearly half the countries in the world boast "their own declarations of independence."[32] Other chapters in this book similarly display the power of the Declaration to inspire.

Despite its original purpose, the Declaration has long been used as a rhetorical figure to register citizens' opposition to their government. While the Declaration originally functioned to rally opposition to King George III and support for the new nation, the years following the Revolutionary War illustrated how populist discontent, bolstered by the Declaration's rhetorical power, could not be shut off as easily as elected officials would prefer. For example, following years of supportive writings in the 1770s for a revolutionary spirit, Thomas Paine's public exhortations were forced to evolve to suggest 1780s protests against their new government exhibited "irrationality" and "delusion."[33] Shays's Rebellion, an armed revolt of former soldiers turned farmers in 1786–87, was launched and maintained by those who argued that the economic policies of colonial Massachusetts were fundamentally no different than the treatment of the colonists at the hands of King George.[34] Shays's Rebellion is partially responsible for the strength of federal power enshrined in our Constitution,[35] as this event ushered in new federal powers in response to claims of sovereign rights. Events like Shays's Rebellion, violent or otherwise, not only convinced US elites of the need to respond but in some ways offered a model as powerful as the Declaration itself.

The repeated use of the Declaration as symbolic justification is central to the violence of sovereign citizens' agenda. The Declaration is repeatedly invoked to justify opposition to perceived tyranny—whether British or US American. Prior to the bombing of the Federal Building in Oklahoma City, for instance, McVeigh revealed in letters to friends how he had come to understand the US American government as no different than the British monarchy of King George.[36] His screed was scrawled on a copy of the Declaration, a choice that makes clear that for McVeigh, the Declaration was not only a living rhetorical artifact but one whose symbolic power could continue to be leveraged materially to justify violent bloodshed. In the US Senate hearings following the Oklahoma City bombing, John Trochmann, co-founder of a Montana militia and an avowed sovereign citizen, entered a copy of the Declaration of Independence into the record annotated with a list of grievances against the current US American government.[37] More recently, during a 2023 interview, John Eastman, the founding director of the Center for Constitutional Jurisprudence and an indicted legal advisor for President Trump, invoked the Declaration of Independence as warrant for President Trump's efforts to overturn the results of the 2020 election. "There's actually a provision in the Declaration of Independence that a people will suffer abuses while they remain sufferable, tolerable while they remain tolerable," Eastman, author of the so-called coup memos, explained.[38]

Sovereign citizens invoke the Declaration for these violent political actions, usually without any basic legal foundation. Though invoking the Declaration in a US American legal context has little precedential value, there remains some ambiguity even among mainstream scholars. Most, though not all, legal scholars believe, as Ian Mylchreest has explained, the Declaration "technically has no legal effect."[39] However, some mainstream scholars defend the legal import of the Declaration to suggest it possesses value at least in clarifying the meaning of other documents.[40] In addition, even when denying the legal power of the Declaration, our highest court has affirmed its rhetorical value. For instance, while Supreme Court Justice Scalia explained in *Troxel v. Granville* (2000) that the Declaration "is not a legal prescription conferring powers upon the courts," he began his opinion by not only citing the Declaration's "unalienable rights" but pointing to those rights as having been ordained by our "Creator."[41]

It is useful to think of these invocations as possessing a logic fueled by the trope known as metonymy. In rhetoric, a trope is "any figure that changes the normal, literal, or conventional meaning" of symbolic communication.[42] In other words, tropes are one way we name understandings of figural representation. While none of the above examples confer legal meaning in any court or legislative context, it would be a mistake to suggest that those using the Declaration to justify their violent protest were simply, as Thomas Paine held, "irrational." In particular, the use of the Declaration is situated as a metaphoric anchor, where its invocation signifies a set of values associated with it. Claire Sisco King argues that there are varied rhetorical logics manifest in the metonymic representations of celebrities.[43] Fans negotiate their rhetorical view of the world through and against the celebrity figure. Similarly, in the discourses of sovereign citizens, the Declaration is used as a pathological demand for freedom from governance, by violence if necessary. If tropes are the "names given to the logic of representation,"[44] for sovereign citizens the Declaration is a trope above all others. If metonymy is "a form of substitution in which something that is associated with x is substituted for x,"[45] for sovereign citizens the Declaration indexes a string of political violence from the revolution and Shays's Rebellion to the Oklahoma City bombing and the attack on the Capitol. Other scholars have described metonymy as "association by some contiguous trait."[46] Here, its practitioners are suggesting that the Declaration itself has been wielded against tyranny and therefore justifies any sovereign citizen's revolt against tyranny. In effect, the invocation of the Declaration becomes a trope that substitutes for the totality of that claim; the Declaration thus becomes an invocation of antigovernment action.

For sovereign citizens, the metonymic move from the historical Declaration to an ongoing demand for violence against tyranny is not an unusual reading of the document. Despite the limited legal value of the Declaration, it is predominantly viewed as an important historical document with vibrant cultural cachet. For example, while most US citizens cannot name a single Supreme Court Justice,[47] almost 60 percent understand the Fourth of July as a holiday commemorating the signing of the Declaration of Independence.[48] In other words, simply invoking the Declaration in a public discussion necessarily carries with it the power of the nationalistic pride, patriotism, and reverence reserved for the Declaration. Generally, to suggest that one's actions are made reasonable by employing a metonymous analogy to the Declaration imbues one's actions with a sense of solemnity. Whether the average US American agrees with the comparison is obviously a different matter altogether. But SCM actors invoke the Declaration as an immediate warrant justifying their response to any state-based "violation," real or imagined, everything from obeying basic traffic laws to not assaulting or murdering law enforcement. Sovereign citizens often transfer the rhetorical appeal of the Declaration to the violent actions they undertake in an almost singular move in which the Declaration operates with supreme rhetorical force. SCM rhetorics make use of the Declaration in a way that conveys the value of the Declaration within US Americans' "historical imagination,"[49] without the requirement that their specific actions be understood by audiences as reasonable. The SCM invokes the Declaration to act against all government as tyrannical in nature.

The Declaration's Aesthetic Appeal and the Trope of Synecdoche

Communities are constructed rhetorically, through discourses, and the more affectively powerful a message is, the faster it circulates. Benedict Anderson famously has suggested that "all communities . . . are imagined. Communities are to be distinguished not by their falsity/genuineness but by the *style* in which they are imagined."[50] What Anderson suggests was not that the authenticity of a community is at issue but that "they are speculatively established."[51] Rhetoricians have long understood that the construction of any community, and in fact the political identities that draw us toward and make us identify with a political community, is accomplished rhetorically.[52] In other words, these communities "emerge through our capacity to communicate with and imagine one another."[53] Our capacity to imagine one another is greatly related to the circulation of discourses that shape our imaginations. Given the prominence of digital communication today, the circulation of these discourses is mobilized and spread through affective connections.[54]

"Affect," a rhetorical term denoting a nearly ineffable, unconscious marker, related to sense, feeling, or emotion, speeds the circulation of discourses and the ideologies implied by those discourses across digital networks.[55] In other words, especially in digital networks, viscerally affective discourses, messages that evoke a strong sense of anger, humor, and so forth, spread virally much more often and much further than other messages.

Anti-government groups use the language of their organizations—how they communicate publicly, as well as in their private discussions—to express and create support for their ideological beliefs, but also to learn from similar groups. Ideologies, together with the symbols and language used to communicate those ideologies, constantly shift and adapt to changing events in the world.[56] All ideologies existing for any significant period of time undergo a process of syncretism—the successful or attempted merging of multiple views into a singular understanding.[57] While the word *syncretism* is generally used in a religious context, it applies to all ideologies—those of liberals, conservatives, pacifists, and even terrorists.[58] This helps to explain why one group's messages are often combined with other groups' messages.

Extremist and reactionary groups are connected through actual understandings of the world as well as through the language they use.[59] The symbols they display, therefore, send both information and argument and convey implied meaning without explicit acknowledgment. At the present time, SCM discourses intermingle with anti-vaccine rhetorics and QAnon logics in a networked morass of related conspiracy and defiance.[60] The connection these discourses create between related yet distinct groups collectively constructs a shared language where extremists can recruit and reinforce each other.[61] In today's world, recruitment is not limited by nation-state borders. For example, though sovereign citizen groups have previously been restricted largely to North America, global digital connections, most often through social media, mean that sovereign citizen protests in Quebec can inspire anti-mask protests in Singapore, anti-police violence in Melbourne, or "Citizen of the USSR" tax protests in Moscow.[62]

The language of SCM discourses builds internal community, creates distrust of nonbelievers, and offers a justification for nearly any desired anti-government action. For those who identify with the written or spoken words of SCM texts, other similar believers exist within a real or imagined community. Like the discourses of nearly any ideology, common beliefs create bonds of similarity, resulting in community. Similarly, especially given the well-outside-the-mainstream legal and historical views for which SCM discourses hold meaning, nonbelievers are understood as either potential recruits or enemies of the sovereign community. In short, believers' uncritical acceptance of SCM discourses, as well as the ego-protecting denunciation of nonbelievers, results in a "binding effect," strengthening the in-group in itself and increasing the rejection of outsiders.[63] Moreover, the resulting bonds created within the sovereign in-group encourage members to accept increasingly conspiratorial thoughts as long as they are discursively connected to SCM ideologies.[64] One explanation for the success of SCM discourses lies in the aesthetic appropriation of the Declaration of Independence.

The Western political tradition traces its origins from the time of Isocrates through the aesthetic approaches of Augustine and Machiavelli and supported by the writings of Hume, Locke, and Jefferson.[65] Since at least Plato and Aristotle, Western conceptions of knowledge have been inextricably bound to understandings of virtue and beauty.[66] Poetry, art, and even language itself not only communicate a feeling but help contour a people's sense of community—and the collectively imagined community spirit that should be embodied and improved. We name this phenomenon "aesthetics." Considerations of what is good or what is just are at the heart of our conceptions of what it means to "be" human. For many, these conceptions of what is good—in art, but also in knowledge production and political governance—represent the human expression of the divine.[67] Those considerations, often expressed as our ideals, not only help shape our cultural norms of what we value but lay the foundation for the political arrangements in which humans thrive. Aesthetics, then, undergird how we conceptualize our best version of ourselves, our lives, and our politics, as well as how we represent expressions and arrangements blessed by God.

Our collective understanding of the Declaration is as much aesthetic as it is textual.[68] As a representation of the country's founding, the Declaration of Independence stands as an aesthetic construction of what is beautiful, good, and ordained by God—the rhetorical construction of a free and fair polity. The very appearance of the Declaration supports a set of visceral meanings beyond what the words of the Declaration itself convey. As Crispin Sartwell explains, "Few Americans can recite it, but many Americans can conjure up the image of a yellowed parchment with calligraphy."[69] And US Americans are not the only ones. For instance, during the early months of the COVID-19 pandemic, some British businesses placed copies of the Declaration in their storefronts "believ[ing] that placing a copy in a window entitled them to ignore government orders to close."[70] Timothy Saunders suggests that perhaps the most aesthetically powerful aspect of the Declaration, what helped it truly achieve its "revolutionary act," was its restarting of US history by rhetorically constructing a beautiful people—"an innovatively rational and fair people and polity."[71]

Aesthetics help explain why Thomas Jefferson was chosen to draft the Declaration; we can see traces of that decision even today. John Adams was initially approached to write the Declaration but instead suggested that Jefferson's aesthetic style was more appropriate.[72] Adams was clearly a strong writer, but Jefferson's writings were well known for their frequent use of "aesthetic images and metaphors."[73] What's more, Jefferson believed in the importance of aesthetics and elsewhere explained that "we . . . have an innate sense of what we call *the beautiful* . . . that is exercised . . . through . . . the imagination directly, as imagery, style, or measure in prose or poetry."[74] Metaphors of the body ("fatiguing . . . legislative bodies," "manly firmness," "swarms of Officers") abound in the Declaration, but political aesthetics are not merely textual. As Sartwell rightly notes, "a politics is an aesthetic environment."[75] While Jefferson's rhetorical skills may have contributed to his selection as the first-draft writer, his ability to craft a document with echoes of the Petition of Right, the English Bill of Rights, and the Virginia Declaration of Rights certainly helps explain how we understand the document today.[76] Yet the traces of these earlier documents are only just that—traces. There is an aesthetic poetry found in the Declaration that partially explains its popularity, but some of this poetry is the nearly indescribable trace of thoughts and images, markers of a larger aesthetic ecosystem. These traces are what is often displayed in SCM discourses.

SCM discourses emulate the Declaration in an effort to capture its aesthetic essence and transfer that essence into political argument. The Southern Poverty Law Center, one of the foremost sources of publicly available information on extremists, suggests that SCM discourses employ a "bizarre use of language" and that "sovereigns see secret meaning in the use or non-use of capitalized letters."[77] Other commenters, including federal and state courts of appeal, have understood SCM rhetorical practices as "rambling," "largely incoherent," or "frivolous."[78] But rather than a rambling set of incoherencies, SCM discourse should be understood as a "coherent, internally consistent field of meaning."[79] For instance, SCM discourses that include what appears to be "bizarre" use of capitalization should instead be understood as following an aesthetic model offered by the Declaration. The rules of grammar and spelling of the eighteenth century as to when words could be capitalized were much more generous than today: sometimes every noun in a passage might be capitalized.[80] In SCM discourses, especially in legal filings, it is common for sovereign citizens to imitate a pattern of capitalization similar to that found in the Declaration. So common is this practice, in fact, that when courts are faced with SCM defendants, they will sometimes *un*capitalize words from their filings when reciting back the facts of the case and then note the deletion."[81]

Similarly, the Declaration refers to "Citizens" with a capital C. A brief foray into SCM discourses here is instructive: "Becoming the Sovereign Citizen you were born to be, which is the master over the legal system rather than the servant you are now as a statutory citizen. (Note the Capitalization of the letter C) You were born a Sovereign but it only lasted a few hours or maybe a day at the most before you were illegally brought into the system by contract known as a birth certificate. That certificate made you a servant to the world we know as the UNITED STATES and the so called American way."[82] The Benefits of Being a Sovereign website suggests that potential adherents not only "note the capitalization" but imitates the Declaration's all-capitalized "UNITED STATES." As Kalinowski explains, "Typography continues to be important to many sovereign citizens. Some sovereign citizens write their personal names with nonstandard capitalization and punctuation in what they claim is a manner that shields them from government control."[83]

Sovereign conceptions of the law are premised in a figuration of the law where the aesthetic pageantry that accompanies legal proceedings and knowledge becomes not just a stand-in for the law but the actual power of the law. The legal system, as Pierre Schlag reminds us, is in fact "an aesthetic enterprise" where even "legal professionals can be taken in by aesthetic images for the simple reason that the aesthetics are taken to be the articulation of law itself."[84] But SCM discourses are not simply the confusion between appearance and reality. Instead, the aesthetic appropriation of the Declaration represents one of the ways SCM discourses attempt to create slippage between conspiracy and reality.

Synecdoche, a rhetorical figure in which a part comes to represent the whole, is one way to construct a coherent illusion of truth through the use of rhetorical figures, thereby bolstering an "aesthetics of conspiracy verisimilitude."[85] For instance, "all hands on deck" transforms the hail for all sailors to a call for a part of the sailors' bodies. Similarly, the Pepe the Frog meme functioned as a synecdochal slight-of-hand for the Alt-Right during the past decade, as Pepe came to stand in for a whole host of ideological beliefs.[86] In conspiratorial discourse, as which SCM rhetorics certainly qualify, the "aesthetic . . . dimension of fictional narrative" is often found to be more persuasive for audiences than an actual, truthful understanding.[87]

The ideological underpinnings of the aesthetic transference of the Declaration's power into modern-day instantiations of power is warranted through SCM beliefs in ritual as the defining characteristic of the law. Sovereign ideology is propelled by understandings of the law not as procedures involving certain rituals but as proceedings fundamentally *about* rituals. Some of this is likely premised on a misunderstanding as to how the US legal system works, while some is rightly characterized as wishful thinking.[88] Legal scholars often consider that for sovereign citizens, their rhetorical interruptions of the normal flow of the law are not simply "'akin' to a magical ritual—they *are* a magical ritual" (emphasis mine).[89] For legal scholars to characterize this transformation as "magic" makes sense given the law's ostensible rejection of the metaphysical. But as scholars of rhetoric can attest, a more satisfying answer takes seriously the views of sovereign citizens and considers how discursive communities are shaped, and aberrant views become naturalized. And taking seriously their rhetorical constructions is especially necessary in view not only of the risk such people may pose but of the risk that their discourses may strengthen those of other extremists.

Conclusion

The discourses shaping the beliefs of sovereign citizenship, especially their reliance on jargon and pseudolaw, exist as a ready-made template for antistate activity and may be leveraged by related groups to justify their own distinct and potentially more violent interpretations of the world. Besides serving as a tactic against the court system, however, SCM discourses are particularly appealing to adjacent reactionary and extremist groups. At root, pseudolaw and the aesthetic practices that accompany it are deeply oppositional to centralized authority, yet also surprisingly "politically agnostic," and have been resoundingly rejected by established courts who have encountered them.[90] SCM discourses and practices, especially pseudolaw, have become extremely attractive to adjacent reactionary and extremist groups who may find willing recruits in sovereign citizen communities or vice versa. These seemingly divergent groups may thus become incubators for recruitment across a variety of extremist groups.

Strong digital networks of support in ideological enclaves, or echo chambers, are often associated with radicalization and militancy.[91] The rapid circulation of these ideas via social media or other digital networks is often facilitated through affective connections.[92] The construction of the Declaration as a metonym for depoliticized opposition to state governance, as well as the appropriation of the Declaration's aesthetic appeal through syndecdoche, offers an especially effective affective connection to audiences, one that not only provides a strong constitutive means for identity creation but also speeds the circulation of conspiratorial ideologies. While many adherents of SCM discourses will likely engage in little more than an angry interaction with law enforcement following a traffic stop, the ideologies underpinning these discourses pervert the Declaration's promise of a rational and fair people and polity. Understanding the mechanisms by which SCM discourses operate, then, are necessary both to asssure a functioning democracy and to lessen the likelihood of another Oklahoma City.

NOTES

1. *Alfred P. Murrah Federal Building Bombing.*
2. Goldstein, "To Kill and Die," 206.
3. Goldstein, "To Kill and Die," 207.
4. Diani, "Concept of Social Movement," 3.
5. Jensen, "Analyzing Social Movement Rhetoric." For more recent trends in social movement work, see Crick, *Rhetoric of Social Movements.*
6. Morris III and Browne, *Readings on the Rhetoric,* 1.
7. Morris III and Browne, *Readings on the Rhetoric,* 1.
8. Sarteschi, *Sovereign Citizens;* Dew and Wright, "God's Law"; Holly Christensen, "Sovereign Citizens: The Uses and Abuses of the Judicial System," *Penn State Law Review: Forum Blog,* April 21, 2022, https:// www.pennstatelawreview.org/the-forum/sovereign-citizens-the-uses-and-abuses-of-the-judicial-sy/.
9. Sarteschi, "Sovereign Citizens: A Narrative Review." This a paraphrase of Sarteschi.
10. Sarteschi, "Sovereign Citizens: A Narrative Review."
11. Sarteschi, "Sovereign Citizens: A Narrative Review."
12. Miller and Rivas, *Year in Hate.*
13. Southern Poverty Law Center, "Ideologies," Southern Poverty Law Center, 2022, https://www.splcenter.org/fighting-hate/extremist-files/ideology/sovereign-citizens-movement.
14. Jonathan Jarry, "Belief in Conspiracy Theories Is Probably Not Getting Worse over Time." *Office for Science and Society,* McGill University, July 28, 2022, https://www.mcgill.ca/oss/article/critical-thinking/belief-conspiracy-theories-probably-not-getting-worse-over-time.
15. Sarah Maslin Nir, "She Bought Her Dream Home, Then a 'Sovereign Citizen' Changed the Locks," *New York Times,* September 26, 2021, https://www.nytimes.com/2021/09/26/ nyregion/moors-newark.html.
16. Nir, "She Bought Her Dream Home."
17. ABC News, "Anti-government Sovereign Citizens Taking Foreclosed Homes Using Phony Deeds, Authorities Say," ABC News, August 20, 2021, https://abcnews.go.com/US/georgia-battling-sovereign-citizens-squatting-foreclosed-homes/story?id=11445382.
18. Barrows, "Sovereigns, Freemen, and Desperate Souls."

19. Sarteschi, "Sovereign Citizens: A Narrative Review."

20. *H.I.R.M. J.M. Sovereign*, 10.

21. USA the Republic, "The True History," USA-the-Republic, 2022, http://www.usa-the-republic.com/revenue/true_history/Chap1.html.

22. *H.I.R.M. J.M. Sovereign*, 14–19.

23. McRoberts, "Tinfoil Hats."

24. Byford, *Conspiracy Theories.*

25. Sarteschi, "Sovereign Citizens: More than Paper Terrorists."

26. Alexander, "Sovereign Citizens."

27. Pometto, *Sovereign Citizens.*

28. Sarteschi, "Sovereign Citizens"; Jordan Fischer, "Sovereign Citizen Proud Boy Convicted on All Counts in Jan. 6 Bench . . . ," WUSA9-CBS, October 3, 2023, https://www.wusa9.com/article/news/national/capitol-riots/sovereign-citizen-proud-boy-convicted-on-all-counts-in-jan-6-bench-trial-marc-anthony-bru-vancouver-washington-militia/65-d44224b4-f046-4221-9136-d152d28166dc.

29. McGee, "'Social Movement.'"

30. Dow, "Declaration of Independence."

31. Lucas, "Stylistic Artistry," 25.

32. Armitage, *Declaration of Independence*, 3.

33. Engels, *Enemyship*, 71–72.

34. Richards, *Shays's Rebellion.*

35. Richards, *Shays's Rebellion.*

36. Michel and Herbeck, *American Terrorist*, 161.

37. Goldstein, "To Kill and Die"; John Mints, "Militias Meet the Senate with Conspiracies to Share," *Washington Post*, June 16, 1995, https://www.washingtonpost.com/archive/politics/1995/06/16/militias-meet-the-senate-with-conspiracies-to-share/7d0e9384-aa22-47f3-ba6b-8465fed9f447/.

38. Josh Kovensky, "Eastman Reiterates Support for Full Insurrection," TPM—Talking Points Memo, August 4, 2023, https://talkingpointsmemo.com/news/eastman-reiterates-support-for-full-insurrection.

39. Mylchreest, "Influence of the Declaration of Independence."

40. Schauer, "Why the Declaration."

41. *Troxel v. Granville* (99-138) 530 U.S. 57 (2000).

42. Jasinski, *Sourcebook*, 257.

43. King, *Mapping the Stars.*

44. Hahner, *To Become an American*, 23.

45. Jasinski, *Sourcebook*, 551.

46. Matheson, "Psychotic Discourse," 193.

47. Tim Marcin, "Half of Americans Can't Name a Supreme Court Justice, Poll Finds," *Newsweek*, August 28, 2018, https://www.newsweek.com/half-americans-cant-name-supreme-court-justice-poll-finds-1093404.

48. Claudia Dimuro, "Over 40% of Americans Don't Know Why We Celebrate July 4: Report," PennLive, July 3, 2023, https://www.pennlive.com/life/2023/07/over-40-of-americans-dont-know-why-we-celebrate-july-4-report.html.

49. White, *Metahistory.*

50. Anderson, *Imagined Communities*, 6; emphasis mine.

51. Cowan, "Constitutive Rhetoric of Late Nationalism," 188.

52. Charland, "Constitutive Rhetoric."

53. Cowan, "Constitutive Rhetoric of Late Nationalism," 185.

54. Chaput, "Trumponomics."

55. Chaput, "Trumponomics."

56. Smelser, *Faces of Terrorism*, 59.
57. Varda, "Drew Ali."
58. Smelser, *Faces of Terrorism*, 58.
59. Parkin, Mills, and Gruenewald, "Far-Right Extremism's Threat."
60. Miller and Rivas, *Year in Hate*.
61. Miller and Rivas, *Year in Hate*.
62. Matthew Luxmoore, "Flouting the Law in Nostalgia's Name: Russia's Growing Movement of 'Soviet Citizens,'" Radio Free Europe Radio Liberty, May 25, 2019, https://www.rferl.org/a/flouting-law-in-nostalgia-s-name-russia-s-growing-movement-of-soviet-citizens-/29962523.html.; Max Matza, "What Is the 'Sovereign Citizen' Movement?," BBC News, August 5, 2020, https://www.bbc.com/news/world-us-canada-53654318.
63. McRoberts, "Tinfoil Hats," 658.
64. McRoberts, "Tinfoil Hats," 658.
65. Sartwell, *Political Aesthetics*, 129.
66. Sartwell, *Political Aesthetics*, 130; Marshall, "Art and Aesthetics."
67. Houlgate, "Hegel's Aesthetics."
68. Saunders, "Aesthetic Understanding," 142.
69. Sartwell, *Political Aesthetics*, 42.
70. Saunders, "Aesthetic Understanding," 136.
71. Saunders, "Aesthetic Understanding," 142.
72. Sartwell, *Political Aesthetics*. There is some dispute about why Jefferson was chosen, with several scholars suggesting it was because Jefferson "had the fewest enemies in Congress." Jeffrey Rosen and David Rubenstein, "Why Did Jefferson Draft the Declaration of Independence?," National Constitution Center, April 13, 2015, https://constitutioncenter.org/blog/why-did-jefferson-draft-the-declaration-of-independence.
73. Quinby, "Thomas Jefferson," 339.
74. Foley, *Jeffersonian Cyclopedia*, 592; emphasis in original. This quote is from an 1814 letter from Jefferson to Thomas Law.
75. Sartwell, *Political Aesthetics*, 2.
76. Dow, "Declaration of Independence."
77. Southern Poverty Law Center, "The Sovereigns: A Dictionary of the Peculiar," *Intelligence Report*, Fall 2010, https://www.splcenter.org/fighting-hate/intelligence-report/2010/sovereigns-dictionary-peculiar.
78. *Brandon Collins v. State of Wisconsin*, United States Court of Appeals, Seventh Circuit, No. 16-4119 (2017), https://caselaw.findlaw.com/court/us-7th-circuit/1852288.html.
79. Matheson, "Psychotic Discourse."
80. Armstrong, *Brushing Up on Grammar*, 167.
81. *Furr v. Ruehlman*, 170 Ohio St.3d 386, 2023-Ohio-481.
82. Joseph Clark, "The Benefits of Being a Sovereign," Discharge Debt, https://discharge-debt.com/id73.htm.
83. Kalinowski IV, "Legal Response."
84. Schlag, "Aesthetics of American Law," 1049, 1114.
85. Pezzini and Terracciano, "Negationist Rhetoric," 144.
86. Woods and Hahner, *Make America Meme Again*, 83.
87. Pezzini and Terracciano, "Negationist Rhetoric," 154.
88. Netolitzky, "Organized Pseudolegal Argument."
89. Netolitzky, "Organized Pseudolegal Argument," 1085.
90. Netolitzky, "A Revolting Itch."
91. Anastasio et al., "How Emotional Traits and Practices."
92. Lim, "Algorithmic Enclaves."

BIBLIOGRAPHY

Alexander, Dean C. "Sovereign Citizens: Threats and Law Enforcement Responses." *Security Magazine*, December 30, 2020. https://www.securitymagazine.com/articles/94007-sovereign-citizens-threats-and-law-enforcement-responses.

Alfred P. Murrah Federal Building Bombing, April 19, 1995: Final Report. Stillwater, OK: Fire Protection Publication, 1996.

Anastasio, Natalie, Arie Perliger, and Neil Shortland. "How Emotional Traits and Practices Lead to Support in Acts of Political Violence." *Studies in Conflict and Terrorism* 46, no. 10 (2023): 1912–32.

Anderson, Benedict. *Imagined Communities: Reflections on the Origin and Spread of Nationalism*. London: Verso, 2006.

Armitage, David. *The Declaration of Independence: A Global History*. Cambridge, MA: Harvard University Press, 2007.

Armstrong, Joyce. *Brushing Up on Grammar*. Santa Barbara, CA: ABC-CLIO, 2010.

Barrows, Samuel. "Sovereigns, Freemen, and Desperate Souls: Towards a Rigorous Understanding of Pseudolitigation Tactics in United States Courts." *Boston College Law Review* 62, no. 3 (2021): 905–40. https://bclawreview.bc.edu/articles/89.

Byford, Jovan. *Conspiracy Theories: A Critical Introduction*. London: Palgrave Macmillan, 2011.

Chaput, Catherine. "Trumponomics, Neoliberal Branding, and the Rhetorical Circulation of Affect." *Advances in the History of Rhetoric* 21, no. 2 (2018): 194–209.

Charland, Maurice. "Constitutive Rhetoric: The Case of the *Peuple Quebecois*." *Quarterly Journal of Speech* 73, no. 2 (1987): 133–50.

Cowan, Jake. "The Constitutive Rhetoric of Late Nationalism: Imagined Communities After the Digital Revolution." *Rhetoric Review* 40, no. 2 (2021): 183–97.

Crick, Nathan. *The Rhetoric of Social Movements: Networks, Power, and New Media*. New York: Routledge, 2021.

Dew, Spencer, and Jamie Wright. "God's Law: Universal Truth According to Religious Sovereign Citizens." University of Chicago Divinity School: Sightings, October 15, 2015. https://divinity.uchicago.edu/sightings/articles/gods-law-universal-truth-according-religious-sovereign-citizens.

Diani, Mario. "The Concept of Social Movement." *The Sociological Review* 40, no. 1 (February 1992): 1–25. https://doi.org/10.1111/j.1467-954x.1992.tb02943.x.

Dow, Douglas. "Declaration of Independence." *The Free Speech Center*, February 19, 2024. https://firstamendment.mtsu.edu/article/declaration-of-independence/.

Engels, Jeremy. *Enemyship: Democracy and Counter-revolution in the Early Republic*. East Lansing: Michigan State University Press, 2010.

Foley, John P. *The Jeffersonian Cyclopedia: A Comprehensive Collection of the Views of Thomas Jefferson*. New York: Funk & Wagnalls, 1900.

Goldstein, Jared A. "To Kill and Die for the Constitution: Nullification and Insurrectionary Violence." In *Nullification and Secession in Modern Constitutional Thought*, edited by Sanford Levinson, 179–222. Lawrence: University of Kansas Press, 2016.

Hahner, Leslie A. *To Become an American*. East Lansing: Michigan State University Press, 2017.

H.I.R.M. J.M. Sovereign: Godsent™: Title 4 Flag Says You're Schwag; The Sovereign Citizen's Handbook. 3rd ed. Self-published: CreateSpace, 2019.

Houlgate, Stephen. "Hegel's Aesthetics." In *Stanford Encyclopedia of Philosophy*, edited by Edward N. Zalta. Stanford, CA: Metaphysics Research Lab, Center for the Study of Language and Information, Stanford University, 2020. https://plato.stanford.edu/entries/hegel-aesthetics/.

Jasinski, James. *Sourcebook on Rhetoric.* Thousand Oaks, CA: Sage, 2001.

Jensen, Richard J. "Analyzing Social Movement Rhetoric." *Rhetoric Review* 25, no. 4 (2006): 372–75.

Kalinowski IV, Caesar. "A Legal Response to the Sovereign Citizen Movement." *Montana Law Review* 80, no. 2 (2019): 153–210.

King, Claire Sisco. *Mapping the Stars: Celebrity, Metonymy, and the Networked Politics of Identity.* Athens: Ohio State University Press, 2023.

Lim, Merlyna. "Algorithmic Enclaves: Affective Politics and Algorithms in the Neoliberal Social Media Landscape." In *Affective Politics of Digital Media: Propaganda by Other Means,* edited by Megan Boler and Elizabeth Davis, 186–203. New York: Routledge, 2020.

Lucas, Stephen. "The Stylistic Artistry of the Declaration of Independence." *Prologue: Quarterly of the National Archives* 22, no. 1 (1990): 24–43.

Marshall, John S. "Art and Aesthetics in Aristotle." *Journal of Aesthetics and Art Criticism* 12, no. 2 (1953): 228–31.

Matheson, Calum Lister. "Psychotic Discourse: The Rhetoric of the Sovereign Citizen Movement." *Rhetoric Society Quarterly* 48, no. 2 (2018): 187–206.

McGee, Michael Calvin. "'Social Movement': Phenomenon or Meaning?" *Central States Speech Journal* 31, no. 4 (1980): 233–44. https://doi.org/10.1080/10510978009368063.

McRoberts, Colin. "Tinfoil Hats and Powdered Wigs: Thoughts on Pseudolaw." *Washburn Law Journal* 58, no. 3 (2019): 637–68.

Michel, Lou, and Dan Herbeck. *American Terrorist: Timothy McVeigh and the Oklahoma City Bombing.* New York: HarperCollins, 2001.

Miller, Cassie, and Rachel Carroll Rivas. *The Year in Hate and Extremism Report 2021.* Southern Poverty Law Center, March 9, 2022. https://www.splcenter.org/20220309/year-hate-extremism-report-2021.

Morris, Charles E., III and Stephen H. Browne. *Readings on the Rhetoric of Social Protest.* 2nd ed. State College, PA: Strata Publishing, 2013.

Mylchreest, Ian. "The Influence of the Declaration of Independence Through History: How American Politicians, and the Supreme Court, Have Invoked It." FindLaw, July 4, 2002. https://supreme.findlaw.com/legal-commentary/the-influence-of-the-declaration-of-independence-through-history.html#bio.

Netolitzky, Donald. "Organized Pseudolegal Argument as Magic and Ceremony." *Alberta Law Review* 55, no. 4 (2018): 1045–87.

———. "A Revolting Itch: Pseudolaw as a Social Adjuvant." *Politics, Religion and Ideology* 22, no. 2 (2021): 164–88. DOI: 10.1080/21567689.2021.1924691.

Parkin, Williams S., Coleen E. Mills, and Jeff Gruenewald. "Far-Right Extremism's Threat to Police Safety and the Organizational Legitimacy of Law Enforcement in the United States." *Criminology, Criminal Justice, Law and Society* 22, no. 2 (2021). https://ccjls.scholasticahq.com/article/26321-far-right-extremism-s-threat-to-police-safety-and-the-organizational-legitimacy-of-law-enforcement-in-the-united-states.

Pezzini, Isabella, and Bianca Terracciano. "Negationist Rhetoric and Post-truth Figures: Transversal Research in Social Media in the COVID-19 Era." *Estudos semióticos* 18, no. 2 (2022): 135–59.

Pometto, Joe. *Sovereign Citizens: Deconstructing, Decoding and Deflating the World's Most Notorious Anti-government Movement.* Self-published, 2020.

Quinby, Lee. "Thomas Jefferson: The Virtue of Aesthetics and the Aesthetics of Virtue." *American Historical Review* 87, no. 2 (1982): 337–56.

Richards, Leonard L. *Shays's Rebellion: The American Revolution's Final Battle.* Philadelphia: University of Pennsylvania Press, 2014.

Sarteschi, Christine M. "Sovereign Citizens: More than Paper Terrorists." Just Security, July 5, 2021. https://www.justsecurity.org/77328/sovereign-citizens-more-than-paper-terrorists/.

———. "Sovereign Citizens: A Narrative Review with Implications of Violence Law Enforcement." Aggression and Violent Behavior 60 (2021). https://doi.org/10.1016/j.avb.2020.101509.

———. *Sovereign Citizens: A Psychological and Criminological Analysis.* New York: Springer, 2020.

Sartwell, Crispin. *Political Aesthetics.* Ithaca, NY: Cornell University Press, 2011.

Saunders, Timothy. "Aesthetic Understanding and Written Culture." In *Språk, Tekst og Medvit,* edited by Tor Arne Haugen, Svenn-Arve Myklebost, Endre Brunstad, and Stig Jarle Helset. 2021. https://press.nordicopenaccess.no/index.php/noasp/catalog/view/146/733/5505-1.

Schauer, Frederick. "Why the Declaration of Independence Is Not Law—and Why It Could Be." *South Carolina Law Review* 89 (2016): 619–36.

Schlag, Pierre. "The Aesthetics of American Law." *Harvard Law Review* 115, no. 4 (February 2002): 1047–1118.

Smelser, Neil J. *The Faces of Terrorism: Social and Psychological Dimensions.* Princeton, NJ: Princeton University Press, 2009.

Varda, Scott J. "Drew Ali and the Moorish Science Temple of America: A Minor Rhetoric of Black Nationalism." *Rhetoric and Public Affairs* 16, no. 4 (2013): 685–718.

White, Hayden. *Metahistory: The Historical Imagination in Nineteenth-Century Europe.* Baltimore: Johns Hopkins University Press, 1979.

Woods, Heather S., and Leslie A. Hahner. *Make America Meme Again.* New York: Peter Lang, 2019.

PART 3

CLAIMS TO EQUALITY

8

WE ARE THE TRUE AMERICANS: THE DECLARATION OF INDEPENDENCE AND RADICAL, ANTI-CAPITALIST, WORKING-CLASS MOVEMENTS

Mary Anne Trasciatti

US Americans are encouraged to believe that capitalism promotes freedom and democracy. However, resistance to that idea has deep roots among workers in the United States that extend back to the nation's beginning. The Declaration of Independence inspired and nurtured this anti-capitalist resistance. Unlike in every other industrializing nation in the nineteenth century, the democratic impact of the US political revolution on working-class white males preceded the impact of the Industrial Revolution. The legacy of the US American Revolution made possible the inclusion of white male workers into active citizenry. These citizen workers saw from the beginning that popular democracy was no guarantee of freedom from economic exploitation in a capitalist society.[1] As African American, women, and immigrant workers claimed their own citizenship rights, they too found their liberties compromised in a society structured by class rule. Many workers believed the Revolution had been betrayed by the capitalist class. They demanded the abolition of capitalism and the wage labor system to realize the Declaration of Independence's promise of liberty and equality for all.

Discontent with industrialization and a political system that was unwilling to address or openly hostile to the interests of working people intensified at the end of the nineteenth century. Workers in the United States, many of them immigrants, channeled their discontent into international revolutionary movements such as anarchism, socialism, and communism. These movements shared the goal of abolishing capitalism and transferring control of the means of production to workers, but they held diverse views on the nature of government and the validity of the state, and they prescribed different methods for achieving their aims. Whatever their differences, the internationalism, efforts to organize among the most marginal workers, and militant opposition to the economic and political status quo that typified these movements led authorities to lump them together and brand them "un-American." Events such as the Paris Commune (1871), the Haymarket affair (1886), and the assassination of European and US American heads of state at the turn of the century, including US President William McKinley, were used to legitimate vilification of radicals, an effort that intensified after the Bolshevik Revolution of 1917.[2] Movement leaders and members attempted to counter this branding and broaden the appeal of their ideas to the US working class by re-appropriating the language and symbols of US American political rhetoric. Like antebellum workers before them, they claimed that capitalism was a tyrannical force that had undermined the egalitarian aims of the Revolution and rendered the Declaration of Independence hollow. As they sought to reframe ideas depicted as un-American, anti-capitalist radicals reimagined the Declaration in ways that aligned with their respective ideologies. By making the Declaration their own, they claimed a place for themselves in a US American tradition of radicalism and the right to revolution. This chapter will trace the emergence of the tradition of using the Declaration in arguments against economic exploitation, explore how that tradition developed in anarchist, socialist, and communist movements, and consider how it might inspire contemporary activists in their struggle against unfettered capitalism and the gross inequality it engenders.

Antebellum Antecedents

The eighteenth-century struggle against British rule bolstered the self-esteem of workers who took part in it and eroded their willingness to defer to their "betters." In the antebellum period, white workers took inspiration from the Revolution's promise of social equality and expanding political democracy to protest the increasing exploitation, discipline, and surveillance of industrial society.[3] Many argued that capitalism had eroded the very liberties for which the Revolutionary War had been fought and called for the overthrow of the economic system. Haunted by the specter of chattel slavery, antebellum workers saw long workdays, wage labor, mechanization of industry, and wealth concentration as creating bonds of servitude that threatened to eradicate free labor.[4] As they sought to return to a pre-industrial and, in their view, more egalitarian past, they used the Declaration of Independence to highlight contradictions between the ideals upon which the nation was founded and the realities of working-class life in the United States.

In 1834, participants in the Trades' Union National Convention argued that a two-tier educational system in which good schools were available only to middle-class students kept working people ignorant and violated the Declaration of Independence's promise of social equality.[5] A year later, shoemakers in Philadelphia expressed outrage at how wage work enslaved them to employers. They noted with irony, "We celebrate the Declaration of Independence, but we are not independent!"[6] In 1844, a petition published in the *Working Man's Advocate*, one of the first labor newspapers in the United States, claimed that concentrated land ownership forced many US American workers into a state of dependency as tenants of large landowners, a condition that violated the republican theory laid down in the Declaration of Independence.[7] In its 1846 report to a labor convention about their petition drive for a ten-hour day (a typical workday ranged from twelve to fourteen hours), members of the Lowell Female Labor Reform Association asserted the readiness of women factory workers to issue their own declaration of independence if the drive was not successful.[8] Although Massachusetts legislators did not respond to their petitions for a ten-hour day, there is no evidence that Lowell's women workers drafted a declaration of independence. Had they done so they would have been in good company. At least six alternate declarations of independence for workers appeared prior to the Civil War. Typically, these declarations were presented on the Fourth of July.

From the 1790s until the end of the nineteenth century, Philip Foner observes, US American labor celebrated the Fourth of July as *its* day. By the 1830s, working-class celebrations of July 4th featuring labor-themed parades, banquets, festivals, toasts, songs, and new declarations of independence had become a staple of working-class culture.[9] The declarations aimed to galvanize workers into a movement to make the United States the kind of nation for which their revolutionary ancestors had fought and died but failed to achieve. One such document, penned in 1844 by land reformer Lewis Masquerier, titled "A Declaration of Independence of the Producing from the Non-producing Class," called for the abolition of landlordism, rent paying, and the wage system.[10] Although workers supported land reform as a way to escape wage labor, they were unable to realize this goal.

In their struggle against what they called "wage slavery," antebellum white workers failed to see that their fate was tied to that of Black workers condemned to chattel slavery. Foner observes that in all of the Fourth of July celebrations from the 1790s to 1845, "not a single reference was made by a labor spokesman between the opening sentences of the Declaration of Independence and the continued existence of slavery for millions of black workers and not a single toast was drunk to the abolition of slavery."[11] In the 1850s, German American socialists, many of them Marxists, argued that no further advances for wageworkers were possible until the abolition of chattel slavery in the United States. It was not until after the Civil War, however, that white workers openly acknowledged the contradiction between slavery and the Declaration of Independence.

The Emergence of Radical Anti-capitalism

In the late nineteenth century, the rise of national industries; introduction of machinery that deskilled labor; arrival of hundreds of thousands of economically precarious, socially marginal, and politically disenfranchised immigrants; and economic cycles of boom and bust fueled the growth of revolutionary anti-capitalist, working-class movements in the United States. The rise of radicalism was not a uniquely US American phenomenon. In 1871, after France's defeat in the Franco-Prussian war and the establishment of a conservative regime, Parisian workers led an insurrection against the government. They took over the city and created a socialist government (La Commune de Paris) that lasted for seventy-two days until French soldiers entered Paris and executed as many as twenty thousand Communards during "Bloody Week" at the end of May in 1871.[12] While radicals in the United States drew inspiration from the Paris Commune, many political officials grew uneasy about the prospect of worker-led mobs seizing control of US American cities, especially during periods of conflict between labor and capital, such as the Great Railroad Strike of 1877.[13]

The Paris Commune did not trigger a rash of worker-led seizures of US American cities, but workers found other ways to express their growing dissatisfaction with a system that to them clearly benefited the few at the expense of the many. The July 4, 1876, centennial of the Revolution provided an opportunity to highlight the damage that capitalism had wreaked on working-class life. In Chicago, members of the Workingman's Party of Illinois, established in 1873 after a massive demonstration of unemployed workers, adopted a new Declaration of Independence. It called for a second US American revolution to correct inequalities that existed because of willful neglect on the part of elected officials who had been corrupted by the "power of capital." Two weeks after they presented the declaration, the party joined with other organizations to form what would eventually come to be called the Socialist Labor Party (SLP). In the 1880s, several sections of the SLP seceded and swelled the ranks of the International Working People's Association, but panic about anarchists inspired by the recent Haymarket affair cut short this trend.[14]

Anarchists and the Rejection of Involuntary Rule

On May 4, 1886, a bomb exploded during a labor rally in Chicago's Haymarket Square, killing one police officer and wounding several others. Authorities suspected anarchists had detonated the bomb, but they had no proof. A raid on the office of an anarchist newspaper provided justification for the arrest of eight men, who were charged with the bombing. Five of them were German immigrants; all were anarchists who embraced an anti-statist philosophy that rejected all forms of involuntary hierarchical rule. The defendants were tried and found guilty, and all but one were sentenced to death by hanging. The trial and sentence divided public opinion. The apparent injustice of the verdict outraged radicals, who staged protests in the United States and around the world. At the same time, press coverage that presented the defendants as bloodthirsty revolutionaries inspired fear of immigrants and revulsion for anarchism among many other US Americans.[15]

Arguably, the most feared—and famous—anarchist of the era was Lithuanian-born Emma Goldman, who emigrated to the United States in 1885.[16] Eight years later, Goldman was arrested and prosecuted for aiding and abetting unlawful assembly by speaking at a demonstration of the unemployed in Manhattan's Union Square. Sentenced to a year's imprisonment on Blackwell's Island, she used the time to burnish her English-language skills. After her release, Goldman began lecturing and writing in English to expand the reach of anarchism beyond Russian- and German-speaking immigrants. From her first English-language publications, Alice Béja notes, Goldman referred to the founding of the United States and the nation's putative ideals of freedom and equality.[17] It was not long before Goldman was drawing thousands to her lectures.

On September 6, 1901, in Buffalo, New York, a gunman killed US president William McKinley. The gunman, Leon Czolgosz, claimed that he had killed the president because he was an anarchist and did not believe in a republican form of government or any type of ruler. He also claimed to have been inspired to commit the deed after hearing Goldman speak. Czolgosz, who likely was mentally ill, was executed in the electric chair. Although it is unlikely that he was an anarchist, that four heads of state in Europe had been assassinated by anarchists at the turn of the twentieth century—President Sadi Carnot of France (1894), Prime Minister Antonio Canovas del Castillo of Spain (1897), Empress Elizabeth of Austria (1898), and King Umberto I of Italy (1900)—made his claim believable.[18]

In October 1901, Goldman published a defense of Czolgosz in the English-language anarchist newspaper *Free Society*. Titled "The Tragedy at Buffalo," it began with a wallop: "Never before in the history of governments has the sound of a pistol shot so startled, terrorized, and horrified the self-satisfied, indifferent, contented, and indolent public, as has the one fired by Leon Czolgosz when he struck down William McKinley, president of the money kings and trust magnates of this country." In the tradition of working-class activists before her, Goldman used the Declaration of Independence to highlight contradictions between the founding ideals of the nation and conditions of grinding inequality since the Civil War, brought about by unfettered capitalism.

> For more than thirty years a small band of parasites have robbed the American people, and trampled upon the fundamental principles laid down by the forefathers of this country, guaranteeing to every man, woman and child, 'Life, liberty, and the pursuit of happiness.' For thirty years they have been increasing their wealth and power at the expense of the vast mass of workers, thereby enlarging the army of the unemployed, the hungry, homeless, and friendless portion of humanity, tramping the country from east to west and north to south, in a vain search for work.[19]

Goldman's grim depiction of conditions in the United States upended the idea of the nation as a haven for the oppressed of Europe. As she saw it, the United States was no different from Europe, and the blame lay squarely with corrupt politicians and greedy capitalists. Goldman countered efforts to tie Czolgosz's assassination of McKinley to his Slavic origins (he was the son of Polish-Russian immigrants) and the influence of foreign agitators like herself by defending his act as an outgrowth of his Americanism. "Who can tell how many times this American child has gloried in the celebration of the 4th of July, or on Decoration Day, when he faithfully honored the nation's dead? Who knows but what he, too, was willing to 'fight for his country and die for her liberty': until it dawned upon him that those he belonged to have no country because they have been robbed of all that they have produced: until he saw that all the liberty and independence of his youthful dreams are but a farce."[20] In short, Goldman argued that Czolgosz assassinated the president when he realized that the promise of the United States had been stolen by businessmen and the politicians whom they kept in their pockets.

Goldman returned to the Declaration nine years later for a Fourth of July contest sponsored by the *Boston Globe* in 1909. She won the contest, but the *Globe* refused to print her entry, so she published it in her newspaper *Mother Earth*. Goldman's new declaration, which followed the form of the eighteenth-century original, was a clear, succinct statement of anarchist political philosophy. She expanded the scope of the Declaration's natural rights claims to include "all human beings, irrespective of race, color, or sex" who "are born with the equal right to share at the table of life" and derided government as a force "which exists but to maintain special privilege and property rights" and "coerces man into submission and therefore robs him of dignity, self-respect, and life."[21]

In Goldman's version, the tyranny that had replaced monarchy was that of "American kings of capital and authority." Theirs, wrote Goldman, "is the history of repeated crimes, injustice, oppression, outrage, and abuse, all aiming at the suppression of individual liberties and the exploitation of the people." She closed the document with an attack on every form of economic, political, and social oppression stemming from "the sacredness of property, the respect for man-made law, the fear of the Church, the cowardice of public opinion, the stupid arrogance of national, racial, religious, and sex superiority, and from the narrow puritanical conception of human life." Although there were no other signatories, Goldman pledged support for the new declaration from "the lovers of liberty" who "joyfully consecrate their uncompromising devotion, their energy and intelligence, their solidarity and their lives."[22] A decade after she penned these words, during the crackdown on radicals that marked the post–World War I Red Scare, Goldman was deported to Russia.

Socialists and the Liberty of US American Workers

Anarchists like Goldman served as convenient scapegoats during periods of labor militancy. Eugene Debs addressed panic about anarchists in a piece he wrote for the *Locomotive Fireman's Magazine* in 1894. Titled "The Fourth of July," the piece was a response to another article, "Thoughts for the Fourth," by Samuel J. Niccolls, pastor of the Second Presbyterian Church of St. Louis, which had been published in the St. Louis *Globe Democrat.* Niccolls's article appeared during the Pullman Strike, a widespread strike and boycott by railway workers that erupted in response to wage cuts and firings. Led by Debs and the American Railway Union, the strike involved anywhere from 125,000 to 250,000 workers and shut down most of the freight and passenger traffic in twenty-seven states west of Chicago.[23] In response to growing militancy among the strikers, Attorney General Richard Olney sought an injunction against the strike and its leaders. President Grover Cleveland dispatched federal troops to Chicago to enforce the injunction. When violence broke out, the troops fired into a crowd, killing at least thirty people and wounding several others. Many US Americans saw the Pullman strike as evidence that the nation had a "labor problem." Niccolls was among them.

In his Fourth of July article, Niccolls professed concern for the "prevailing lawlessness of the times," which he attributed to immigrant anarchists, "the avowed foes of all government . . . earnestly laboring to bring society into that disorganized and debased condition in which there shall be no law save that which seems best to each man," and the militancy of labor. Although he claimed to have sympathy for wage earners "in their efforts to secure themselves from the oppression of capital," Niccolls criticized the tactics of the Pullman strikers and the disruptive effects of the strike.[24]

Debs had been a labor moderate, but the violent repression of the Pullman Strike radicalized him and transformed him into a socialist. In his rebuttal of Niccolls, Debs recalled a US tradition of struggle against tyranny. "The American people . . . will not yield their rights, their liberties, their independence, and go down to degradation without a struggle." He acknowledged that there were anarchists in the United States and that "some of them have been imported," but he noted that radicals were born of exploitation. Such had been the case with the colonists under British rule. "Prior to July 4th, 1776, the colonies were full of agitators. They defied courts and their injunctions. They flung defiance into the very teeth of the British king, his generals, and his soldiers. There was riot and bloodshed, battles, defeats, and victories. Washington and his compatriots were denounced as anarchists, nihilists, rebels, and traitors." Turning to his own time, Debs noted how exploitative conditions were again providing fertile ground for radicalism. "Bad laws enacted, under cover of which, courts, governors, and presidents issue despotic decrees which crush the masses and protect plutocrats, trusts, and corporations, will now, as certainly as in 1774–84[,] produce rebellion." If working people had the heel of oppression on their necks, there could be no celebration of Independence Day. "The grand old 4th of July, as a national holiday[,] is a thing of the past. That men are 'created equal' is denounced as a vagary, the hallucination of a diseased brain, and the 'inalienable rights of life, liberty, and the pursuit of happiness' have been relegated to the limbo of shams."[25]

As he toggled between the US American Revolution and the recent events of the Pullman Strike, Debs re-imagined the Declaration of Independence as a recitation of the causes of a "great strike" for liberty. The strike metaphor allowed Debs to compare the disruptive effects of the rail strike with the disruption caused by the quest for independence from Britain. "The authors of the strike knew there would be great inconvenience to the people of the colonies; that trade and commerce would be crippled; that untold sacrifices and sufferings would result, but the leaders did not heed such ravings. There was a principle involved, and they struck for a principle." His point was that disruption of the status quo is warranted when there is just cause for a strike, whether political or economic. In 1776, the battle cry was "liberty"; in 1894, it was "wages."[26]

Although he displayed empathy for those whose exploitation was so extreme that it drove them to anarchism, Debs was no anarchist. On the contrary, he retained faith in US political institutions throughout his life, which included five bids for the US presidency between 1900 and 1920. It is no surprise, then, that he insisted the best hope for "preserving something of the old glory for the 4th of July" was the ballot. The election of honest men, he hoped, could rescue the Fourth of July from "eternal odium."[27]

After the Pullman Strike ended, Debs served six months in the McHenry County Jail in Woodstock, Illinois. He was released on November 22, 1895. Upon his release, he spoke to a crowd that had assembled to cheer his freedom. He began his speech with a reference to the Declaration of Independence. "Manifestly the spirit of '76 still survives. The fires of liberty and noble aspirations are not yet extinguished. I greet you tonight as lovers of liberty and as despisers of despotism. I comprehend the significance of this demonstration and appreciate the honor that makes it possible for me to be your guest on such an occasion. The vindication and glorification of American principles of government, as proclaimed to the world in the Declaration of Independence, is the high purpose of this convocation."[28]

Debs lamented how corporations were stealing the liberty of US American workers, which had been declared on July 4, 1776, and codified eight years later in the Constitution. A prime example was the injunction issued against the Pullman Strike. "I challenge the world to assign a reason why a judge, under the solemn obligation of an oath to obey the constitution, should in a temple dedicated to justice, stab the Magna Carta of American liberty to death in the interests of corporations that labor might be disrobed of its inalienable rights and those who advocated its claim to justice imprisoned as if they were felons?"[29] Although powerful forces had arrayed themselves against working people, Debs expressed "an abiding faith in the ultimate triumph of the right" and took heart from the crowd that had gathered to cheer his release. The workers assembled before him, along with other "American lovers of Liberty," he posited, were setting in motion forces "to rescue their constitutional liberties from the grasp of monopoly and its mercenary hirelings." Again, he praised the ballot, which he depicted as the birthright of US American workers, the most powerful force they had at their disposal. "Their fathers were free born—their sovereignty none denied and their children yet have the ballot. It has been called 'a weapon that executes a free man's will as lightning does the will of God.'"[30] Of course, he was talking here about a "weapon" for the working class that was available at the time only to US-born male workers.

Debs ran for president for the first time in 1900. He earned over 87,000 votes on the Social Democratic Party ticket in a campaign that was largely viewed as a rematch between Republican William McKinley and Democrat William Jennings Bryan. On July 4, 1901, just weeks before the founding convention of the Socialist Party of America, he delivered an Independence Day address. His salutation to the crowd—"Ladies, Gentlemen, Comrades"—combined politesse with radical socialism. After opening comments about the current "marvelous age," he spoke of the situation in 1776: "A little over a century ago, the inhabitants of this country were not citizens. They were ruled by a foreign king. They petitioned for relief. Their petitions were disregarded. They objected to taxation without representation. Their protests were scorned. Finally they revolted. They issued the Declaration of Independence and enunciated the proposition that men are created equal." As numerous working-class radicals before him had done, Debs pointed out the unfinished nature of the Revolution. "But the founders of this republic had only vague conceptions of democracy. The working class as we understand it today were not represented in the Constitutional Convention. The founders of the republic in declaring that men were equal evidently meant themselves alone." The working class to which Debs referred included Black workers. They were not represented at the Constitutional Convention because they "had been reduced to a state of abject slavery." The institution of slavery, Debs thundered, "was in conflict with the spirit of the Declaration, with the genius of free institutions, and yet it was incorporated in them." He excoriated politicians who ignored the glaring contradiction between the words of the Declaration and the history of slavery while they bloviated about freedom on the Fourth of July:

> Thousands of orators all over this broad land will glorify the institutions under which we live. In pride they will point toward Old Glory and declare that it is a flag that waves over a free country. In these modern days we hear very much about that flag and about the institutions over which it waves. I am not one of those who worships the flag. I have no respect for the stars and stripes, or for any other flag that symbolizes slavery. It does not matter to me what others may think, say, or do. I propose to preserve the integrity of my soul.[31]

The institution of chattel slavery had been eradicated by the Civil War, a struggle whose "greatest and noblest figure," according to Debs, was John Brown, but another form of slavery likewise antithetical to the Declaration of Independence remained: wage slavery.

Debs saw the Fourth of July as an occasion to denounce capitalism and advocate for a socialist government that would abolish the wage system and transfer ownership of the means of production to workers. "Arouse, ye slaves! Declare war, not on the capitalist, but on the capitalist system, and if it should be your fate or fortune to suffer in years to come, that suffering will not be result of your own deliberate act. I am for the freedom of the working class. Though my heart yearns for the freedom of men, I am powerless. Only the working class itself can achieve its emancipation."[32]

The Pullman Strike had convinced Debs that unions could not protect the rights of workers unless US political institutions changed. "You workingmen have as much to do with the control of this government as if you inhabited Mars or some other planet," he told his Fourth of July audience. "The capitalist class rules in absolutely every department of our government." For this reason, Debs argued, "while organization is necessary on the economic field, it is vastly more important on the political field." He insisted on the necessity of voting for candidates who would fight for workers' interests, but he was critical of the Democratic and Republican parties, because both ultimately served the interests of capital. A socialist political party offered the only means of "throwing over the capitalist" and creating a society based on principles of equality and liberty such as were laid out in the Declaration of Independence.[33]

Debs was not alone. Articles in the *International Socialist Review* (*ISR*), the monthly magazine of the Socialist Party of America, reveal that socialists incorporated the Declaration of Independence into discussions of various topics. Among them was the so-called Negro problem, which Debs wrote about in 1903. He compared the founders of the nation unfavorably to Karl Marx. The former claimed freedom for all in the Declaration of Independence, and then in the Constitution they denied freedom to enslaved Blacks. In contrast, "When Marx said: 'Workingmen of all countries unite,' he gave concrete expression to the socialist philosophy of the class struggle; unlike the framers of the declaration of independence who announced that 'all men are created equal' and then basely repudiated their own doctrine." As Debs noted, Marx's inclusive vision of the working class embraced all toilers in all lands, "regardless of race, sex, creed or any other condition whatsoever." On the issue of racial inclusivity, Debs was clear: as the party of the working class, socialists would not allow themselves to be divided "by any specious appeal to race prejudice."[34]

Black radicals such as W. E. B. DuBois and A. Philip Randolph admired Debs for this position, which was at odds with that of most white socialists, including I. M. Robbins, who, beginning in 1908, wrote several articles for the *ILR* on the Negro. In one of those articles, Robbins claimed that slavery had a "harmful, demoralizing effects upon the white population of the South" but that "it proved to be a school of civilization for the savage Negro." Robbins also pointed to Jefferson's inconsistency in penning the Declaration of Independence while upholding the institution of slavery. "In his famous Declaration of Independence Jefferson had originally included a few sentences, accusing England of the shame of introducing slavery in the colonies for its personal advantage. But Adams, the Northerner opponent of slavery, influenced Jefferson to strike out this paragraph, so as not to call forth the displeasure of the South." Thus, unlike Debs, Robbins excused Jefferson for making a necessary political calculation to save the project of national independence.[35]

For the next decade, socialists continued to incorporate the Declaration in arguments on a variety of topics, including support for strikes and opposition to military preparedness in the lead-up to World War I and to conscription once the United States entered the war.

Communists and Twentieth-Century Americanism

Arguably, the most consequential statement about the US American Revolution for twentieth-century anti-capitalist radical movements around the globe initially surfaced not in the United States but in Russia. The success of the November 1917 Bolshevik Revolution, in which a working-class party of 20,000 led by Vladimir Lenin won control of a massive, two-hundred-year-old, overwhelmingly rural empire with approximately 125 million people, in the words of journalist John Reed, "shook the world."[36] On August 20, 1918, *Pravda*, the official newspaper of the Communist Party of Russia, published Lenin's "Letter to American Workers," his report on the Russian revolution and the obstacles that remained before its goals would be realized. Lenin depicted the Central Powers, as well as Russia's former wartime allies, who now mounted a counterrevolutionary offensive against the Bolsheviks, as conducting wholesale slaughter in a grab for spoils, market profits, and control of colonies. In contrast to the current "imperialist slaughter of nations," Lenin remembered the US American Revolution as a genuine war of liberation. "The history of modern, civilised America opened with one of those great, really liberating, really revolutionary wars of which there have been so few compared to the vast number of wars of conquest which, like the present imperialist war, were caused by squabbles among kings, landowners or capitalists over the division of usurped lands or ill-gotten gains. That was the war the American people waged against the British robbers who oppressed America and held her in colonial slavery."[37]

In December 1918, an abridged version of the letter appeared in two US socialist publications: *The Class Struggle* (New York) and *The Revolutionary Age* (Boston). The letter evoked keen interest among readers, and it was circulated as a reprint and frequently republished in various newspapers around the United States and western Europe. In September 1919, a split in the Socialist Party led to the founding of the Communist Party of the United States (CPUSA). Rising inequality and worker unrest convinced members of the fledgling party that a successful worker-led uprising against capitalism in the United States was just around the corner. Instead of another liberating revolutionary war, however, these radicals witnessed the defeat of working-class movements at home and around the globe and the rise of fascist regimes in the 1920s.[38]

It was not until 1934 that Lenin's "Letter to American Workers" re-emerged in a pamphlet published by International Publishers, a New York–based company that specializes in Marxist works. That year also saw the beginning of US American communism's most influential period: the Popular Front, a broad alliance of communist, socialist, and liberal organizations to defend bourgeois democracy against a common fascist threat. Popular Front politics entailed downplaying anti-capitalist revolutionary rhetoric in favor of emphasis on broad alliances, labor advocacy, support for New Deal policies, and commitment to antifascism.[39] While Popular Front communists deemphasized the rhetoric of Bolshevik-style revolution, they hailed the US American Revolution and the Declaration of Independence that had launched it. The party's 1934 manifesto, issued at its Eighth Convention, stated that the CPUSA alone carried "forward the revolutionary traditions of 1776 and 1861" and that the "new government" mentioned in the Declaration of Independence was nothing other than the dictatorship of the proletariat in the form of "workers' and farmers' councils."[40]

Lenin's "Letter" inspired Earl Browder, secretary general of the CPUSA. In a 1935 pamphlet, *Communism in the United States,* Browder posed the question "What is Americanism?" In reply, he echoed the rhetoric of the Eighth Convention: "Today, the only Party that carries forward the revolutionary traditions of 1776 and 1861, under the present-day conditions and relationship of classes, is the Communist Party. . . . Only the Communist Party brings sharply forward and applies to the problems of today that old basic document of 'Americanism,' the Declaration of Independence."[41]

Popular Front communists did not take an uncritical view of US American political traditions. They had no qualms about acknowledging the foibles of the founding generation even as they praised their contributions to the Revolution. A February 1935 *Daily Worker* article by Leo Thompson, a member of the Young Communist League, is illustrative. Thompson called upon US American youth to reject sentimental myths about the first president and his "rich fellow-merchants" but also celebrate the "useful, progressive, REVOLUTIONARY part" he played in US history. "The Revolution of 1776, the Declaration of Independence, the Civil War of 1860–1864 . . . prove that Revolution and Civil War are not 'treasonable,' 'foreign,' 'Red,' or 'un-American' ideas," because "AMERICA WAS BORN IN REVOLUTION."[42]

As Fraser Ottanelli explains, Popular Front communism borrowed heavily from historians Charles and Mary Beard, Carl Becker, and Vernon Parrington, who argued that economic forces propelled US history.[43] Informed by this historical paradigm, communists had no reason to rewrite the Declaration of Independence. They simply reinterpreted the document as a validation of Marxist historical materialism and Soviet-style communism.

> Applying the Declaration of Independence to present-day conditions, the Communist Party points out that never was there such a mass of people so completely deprived of all semblance of "the right to life, liberty and pursuit of happiness." Never were there such "destructive"

> effects upon these rights by "any form of government," as those exerted today by the existing form of government in the United States. Never have the exploited masses suffered such a "long train of abuses" or been so "reduced under absolute despotism" as today under capitalist rule. The "principle" which must provide the foundation of the "new government" mentioned in the Declaration of Independence is, in 1934, the principle of the dictatorship of the proletariat; the new form is the form of the workers' and farmers' councils—the Soviet power.[44]

Throughout the Popular Front period, Browder answered the party's critics by positing links between the nation's origins and the present CPUSA program. In a 1936 pamphlet, titled *Who Are the Americans?*, he observed that "the Declaration of Independence was for that time what the Communist Manifesto is for ours." So perfect was the analogy, one could "copy all the most hysterical Hearst editorials of today against Moscow, Lenin, Stalin; substitute the words America, Washington, Jefferson; and the result is an almost verbatim copy of the diatribes of English and European reactionary politicians in the closing years of the eighteenth century against our American founding fathers." Browder pointed out how efforts by the oppressed to liberate themselves always met with opposition from the powerful. Those among the eighteenth-century British establishment who were threatened by popular democracy attempted to derail the very idea of revolution by labeling it "an alien doctrine imposed from America," just as US American capitalists now deemed it "imported from Moscow." To ignore the "revolutionary kernel" that lies at the heart of US history was to ignore the truth of the nation's origins and render Fourth of July observances nothing more than "the strutting of marionettes and stuffed shirts" and "spread eagle oratory." Browder claimed that communists were true heirs of the nation's revolutionary traditions because they were the only ones applying those traditions to the present moment. "We are the Americans and Communism is the Americanism of the twentieth century."[45] This statement encapsulated the party's Popular Front strategy. It depicted communism as a democratic movement central to US history and rebutted those who branded the policies and ideology of the CPUSA un-American.

Their embrace of US American political traditions meant that communists planted their ideological roots in soil that included not only Marx, Lenin, and Stalin but the founding generation as well. The preamble to the CPUSA's new constitution made the case explicitly, stating that US American communists "carried forward today the traditions of Jefferson, Paine,

Jackson, and Lincoln, and of the Declaration of Independence."[46] Thus, Popular Front communism framed the Declaration of Independence as a key statement of revolutionary principles that shook the earth at the time of their proclamation and continued to reverberate in the present struggle against political repression at home and fascism abroad.

The Popular Front disintegrated with the signing of the Nazi-Soviet nonaggression pact in August 1939.[47] This development left communists in the United States in a difficult position. Although they remained anti-fascist in principle, defense of the Soviet Union now required reframing the war in Europe from an anti-fascist struggle to an imperialist competition and President Roosevelt from a bourgeois ally in the struggle against fascism to a tool of Wall Street in the service of empire and capital. The difficulty lasted fewer than two years. Hitler's June 21, 1941, invasion of the Soviet Union voided the Nazi-Soviet Pact and recast the party's relationship to the war and to Roosevelt. For the remainder of the war, communists found inspiration in the US American Revolution for the struggle against fascism. This inspiration was qualified. Communists acknowledged that Jefferson's masterpiece, the Declaration of Independence, was an imperfect document. As evidence, they typically cited the passage condemning the slave trade that was stricken from the final version to appease Southern slaveholders.[48] Despite leaving the institution of slavery unchallenged in the Declaration, Jefferson was lauded by communists for sweeping away the ruins of British imperialism and "thinking first and foremost of the creation of a new society, a new perspective, a new outlook, a new day."[49]

After the end of World War II, competition between the United States and the Soviet Union for global dominance fostered a climate of intense political repression against US American communists.[50] The Cold War and McCarthyism forced a separation of the labor movement from the anti-capitalist Left as unions expelled radical members to avoid being vilified as "red" and hence un-American. Another casualty of that competition was memory of the US American tradition of revolutionary radicalism that had nourished many activists on the front lines of class struggle for over a century. These combined developments have hobbled efforts by workers to fight together against economic exploitation and political marginalization. Historically, the key to a vibrant US American labor movement has been the presence of a core group of radical activists dedicated to class struggle who ignite the spark of collective action among fellow workers. As economic and social inequality again reach crisis levels, radicals seeking to reinvigorate the labor movement and democracy can reclaim that tradition—especially, but not only, the

Declaration of Independence—even as they point out its shortcomings, to popularize their ideas and inspire fellow workers in the latest round of struggle for freedom from the tyranny of unfettered capitalism.

NOTES

1. Montgomery, *Citizen Worker*, 1–12.

2. Goldstein provides an overview of repressive campaigns against working-class radicals in the United States; see *Political Repression in Modern America*.

3. Montgomery, *Citizen Worker*, 13–51.

4. Ware, *Industrial Worker*, 198–226.

5. National Trades' Union, "Convention of 1834," 207.

6. General Trades Union of the City and County of Philadelphia, "The Cordwainers," 21.

7. Commons, *Documentary History*, 7:317.

8. Commons, *Documentary History*, 8:118.

9. Foner, *Other People*, 1–3.

10. Foner, *Other People*, 13.

11. Foner, *Other People*, 16.

12. Eichner, *Paris Commune*.

13. See, e.g., Simon, *Alternative History*.

14. Kipnis, *American Socialist Movement*, 11.

15. Green covers the trial and its aftermath in *Death in the Haymarket*.

16. For a reconstruction of Goldman's life in the United States through primary texts, see Falk, *Documentary History*, vols. 1 and 2.

17. Béja, "'Dreaming (Un)American Dreams,'" 7.

18. Pernicone and Ottanelli, *Assassins*.

19. Goldman, "Tragedy at Buffalo," 471–78.

20. Goldman, "Tragedy at Buffalo," 471–78.

21. Goldman, "New Declaration of Independence," 137.

22. Goldman, "New Declaration of Independence."

23. On Debs, see Salvatore, *Eugene V. Debs*. A succinct and informative account of the Pullman Strike is Brecher, *Strike!*, 85–93.

24. Quoted in Debs, "Fourth of July," 874.

25. Debs, "Fourth of July," 873.

26. Debs, "Fourth of July," 874.

27. Debs, "Fourth of July," 874.

28. Debs, "Liberty," 3.

29. Debs, "Liberty," 20–21.

30. Debs, "Liberty," 3, 11.

31. Debs, "Independence Day."

32. Debs, "Independence Day."

33. Debs, "Independence Day."

34. Debs, "Negro in the Class Struggle," 259.

35. Robbins, "Economic Aspects," 548, 550.

36. Reed, *Ten Days*. A classic history of the Bolshevik Revolution is Sheila Fitzpatrick, *Russian Revolution*.

37. V. I. Lenin, "Letter to American Workers," *Pravda*, August 22, 1918.

38. On the founding of the Communist Party, see Draper, *American Communism*, 9–95.

39. On Popular Front Communism, see Ottanelli, *Communist Party*.

40. "Against the 'New Deal,'" 27.

41. Browder, "Communism," 18.

42. Leo Thompson, "Washington Was Called 'Traitor' for Civil War Against King George and Tory Hired Lackeys," *Daily Worker*, February 22, 1935, 2.

43. Ottanelli, *Communist Party*, 122.

44. Browder, "Communism," 18–19.

45. Browder, *Who Are the Americans?*, 12.

46. "Constitution and Bylaws of the Communist Party U.S.A."

47. Isserman, *Which Side Were You On?*, 32–54.

48. Meyers, "Thomas Jefferson," 523.

49. Bowers, "Jefferson," 15.

50. Belknap, *Cold War Political Justice*; Schrecker, *Many Are the Crimes*.

BIBLIOGRAPHY

"Against the 'New Deal' of Hunger, Fascism, and War! For the Revolutionary Solution of the Crisis." In *The Way Out, A Program for American Labor: Manifesto and Principal Resolutions Adopted by the Eighth Convention of the Communist Party of the U.S.A., Held in Cleveland, Ohio, April 2–8, 1934*, 20–30. New York: Workers Library, 1934.

Béja, Alice. "'Dreaming (Un)American Dreams': Anarchists and the Struggle to Define Americanism." *Journal for the Study of Radicalism* 13 (2019): 1–18.

Belknap, Michael R. *Cold War Political Justice: The Smith Act, the Communist Party, and American Civil Liberties*. Westport, CT: Greenwood Press, 1977.

Bowers, Claude C. "Jefferson and the American Way of Life." In *The Heritage of Jefferson*, edited by Claude C. Bowers and Earl Browder, 11–27. New York: Workers School, 1943.

Brecher, Jeremy. *Strike!* Oakland, CA: PM Press, 2015.

Browder, Earl. "Communism in the United States." New York: International Publishers, 1935.

———. *Who Are the Americans?* New York: International Publishers, 1936.

Commons, John R. *A Documentary History of American Industrial Society*. Vol. 7. Cleveland: Arthur H. Clark, 1910.

———. *A Documentary History of American Industrial Society*. Vol. 8. Cleveland: Arthur H. Clark, 1910.

"Constitution and Bylaws of the Communist Party U.S.A." In Fraser M. Ottanelli, *The Communist Party of the United States: From the Depression to World War II*, 5–6. New Brunswick, NJ: Rutgers University Press, 1991.

Debs, Eugene V. "The Fourth of July." *Locomotive Firemen's Magazine*, September 1894, 872–74.

———. "Independence Day Address," July 4, 1901. https://jacobin.com/2020/07/eugene-debs-independence-day-address-fourth-july.

———. "Liberty: A Speech Delivered at Battery D, Chicago, on Release from Woodstock Jail, November 22, 1895." Chicago: Charles H. Kerr, 1911.

———. "The Negro in the Class Struggle." *International Socialist Review* 4, no. 5 (November 1903): 357–60.

Draper, Theodore. *American Communism and Soviet Russia*. New York: Octagon Books, 1977.

Eichner, Carolyn J. *The Paris Commune: A Brief History*. New Brunswick, NJ: Rutgers University Press, 2022.

Falk, Candace, ed. *Emma Goldman: A Documentary History of the American Years*, vol. 1: *Made for America 1890–1901*. Urbana: University of Illinois Press, 2003.

———, ed. *Emma Goldman: A Documentary History of the American Years*, vol. 2: *Making Speech Free, 1902–1909*. Urbana: University of Illinois Press, 2008.

Fitzpatrick, Sheila. *The Russian Revolution*. 4th ed. Oxford: Oxford University Press, 2017.

Foner, Philip. *We, the Other People: Alternative Declarations of Independence by Labor Groups, Farmers, Woman's Rights Advocates, Socialists, and Blacks, 1829–1975*. Urbana: University of Illinois Press, 1976.

General Trades Union of the City and County of Philadelphia. "The Cordwainers." In *A Documentary History of American Industrial Society*, vol. 6, edited by John R. Commons, 21. Cleveland: Arthur H. Clark, 1910.

Goldman, Emma. "A New Declaration of Independence." *Mother Earth* 4, no. 5 (July 1909): 137–38.

———. "The Tragedy at Buffalo." In Falk, *Emma Goldman*, 471–78.

Goldstein, Robert Justin. *Political Repression in Modern America: From 1870 to the Present*. Boston: G. K. Hall, 1978.

Green, James. *Death in the Haymarket: A Story of Chicago, the First Labor Movement and the Bombing That Divided Gilded Age America*. New York: Anchor Books, 2007.

Isserman, Maurice. *Which Side Were You On? The American Communist Party During the Second World War*. Middletown, CT: Wesleyan University Press, 1982.

Kipnis, Ira. *The American Socialist Movement, 1897–1912*. 1952. Chicago: Haymarket Books, 2004.

Meyers, Frank. "Thomas Jefferson—Leader of the Nation." *The Communist* 21, no. 6 (July 1942): 522–33.

Montgomery, David. *Citizen Worker: The Experience of Workers in the United States with Democracy and the Free Market During the Nineteenth Century*. Cambridge: Cambridge University Press, 1993.

National Trades' Union. "The Convention of 1834." In Commons, *Documentary History of American Industrial Society*, 6:207.

Ottanelli, Fraser M. *The Communist Party of the United States: From the Depression to World War II*. New Brunswick, NJ: Rutgers University Press, 1991.

Pernicone, Nunzio, and Fraser M. Ottanelli. *Assassins Against the Old Order: Italian Anarchist Violence in Fin de Siècle Europe*. Urbana: University of Illinois Press, 2018.

Reed, John. *Ten Days That Shook the World*. New York: Penguin, 2007.

Robbins, I. M. "The Economic Aspects of the Negro Problem." *International Socialist Review* 8 (March 1908): 548–54.

Salvatore, Nick. *Eugene V. Debs: Citizen and Socialist*. Urbana: University of Illinois Press, 2007.

Schrecker, Ellen. *Many Are the Crimes: McCarthyism in America*. Boston: Little, Brown, 1998.

Simon, Ed. *An Alternative History of Pittsburgh*. Lakewood, OH: Belt Publishing, 2021.

Ware, Norman. *The Industrial Worker, 1840–1860*. Chicago: Ivan R. Dee, 1990.

9

THE DECLARATION OF INDEPENDENCE AND CIVIL RIGHTS: THE LONG MOVEMENT AND COUNTERMOVEMENT

Davis W. Houck

The Declaration of Independence is first and foremost a rhetorical text. That is, the document's principal value is to warrant public arguments. Those arguments range across the ideological spectrum, as I will illustrate in what follows. Whether it's to bludgeon "America-hating leftists" or its phrases are appropriated by civil rights activists, Jefferson's draft and the Continental Congress's edits function as explosive fodder not just on July 4 but on countless and diverse rhetorical occasions. The Declaration shows up in some curious places, even as the meaning of its key terms continues to evolve.

My point of departure in this chapter is the very particular context of America's "long civil rights movement." Most scholars agree that the nation's "short civil rights movement" can be periodized as either 1954–65 or 1954–68. That brief period—whether twelve or fifteen years—is characterized by mass protest, intense media coverage, legal challenges and changes, and charismatic national leadership. While scholars understand the benefits of the convenient periodization of the movement, they also know it to be something of a fiction; movements rarely experience such sudden beginnings and endings, thus the "long civil rights movement."

I begin with the Declaration and move across nearly 250 years of American history, with an eye on how the document and its language are leveraged in arguments for and often against legal rights of enslaved Africans and later Black American citizens. I move quickly through huge swaths of discourse recorded in many places. As a first in the field of rhetorical studies, I hope only to note some suggestive beginnings. Curiously, rhetorical scholars—and I only count two—have attempted to understand the rhetorical power of the document in its antecedents, not its prospects.[1] I move in the opposite chronological direction. Not surprisingly, because the Declaration is *the* defining text of what it means to be a US American, its language functions as a fulcrum in countless debates involving the civil rights of Black (and white) Americans; furthermore, the intent and meaning of the document are almost always at issue.

Before examining those public arguments, however, we should note the passage on slavery that Jefferson drafted, his small Committee of Five apparently approved, but that was later removed from the final draft by elected officials from Georgia and South Carolina. It reads:

> He has waged cruel war against human nature itself, violating its most sacred rights of life and liberty in the persons of a distant people who never offended him, captivating and carrying them into slavery in another hemisphere or to incur miserable death in their transportation thither. This piratical warfare, the opprobrium of infidel powers, is the warfare of the Christian King of Great Britain. Determined to keep open a market where Men should be bought and sold, he has prostituted his negative for suppressing every legislative attempt to prohibit or restrain this execrable commerce; and that this assemblage of horrors might want no fact of distinguished die, he is now exciting these very people to rise in arms among us, and to purchase that liberty of which he deprived them, by murdering the people upon whom he also obtruded them; thus paying off former crimes committed against the liberties of one people, with crimes which he urges them to commit crimes against the lives of another.[2]

First things first: Jefferson refers to enslaved Africans as "human," "persons" and "people," however "distant," by which I take him to mean geographically, not phylogenetically. Jefferson is careful not to mention the domestic slave trade, nor life on an indigo plantation in southeast Georgia. No, King George III, whose "Christianity" is conspicuous by its rhetorical presence, wages a cruel and "piratical" war in human souls whose end is twofold: profit and strategic military advantage. Regarding the latter, Jefferson alludes to Virginia's royal governor, the Earl of Dunmore, whose proclamation in May 1775 promised to free any enslaved person willing to fight on the British side, in his "Ethiopian Regiment."[3] The promise of emancipation stoked fears among colonists that a mass slave revolt was imminent.

The deleted section reads like a proto-abolitionist text. "Execrable commerce," "assemblage of horrors," and the "miserable death" of buying and selling human beings sits uncomfortably next to the fact that twelve of the thirteen original states had legalized slavery. Indeed, before the Declaration had even been drafted, the English polymath Samuel Johnson noted rather acidly, "How is it that we hear the loudest yelps for liberty among the drivers of negroes?"[4] Jefferson, of course, was not unaware of the preamble's claim that if all men were created equal by a divine source, and therefore shared the unalienable rights of life, liberty, and the pursuit of happiness, enslaved (and free) Africans posed a rather substantial problem.

Benjamin Banneker was perhaps the first Black person, free or enslaved, to call Jefferson out for his rank hypocrisy. Banneker wrote to Jefferson on August 19, 1791. He noted that Jefferson's "abhorrence [of slavery] was so excited" that it led him to author the Declaration, whose preamble he then quotes at some length. And yet, Jefferson had counteracted God's mercies by "detaining by fraud and violence so numerous a part of my brethren under groaning captivity and cruel oppression, that you should at the same time be found guilty of that most criminal act, which you professedly detested in others, with respect to yourselves."[5] Banneker's private letter begins a nearly sixty-year period of American history during which the promises of the Declaration and the realities of chattel slavery—the "criminal act" being a cruel hypocrisy—coexist in querulous tension.

Like Jefferson, an anonymous "Republican" writing in *The North-Carolina Journal* (Halifax, NC) on the twenty-year anniversary of the Declaration's signing drew attention to a God of "justice and mercy" whose ears were open to the call of the oppressed, and who would one day, "not very remote," "break the dire chain, that holds the slave, and heal those wounds the tyrant gave." While noting the "amazing contrast" between a professed liberty and the practice of oppression, the writer quotes the Declaration's preamble at length to conclude: "Here was an effort of reason which did honor to human nature; but how little consistency is there in the human character, when prejudice is substituted for justice and when private interest usurps the empire of reason." How "very absurd" that on this Independence Day "a part of the human race" is "sold like cattle from one imperious master to another."[6] At this relatively early date in the Declaration's existence, the problem of theory and practice was syllogistic in nature: reason dictated that "black men" were a minor premise of "all men" and should therefore be able to exercise the same rights as white men. As the nineteenth century unfolded, though, proslavery speakers and writers would amend the major premise with a five-letter adjective.

Portending that fierce hermeneutical debate back in 1813, James Forten, a free Black man in Philadelphia, penned *A Series of Letters by a Man of Color.* One such letter took up the issue of the "all men" then just under question in a piece of proposed Pennsylvania legislation. Wrote Forten, "They [the founders] did not particularize white and black because they never supposed it would be a question whether *we were men or not.*" No, the "all men" did not need to be preceded by an adjective of "white" or "black" because even as the founders "knew we were deeper skinned than they were," they still "acknowledged us as men, and found that many an honest heart beat beneath a dusky bosom." Forten asked, "Has the God who made the white man and the black left any record declaring us a different species? Are we not sustained by the same power, supported by the same food, hurt by the same wounds, wounded by the same wrongs, pleased with the same delights, and propagated by the same means?"[7] The questions needed no answers; as such, Forten concludes, let us "be considered as men." As I will later illustrate, Forten's first query regarding God's archive will feature a different, and directly stated, answer by Mississippi segregationists a century and a half later.

Sixteen years after Forten's missive, David Walker's tectonic four-part *Appeal to the Colored Citizens of the World* was published. The Bostonian scared the hell out of whites and Blacks, especially since he argued that submissive slaves shouldn't wear out their knees praying for their earthly deliverance. Walker's appeal stopped well short of advocating for a nonviolent solution; in fact, less than two years after the *Appeal*'s publication, Nat Turner's murderous rebellion quickly became slavers' worst nightmare. While Walker makes specific mention of the preamble's "We hold these truths to be self evident" and the vast distance between democratic theory and practice, more interesting is his mention of a different part of the Declaration: "Hear your language further! 'But when a long train of abuses and usurpation, pursuing invariably the same object, evinces a design to reduce them under absolute despotism, it is their right, it is their duty, to throw off such government, and to provide new guards for their future security.' Now, Americans! I ask you candidly, was your sufferings under Great Britain, one hundredth part as cruel and tyrannical as you have rendered ours under you?"[8] Like Forten's letter, Walker's question needs no answer, but the suppressed conclusion might have attracted the attention of whites in the North and South: Blacks, too, could "throw off" the despotism of slavery; they would certainly be warranted in such revolutionary action.

Walker's *Appeal* was part of a nascent movement, centered in the Northeast, to abolish slavery, and perhaps no voice was as consistent and persuasive as William Lloyd Garrison's. His influential newspaper, *The Liberator*, began publishing in 1831. In its inaugural issue, he too reached for the Declaration's preamble in warranting his cause: "Assenting to the 'self-evident truth' maintained in the American Declaration of Independence, 'that all men are created equal, and endowed by their Creator with certain inalienable rights—among which are life, liberty and the pursuit of happiness,' I shall strenuously contend for the immediate enfranchisement of our slave population." Unlike other abolitionists who urged a gradual emancipation of the enslaved, Garrison famously roared:

> I am aware, that many object to the severity of my language; but is there not cause for severity? I will be as harsh as truth, and as uncompromising as justice. On this subject, I do not wish to think, or speak, or write, with moderation. No! No! Tell a man whose house is on fire, to give a moderate alarm; tell him to moderately rescue his wife from the hand of the ravisher; tell the mother to gradually extricate her babe from the fire into which it has fallen;—but urge me not to use moderation in a cause like the present. I am in earnest—I will not equivocate—I will not excuse—I will not retreat a single inch—AND I WILL BE HEARD.[9]

Even in 1831, the caps lock denoted shouting, and Garrison's persuasive voice was in fact heard. Unlike the American Colonization Society, which advocated for free Blacks to return to the west coast of African (Liberia, specifically), Garrisonian abolition called for the enslaved's immediate freedom on American shores.

One of the many escaped slaves who heard Garrison's abolitionist voice was a young Frederick Douglass, who was destined to become America's most famous abolitionist and one of the nation's most accomplished speakers. Douglass's big break as an orator occurred on August 12, 1841, at a meeting of the Massachusetts Anti-Slavery Society on Nantucket Island. Eleven years later Douglass gave a speech whose fame continues to grow in the present day. "What to the Slave Is the Fourth of July?," delivered before the Rochester Ladies' Anti-Slavery Society on July 5, 1852, "was nothing less than the rhetorical masterpiece of American abolitionism."[10] I will get to that address in a moment, but it's worth pausing to ask why Douglass chose July 5 as the date of his speech. Many African Americans called attention to the Declaration's unfulfilled promises by holding an observance on July 5. Twenty years to the day before Douglass's oration pierced the nation's eyes and ears,

Connecticut community leader Peter Osborne explained to his "fellow citizens" of New Haven what the Fifth of July represented: "On account of the misfortune of our color, our Fourth of July comes on the fifth. But I hope and trust that when the Declaration of Independence is fully executed, which declares that all men, without respect to person, were born free and equal, we may then have our Fourth of July on the fourth."[11] Osborne glimpsed that day "approaching very fast," since signs in every part of the country were "favorable." With the "Declaration of Independence in one hand and the Holy Bible in the other," the enemy could be vanquished.

A generation later and the nation's preeminent abolitionist could only lament "that the character and conduct of this nation never looked blacker to me than on this Fourth of July." As a Black man invited to deliver what his interlocutors likely assumed would be a paean to a Declaration that he'd previously praised, Douglass probably had the better citizens of Rochester squirming: "Fellow citizens, pardon me, allow me to ask, what am I called upon to speak here today? What have I, or those I represent, to do with your national independence?"[12] More specific questions gathered force: "Are the great principles of political freedom and of natural justice, embodied in the Declaration of Independence, extended to us?" His answers were also intimate, foregrounding the first person: "I am not included within the pale of this glorious anniversary! Your high independence only reveals the immeasurable distance between us. . . . The rich inheritance of justice, liberty, prosperity and independence, bequeathed by your fathers, is shared by you, not by me." Douglass's indictment of the invitation was almost complete: "This Fourth of July is *yours*, not *mine*. *You* may rejoice, *I* must mourn." I'm guessing things were mighty awkward at this point in Corinthian Hall.

But even if the invitation functioned as a personal insult, Douglass wasn't going to waste the occasion merely on detailing first-person effrontery. No, he quickly brought the slave into the center of the esteemed hall: "What, to the American slave, is your Fourth of July? . . . a day that reveals to him, more than all other days in the year, the gross injustice and cruelty to which he is the constant victim." Those revelations poured forth with the accumulating force of a devastating avalanche: "To him, your celebration is a sham; your boasted liberty an unholy license; your national greatness swelling vanity; your sounds of rejoicing are empty and heartless; your denunciation of tyrants brass-fronted impudence; your shouts of liberty and equality hollow mockery; your prayers and hymns, your sermons and thanksgivings, with all your religious parade and solemnity, are to [h]im mere bombast, fraud, deception, impiety and hypocrisy—a thin veil to cover up crimes which would disgrace a nation of savages." Notice that each of Douglass's accusations are oral and rhetorical in character; each involves the inherited speech of an unfeeling and frankly unintelligent nation hypocritical to its core.

Rendered metaphorically as natural destruction and devastation, Douglass's solutions were, of necessity, also rhetorical: "It is not the light that is needed, but fire; it is not the gentle shower, but thunder. We need the storm, the whirlwind, and the earthquake. The feeling of the nation must be quickened; the conscience of the nation must be roused; the propriety of the nation must be startled; the hypocrisy of the nation must be exposed; and its crimes against God and man must be proclaimed and denounced." Feelings quickened, consciences roused, propriety startled, hypocrisy exposed, and crimes proclaimed and denounced—these uniquely rhetorical acts and arts comprised Douglass's ambition. And borrowing from his mentor and friend, "'I will not equivocate; I will not excuse'; I will use the severest language I can command; and yet not one word shall escape me that any man, whose judgement is not blinded by prejudice, or who is not at heart a slaveholder, shall not confess to be right and just." And so he did. We are still reckoning with Douglass's speech delivered on The Day After.

Despite the "darkness" and "degeneracy" of the moment, Douglass closed his lengthy address by declaring that he drew "encouragement from the Declaration of Independence [and] the great principles it contains." That document, plus technology's shrinking of the globe and the corresponding expansion of knowledge gave Douglass hope about "the inevitable downfall of slavery." Perhaps Douglass also sensed a quickening crucible. The Mexican-American War brought the slave question to a fevered boil: with potentially millions of new acres captured from Mexico, would these territories be free or slave? David Wilmot's "Proviso" aimed to make any new territory gained from Mexico free; some of his congressional colleagues had other ideas.[13] The Compromise of 1850 temporarily defused the crucible, but only for four short years. With passage of the Kansas-Nebraska Act in 1854, war drums could be heard across the North and South.

That act and its adjudication of the slave question through popular sovereignty awakened a Springfield, Illinois, attorney. Stephen Douglas and Abraham Lincoln would eventually square off across Illinois in seven lengthy and memorable debates, the question of slavery in the territories animating that debate. Not surprisingly, the Declaration and its meaning was at the center of arguably the most famous political debates in American history. Before the Lincoln-Douglas debates took place in the late summer of 1858, the Dred Scott case was adjudicated by the US Supreme Court in March 1857. Chief

Justice Roger Taney, writing infamously for the 7-2 majority, concluded that Blacks, both free and enslaved, "had no rights which the white man was bound to respect."[14] More relevant to my purpose is some of the legal reasoning used to reach that conclusion. According to Kate Masur, "Taney insisted that no one could have imagined free African Americans as citizens when the nation was founded. . . . Taney confidently claimed that the nation's founders never meant for the Declaration to apply to people of African descent."[15]

Three months later, and more than a year before the debates with Lincoln got underway, Stephen Douglas could hardly contain himself in a speech delivered in Lincoln's adopted hometown of Springfield. If "perfect equality" were to exist between Black men and white men, Douglas conjectured, not only would all slaves be set free, but they could vote, outvote any white minority, and also run for any political office—including president. But what really worried "The Little Giant" was a far more explosive civil right: "If their [Republicans'] interpretation of the Declaration of Independence is correct, . . . we shall be compelled . . . to go one step further: repeal all laws making any distinction whatever on account of race and color, and authorize negroes to marry white women on an equality with white men (immense cheering)."[16] Douglas didn't need to specify "negro men"—but he certainly felt compelled to specify "white women." The fevered nightmare of generations of mostly Southern white men would animate countless lynch parties—once a slaver's corporeal investment had been depreciated to the point of obsolescence by the Emancipation Proclamation and the Thirteenth Amendment. Unlike the "Negro rapist" of the late nineteenth and early twentieth centuries, the slippery slope of future (legal) interracial sex in 1857 was premised on a consensual and promiscuous white womanhood. That womanhood would need careful surveillance and protection in the post-Reconstruction era. Later still, interracial sex would be placed at the center of a communist conspiracy designed to diminish the collective cognitive capacity of the nation. Meanwhile, white men kept having sex (consensual and otherwise) with Black women.

No doubt Lincoln had listened to Douglas in Springfield. A few short weeks later he raised this question in a speech he delivered in Chicago: "I should like to know, if taking this old Declaration of Independence, which declares that all men are equal upon principle, and making exceptions to it, where will it stop? If one man says it does not mean a negro, why may not another man say it does not mean another man? If the Declaration is not the truth, let us get the statute book in which we find it and tear it out."[17]

At Galesburg, during their fifth debate on October 7, 1858, Douglas replied directly to Lincoln's July 1857 challenge, "I should like to know." The Little Giant didn't mince words: "I tell you that this Chicago doctrine of Lincoln's declaring that the negro and the white man are made equal by the Declaration of Independence and by Divine Providence is a monstrous heresy. The signers of the Declaration of Independence never dreamed of the negro when they were writing that document. They referred to white men, to men of European birth and European descent, when they declared the equality of all men."[18] Douglas's proof for his claim came from three facts: Jefferson continued to own slaves; all of the original thirteen colonies "were slaveholding colonies"; and so the signers of the Declaration represented constituencies who approved of the practice.

As Masur argues, "Lincoln needed to tread carefully. The Democrats were poised to construe anything he said as advocacy of interracial sex."[19] Earlier in the debates Lincoln had stated, "I do not understand that because I do not want a negro woman for a slave I must necessarily want her for a wife (cheers and laughter). My understanding is that I can just let her alone. I am now in my fiftieth year, and I certainly never have had a black woman for either a slave or a wife."[20] A clever response, to be sure. But Lincoln's retort carefully skirted the real issue: Black men having sex with white women, not the other way around. Democrats couldn't be bothered with white men having sex with Black women. And so the pre-abolitionist Lincoln and the proslavery Douglas both understood that the Declaration's "All men" being created equal led very quickly in the public's imagination to the bedroom.

While Lincoln and Douglas performed their hermeneutical dance around the state of Illinois in the summer and fall of 1858, the latter won the battle, but Lincoln won the war. Just five short years later, Lincoln's 269-word speech at Gettysburg enshrined his view of the Declaration before a war-weary nation. It's a view that still holds sway three centuries on.

Some of the arguments changed immediately following the Civil War. In surveying several Southern newspapers following Appomattox and the summer of 1865, and the impending abolition of slavery via the Thirteenth Amendment, I was curious to see how the nation's newspapers editorialized. In Columbus, Ohio, hardly a hotbed of proslavery fervor, the *Statesman* featured an argument familiar to twenty-first-century ears: "Where the orator is an Abolitionist, the declaration that 'all men are created equal' will serve as the foundation for a grandiloquent oration, wherein the Black man will be made to figure almost exclusively." White men were here understood as excluded in the syllogism. Furthermore, a new part of the Declaration entered public argument: "And the declaration that to secure 'life, liberty, and the pursuit of happiness' 'Governments are instituted among men, deriving their just powers from the consent of the governed,' will be ignored, unless it can be twisted so as to have reference to the Black man alone."[21] With federal occupation across the South, and with the citizenship status of countless Johnny Rebs in limbo, there was no "consent of the governed." This argument was specified further by several writers, who began using Jefferson's bill of particulars against King George III to argue that they were now the real colonials. The *Hinds County Gazette* in Mississippi wrote, "We regret that we cannot now enjoy the 4th of July—that our veneration for the day has passed away. . . . Who can love a country that has plundered and devastated one of its sections—now holds eight millions of its citizens in a state of vassalage—has forcibly taken from them their wealth—has destroyed the market for their chief agricultural production—loads them with the heaviest rates of taxation known to civilization or uncivilization, and yet does not permit them, in any form, to participate in the government?"[22] The *Vicksburg Daily Times* could only ask "by what strange freak of national lunacy the negro has been permitted to monopolize the Fourth of July."[23]

Several newspapers tried to maintain the line of reasoning popularized by Douglas, that the original intent of the founders was that "all men" meant white men only. Not surprisingly, other editorials used the North's victory and the end of slavery to rub it in. From Alton, Illinois, the same Mississippi River city infamous for the murder of newspaper editor Elijah P. Lovejoy, the *Telegraph* was eager to hear the Declaration read in South Carolina, "not as it has heretofore been done in that tory and rebel State, as a collection of mere abstract sentences, but as declaring living practical truths, which must hereafter exert a controlling influence over the people and become the basis of the civil government of even that proud, overbearing, domineering and fire-eating state."[24] Free-staters like Illinois might plausibly gloat in the war's aftermath, but we know that the "hereafter" of the *Telegraph*'s editorial would last a mere two decades.

But as Reconstruction ended and the South looked to repeal the gains of the remarkable legislation of that period, the meaning of key phrases in the Declaration evolved yet again. Southern state constitutions were rewritten in the late nineteenth and early twentieth centuries with one principal aim: disenfranchising Black voters. The *Richmond Dispatch*, for example, claimed that nothing in the Declaration forbade state legislatures from disenfranchising its erstwhile Black voters. Jefferson's "inalienable right" was, they argued, not a right to vote. Furthermore, "if the people of the Southern

States have become convinced that the elective franchise in the hands of vicious and ignorant citizens is destructive of their rights to life, liberty, and the pursuit of happiness, the Declaration of Independence itself" warrants such measures.[25] The *Virginian-Pilot* offered a different argument: the Declaration certainly allowed for Blacks to govern themselves—but not a "highly civilized enlightened and sensitive people." For an "infinitely lower people" to try and govern their betters was "the political creed of the devil."[26]

While some still clung to the idea that "all men" did not include Black US Americans—a status created by the Fourteenth Amendment—that argument increasingly found less public expression. Regardless of Jefferson and the founders' intent, the matter had been codified in federal law, thus, as the *Chicago Tribune* wrote, "fully vindicat[ing]" an expansive reading of "all men."[27] Massachusetts senator Charles Sumner understood the fulfillment of the Declaration's promises in the election of Mississippi senator Hiram Revels: "Today we make the Declaration a reality. . . . The Declaration was only half established by Independence. The greatest duty remained behind. In assuring the equal rights of all we complete the work."[28] Of course, once federal troops and the Freedman's Bureau fled north, Southern states quickly enacted segregation laws designed to (re)create its vaunted "way of life," a separate and superior society in which "all men" might have been created equal but were second-class citizens in practice.

For some Black writers and organizations, though, the matter of "all men" had been decisively settled in their favor; if the Declaration's promises had not yet been fully redeemed, the process had begun. Perhaps it's not surprising to see the Declaration's language show up in some unexpected places, most notably Marcus Garvey's United Negro Improvement Association (UNIA). Garvey's organization, international in scope and defiantly separatist in rhetorical practice, grew very quickly following the close of World War I. By the summer of 1920, the organization could boast of an international convention held in Harlem and attended by more than twenty thousand people. Over the course of a month, the UNIA hammered out a "Declaration of Rights of the Negro Peoples of the World." The first item of its declaration read, "Be it known to all men that whereas all men are created equal and entitled to the rights of life, liberty and the pursuit of happiness, and because of this, we the duly elected representatives of the Negro peoples of the world, invoking the aid of the just and Almighty God, do declare all men, women and children of our blood throughout the world free denizens, and do claim them as free citizens of Africa, the Motherland of all Negroes."[29] It was a whopper of a declaration; it was also a declaration grounded explicitly on the one recorded 144 years earlier in Philadelphia.

James Cone's claim that Black nationalist groups such as the UNIA "do not define their significance and purpose as a people by appealing to the Declaration of Independence" and other sacred civic documents might ring true, but in this case Garvey and his acolytes grounded their declaration in words very familiar to Americans—white and Black.[30] If the opening wasn't explicit enough, the fifty-fourth and closing item brought the UNIA's declaration full circle: "We want all men to know that we shall maintain and contend for the freedom and equality of every man, woman and child of our race with our lives, our fortune and our sacred honor." The irony of employing a document that many in the eighteenth and nineteenth centuries had read as a proslavery document was likely not lost on the UNIA delegates; they now turned the tables to make their declaration, if not a Black supremacist document, certainly a Black separatist one.

Forty-six years later, another Black separatist organization employed a similar rhetorical tactic: in the Black Panther Party's platform and program, Huey P. Newton and Bobby Seale outlined "What We Want, What We Believe" in ten concise points. What makes the document interesting to us isn't their call for freeing all Black prisoners or exempting Black men from military service, but how the platform closes: following their final point, the document then reprints, in full, the entire preamble to the Declaration of Independence.[31] I was initially flummoxed as to what rhetorical function was fulfilled by the inclusion. Unlike the UNIA, which used key Declaration phrases to cast its ambitions anew, the Newton-Seale document doesn't use the preamble to comment on the Black Panther agenda in an explicit way; it's apparently just a cut-and-paste.

A closer look, though, indicates how they wanted readers to understand their use of the iconic American text. Only two sentences in the preamble are italicized in the platform; both of them deal with the right to "abolish" or "throw off" extant government in order to "institute a new government" and "to provide new guards for their future security." In other words, by italicizing and thus highlighting this part of the preamble, the Black Panthers ground their program of Black nationalism squarely on the premise that the federal government had in fact "become destructive" of the ends of life, liberty, and the pursuit of happiness. The Panthers remind us that the Declaration was in word and deed a revolutionary text. Malcolm X reminds us too, a fact with which Newton and Seale were, no doubt, very familiar. Following his formal March 1964 break with the Nation of Islam, Malcolm delivered a version of his "Ballot or Bullet" speech before the Militant Labor Forum in New York City. "If George Washington didn't get independence for this country non-violently," he stated, "and if Patrick Henry didn't come up with a non-violent statement, and you taught me to look upon them as patriots and heroes, then it's time for you to realize that I have studied your books as well." Furthermore, 22 million American Negroes did not care, like the nation's founders, that the odds of victory might be long. They were "ready, willing and justified to do the same thing today to bring about independence for our people that your forefathers did to bring about independence for your people."[32] Malcolm was not preaching some back-to-Africa bullshit preferred by the racists of the American Colonization Society or the resettlement grift of the Black Star Line of Garveyism. No, this was revolution on American soil with Black-owned munitions—justified by American documents.

Speaking of revolution, one of the most revolutionary documents ever produced on civil rights by a presidential administration was Harry Truman's President's Committee on Civil Rights (PCCR). As Steven R. Goldzwig documents, it reads like a blueprint of where the nation was headed as the short civil rights movement neared.[33] Less than one year after the committee was formed, Truman had their report; it was titled "To Secure These Rights." Truman did not miss the parallel: "I notice that the title of this report is taken from the Declaration of Independence. I hope this Committee has given us as broad a document as that—an American charter of human freedom in our time." Indeed, they had. The nation was still ten years away from its first piece of federal civil rights legislation, but the recommendations of the PCCR would be seen as very radical, especially by the Deep South. Not surprisingly, the Declaration was used to round some of its edges: "There is no essential conflict between freedom and government. Bills of rights restrain government from abridging individual civil liberties, while government itself by sound legislative policies protects citizens against the aggressions of others seeking to push their freedoms too far. Thus in the words of the Declaration of Independence: 'Man is endowed by his Creator with certain inalienable rights. Among these are life, liberty, and the pursuit of happiness. To secure these rights, *governments are instituted among men.*'"[34] The country waited to learn what those "sound policies" might be.

One of the policies not recommended by the PCCR was the immediate integration of public schools in the Deep South; even in 1947, such a possibility was too radical. And so when the US Supreme Court unanimously adjudicated the five school segregation cases constituting *Brown v. Topeka Board of Education*, seven short years later, the backlash was swift, extensive, and lethal. The White Citizens' Councils formed just months later in Indianola, Mississippi, and spread rapidly across the former Confederacy. Because it was nine members of the Court forcing southerners to change their "way of life," the analogies to King George III were legion. Mississippi's John Bell Williams railed to his colleagues in the US House of Representatives that this ruling did not represent the "consent of the governed."[35] Left implied was that white southerners were not obliged to follow the law. The state's arch-racist senator, James O. Eastland, went a step further, telling audiences of Citizens' Councils that they were in fact obligated to disobey it. The justifications for disobedience weren't simply that nine federal judges shouldn't speak for the South—that was just one part of the issue. Far bigger in the southern imagination was the old Douglas canard: the "all men" of the Declaration were all white men.[36] The executive director of the councils, Robert Patterson, told an audience in Chattanooga that "modern propagandists" had misled the nation, that "the races are not equal when judged by the white man's standards" and "the negro as a race does not measure up to the white man's standards in a white society."[37] Like Douglas, Patterson also claimed to be angered by the inevitability that black men would soon be having sex with his white daughters, projection being one helluva drug. The legal mastermind of the councils was Brookhaven jurist Tom Brady (rhymes with *daddy*). Like Patterson, he urged Negroes to honor the Fourth of July, since "they could [then] develop within the framework of an existing civilization bought with the sweat and blood of members of the white race."[38] The irony is palpable: that civilization had been purchased, literally, with generations of Black bodies, but the clueless paternalism of the councils was ever-present.

Countering the rhetoric of the pro-segregationists at every turn, Dr. Martin Luther King Jr. and scores of other speakers wielded the text of the Declaration to great effect. In fact, the anthem of the short civil rights movement, King's "I Have a Dream" address, featured its words from the outset, cast metaphorically as a form of currency: "When the architects of our republic wrote the magnificent words of the Constitution and the Declaration of Independence, they were signing a promissory note to which every American was to fall heir. This note was a promise that all men—yes, Black men as well as white men—would be guaranteed the unalienable rights of life, liberty and the pursuit of happiness."[39] King and other movement leaders knew that they had some wind at their backs at the March on Washington; one very encouraging breeze came from President Kennedy, who on June 11 had declared on national television that civil rights was a "moral issue." Furthermore, and invoking the Declaration: "This nation was founded by men of many nations and backgrounds. It was founded on the principle that all men are created equal."[40] Just a few hours later, from a honeysuckle hedge in North Jackson, Mississippi, Byron de la Beckwith shot and killed Medgar Evers in his driveway. Beckwith was an officeholder in the Leflore County Sons of the American Revolution. Before Evers could even be buried with full military honors at Arlington National Cemetery, George McGovern had this to say: "We may be better able to comprehend the message of Birmingham and Jackson in 1963 if we see it as a continuance of the forces unleashed at Philadelphia and Boston in 1776. For it seems to me that the Negro is saying to the white man: '[I]f we are not accepted as your brothers, you cannot hold the birthright of America. If we are not free and equal, you cannot be free and equal. If we are not full members of society, your pursuit of happiness is endangered.' . . . The Negro, in short, is echoing the words which Adams and Paine and Jefferson dispatched to King George and to their fellow colonists nearly two centuries ago."[41]

In closing, I should mention the Trump administration's ill-fated and tardily conceived *1776 Project*. It's tempting to dismiss the entire effort as a racist rejoinder to the *1619 Project*. In an administration whose support for white supremacy was unapologetic for four long years, that's easy to do. But in reading their report, issued on January 18, just two days before Trump fled to his perdition in Palm Beach and criminal indictments dizzying in their specifics, one paragraph caught my eye; it reads: "The foundation of our Republic planted the seeds of the death of slavery in America. The Declaration's unqualified proclamation of human equality flatly contradicted the existence of human bondage and, along with the Constitution's compromises understood in light of that proposition, set the stage for abolition. Indeed, the movement to abolish slavery *that first began in the United States* led the way in bringing about the end of legal slavery."[42] We can quibble with the claim that we were "first"; the United States has a thing with being number one. We weren't. We might also quibble with "unqualified." As I've documented here, many felt "all men" was unqualified precisely because it didn't need to be; to say that "all white men were created equal" was too obvious to need spelling out.

But this claim by the *1776 Project* is pure Douglass. Those "seeds," though, were cultivated over 250 long years, and in doing that work many people lost their lives and their livelihoods. What the *1776 Project* report refuses to say is that there was nothing foreordained, or in keeping with the metaphor, "natural," about slavery's end in the United States. We don't need Ken Burns to remind us that the country fought a long civil war over that seeded furrow; both sides of its channels are still caked with the blood of more than 600,000 young men. What the language of the *1776 Project* report does suggest, though, is that a meaning of that document is beginning to solidify. Yes, that "all men" meant all white and Black men. Perhaps that "all men" meant all white and Black and Brown women, too. Perhaps one day even that "all men" means all genders, all sexualities, all religions, and all nationalities.

Perhaps.

NOTES

1. Howell, "Declaration of Independence"; Lucas, "Rhetorical Ancestry."

2. Thomas Jefferson, draft of Declaration of Independence, https://www.loc.gov/exhibits/declara/ruffdrft.html.

3. Hannah-Jones et al., *1619 Project*, 14.

4. Johnson, "Taxation No Tyranny."

5. Banneker to Jefferson, in Kendricks and Levitt, *Afro-American Voices*, 45–46.

6. A Republican, *North Carolina Journal* (Halifax, NC), July 4, 1796, 4.

7. "A Philadelphia Negro Condemns Discriminatory Proposals, 1813," in Aptheker, *Documentary History*, 61, 62.

8. David Walker, *Walker's Appeal, in Four Articles; Together with a Preamble, to the Coloured Citizens of the World, but in Particular, and Very Expressly, to Those of the United States of America, Written in Boston, State of Massachusetts*, September 28, 1829, https://docsouth.unc.edu/nc/walker/walker.html.

9. William Lloyd Garrison, "Letter to the Public," January 1, 1831, https://teachingamericanhistory.org/document/to-the-public/.

10. Blight, *Frederick Douglass*, 230.

11. Osborne, "American Negro's Fourth of July, 1832," in Aptheker, *Documentary History*, 137.

12. Frederick Douglass, "What to the Slave Is the Fourth of July?," July 5, 1852, https://www.loc.gov/resource/sn84026366/1852-07-09/ed-1/?sp=1&st=gallery&loclr=blogser.

13. E. Foner, *Fiery Trial*, 51–52.

14. Masur, *Until Justice Be Done*, 256.

15. Masur, *Until Justice Be Done*, 259.

16. Stephen A. Douglas, "Speech," *Ottawa Free Trader* (IL), June 27, 1857, 1.

17. Abraham Lincoln, Speech of July 10, 1858, https://quod.lib.umich.edu/l/lincoln/lincoln2/1:526?rgn=div1;view=fulltext.

18. See https://www.nps.gov/liho/learn/historyculture/debate5.htm.

19. Masur, *Until Justice Be Done*, 263.

20. Abraham Lincoln, Speech of September 18, 1858, https://quod.lib.umich.edu/l/lincoln/lincoln3/1:20.1?rgn=div2;view=fulltext.

21. "The Day We Celebrate," 2.

22. *Hinds County Gazette*, June 29, 1866, 2.

23. *Vicksburg Daily Times* (reprinted from the *Richmond Times*), July 12, 1866, 2.

24. "The Fourth in South Carolina," *Alton Telegraph*, July 2, 1865, 2.

25. "Dressed Down," *Richmond Dispatch* (quoting the *Buffalo Evening Times*), August 23, 1900, 4.

26. "The South and Imperialism," *Virginian-Pilot*, July 26, 1900, 4.

27. *Chicago Tribune*, July 2, 1866, 2.

28. Quoted in Dray, *Capitol Men*, 72.

29. United Negro Improvement Association, "Declaration of Rights of the Negro Peoples of the World," https://historymatters.gmu.edu/d/5122/.

30. Cone, *Martin and Malcolm and America*, 9.

31. See "What We Want, What We Believe," in P. Foner, *Black Panthers Speak*, 2–4.

32. Malcolm X, "The Ballot or the Bullet," https://mronline.org/2022/07/11/speech-the-black-revolution-is-part-of-world-wide-struggle-malcolm-x-1964/.

33. Goldzwig, "Inaugurating the Second Reconstruction," 83–113.

34. President's Committee on Civil Rights, "To Secure These Rights," https://www.trumanlibrary.gov/library/to-secure-these-rights.

35. John Bell Williams, *Interposition: The Barrier Against Tyranny*, January 25, 1956, https://egrove.olemiss.edu/citizens_pamph/44/.

36. Eastland, "Speech."

37. Robert Patterson, "The Truth Cries Out: An Address to the Annual Leadership Conference of the Citizens' Councils of America," Chattanooga, Tennessee, January 8, 1966, https://catalog.libraries.psu.edu/catalog/36151832.

38. Quoted in "Judge Tom Brady's 'Black Monday,'" *McComb Enterprise Journal*, September 2, 1954, 2.

39. Martin Luther King Jr., "I Have a Dream" (speech), August 28, 1963, https://www.npr.org/2010/01/18/122701268/i-have-a-dream-speech-in-its-entirety.

40. John F. Kennedy, "Address to the Nation on Civil Rights," June 11, 1963, https://www.jfklibrary.org/learn/about-jfk/historic-speeches/televised-address-to-the-nation-on-civil-rights.

41. George McGovern, "The Continuing American Revolution and the American Negro" (speech), June 15, 1963, New York City, https://www.jfklibrary.org/asset-viewer/archives/BMPP#id9.

42. "1776 Project," https://trumpwhitehouse.archives.gov/wp-content/uploads/2021/01/The-Presidents-Advisory-1776-Commission-Final-Report.pdf.

BIBLIOGRAPHY

Aptheker, Herbert, ed. *A Documentary History of the Negro People in the United States*. New York: Citadel, 1951.

Blight, David W. *Frederick Douglass: Prophet of Freedom*. New York: Simon and Schuster, 2018.

Cone, James H. *Martin and Malcolm and America: A Dream or a Nightmare*. Maryknoll, NY: Orbis, 1991.

Dray, Philip. *Capitol Men: The Epic Story of Reconstruction Told Through the Lives of the First Black Congressmen*. New York: Mariner, 2008.

James O. Eastland. Speech before the Association of Citizens' Councils of America, Jackson, MS, December 1, 1955, James O. Eastland Papers, University of Mississippi, Oxford.

Foner, Eric. *The Fiery Trial: Abraham Lincoln and American Slavery*. New York: W. W. Norton, 2011.

Foner, Philip S., ed. *The Black Panthers Speak*. Cambridge, MA: Da Capo, 1995.

Goldzwig, Steven R. "Inaugurating the Second Reconstruction: President Truman's Committee on Civil Rights." In *Civil Rights Rhetoric and the American Presidency*, edited by James Arnt Aune and Enrique D. Rigsby, 83–113. College Station: Texas A&M University Press, 2005.

Hannah-Jones, Nikole, Caitlin Roper, Ilena Silverman, and Jake Silverstein, eds. *The 1619 Project: A New Origin Story*. New York: One World, 2019.

Howell, Wilbur Samuel. "The Declaration of Independence: Some Adventures with America's Political Masterpiece." *Quarterly Journal of Speech* 62 (1976): 221–33.
Johnson, Samuel. "Taxation No Tyranny." In *The Works of Samuel Johnson*, 14:93–144. Troy, NY: Pafraets & Company, 1913. https://www.samueljohnson.com/tnt.html.
Kendricks, Ralph, and Claudette Levitt, eds. *Afro-American Voices 1770s–1970s*. New York: Oxford University Press, 1970.
Lucas, Stephen E. "The Rhetorical Ancestry of the Declaration of Independence." *Rhetoric and Public Affairs* 1 (1998): 143–84.
Masur, Kate. *Until Justice Be Done: America's First Civil Rights Movement, from the Revolution to Reconstruction*. New York: Norton, 2021.

10

FROM BLACK LIVES MATTER TO THE SYRIAN REVOLUTION: HOW DO "WE THE PEOPLE" RENDER OUR STRUGGLES VISIBLE?

Noor Ghazal Aswad

On July 3, 2020, ahead of the flashy fireworks, military flyover, and presidential speech planned by President Trump at South Dakota's Black Hills in celebration of Independence Day, protestors blocked the access road to Mount Rushmore with a line of vans. The activists, made up mostly of Native Americans, cried out, "Respect our right to exist or expect our resistance. . . . We are orphans crying in the night and we will keep making noise until they hear us."[1] The South Dakota National Guard arrived an hour later, arrested the protestors, and declared the gathering an "unlawful assembly." Similar protests occurred in Washington, DC; Chicago; Los Angeles; and other cities and towns across the country. While the protests in South Dakota centered around the stolen lands of the Black Hills from the Lakota Sioux, those in Washington near the National Mall concentrated on Black lives and the irony that the Independence Day holiday "doesn't really mean anything when Black people weren't free on July 4th and those same liberties weren't afforded to us."[2] In Chicago, Rabbi Michael Ben Yosef took a knee in silence for eight minutes and forty-six seconds, in memory of George Floyd, the African American man unjustly murdered by police. He later argued that the Declaration failed to actualize the rights of minorities: "Independence for people of color has not been part of our livelihood. We're constantly murdered, harassed because of police brutality all over the country. The concept of freedom does not seem to come to our doorstep, even though we've been here 400 years."[3]

This rhetoric reflects a growing popular sentiment toward Independence Day following the reckoning on racial equality in the United States.[4]

George Floyd's death and the multitude of Black people killed wrongfully before and after him have created in some a reluctance to celebrate July 4th, the day in which the nation's founding document was signed.[5] Those citing the hypocritical celebration of freedom are driven by the conviction that the "we" in the Declaration was narrowly defined and never meant to include either Indigenous peoples or the enslaved Africans of the time and continues to offer an exclusionary vision of the nation.[6] Black Lives Matter activists and scholars insist that the Declaration be reread through the prism of the United States as a nation embedded in structures of racism, testifying to how the "we" passage in the Declaration rings hollow amid the country's indifference to recurring racist killings.[7]

This chapter opens up this lens through attention to the Declaration of Independence's applicability as a model for challenging dominant power structures in contemporary global struggles for justice and equality. By tracing revolutionary narratives from the Syrian revolution, this chapter highlights the document's diminishing relevance as a tool for transnational activism, suggesting its ideals may no longer adequately address contemporary struggles against colonialism and authoritarianism. Instead, grassroots revolutionaries shift their attention to grassroots political resistance within the United States rooted in the specific experiences of marginalized communities, as opposed to exclusionary discourses perpetuated by those in power. In sum, it addresses the implications of the Syrian case for redefining and reimagining the ideals enshrined in the Declaration. By emphasizing the transformative potential of contemporary revolutionary movements, even those that emerge from different traditions and express different objectives, these social movements offer new possibilities for realizing the principles of freedom, equality, and democracy in ways that were not envisioned by the framers of the Declaration.

With this in mind, the chapter develops over two sections. First, it traces the history of revolutionary activism in Syria to establish a short history of the United States' links to democracy in Syria. Looking to the Syrian revolution of today, I suggest Syrians instituted a different kind of "peoplehood," distinct from dominant notions of a homogenous "people" in the Declaration of Independence and looking toward the larger space of lived experience of those struggling for racial justice in the United States. Second, it anchors the analysis in the sociopolitical subjectivities of Syrians in resistance, drawing on their visual, verbal, and material rhetorics to trace the ways in which the Black Lives Matter movement constitutes a resource for the legitimation of their own revolutionary politics. In doing so, they forge an imagined spatiality in which people around the world are central to a global revolutionary project. In this section are identified the interconnected rhetorical strategies used to make struggles relational in urgent and compelling terms: breath and suffocation, strategic antiracism, and the affective "excess" of the United States. This rhetoric creates a relationality unconstrained by territoriality and state-based sovereignty, while acknowledging the commonalities of resistance. I conclude by contemplating the diminution of the Declaration's rhetorical power in the struggles of Indigenous people and what translocal calls of solidarity teach us about how those on the path to self-determination choose to produce claims for freedom.

Questioning the Timeless Appeal of the Declaration of Independence

Public perception of the Declaration of Independence and the integrity of the US American polity has not always been as negative, either in the United States or elsewhere, as it is now. Valued as one of the great documents of democracy in the United States, historically the Declaration was not only a powerful symbol for those asserting independence from other states but also served as an inspiration for Indigenous revolutionaries of anti-imperial and anti-colonial secession movements around the world.[8] However, despite the historical "universal appeal" of the Declaration of Independence and its proliferation and variegation around the world, a closer look at contemporary social movements in the Middle East and North Africa reveal its limitations in mobilizing for overtly political purposes, especially when struggles are intersectional in nature. Taking the ongoing Syrian revolution as a case study, this chapter shows how Syrian appeals for independence, equality, and liberty were made less in terms of the founding documents of the United States and more in terms of local, Indigenous rhetoric of those in struggle. Arguably, this speaks to a disenchantment with the myth of the United States as a Shining City on a Hill and the international liberal order led by the United States, but also to an erosion of faith in US American constitutionalism amid the racial and economic policies pursued by US American elites.[9]

Although the language of the Declaration of Independence does not appear verbatim in the rhetoric of the Syrian revolutionaries of 2011, the Syrian quest for democracy has historically been intertwined with US American democracy. During World War I, Syrian Arabs who were part of the Arab Revolt fought alongside the Allies against the Ottomans.[10] After the end of the war, a wave of new states embraced postcolonial independence and constitutions upon the cinders of the Ottoman Empire—along with new anthems and flags—as markers of self-determination. Syrian Arabs embraced President Woodrow Wilson's Fourteen Points and visions of a new world order centered on conceptions of self-determination. Although the term "Syrian Arabs" may appear exclusionary, at the time the designation of Syria as an Arab nation was meant to be inclusive, with the intention of uniting Arab speakers of different faiths. Armenians residing in Syria were expected to return to their ancestral homelands, and Kurds (who now predominantly reside in northeastern Syria) were in a distant frontier zone that the King-Crane Commission of 1919, a visiting US American committee of inquiry into the disposition of areas within the former Ottoman Empire and their readiness for independence, never visited.

Rashid Rida, president of the Syrian Arab Congress, wrote in the most widely read newspaper of the day, *Al Manar* (The Lighthouse), that Syrians welcomed "Dr. Wilson's lofty principles of freedom for great and small nations alike, their independence based on equal rights, and the renunciation of the politis of conquest and colonialism."[11] Interestingly, President Wilson's *The State: Elements of Historical and Practical Politics* was considered the leading political textbook of the time and was immensely popular among Syrian politicians.

The Syrian congress presented its resolutions for a new era of constitutional government to Wilson's King-Crane Commission. Arab nationalists were inspired by the example of US American federalism and felt it was the best solution for creating pan-Arab unity.[12] In a bid to build their own sovereign state and establish their capacity for self-rule, on March 8, 1920, the Syrian congress issued its Declaration of Independence, in the name of the people of Greater Syria.[13] Those included were not only Sunni Arabs but Jewish, Greek Orthodox, Shi'ites, and Christian leaders, all of whom pledged allegiance to the constitutional monarchy and King Faisal bin Ali Al-Hashemi. Even as the threat of French invasion loomed, Syrians wrote a 147-article constitution, the most democratic to date in the Middle East, modeled on its Ottoman predecessor and US American federalism.[14]

This fragile yet pivotal moment in twentieth-century Arab politics was to be short-lived. The constitution was never fully ratified. Four months later, Syrians were stripped of their sovereignty and their attempts at democracy dashed. Britain and France, worried that a free democratic regime in Syria threatened their claim to colonial rule elsewhere, reneged on their promise to support Arab independence. Although the King-Crane Commission had established a road for democracy in Syria, US support for Syrian self-determination proved to be just "an empty gesture."[15] Imperialist mapmaking carved up the Middle East under the secret Sykes-Picot Agreement against the plainly formulated wishes of the people.[16] Popular protests flared across Syria to avert outright colonization. But on July 20, 1920, French troops entered Damascus, and decades of colonial rule ensued. After momentous struggles against French colonial occupation and a world war explicitly fought on the basis of preserving international democracy, France withdrew from Syria in 1945. There was a brief stint of democracy followed by a succession of coups and countercoups, after which Syria was ruled by the dictatorship of the Assad family that continues to this day.

Under the Assad dictatorship, Syria became a totatalitarian autocracy, where civil society was severely curtailed and Syrians faced regular mistreatment by the *mukhabarat*, an increasingly formidable mini-state of police and security forces. Under the Ba'ath regime's emergency martial laws of 1963, freedom of expression, freedom of religion, freedom to protest, and freedom to assemble became illegal. After the brutal Hama massacre of the 1980s, in which 25,000–40,000 people were killed,[17] frustration built up for decades. But it wasn't until the torture of schoolchildren in the desert town of Daraa for anti-government graffiti on the walls of a school that revolution was ignited. In 2011, in tandem with the transnational revolutionary wave emerging across the region, Syrians went out into the streets, at first timidly but slowly gaining strength in numbers and in agency, chanting for their freedom "Ash-shab yurid isqat an-nizam" (The people want to bring down the regime). In many ways, "the people want" mirrors "we the people" found in the Declaration of Independence, as Syrians created spaces from which to demand their independence from the tyrannical state, in the face of its abuse of their unalienable rights for life, liberty, and the pursuit of happiness. In this case, the mysterious entity of "the people" referred to a unified resistance against a repressive state apparatus, a resistance that cut across class, political, religious, ethnic, and gender divisions. The "people" were Muslims, Arabs, Kurds, Christians, and Alawites, secular and religious, side by side speaking "not in one voice, but millions."[18] A revolutionary consciousness emerged, of new personal identities instead of inherited ones. Syrians began to revive the original names of places that had been renamed after Assad took power. Soon, revolutionaries raised an "independence flag,"[19] one from times past, which had an additional star and supplanted the red stripes of the Syrian Arab Republic's flag with green. They demanded the lifting of restrictions on freedom of expression, release of prisoners of conscience, legalization of political parties outside of the Ba'ath party, and repeal of the emergency law. And eventually, as the noose of the state tightened around them, they demanded the downfall of a tyrannical government.

While the Syrian activists of the 1920s directly invoked Wilson's principles and US American protection of civil rights and equality of citizens, the Syrian activists of 2011 took a different approach to both how they, as a people, made their claims to autonomy and even how they defined "the people." For them, "the people" were a collectivity of subjects brought together by an acknowledgment of how they were all enmeshed in the same system that oppressed each and every one of them. In doing so, they challenged Western liberal articulations of "the people" predicated on cultural and political homogeneity toward what Michael Hardt and Antoni Negri have defined as a "multitude"—that is, a group composed of innumerable internal differences that cannot be reduced to a single identity but are united by what they have in common, which allows them to communicate and act together against an extraneous entity.[20] The people are on the ground, both figurativly and literally, reshaping the meaning, history, and functions of "the people" as it is normally understood.

This can be seen in individual protestors dancing *dabkeh* (a folkloric circle dance called "dancing of the feet") in unison amid the raining of bombs: their bodies would become in sync, separate but together. The representational force of this performance was powerful: one activist referred to themselves as "كتلة بشرية"—one human mass or body politic, even if these bodies do not have a singular voice.[21] Though the protests were infectious in nature, they were highly localized in nature, crafting multitudes of "new identities" out of the Arab nationalism that had suppressed the internal diversity among Syrians.[22]

Syrians were rearticulating "the people" as a multitude, tearing down the "wall of fear" instituted by those in power without renouncing their own autonomy and difference. Modeling understandings of the "multitude," Omar Aziz, the renowned Syrian intellectual and anarchist dissident, insisted on avoiding the terms "the people" or "the masses"; he preferred the term "humans," seeing the former as hegemonic terms coined by authority as part of a homogenizing cultural force for maintaining their power.[23] In what is characterized by Walter Mignolo as a "delinking,"[24] Syrians took a term used by those in power and remade it into one that spoke to liberation. As a collective entity, Syrian revolutionaries experienced a "direct collision with the notion of 'identity' . . . and [what] constitutes 'Us'"—realizing that the "us" did not encompass the powers that were supposed to protect the people.[25] This started a decolonial rhetoric that concretized their individual character and separated "the people" from their Assadist ruler, evident for instance in the popular chant "He who kills his people is a traitor." The Syrian American activist Amal Hanano describes Syrians' rhetorical imagination of "the people" in this way: "The story of a nation begins and ends with the stories of its people. For over forty years, the authoritarian regime had tried to make the story of Syria, and thus its destiny, the narrative of one person and of one family. When Syrians stood to face the tyrant, his image was shattered into a million pieces that reflected the mulitiplicity of its people."[26]

This wasn't just a matter of words. Bodies were on the line in the face of a massive government crackdown. Syrians took notice of the differences among them and the fact that they were decidedly not a homogenous polity, but they still understood the ways in which they had the capacity for self-determination. Not only this, but with time Syrians nurtured coalitional bonds with the lands on which they lived and, eventually, the lands from which they would be expelled, so much so that the land itself became woven into the very fabric of the revolution.

Relational Ontologies of Breath and Suffocation

After watching the footage of George Floyd pleading for his breath while a police officer pinned his neck to the ground in Minneapolis, the graffiti artist Aziz Asmar had flashbacks of Syrians gasping for breath after sarin gas attacks by the Assad regime. He was inspired to paint Floyd's portrait on the remains of his family's kitchen wall in the city of Binnish, which had been destroyed by the regime's airstrikes. The brightly colored eight-foot mural features Floyd's face, and his last words, "I can't breathe. No to racism," are appended.[27] In an interview, the painter brought to life the scene of George Floyd's murder and how it evoked memories of Syrian suffocation that he had witnessed: "In those hospitals, the victims were crying, and they were asking to breathe. I saw George Floyd pleading with the officer to let him breathe and it reminded me of the way they were killed."[28]

Amid the plethora of images of decimated Syrian cities, the theatricality of the graffiti creates discord with audience expectations as a razed home in a small city in Syria becomes the literal and ideological backdrop for remembering George Floyd. The location of the painting in the middle of a destroyed landscape dramatizes the locality of bodies in crisis and the apocalyptic aftermath of bombing raids. The destruction of life in one place is mapped onto the destruction of life in another; they become strongly identified. Asmar describes the act of painting as one rife with real physical costs and danger: "There are logistical problems. We draw on walls destroyed by bombs. Because of that, it is difficult to draw on them. Sometimes rocks fall on us, and sometimes planes return to bomb the areas in which we are drawing."[29]

As the video of George Floyd's murder went viral, activists in Kafranbel were also taking note. Kafranbel, a small northern town in the Idlib countryside, became an international sensation after global news agencies caught wind of their weekly Friday banners and demonstrations. The group created simple yet eloquent banners to raise awareness about what was happening in Syria and in the hope of reviving the waning attention to the Syrian cause. In many respects, the Syrian revolution has not received the international solidarity or recognition it deserved, and when discussed, it has been obfuscated and mystified in a multitude of ways.[30]

In their intersection of aesthetic experimentation and political activism, the banners exemplify the "embodied process of making solidarity itself."[31] Each banner was hand-made, staged, and signed with the date by the activists who stood behind and around the banner. A calligrapher and translator designed and translated the text from Arabic into multiple languages, such as Turkish, English, Russian, or Chinese, demonstrating not only a media savviness but an ability to think with the interstices between modern and colonial worlds. The locations in which the banners were held were carefully planned, often in public sites of protest or in front of bombed-out buildings. Eventually, when the activists became the target of regime airstrikes and barrel bombs, the photographs were taken in inconspicuous side streets. Because of weak internet service, the activists took pictures of the banners with a Nokia flip phone and sent them to those living outside of Syria to circulate online.[32] As their activism began to generate international attention, giving them access to a wider public audience, the people of Kafranbel put pressure on the activists to stop creating the banners, owing to the conviction that they were the reason for the regime's concentrated air raids on the town. This communication became central to their notion of revolution: the behind-the-scenes operations of the banner-making reveal a drive to initiate a translinguistic and transnational encounter with the world, at great risk to themselves and the people in the town.

On the occasion of George Floyd's murder, the Kafranbel activists reposted an image of a banner made a few years prior in solidarity with Eric

Garner, a Black man who was wrestled to the ground and choked to death on a New York City sidewalk as he rasped, "I can't breathe." The banner, designed by the architect of the Kafranbel banners, Raed Fares, in 2014, states in bold letters: "WE STAND IN SOLIDARITY WITH THE OPPRESSED WHO CANNOT BREATHE."[33] In this case, the re-post was accompanied by a new caption that brought the assassination of Raed Fares in 2018 by extremists and the killing of George Floyd in 2020 into conversation with one another:

> Six years ago, Raed wrote this banner from his city which was under daily bombardment to express his solidarity with a black [*sic*] young man who was killed by the police in New York while he was not armed. Before he was killed, the man was saying, "I cannot breathe." Today, another black man has been killed by Minnesota police, as a policeman put his knee on the neck of the man who was lying on the ground and unable to move, and unable to breathe, and he did not remove his knee until that man had taken his last breath. Our hearts are in solidarity with those on a far-off continent despite our own catastrophes. It burns our hearts and it will not be repeated.[34]

This passage is important for several reasons. The death of George Floyd was a perfect moment to draw attention to the unexpected yet significant parallels with the Syrian liberatory struggle. The novelist Samar Yazbek claims that for Syrians living under the regime, fear was as automatic as breathing; in protesting and allowing themselves to freely express themselves and their revolution, they were breaking free of both of these.[35] Through this juxtaposition, Syrian revolutionaries situate their struggle within the broader context of a global fight for the right to breathe. The theme of suffocation has inspired several public awareness campaigns in Syria, such as the "Do Not Suffocate the Truth" campaign on the anniversary of the Ghouta chemical attack, which stresses the simultaneous denial of breath and memory to those who suffered. As such, although the political heritage and trajectories of the two movements could not be further apart, the "disinterested spectator" is asked to recognize a heterogenous set of subjects based on a shared experience of suffocation. In the absence of obvious racial, ethnic, or geographic kinship, the emotional registers of breath are channeled to indicate the ways in which Raed Fares's, George Floyd's, and Eric Garner's killings are similar. The differences between the three killings are obvious. Nevertheless, these moments created commonality, "despite our own catastrophes."

Analogous experiences of suffocation, their pervasiveness and persistence, are portrayed along the lines of the right to breathe, and breathe freely, as a fundamental human right of *the people.*

Strategic Anti-racism and Affective "Excess" of the United States

Though centered on specific instances of the killing of various Black individuals by the state, these events signal questions of race and historical legacies of slavery. For example, the signifier "Black" locates these killings within their historical, racial, and cultural contexts. The audience is invited to take on the intellectual task of reconsidering the faraway Syrian subject within the history of subjugation of African Americans. The Syrian intellectual and dissident Yassin al-Haj Saleh put this forthrightly and does not mince his words: "Ours is a struggle against racism, though without races."[36] This oxymoronic statement reveals the inherent tension in the conceptualization of the Syrian movement as anti-racist—namely, in its composition of a collective of two historic struggles against racism in which one, however, is "without races." In the same article, this analogy is made explicit: the sovereign state is "busying itself killing Syrian blacks." In this sense, US American slavery is seen to be similar to Assadist authoritarianism in that it depends on the racialization of those it oppresses.

The affinity of the Syrian revolution with questions of race and racism, and the entanglement of Syrians within racial hierarchies, is thus carefully constructed. Though Black Lives Matter does not lend itself to an easy translation to the Syrian context, the rhetoric ventures beyond a shared humanitarian concern with the suffering of others toward a rethinking of political structures writ large and how Syrians have also been subject to a colonial and racialist world system. "Syrian Blacks" implicates Syrians within the hierarchical racialization of the United States and its people, rejecting the individualized subject to instead privilege a construction of "race" within global systems of white supremacy and authoritarianism and the colonized "other." This way of thinking entangles Syrians in racial structures without directly outlining the causal structures of the racialized oppression of individual subjects. The divergent "phenomena" of George Floyd's murder by a white police officer in Minneapolis and Raed Fares's murder by extremists are foregrounded to establish racialized significance for a public so they might understand the events in relation to each other.

Though the rhetoric does not take on the complexity of racial categories in the Syrian context, race is talked about as a non-fixed category attached to political structures. Syria is marked by tyranny toward "the majority"—by and large, Sunni Muslims, who form the majority of the population and are not known for their "otherness," are oppressed by a regime from the Alawite minority sect.[37] Added to this, there is ethnic racism toward Kurdish Syrians, who have historically been exiled from the public space and systematically discriminated against by the regime and by other Syrians. As a minority non-Arab ethnic group, the Kurds had an uneasy relationship with the Assad regime's ideology of Ba'athism, which preached pan-Arab nationalism. Aside from the 120,000 Syrian Kurds stripped of citizenship in 1962, even Kurds with Syrian citizenship face institutional racism. They cannot publish in their language, have cultural festivals, or teach in their language. Admittedly, "ethnic tension" between Arabs and Kurds eventually resulted in the latter splitting from Syrian (Arab) revolutionary groups and an increased marginalization from the wider uprising. As with the previous examples, there are parallels between the racialization of African Americans and Syrians, relying on the commonalities of oppression rather than the specifics of local situations.

For Syrians, connecting their struggle to Black Lives Matter also creates the possibility that their efforts will receive more global attention. The outrage at the death of George Floyd and others provides a point of entry into an explicitly political conversation from which Syrians have been excluded. Indeed, Black Lives Matter has served as a potent mise-en-scène for reflections on solidarity, coalition building, and legal, moral, and political responsibility for injustice within contemporary politics around the globe.[38] As the "social justice yellow brick road" of social movements, this endows Black Lives Matter with a moral clarity, an ideological convergence, that orients activists, allies, scholars, and the broader public toward the Syrian emancipatory struggle in a way that makes it easy to identify the perpetrator and the oppressed.[39] The Syrian revolution may be invoked within the sociopolitical radicalism of Black Lives Matter, debatably one of the most influential social movements of the post–civil rights era, to remedy injustices of erasure through advancing the registers of their resistance that might not have been considered. Similar to Syrians, African Americans live under "domestic colonialism," and their struggles for racial equity are in the vanguard of anti-colonial movements.[40] In contesting constraints of visibility, Syrians do not emphasize identification of a common white supremacist "enemy" with linkages across states or borders so much as establish relationality between those in liberatory struggles. Political bonds are established that anchor the local ontologies and everyday resistance of the multitude struggling for a life of liberty and dignity.

Conclusion

While historically famous activists and reformers, such as Frederick Douglass and Martin Luther King Jr., once called on the language of the Declaration of Independence to make compelling claims for expanding America's racial boundaries, as we approach the 250th anniversary of the Declaration and trace its afterlife beyond the United States, there has been a greater impulse to critique the document as institutionalizing modern racism and limiting our ability to move toward social justice in the twenty-first century. Scholars in the Black radical tradition argue that the Declaration envisioned the nation as white, not "slow[ing] the oncoming train of racism . . . [but] . . . accelerat[ing] it."[41] These thinkers suggest that the US American settler state was built around the exclusions of Indigenous and Black individuals, who thereby suffered dispossession and are *still* excluded from what it means to be a US American citizen.[42] A recent cartoon by Pulitzer Prize–winning political cartoonist Signe Wilkinson explicitly exposes the tension between the lives of Black people and the Declaration of Independence, and how they both draw from and repel one another. The cartoon illustrates two men with their backs to one another, both of them writing. Thomas Jefferson faces in one direction, writing "All men are created equal" on a scroll with an old quill, which he then passes to a young African American facing in the opposite direction, typing "Black Lives Matter" into his computer screen.[43] While some disavow the Declaration outright, there are those who insist that we are the "spiritual descendants" of those who wrote the Declaration of Independence; we testify to how the inability to grant African Americans liberty "violates America's soul"[44] and endeavor to extend to all the full promise of what it is to be a US American.

And so, this chapter offers a vision of what it might mean for the United States to better apply its own ideals through shedding light on Syrian initiations of translinguistic and transnational affective encounters across borders with those in liberatory struggles in the United States. In the latter's departure from its own presumptive values and the state's seeming indifference toward the recurrence of racist killings, this chapter disputes the claim to universal appeal of the founding documents of the United States among wider multiethnic, multiracial, and intersectional popular movements in broader Global South decolonial politics.

In the Declaration of Independence's inability to make effective its own declarations within the domestic affairs of the nation, its suitability as a warrant for social imaginaries outside of coloniality and authoritarian systems is in question. In underlining the Declaration's diminishing validity as a resource from which transnational others may derive their arguments for challenging regnant structures of power, we see how coalitional possibilities may be found instead in the ordinary, everyday political resistance of grassroots iterations of the US American political tradition. Without renouncing their own autonomy and differences, their politics are grounded in the specificity and incommensurability of the grassroots experiences of those at the periphery, those whose position is tenuous within the nation-state, as opposed to the discourses of those who are the purveyors of exclusion.

At the same time, the Syrian case offers implications for how we might redefine and reimagine the ideals enshrined in the Declaration. Against the trope of the "belated" Arab world,[45] the prominent dissident Yassin Haj Saleh insisted that the Syrian revolution was too progressive for the US establishment.[46] In a general disillusionment regarding the United States and its leadership, Syrians were aware of the vast gap between the United States' inspirational rhetoric and its tepid response to the revolution and willingness to be a bystander to Assad's atrocities. So perhaps it is no surprise that Syrians would enunciate a pluriversal alternative to "the people," moving away from universalized notions of the Declaration of Independence and toward the alternative space of lived experience of those struggling for racial justice in the United States. "The people" are agentic, sovereign, and fighting for their right to breathe and live freely as a multitude of diffuse and heterogenous subjects across historical anti-racist and anti-colonial struggles. They are not waiting for the state to protect or deliver their rights; rather, they place their faith in the transformative power of the movements of multitudes to create a new world.

Finally, despite the prominence of the United States in international affairs, it is worth remembering that the Syrian uprising was never about the United States. It was about the desire for a dignified life and a modicum of control over one's own destiny, and about the multitude who came together to announce that "another world is possible." But as much as we all may wish to escape or deny it, the lack of solidarity on the part of the United States was keenly felt by Syrians and transformed their resistance into a language recognizing that there is no singularity that is not also established in the common. From there they took steps toward communal solidarities and political communities, and the creation of what Hardt and Negri call "a movement of movements."[47] The production of the common took place not by withdrawing into local or identity-based certainties, or even by aspiring to the institutional logics of sovereign nation-states, but by traversing the borders within which they were trapped to find other multitudes with whom they might contest the fundamental injustices of an (in)habitable world.

NOTES

1. Mackenzie Huber and Erin Woodiel, "Protesters in Keystone Arrested After Blocking Road to Mount Rushmore for Hours," *USA Today*, July 4, 2020, https://www.usatoday.com/story/news/politics/2020/07/03/keystone-south-dakota-protesters-anti-trump-demonstration-mount-rushmore-rally-fireworks/5374418002/.
2. Grace Hauck, "'We Refuse to Celebrate': July 4th Protesters Say Not All Americans Are Free," *USA Today*, July 4, 2020, https://www.usatoday.com/story/news/nation/2020/07/04/fourth-july-holiday-protests-refuse-celebrate-independence/5372733002/.
3. Hauck, "We Refuse to Celebrate."
4. Courtney Vinopal, "For Some Americans, July 4 Is a Time Not to Celebrate, but Reflect," PBS, July 3, 2020, https://www.pbs.org/newshour/nation/for-some-americans-july-4-is-a-time-not-to-celebrate-but-reflect.
5. Alyson Krueger, "No Sparklers for These Folks: Why Some Americans Are Rethinking July 4th Celebrations," *New York Times*, July 3, 2023, https://www.nytimes.com/2023/07/02/style/rethinking-july-4th-celebrations.html.
6. Stuckey, *Deplorable.*
7. Peter D. Kramer, "The Declaration of Independence, with 2020 Vision," Real Clear Politics, July 2, 2020, https://www.realclearpolitics.com/2020/07/02/the_declaration_of_independence_with_2020_vision_516096.html.
8. Pencak, "Declaration of Independence."
9. Bâli and Rana, "Constitutionalism."
10. Thompson, *How the West Stole Democracy.*
11. Excerpt from the Declaration of Independence in Rida, "Bab Al Tarikh," 442.
12. Tauber, *Formation of Modern Syria and Iraq.*
13. Thompson, *How the West Stole Democracy.*
14. Qasimiyah, *Arab Government in Damascus*; Armitage, *Declaration of Independence.*
15. Thompson, *How the West Stole Democracy*, 132.
16. Cleveland and Bunton, *History of the Modern Middle East.*
17. Lefevre, *Ashes of Hama.*
18. Yassin-Kassab and Al-Shami, *Burning Country*, vii.
19. Al-Haj Saleh, *Impossible Revolution.*
20. Hardt and Negri, *Assembly.*
21. *Our Memory Belongs to Us*, dir. Rami Farah (Final Cut for Real, 2021), https://www.youtube.com/watch?v=MzSMetXYt_w.
22. Al-Haj Saleh, *Impossible Revolution*, 4.
23. Budour Hassan, "Omar Aziz: Rest in Power," Anarchist Library, February 20, 2013, https://theanarchistlibrary.org/library/budour-hassan-omar-aziz-rest-in-power.
24. Mignolo, "Delinking," 452.
25. Omran, "Sect as Homeland," 41.

26. Hanano, "From Hama to Daraya," 91.

27. Aziz Asmar, "#Myanmar Protestors on a Mural in #Idlib," *Syrian Campaign*, April 16, 2021, https://twitter.com/TheSyriaCmpgn/status/1383065227122589697/photo/1.

28. Joseph Hincks, "In Solidarity and as a Symbol of Global Injustices, a Syrian Artist Painted a Mural to George Floyd on a Bombed Idlib Building," *Time Magazine*, June 6, 2020, https://time.com/5849444/george-floyd-mural-idlib-syria/.

29. Aziz Asmar, "Syrian Painter, Binnish 2020," *Youtube*, https://www.youtube.com/watch?v=itlnY3bhkHo.

30. Ghazal Aswad, "Unsafe Homecoming"; Ghazal Aswad, "Reverse Moral Exceptionalism," 354–75; Ghazal Aswad, "Radical Rhetoric," 207–22.

31. Berlant, *Cruel Optimism*, 260.

32. Joyce Karam, "Syria's Revolution Through the Banners of Kafranbel," *Al-Arabiya*, January 11, 2014, https://english.alarabiya.net/perspective/analysis/2014/01/11/Syria-s-revolution-through-the-banners-of-Kafranbel.

33. Occupied Kafranbel Banners, "We Stand with the Oppressed Who Cannot Breathe #BlackLivesMatter," Facebook, May 26, 2020, https://www.facebook.com/kafrnbl/photos/3092542220839197.

34. Occupied Kafranbel Banners, "We Stand with the Oppressed."

35. Yazbek, *Woman in the Crossfire*.

36. Marina Naprushkina, "Surviving Monstrosities: An Interview with Yassin al-Haj Saleh," *Al-Jumhuriya*, June 25, 2020, https://www.aljumhuriya.net/en/content/surviving-monstrosities-interview-yassin-al-haj-saleh.

37. Al-Haj Saleh, *Impossible Revolution*, 41.

38. Binning, "How Black Lives Matter."

39. Binning, "How Black Lives Matter," 27; Johnson, *After Black Lives Matter*.

40. Kelley, *Freedom Dreams*, 73.

41. Parkinson, *Thirteen Clocks*, 11.

42. Gorup, "Subverting the American Paradox," 355–76.

43. Signe Wilkinson, "Thomas Jefferson Passes His Quill to Black Lives Matter," *Philadelphia Inquirer*, July 5, 2020, https://www.inquirer.com/opinion/cartoons/thomas-jefferson-declaration-of-iindependence-black-lives-matter-20200705.html.

44. Richard Lee Abrams, "Black Lives Matter and the Declaration of Independence," October 22, 2020, City Watch, https://www.citywatchla.com/los-angeles/20609-black-lives-matter-and-the-declaration-of-independence.

45. Bardawil, *Revolution and Disenchantment*, 193.

46. Al-Haj Saleh, *Impossible Revolution*.

47. Hardt and Negri, *Assembly*, 87.

BIBLIOGRAPHY

Armitage, David. *The Declaration of Independence: A Global History*. Cambridge, MA: Harvard University Press, 2007.

Bâli, Asli, and Aziz Rana. "Constitutionalism and the American Imperial Imagination." *University of Chicago Law Review* 85, no. 2 (2018): 257–92.

Bardawil, Fadi. *Revolution and Disenchantment: Arab Marxism and the Binds of Emancipation*. Durham, NC: Duke University Press, 2020.

Berlant, Lauren. *Cruel Optimism*. Durham, NC: Duke University Press, 2011.

Binning, Arelle A. "How Black Lives Matter Has Influenced and Interacted with Global Social Movements." Master's thesis, City University of New York, 2019. https://academicworks.cuny.edu/cgi/viewcontent.cgi?article=4182&context=gc_etds.

Cleveland, William L., and Martin Bunton. *A History of the Modern Middle East*. Boulder, CO: Westview Press, 2013.

Daher, Joseph. *Syria After the Uprisings: The Political Economy of State Resilience*. Chicago: Haymarket Books, 2019.

Ghazal Aswad, Noor. "Radical Rhetoric: Towards a Telos of Solidarity." *Rhetoric and Public Affairs* 24, nos. 1–2 (2021): 207–22. doi:10.14321/rhetpublaffa.24.1-2.0207.

———. "Reverse Moral Exceptionalism and the American Left: When Do Villains Become Heroes?" *Quarterly Journal of Speech* 109, no. 4 (2023): 354–75. doi: 10.1080/00335630.2023.2250580.

———. "Unsafe Homecoming: Unraveling Environmental Injustice and Land Dispossession in the Syrian Refugee Crisis." *Environmental Communication* 18, nos. 1–2 (2024): 35–42. doi: 10.1080/17524032.2023.2296831.

Gorup, Michel. "Subverting the American Paradox: Race, Redemption, and Revolution in David Walker's Appeal." *Law, Culture and the Humanities* 17, no. 2 (2021): 355–76.

Haj Saleh, Yassin al-. *The Impossible Revolution: Making Sense of the Syrian Tragedy*. London: Haymarket Books, 2017.

Hanano, Amal. "From Hama to Daraya." In *Critical Muslim 11: Syria* Z, edited by Ziauddin Sardar and Robin Yassin-Kassab. London: Muslim Institute / Hurst, 2014.

Hardt, Michael, and Antonio Negri. *Assembly*. Oxford: Oxford University Press, 2017.

Johnson, Cedric. *After Black Lives Matter: Policing and Anti-capitalist Struggle*. London: Verso, 2023.

Kelley, Robin. *Freedom Dreams: The Black Radical Imagination*. Boston: Beacon Press, 2002.

Lefevre, Raphael. *Ashes of Hama: The Muslim Brotherhood in Syria*. New York: Oxford University Press, 2013.

Mignolo, Walter. "Delinking: The Rhetoric of Modernity, the Logic of Coloniality and the Grammar of De-coloniality." *Cultural Studies* 21, nos. 2–3 (2007): 449–514.

Omran, Rasha. "The Sect as Homeland." In *Critical Muslim 11: Syria* Z, edited by Ziauddin Sardar and Robin Yassin-Kassab. London: Muslim Institute / Hurst Publishers, 2014.

Parkinson, Robert G. *Thirteen Clocks: How Race United the Colonies and Made the Declaration of Independence*. Chapel Hill, NC: University of North Carolina Press, 2021.

Pencak, William. "The Declaration of Independence: Changing Interpretations and a New Hypothesis." *Pennsylvania History* 57, no. 3 (1990): 225–35.

Qasimiyah, Khairiyah. *The Arab Government in Damascus Between 1918 and 1920*. Beirut: Arab Institute for Publishing, 1982.

Rashid, Rida M. "Bab Al Tarikh: Istiqlal Surya wa Al Iraq [A chapter in history: Independence of Syria and Iraq]." *Al Manar* 21, no. 8 (2020): 441–44.

Stuckey, Mary. *Deplorable: The Worst Presidential Campaigns from Jefferson to Trump*. University Park: Pennsylvania State University Press, 2021.

Tauber, Eliezer. *Formation of Modern Syria and Iraq*. London: Frank Cass, 1995.

Thompson, Elizbeth. *How the West Stole Democracy from the Arabs: The Syrian Arab Congress of 1920 and the Destruction of Its Historic Liberal-Islamic Alliance*. New York: Atlantic Monthly Press, 2020.

Yassin-Kassab, Robin, and Leila Al-Shami. *Burning Country: Syrians in Revolution and War*. London: Pluto Press, 2016.

Yazbek, Samar. *A Woman in the Crossfire: Diaries of the Syrian Revolution*. London: Haus, 2011.

II

A MORALLY GROUNDED IDEOGRAPH: VÁCLAV HAVEL'S CONSTITUTIVE RHETORIC IN THE VELVET REVOLUTION

Rebecca Oliver

Václav Havel's leadership in the Velvet Revolution is often seen as one of the most successful and peaceful transitions from authoritarianism to democracy in modern history, which is especially interesting given that it drew inspiration from the principles of the US Declaration of Independence, a document that was integral to an armed rebellion.[1] The Velvet Revolution occurred in 1989 in Czechoslovakia, marking the end of Communist rule and paving the way for establishing a democratic government. Among the key figures in the Velvet Revolution was Václav Havel, a dissident playwright who became a leading voice for democracy and human rights in Czechoslovakia and in the Civic Forum, an opposition movement that played a crucial role in organizing protests and negotiations with the Communist government. The Velvet Revolution was primarily driven by popular protests, demonstrations, and civil disobedience against the Communist Party of Czechoslovakia, which had maintained power since the late 1940s. As the protests grew, the Communist leadership began to lose its prominence. The catalytic event for the revolution was the violent suppression of a student protest in Prague on November 17, 1989, which led to widespread public outrage and increased demands for political change.[2]

Then, on December 10, 1989, Czechoslovakian president Gustáv Husák appointed Václav Havel as the country's new president, marking a significant shift in power. The Communist Party agreed to negotiations with the opposition, which eventually led to the formation of a transitional government that included members of both the opposition and the Communist

Party. Havel was the first non-Communist president of Czechoslovakia in over forty years. In the years following Havel's leadership, Czechoslovakia transitioned to a democratic system, held free elections, and embarked on a path of political and economic reforms.

Havel became a symbol of unity and reconciliation in the new Czech Republic. Specifically, his emphasis on moral authority and commitment to democratic principles helped bridge the gap between the old Communist regime and the new democratic era, and he is remembered as a symbol of moral leadership and a champion of democracy in Central and Eastern Europe.[3] Understanding Havel's public addresses and the various discourses about them helps us understand how claims to morality become associated with ideologies and influence practical politics. Since dominant worldviews control the discourse and thus maintain the worldviews of the privileged, and since Havel's discourse was delivered at a time of transition in power, this analysis explores how power is both maintained and sometimes undermined.

This chapter explores how Václav Havel's presidency drew from the ideals associated with the US Declaration of Independence, which he formulated as what I term a "morally grounded ideograph." While Havel did not often rely explicitly on the US Declaration, its influence on his rhetoric is clear. In making this case, I analyze how the form of this ideograph (an abstract term used by rhetoricians to denote an ideologically complicated concept) was employed to unify the people of Czechoslovakia under Havel by rendering morality and independence inseparable ideals. First, Czechoslovakia's Declaration of Independence was paralleled with the US Declaration of Independence. Second, Havel relied on scapegoating to reframe the definition of his political rhetoric as "political morality" in the fight against oppression by one-party rule. Third, he created an ideograph using the US Declaration of Independence in a way that grounded the argument for independence in morality, as the original Declaration of Independence did for the US revolution, but using morality as a way to avoid rather than justify the violence of revolution.

Reorienting Czechoslovakia

Czechoslovakia has a long history of being ruled by oppressors and of tensions along geographic and civil divisions. This history includes an official Declaration of Independence in 1918, which was written long before but was still influential in the events of 1989. Both the original US Declaration and the later Czech versions serve as referents for the orientational metaphor Havel used to link his nation to the United States and ultimately create a morally grounded ideograph. Orientational metaphors are used to further illustrate how a referent is a known point of reference as it relates to an unknown concept to which a speaker hopes to link; such metaphors orient an audience toward a new idea by using an existing one. In his address to congress in 1990, Havel said, "Thanks to the great support of your President (Woodrow) Wilson, our first president, Tomas Garrigue Masaryk, founded our modern independent state. He founded it, as you know, on the same principles on which the United States of America had been founded, as Masaryk's manuscripts held by the Library of Congress testify. In the meantime, the United States made enormous strides. It became the most powerful nation on earth, and it understood the responsibility that flowed from this."[4] He argued that the example of the United States was fundamental to the establishment of a principled government in his own nation. This reference to the United States was echoed by US President George H. W. Bush, who in 1991 announced a "Joint Declaration of the United States and the Czech and Slovak Federal Republic." That declaration calls upon common themes that were first employed by Havel, showing that Havel's effort to draw parallels between the two nations was successful.[5] Among the themes laid out by Havel were revival, rebirth, and renewal, all of which were echoed in public discourse at the time.

First of all, in regard to revival, many people responded to Havel's early addresses by taking them as a call for the revival of democracy on the part of the people of Czechoslovakia and Europe more broadly to oppose the constraints of socialism, a revival of democracy that would be free of the misleading and corrupt practices associated with Soviet rule. Michael Simmons of *The Guardian*, for example, explicitly recognized Havel's willingness to deviate from the Soviet practice of denying difficult truths in public messaging, reporting, "Havel ha[s] delivered a presidential address which could not have diverged more sharply from the usual practice of telling the nation that everything was fine in the best of socialist worlds."[6]

Second, the idea of rebirth in the 1918 Czechoslovakian Declaration of Independence is related to the idea of birth in the US Declaration of Independence. In the latter document, the United States is figured as a new creation, a birth rather than a rebirth.[7] The US Declaration of Independence, which gave birth to the American Revolution, thus informs the Czechoslovakian Declaration of Independence, but this revolution is depicted as a return, a re-creation, not a new entity. It breaks with the US model in that, being a return, it becomes possible to accomplish the transition peacefully. Unlike some other parts of the former Eastern Bloc, this transition in Czechoslovakia occurred without significant violence or conflict.

Third, the idea of renewal refers to Havel's support of the new nation's joining NATO alongside the United States, to become an ally of the West. Havel was a strong advocate for the Czech Republic's membership in NATO, which he believed was crucial for the security and stability of the Czech Republic and the broader region of Central Europe. Before becoming a full member, the Czech Republic, along with other Central and Eastern European countries, participated in NATO's Partnership for Peace (PfP) program. This program allowed for military cooperation, joint exercises, and the development of interoperability between PfP countries and NATO member states.[8] Much of Havel's enthusiasm for NATO came from his admiration for the United States. During various speeches he told the story of his trip to the United States in 1968, saying how thankful he was for the United States' role in defending freedom in Europe.[9] Specifically, in a speech at NATO in 1991, he even apologized to Western democracies "for all the lies that my predecessors, on behalf of the same peoples, were for years telling about you."[10] It was in this particular speech that he explained the central parallel between the United States and the Czech Republic, saying that Eastern European countries needed to accept that the Western alliance was a "democratic, defensive community."[11] The Czech Republic, in other words, in its renewed form, was now able to join this community, leaving the Soviet community behind.

In regard to all Havel's speeches during this period, public opinion surrounding his presidential rhetoric about the United States indicates that he had achieved harmony through a paradoxical leadership style.[12] While focusing on themes of rebirth, renewal, and revival, Havel used the past to his nation's advantage by drawing parallels between the 1918 Czechoslovakian Declaration and the US Declaration of Independence, allowing him to maintain a clear grounding in his own nation's history while also forging new ties with Western, and especially US American, allies.

Creating More Moral Leadership—and a More Moral Nation

Havel, like other political leaders, aimed to bolster his status through claims to a superior morality, although, in Havel's case, he was referring to the virtue of entire political systems rather than individuals. To accomplish this, he employs scapegoating rhetoric to rid himself and his people of lingering guilt from the years of Communist rule. Literary theorist Kenneth Burke writes that scapegoating is a cathartic process that purifies the rhetor and separates them from "the other,"[13] which in Havel's case are the Communist leaders of the Eastern Bloc. For example, in line with the first step of the scapegoating process, Havel draws a contrast between his new government and an enemy, the corrupt previous regime, that is lacking in moral standards and character:[14] "I was living in a country ruled by the most conservative Communist government in Europe, and our society slumbered beneath the pall of a totalitarian system. Today, less than four months later, I'm speaking to you as the representative of a country that has set out on the road to democracy, a country where there is complete freedom of speech, which is getting ready for free elections, and which wants to create a prosperous market economy and its own foreign policy."[15] Here, he associates his country's progress and prosperity with his nation's newfound freedom, thus justifying the political change through reference to its results.

Taking the second step of scapegoating, Havel situated himself as the voice of reason against the corruption of the Communist government. In a 1990 speech to the Council of Europe, he said, "Throughout my life, whenever my thoughts have turned to social affairs, politics, moral questions, and life in general, there has always been some reasonable person ready to point out sooner or later, very reasonably and in the name of reason, that I should be reasonable too, cast aside my eccentric ideas, and acknowledge that nothing can change for the better because the world is divided once and for all into two worlds."[16] Havel positioned himself as someone able to mediate between these two worlds and asserts that he is capable of handling the threat posed by communism. In other words, he argues that because of his ability to accept his own flaws and proceed on the basis of reason, he knows best how to cope with the various threats posed by communism and how to move the country forward to a democratic future. He makes direct reference to the Soviet Union and its failures and then says, "All of this taught us to see the world in bipolar terms as two enormous forces—one a defender of freedom, the other a source of nightmares. Europe became the point of friction between these two powers, and thus it turned into a single enormous arsenal divided into two parts."[17] That history was one of division; the future Havel envisions transcends that division and offered unity.

Havel and the Declaration: A Moral Ideograph

An ideograph is a term or expression characterized by an imprecise definition, referring to a broad and unclear range of concepts—terms such as "equality" and "justice." Because they help to unify broad coalitions of people, ideographs are very useful politically. And for social movements such as the Velvet Revolution that create "changes in social reality through changes in meanings of 'foundational' rhetorical forms,"[18] ideographs can help activists join calls for change to arguments about stability. Because of their vagueness, ideographs are able to convey a message that lacks specificity while still resonating emotionally.[19] To put it differently, when individuals encounter an ideograph, its impact is typically not due to its precise definition but rather to the emotions it evokes. This characteristic makes ideographs particularly valuable to persuasive speakers, as their inherent ambiguity allows them to substitute widely accepted words for intricate ideas.

Moreover, since ideographs tend to carry multiple connotations of morality, they can enhance a speaker's emotional appeal. Ideographs are not exclusive to politics, but they are influential elements of political discourse. In the case of Havel, terms such as "democracy," "morality," and "independence" all denote an ideology, but they lack a specific referent. Each of them has many different meanings and interpretations, which enables such ideographs to sway individuals emotionally without necessarily conveying a precise purpose or meaning. As president, Havel was able to use the ideograph as an effective device to unify a nation in transition while also bolstering his own status as leader. He made use of the inherent ambiguity found in words, speeches, and philosophies:[20] leaders tell stories about a group called "the people," and when people see themselves in those stories, they endorse both that definition of the nation and the right of the leader to govern it.[21]

Constitutive rhetoric—here, the process of creating a people by resolving their contradictions—is one of the main ways a president tells the people stories about themselves. In the early days of his presidency, Havel had to both move forward and break away from the precedent set by the previous government. However, he could not fail to recognize that a part of his people's identity would always be connected in some way to what came before they were democratized under his leadership. It is the nature of a declaration of independence to remember previous struggles, to use them as motivation for change.[22] Successful constitutive rhetoric resolves contradictions that emerge in identities stretched by the tensions that come naturally in social life. In Havel's case, he recognized that in moving forward there would still be contradictions in the identity of this new Czech people, owing to the residue of who they were before, and reconciled these tensions through specific claims to morality.

The president of a nation is often charged with telling these constitutive stories,[23] whose rhetoric defines political reality.[24] The social realities in presidential rhetoric are not given; within limits, presidents have flexibility in how they describe the political world. To enact a presidential purpose is to plead a case or make a claim as to what the presidency should be and how it should be.[25] Presidents therefore must make strategic choices in deciding how to persuasively describe the world so that their constituents will recognize those descriptions as reflecting reality and providing a vision of the future that they see as desirable.

How a message is conveyed in a presidential address is concerned with "form"—the kind of speech a president makes needs to fit with the content of the speech and the occasion where the speech is given.[26] Presidents of the United States, for example, commonly give inaugurals, grant pardons, and deliver State of the Union addresses.[27] Each of these kinds of speech gives audiences certain kinds of expectations, and presidents generally do well to meet those expectations.[28] Presidents choose a form or genre depending on the context of a speech[29]—that is, a combination of geographical place, the kind of audience a speaker is addressing, the reason they are speaking at this moment to these people, and what they hope to achieve by giving the speech: public support for a policy, specific support for themselves, and so on. This created real challenges and opportunities for Havel when he came to power in 1989.

Havel certainly found his key moment during his presidency following the Velvet Revolution. He was handed an audience who lacked identity in the wake of great change; his task was to give that audience an identity. But this identity had to be one that was consistent with the audience's historical understanding of what it meant to be Czech, as well as one that would set his people and himself apart from the former communists—in the same way that the US Declaration of Independence was made appealing to an audience that lacked identity in the face of leaving behind their nation and their nation's type of government. Havel seized this opportunity and paralleled the experiences of his people with those of the US American people in the examples he used during his addresses.[30] In this way he established an identity for himself and his people through the lens of democratic government while also making democracy appear morally superior to communism. His rise to the leadership of the revolution was propelled by his moral credibility and adept articulation of the people's demands.[31] For Havel, then, the use of words such as "democracy" as ideographs always carried moral implications: democracy was preferable to communism because it was more moral, and morality ought to be the standard by which nations are judged.

Havel found himself in a moment of transition that called for independence grounded in the morality of overcoming folly. Instead of proudly highlighting the accomplishments of his people or his own governance, his primary focus was on the inherent folly of human endeavors.[32] He explored the complexities of individuals, nations, and governments in their human condition, often constrained and rendered ludicrous by their limitations or endeavors to surpass them. In other words, the recognition of one's folly is the morally just thing to do. This "morality" was a blanket term or ideograph for a variety of emotions that would be evoked in Havel's audience as his morally grounded ideograph demonized communism, bridging the old and new with democratic reforms and cooperative foreign policy.

To begin fully formulating his morally grounded ideograph, Havel first had to create a connection between Czechoslovakia's Declaration of Independence in 1989 and the US Declaration of Independence. Havel did not rely on the US Declaration directly; rather, the Czechoslovakian Declaration was more a manifestation of what he aspired to create in his ideograph. The US Declaration inspired but did not a directly influence the Czechoslovakian Declaration. The two share similarities, but each came into existence and was communicated within the boundaries of its particular situation. While the US Declaration announced the birth of a new nation from the oppression of British rule, the Czechoslovakian Declaration was about the *re*birth of a democratic nation after Communist oppression. Both peoples had been oppressed, but in different ways and by different political systems. The Czechoslovakian Declaration was a reclaiming of what had been lost to "folly" during Communist control and called for a return to the historical values of recognizing it as such and moving forward. Havel was reflective, using the history of the Czech people to inform his ideograph. In this way. Havel's rhetoric and the Czechoslovakian Declaration are, in essence, more realistic than the US Declaration, which posits the United States as a divine nation, blessed by God, that is not guilty of folly. By contrast, Havel's rhetoric is characterized by an awareness and understanding of past moral failures to achieve a better moral grounding in the future.

Within the context of leaving behind the Communist regime, Havel juxtaposes communism and morality. His speeches given early in his presidency reflect a disgust with the belief that communism can bring about equality. He argues instead that communism provides a false sense of idealism that can never be brought to fruition, a delusion that has brought the Eastern Bloc into a state of tyranny. In his Independence Day commemorative address Havel says, "In my opinion, there is only one thing necessary: that we should all awaken within ourselves responsibility, and that we should mobilize such characteristics as a healthy reason, a sense of perspective, matter-of-factness, broad-mindedness, courage for the truth, and understanding for others." The type of democracy he calls for is one that embodies that basic call for moral clarity.

In his 1990 address to Congress, Havel begins with humility about his beginnings as a playwright who never saw himself as a political leader. It is this sense of humility that sets him apart from the autocracy of his predecessors as he then begins to discuss how "the human face of the world is changing so rapidly that none of the familiar political speedometers are adequate."[33] In other words, Havel is not only claiming that communism should be thrown out but also saying that how we gauge what is just, fair, and equal in government should be thrown out with it as we reassess what really matters in a changing world. Focusing on the "human face" defines morality as concerning not material things or the means of production but who produces it and what matters to them. Havel uses the history of his people's oppression to explain why this refocus on the "human face" of the world is necessary, recalling the traumatic events that befell them under communism. The elements of humility in this speech, followed by the recognition of rapid change and a call to throw out the way we think of government by refocusing on the "human face" of the world, culminate in an exemplar of Havel's morally grounded ideograph, a device used broadly in his presidential rhetoric beyond that moment.

Conclusion

When Václav Havel passed away in 2011, Jan Kavan, former foreign minister of the Czech Republic from 1998 until 2002, wrote, "Václav Havel was undoubtedly one of the greatest Europeans of our generation, a man who fully deserves the unquestionable respect both of his country and the world."[34] Havel was known as someone who hated conflict, but he was also a brave defender of his nation, endowing his position as president with moral superiority. Havel's success in transitioning his nation to democracy is the reason he is remembered as "one of the greatest Europeans of our generation." An examination of public discourse about Havel, his speeches, and their references to similarities between the United States' and the Czech Republic's Declarations of Independence in 1776 and 1918, respectively, reveals that his success is tied to his use of the "morally grounded ideograph," which defined his presidency as aligning with the same principles of democracy as those articulated in the US Declaration of Independence. The US Declaration, with its themes of morality, carries a rhetorical significance that has transcended the bounds of time and has been used to orient metaphors constituting nations as morally grounded democracies. By referencing the US Declaration and the 1918 Czechoslovakian Declaration, Havel established his identity and his idea of democracy as being morally righteous and then reconstituted the Czech people accordingly by resolving the contradictions in their identity attributable to the previous, immoral Communist regime. This all may be seen to culminate in the morally grounded ideograph that serves as an exemplar in Havel's 1990 address to Congress.

NOTES

1. Martin Palouš, "Introductory Remarks: Solidarity of the Shaken Day," Václav Havel Library Foundation, Encounters with America, March 30, 2015, 4.
2. Michael Simmons, "Czechoslovakia's Velvet Revolution," *The Guardian*, November 13, 2019, https://www.theguardian.com/world/from-the-archive-blog/2019/nov/13/czechoslovakia-velvet-revolution-november-1989.
3. Desai, *Václav Havel's Economic Legacy*.
4. Václav Havel, Speech to Congress, February 21, 1990, https://www.washingtonpost.com/archive/politics/1990/02/22/text-of-havels-speech-to-congress/df98e177-778e-4c26-bd96-980089c4fcb2/.
5. Joint Declaration of the United States and the Czech and Slovak Federal Republic, October 22, 1991, https://www.presidency.ucsb.edu/documents/joint-declaration-the-united-states-and-the-czech-and-slovak-federal-republic.
6. Simmons, "Czechoslovakia's Velvet Revolution."
7. Morgan, *Birth of the Republic*, 39.
8. NATO Review, "Václav Havel: Remembering the Big Little Man," https://www.nato.int/docu/review/articles/2012/05/07/Václav-havel-remembering-the-big-little-man/index.html.
9. Zantovsky, "In Search of Allies."
10. Václav Havel, Speech to NATO, March 21, 1991, https://www.washingtonpost.com/archive/politics/1991/03/22/havel-urges-nato-to-seek-ties-with-easts-new-democracies/5d992dce-a345-461e-8393-b93cc7b2e2ea/Havel.
11. Havel, Speech to NATO.
12. NATO Review, *Václav Havel*.
13. Burke, *Permanence and Change*, 14–16.
14. Pankaj Mishra, "Václav Havel's Lessons on How to Create a Parallel Polis," *New Yorker*, February 8, 2017.
15. Havel, Speech to Congress.
16. Václav Havel, Speech to the Assembly, March 10, 1990, http://www.assembly.coe.int/nw/xml/Speeches/Speech-XML2HTML-EN.asp?SpeechID=88.
17. Havel, Speech to Congress.
18. DeLuca, "Meditations on Image Events."
19. McGee, "The 'Ideograph.'"
20. Klicperová-Baker, "Czech Rhetoric of 1989," 107.
21. Klicperová-Baker, "Czech Rhetoric of 1989," 108.
22. Milford, "National Identity."
23. Zarefsky, "Presidential Rhetoric," 610.

24. Stuckey, "Rethinking the Rhetorical Presidency," 40.
25. Dorsey, "Frontier Myth in Presidential Rhetoric," 17.
26. Campbell and Jamieson, *Presidents Creating the Presidency*, 21.
27. Campbell and Jamieson, *Presidents Creating the Presidency*, 23.
28. Campbell and Jamieson, *Form and Genre*, 3.
29. Zarefsky, "Presidential Rhetoric," 611.
30. Havel, Speech to Congress.
31. Klicperová-Baker, "Czech Rhetoric of 1989."
32. Zagacki, "Václav Havel and the Rhetoric of Folly," 20.
33. Bruce Sterling, "Václav Havel: What Communism Still Teaches Us," *Wired*, April 16, 2013, https://www.wired.com/2013/04/vaclav-havel-what-communism-still-teaches-us/.
34. Jan Kavan, "Remembering Václav Havel," *The Nation*, January 6, 2012, https://www.thenation.com/article/archive/remembering-Václav-havel/.

BIBLIOGRAPHY

Burke, Kenneth. *Permanence and Change: An Anatomy of Purpose*. Berkeley: University of California Press, 1984.

Campbell, Karlyn Kohrs, and Kathleen Hall Jamieson. *Form and Genre: Shaping Rhetorical Action*. Annandale, VA: Speech Communication Association, 1978.

———. *Presidents Creating the Presidency: Deeds Done in Words*. Chicago: University of Chicago Press, 2008.

DeLuca, Kevin Michael. "Meditations on Image Events: The Possibilities and Consequences for Rhetorical Theory or Critical Rhetoric, Social Movements, and Environmental Politics: An Assemblage of Fragments." PhD diss., University of Iowa, 1996.

Desai, Raj M. *Václav Havel's Economic Legacy*. Washington, DC: Brookings, 2011.

Dorsey, Leroy G. "The Frontier Myth in Presidential Rhetoric: Theodore Roosevelt's Campaign for Conservation." *Western Journal of Communication* 59, no. 1 (1995): 1–19.

Klicperová-Baker, Martina. "Czech Rhetoric of 1989 and Václav Havel." *Advances in the History of Rhetoric* 18 (2015): S87–108.

McGee, Michael Calvin. "The 'Ideograph': A Link Between Rhetoric and Ideology." *Quarterly Journal of Speech* 66, no. 1 (1980): 1–16.

Milford, Mike. "National Identity, Crisis, and the Inaugural Genre: George W. Bush and 9/11." *Southern Communication Journal* 81, no. 1 (2016): 18–31.

Morgan, Edmund S. *The Birth of the Republic, 1763–89*. Chicago: University of Chicago Press, 2012.

Stuckey, Mary E. "Rethinking the Rhetorical Presidency and Presidential Rhetoric." *Review of Communication* 10, no. 1 (2010): 38–52.

Zagacki, Kenneth S. "Vaclav Havel and the Rhetoric of Folly." *Southern Communication Journal* 62 no. 1 (1996): 17–30.

Zantovsky, Michael. "In Search of Allies: Vaclav Havel and the Expansion of NATO." *World Affairs* 177, no. 4 (2014): 47–58.

Zarefsky, David. "Presidential Rhetoric and the Power of Definition." *Presidential Studies Quarterly* 34, no. 3 (2004): 607–19.

PART 4

THE SEMI-SACRED DECLARATION

12

"THAT WAS THE FIRST TIME IN HISTORY THAT ANYONE BOTHERED TO WRITE THAT DOWN": MYTHOLOGIZING THE DECLARATION OF INDEPENDENCE IN *THE WEST WING*

Christopher J. Wernecke and Ann E. Burnette

Although its final episode aired almost twenty years ago, *The West Wing* (*TWW*) still commands the attention of fans, writers, critics, and scholars alike. In addition to its twenty-six Primetime Emmy Awards and its consistent position as one of the best-written television shows of all time, *TWW*'s continued presence on popular streaming services such as Netflix (2016–20) and Max (2021–) has introduced its relatable characters, memorable narrative arcs, and portrayal of American politics to a new generation of viewers.[1] While fictional, much of the show's critical praise and enduring popularity stems from its seemingly authentic portrayal of the modern American presidency, a portrayal that encompasses the lives and roles of various West Wing staffers and high-ranking officials, as well as its nuanced exploration of real-world social, economic, religious, and ideological issues.

TWW's connection to reality, however, also extends beyond its setting. The show often blends real people, places, and events from US American history together with people, places, and events from its own fiction. In particular, *TWW*'s blending together of history and fiction when invoking the Declaration of Independence exerts a rhetorical force that has yet to be fully examined. While the show's employment of the Declaration can be said to be largely representative of the document's framing across much of US American political and popular culture—a celebratory, if not overtly heroic, framework that is intimate, evocative, reverent, and altogether imbued with significant affect—there is an elusive pull to *TWW*'s framing of the Declaration that is distinct from other artifacts of popular culture that similarly feature the document. Indeed, *TWW*'s unique position as a fiction more firmly rooted in historical reality distinguishes it from films such as *National Treasure* (2004) and *The Patriot* (2000), which, we contend, ultimately conceals the true extent of both the show and the Declaration's ideological power.

This chapter argues that *TWW*'s celebratory, intimate, and affect-infused framing of the Declaration constitutes a mythic form of rhetoric that helps fuel the larger mythos surrounding America's founding.[2] In reifying the mythology of America's founding via its treatment of the Declaration, *TWW* functions in concert with past, present, and largely hegemonic US American political discourses. Indeed, as Mary Stuckey notes in this volume's introduction, the Declaration's iconicity has helped instantiate and legitimize some of humanity's best and worst ideologies both in the United States and around the world. Echoing this, we believe the ideological implications emanating from the Declaration's mythic ethos in popular culture to be not only relevant in deliberations regarding the document's symbolic import but also consequential in the material and bodily entailments of the document as well. More simply, this chapter positions the mythologized nature of America's Declaration of Independence in popular culture as a source crucial to the document's rhetorical power today—a power that manifests in a variety of policy decisions and political actions, impacting the everyday lives of a great many people.

To properly explicate our argument, this chapter is organized in four parts. First, we further situate *TWW*'s staying power in American popular culture and consider existing scholarly critiques of the show. Second, we briefly sketch the contours of mythic rhetorical criticism through a review of relevant scholarship within rhetorical studies. Here, we identify an often-overlooked aspect of mythic criticism—the role of the nondiscursive in mythic rhetoric. Accordingly, then, we use this chapter's third section to analyze multimodal elements from two episodes of *TWW*, "What Kind of Day Has It Been?" (season 1, episode 22) and "Jefferson Lives" (season 5, episode 3),[3] demonstrating *how* the Declaration is crafted with mythic sinews—that is, we consider the show's use of not only language, but also music, lighting, and editing techniques to demonstrate how *TWW* mythologizes the Declaration. We then conclude by discussing the various implications engendered by a mythologized Declaration.

The West Wing's Enduring Popularity

Created by Aaron Sorkin, *TWW* debuted in September 1999 and ran for seven seasons, ending in May 2006. *TWW* chronicled the fictional presidency of

Josiah Bartlet and the workings of his closest West Wing staff, drawing critical acclaim and high ratings throughout its initial run on NBC. The show's twenty-six Primetime Emmy Awards included four consecutive Outstanding Drama Series Awards from 2000 to 2003. The series also won three Golden Globe Awards and two Peabody Awards. At its peak, the show boasted 17 million audience members.[4] Viewers and critics alike celebrated the show's depiction of presidential politics as momentous, fast-paced, and driven largely by the values of democracy. Putting *TWW* in stark political context, media critic Brian Moylan of *The Guardian* described the show as "presenting the sort of government that many viewers wish we had when it was airing in the depths of the Bush administration."[5] As the series' run came to a close, media critic Janine Gibson lamented the things that she would miss *learning* about when the show ended, which included filibusters, the lawmaking process, and "President Andrew Jackson's big block of cheese."[6]

Not only was *TWW* popular during its primetime run, it has also enjoyed a rich afterlife. In March 2016, actor Joshua Malina, who played Deputy Communications Director Will Bailey for the last four years of the series, announced that he and co-host Hrishikesh Hirway were launching a podcast dedicated to the series, *The West Wing Weekly*.[7] Each episode of the podcast focused on one episode of *TWW*—covering all 156 episodes of the series while also recording several additional episodes featuring many of *TWW*'s writers, actors, and producers. In honor of the tenth anniversary of the show's last episode, Moylan further observed that *TWW* "has really never gone away" and that it provided the opportunity for viewers "to escape with President Bartlet"—a sentiment that later grew among at least some people following Donald Trump's election in 2016.[8]

Now nearly a quarter century after its debut, *TWW*'s popularity and influence continues to be readily evident. In a 2022 Ipsos poll of American television viewers, for instance, respondents named *TWW* as the most "realistic depiction of what happens in Washington."[9] Moreover, during the 2020 US presidential election HBO hosted a unique reunion for *TWW* that functioned as a "get out the vote" public service announcement via a stage recreation of the season 3 episode "Hartsfield Landing." With all of the cast (aside from the late John Spencer) reprising their roles for the stage reproduction, the reunion also featured messages from prominent figures associated with the pro-voting organization *When We All Vote*, such as Michelle Obama, Lin-Manuel Miranda, and Samuel L. Jackson. The reunion further illustrated Scott's contention that *TWW* "wrote a new generation's rulebook on how to be an emerging political cohort with high-minded idealism and civic activism at the heart of its agenda."[10]

Scholars from a variety of disciplines, including communication, political science, mass media, and religious studies, have analyzed *TWW* and its effect on popular culture and perceptions of the political process. One topic of enduring interest is *TWW*'s representation of American democracy and the presidency. Trevor Parry-Giles and Shawn Parry-Giles argue that *TWW* promulgated a romantic image of "nobler, better U.S. politics."[11] To an extent, Parry-Giles and Parry-Giles write in another analysis, *TWW* also "disrupts images of traditional political power, depicting a chaotic, inclusive, and communal presidentiality dominated by a collectivity of appealing heroes."[12] Anne Ulrich contends that *TWW* addressed its audience "as citizens" and showed them "the process of making political rhetoric."[13] In this way, Ulrich explains, the show provided a model of citizenship and invited its audience to feel a connection with democracy.[14] Janet McCabe additionally describes a "vibrant conversation about the meaning of American democracy" that the series promoted.[15] Lance Holbert et al. argue that *TWW* framed the presidency in a way that is comparable to the way news media frame the presidency.[16] Kay Richardson similarly contends that *TWW* made the "dark art" of spin look good.[17] Finally, Christina Littlefield et al. describe *TWW*'s larger vision as a civil religion that celebrates democracy and is based in Judeo-Christian values.[18]

Meanwhile, several feminist critiques of *TWW* have considered the show's messages regarding sex and gender. Laura Shepherd analyzes the feminism(s) represented in the show and concludes that the overall feminist message of the show is "limited and limiting."[19] Shane Semmler et al. explore the extent to which a fictional female president depicted on a television show could facilitate Americans' acceptance of a real woman president and ultimately conclude that *TWW* reified an emphasis on "masculine" political issues that consequently place women candidates and politicians at a disadvantage.[20]

In analyses more closely related to ours, a few scholarly treatments of *TWW* have commented specifically on the ways in which the show featured the Declaration of Independence. For example, Parry-Giles and Parry-Giles note that *TWW* positions its fictional executive, President Josiah (Jed) Bartlet (portrayed by Martin Sheen), as a direct lineal descendant of Dr. Josiah Bartlett, a real signatory of the Declaration of Independence. Parry-Giles and Parry-Giles argue that this lineage ultimately cements the narrative of a white, patrilineal relationship with the Declaration of Independence.[21] Ulrich similarly contends that Jed Bartlet's connection to the Declaration bolsters his credibility and further advances perceptions of him as both an intellectual and a charismatic president.[22] Finally, Littlefield et al. use references to the Declaration of Independence as a variable in examining how *TWW* portrays civil religion.[23]

Positioning a Multimodal Mythic Criticism

While the scale and scope of mythic criticism has long been debated by scholars in rhetorical studies,[24] many agree with Kenneth Burke's assessment that mythic rhetoric functions as a catalyst for identification. Summarizing Burke's view, Robert Rowland and David Frank write that myths foster "communal identification" by connecting a group's members in the present to their members of the past through "sacred stories that inspire action."[25] The "most appealing" myths romanticize a collective's origins by framing their emergence as cosmically preordained or so consequential that the group's very creation influences the trajectory of the "entire universe."[26] In divinely retelling a people's origin story, myths also help reify the collective's identity for present members by "blur[ring] the line between fact and fiction"—which, in turn, further consecrates certain cultural values and behaviors.[27] Indeed, a number of cultural fables, folklore, and legends frequently function as mythic shorthand, demonstrating mythic rhetoric's lasting power through short, simple, and accessible stories. For example, the story of a young George Washington admitting to his father that he cut down his family's cherry tree is often told to schoolchildren in the United States as both instruction and inspiration. Residing within that blurry space between fact and fiction, the fabled retelling of Washington and the cherry tree valorizes his determined adherence to values of truth, honesty, and personal responsibility while also teaching children to similarly enact these values. In this process, then, the nation's youth yearn to embody Washington, solemnly reciting the fable's timeless mantra: "I cannot tell a lie." Furthermore, because of Washington's revered position as a Revolutionary War hero and the nation's first president, many iterations of the cherry tree tale often imply (if not explicitly state) that values of truth, honesty, and personal responsibility are inherently US American values. In short, the folklore surrounding a prominent figure in a culture's past exerts mythic qualities of identification, sacralizing the community's birth as well as maintaining a belief in their cosmic importance.

The vast majority of critical mythic scholarship in rhetorical studies primarily focuses on the role of discourse in the communication of cultural myths, leaving the role of the nondiscursive either implied or altogether ignored. Put differently, rhetorical examinations of myths have frequently favored *what* is being said in the retelling of a myth over *how* it is being said. For example, even when exploring the evolution of America's frontier myth in films such as *Star Wars*, *E.T.*, the *Alien* franchise, and the larger Western genre, much of Janice Rushing's focus tends toward larger thematic elements emanating from the film's narrative and not on how the film's nondiscursive components contribute to the myth's elasticity.[28] That is, while *scene* is important to a myth's rhetorical power in film and television, the actual construction of the scene, the mise-en-scène—the lighting, music, and camera position, as well the character's nonverbal features and the overall production—remains mostly unexplored in mythic criticism.

To address this inattention to the ways nondiscursive rhetorics contribute to a myth's underlying appeal in popular culture artifacts, our analysis of *TWW*'s mythic framing of the Declaration draws upon scholarship from a variety of critically oriented academic disciplines, including cultural, film, and narrative studies. Importantly, though, our analysis still examines how *TWW* discursively mythologizes the Declaration. Just as Richard Slotkin positions both the visual and the verbal as crucial to understanding the lasting influence of America's frontier mythology across three centuries worth of "literature, folklore, ritual, historiography, and polemics," we similarly maintain that a "single image or phrase" can call forth an affective array of mythic entailments.[29] Especially when combined with multimodal elements of the mise-en-scène, we position the liturgical use of certain "icons, keywords, and historical cliches" as crucial to a myth's abiding presence and power in a culture.[30]

Mythologizing the Declaration of Independence in *The West Wing*

What Kind of Day Has It Been?

In the waning moments of *TWW*'s first-season finale, President Bartlet concludes a student-focused town-hall event in Rosslyn, Virginia, by reminding his audience that he is the direct descendant of a Founding Father, Dr. Josiah Bartlett.[31] As a member of New Hampshire's delegation to the Second Continental Congress, Bartlet's ancestor affixed his name to the document that "announced to the world that we were no longer subjects of King George III, but rather a self-governing people—we hold these truths to be self-evident, they said; that all men are created equal." Bartlet continues: "Strange as it may seem, that was the first time in history that anyone bothered to write that down." As several of the show's main characters thoughtfully look on, a subtle yet poignant musical score accompanies Bartlet as he concludes his remarks by connecting America's past to the present. "Decisions," he says, "are made by those who show up—class dismissed."

Beginning in the discursive realm, Bartlet's remarks at the end of "What Kind of Day Has It Been?" bolster the larger mythos surrounding America's founding by first connecting another enduring cultural myth to the Declaration of Independence—the myth of US American exceptionalism. Defined by David Weiss and Jason Edwards, "American exceptionalism" is "the distinct belief that the United States is unique, if not superior, when compared to other nations"—and this belief, among others, animates the cultural reverence for the Declaration of Independence and the Founding Fathers in the United States today.[32] While it is true that the United States is the only country today that marks its birth with the signing of a document and not by commemorating a day of violence,[33] Bartlet's assertion that the Declaration was the "first time in history that anyone bothered to write" anything related to self-determination and equality down on parchment is demonstrably false.[34] Importantly, though, because the president of the United States is the "definitive and constitutive agent" in the formulation of American collective identity,[35] Bartlet's discourse here carries profound weight both within the fiction of *TWW* and within real American popular and political culture. That is, by "offering the vocabulary and discourses necessary for the larger public to form their national identity and essence," Bartlet's application of America's supposed exceptionalism to the Declaration of Independence further reinforces the mythos of the document and our country's creation.[36]

Next, by reminding his audience of his familial connection to the Declaration of Independence, Bartlet further contributes to the Declaration's mythic position in US American culture and history in two important ways. First, for his immediate audience within the show's fiction, Bartlet's remarks bolster his ethos—not only is Bartlet the president of the United States, he is also an embodied transhistorical link to the nation's sacred past. Second, for his secondary audience, the *TWW*'s viewers, this blending of fact and fiction together creates and sustains a believable history—a history that still maintains a mythic presence. As mentioned above, although *TWW*'s President Bartlet is entirely fictional, Dr. Josiah Bartlett is entirely nonfictional. In addition to signing the Declaration of Independence in 1776, the real Bartlett urged New Hampshire to adopt the US Constitution in 1788 and later served as the state's first governor.[37] The fictional Bartlet, in comparison, holds a PhD in economics, is a Nobel laureate, and also served as governor of New Hampshire. In the discursive resurrection of his ancestral link to the Declaration, then, *TWW*'s Bartlet ultimately initiates an interplay of identification, providing both audiences with additional emotional currency to further invest in the narrative that Bartlet is advancing. In other words, because Bartlet possesses an intimate, familial link to the Declaration—and he shares that link with the students sitting before him, as well as the show's viewers—members of both audiences are, in effect, invited to also feel an intimate connection with the sacred document. In inviting his audience to share in his visceral attachment to America's founding, Bartlet helps to advance our identification with the revered founding generation.

In the nondiscursive realm, *TWW*'s first season finale adds to the mythic weight of the Declaration primarily via two modalities: sound and sight. First, the musical score that accompanies President Bartlet helps sanctify the content of his closing message to students by adding elements of affect and reverence. Indeed, as Bartlet speaks, the music builds slowly and softly behind his voice. Interestingly, though, the music never overtakes Bartlet's voice, nor does Bartlet's voice increase in volume—it remains quiet, sincere, and reflective. The music's subtle crescendo, meanwhile, is only punctuated by (relative) silence twice: when Bartlet directly quotes the Declaration and offers his wistful, exceptionalistic interpretation of the document, and then again at the end of his remarks when he reminds his student audience that "decisions are made by those who show up." In addition to connecting the two discursive messages together to accentuate the ceremonial nature of Bartlet's concluding remarks, this sonic rhetorical strategy helps sustain a solemn atmosphere, a sacralizing aura akin to a religious service.

Working in tandem with its musicality, several visual components further contribute to this scene's mythic mise-en-scène. First among these visual components is the use of lighting. While Bartlet's physical location and bodily presence throughout the scene may have initially dictated the various lighting techniques used, the lighting ultimately "reifies the same romantic images" of the presidency that are "predicated on the power of the white, male hero."[38] Because Bartlet is seated alone on stage, the spotlight is, quite literally, only on him. The stage around Bartlet and his spotlight, meanwhile, remains in darkness. Relatedly, how the scene was edited reinforces the striking visuality created by its lighting. In particular, as Bartlet speaks about the Declaration within the paradigm of US American exceptionalism—all while the music softly builds around his voice—the camera artfully cuts to several members of the president's staff as they thoughtfully look on. The viewer, like Bartlet's staff, cannot help but also observe and listen to Bartlet's interpretation of the Declaration with similar reverence for the document and all that it entails, including the embodied connection to the past onstage before them.

Jefferson Lives

In the third episode of *TWW*'s fifth season, the Declaration occupies a peculiar position—it lives simultaneously in both the narrative's fore- and background. The episode's entire narrative arc occurs on the Fourth of July—Independence Day. Importantly, though, within the larger narrative arc of *TWW*, this episode, titled "Jefferson Lives," is the first episode following the resolution of a particularly dramatic plotline—the abduction of President Bartlet's youngest daughter, Zoe. In addition to the personal trauma endured by the president, his family, and his staff at Zoe's abduction, the situation also triggered a constitutional crisis that, ultimately, demanded a patriotic display of bipartisanship. "Jefferson Lives" chronicles both the personal and political aftermath of Zoe's traumatic ordeal.

Because Zoe is a member of the First Family, her kidnapping was considered an act of terror against the United States. This situation's unique set of exigencies ultimately placed Bartlet's position as both the victim's father and the country's commander-in-chief precariously at odds. Bartlet invoked the Twenty-Fifth Amendment, temporarily transferring power to the next person in the line of succession. Compounding the drama of this plotline, however, the person next in line after Bartlet was not the vice president but the Speaker of the House. In a scenario reminiscent of Spiro Agnew's resignation as Nixon's vice president, Bartlet's vice president had resigned from the office a few episodes prior, leaving the Speaker of the House—a Republican intrinsically opposed to Bartlet's progressivism—next in the presidential line of succession. While the episodes prior to "Jefferson Lives" largely valorized Bartlet's decision to invoke the Twenty-Fifth Amendment (Will Bailey, for example, commented that it was a "fairly stunning act of patriotism" but a "fairly ordinary act of fatherhood"), Bartlet's staff grew increasingly despondent over the political implications of their boss's decision. Party politics, in other words, remained omnipresent—a theme that "Jefferson Lives" subtly explores later.

The episode's title—"Jefferson Lives"—quietly begins to mythologize the Declaration the moment it appears onscreen. The title is a line reportedly whispered by the second president of the United States, John Adams, moments before he died on July 4, 1826—fifty years to the day since the signing of the Declaration of Independence. In an "extraordinary and eerie coincidence," America's third president, Thomas Jefferson, also lay dying on the very same day.[39] "Immortalized in [John] Trumbull's famous painting of the scene" in Independence Hall, elderly Senator Adar monotonously tells Bartlet at one point during the episode, the "two great giants," after "years of friendship and feuding," both died on their "country's birthday." Moreover, as many scholars have noted, the persistent mythos surrounding the Declaration of Independence can also be traced to Jefferson himself. By the close of his tenure in office, Jefferson reviled the presidency to such an extent that the epigraph on his tombstone (per his order) makes no mention of it, featuring instead only three accomplishments: author of the Virginia Statute for Religious Freedom, founder of the University of Virginia, and author of the Declaration of Independence.

While ultimately extolling the power and significance of the Declaration of Independence, this episode also introduces less exalted retellings of the symbolism of Adams and Jefferson dying on the fiftieth anniversary of the signing of the Declaration. Importantly, however, by the end of the episode, the Declaration is reified once again as a mythic foundational document. In an early scene, Zoe Bartlet affectionately anticipates her father's glorified celebration of the Declaration, telling Will Bailey that, for her father, the story behind "Jefferson Lives" is parabolic, that the story's connection to Independence Day "appeals to [her] Dad" because, "you know, hope and irony" and with a "little party politics thrown in," Will adds. This lighthearted tone abruptly ends when, in a later scene, viewers observe President Bartlet listening to the story of Adams and Jefferson being told by the monotonous Senator Adar. Bartlet struggles to maintain his polite composure as the senator drones on, rendering the story boring and on the verge of irrelevant.

The stiffest challenge to the mythic "Jefferson Lives" narrative, however, takes place later in the episode, when Bartlet expresses his frustration over the process of selecting a new vice president to his chief-of-staff, Leo McGarry. Here, Bartlet tells US America's origin story with a certain degree of exasperation. "Two hundred and twenty-seven years ago," Bartlet ruminates, "a bunch of guys got together on the Fourth of July and decided, because they didn't have any cherry bombs, they would declare some self-evident truths." McGarry chides him: "Fed up with democracy, are we?" Bartlet wearily explains that he talked to his initial pick for vice president to let him know that he was no longer being considered for the vice presidency. McGarry asks whether Bartlet wants to fight for his initial pick, and Bartlet, in the next breath, recommits to the democratic experiment. The country, he affirms, deserves "a chain of command that's irrefutable." He invokes another Founder, saying, "Ben Franklin thought the only hope for democracy was if people respected each other enough to compromise." In this way, Bartlet begins to reclaim the mythic greatness of the political system that the Declaration of Independence introduced, priming viewers for the episode's next and final scene.

This episode's framing of the Declaration of Independence is markedly different from its season 1 counterpart examined above. This season 5 episode paints perhaps a more humanized portrait of the founding generation. Throughout "Jefferson Lives," the storybook tale of President Adams's last words regarding his friend and rival, President Jefferson, varies in each retelling, fluctuating between inspirational, boring, and even irrelevant to the modern business of politics. The message concerning the Declaration, however, comes full circle by the end of the episode. The scene immediately following the aforementioned conversation between Bartlet and McGarry reverts to an unmistakably reverent framing. Earlier in the episode, viewers learn that a group of aspiring citizens from primarily Arab countries could not take their citizenship oaths because of a bomb threat. President Bartlet's response in this early scene is: "Let's find them an auditorium where they can safely take their oath." In the episode's final sequence, Bartlet and McGarry visit the auditorium where the group is in the process of repeating the oath. When they are finished, the judge administering the oath recognizes the president, who comes to the front of the room. He addresses the crowd: "My fellow Americans, congratulations and welcome. I hear you had some trouble finding a safe place to take your oath today. Our Founding Fathers were in a similar predicament. In many ways, our great Declaration of Independence was a work order issued under fire . . . one we still struggle to fulfill." With that, Bartlet leads the group in reciting the Pledge of Allegiance for the first time as American citizens. By both explanation and example, Bartlet reiterates the mythic significance of the Declaration of Independence and demonstrates its relevance to today's political world.

The combined power of discursive and nondiscursive rhetorics is apparent during the episode's final sequence. When Bartlet and McGarry arrive at the swearing-in ceremony, they linger in the background as the camera pans across the group repeating their Oath of Allegiance to the United States. The group's members are sober and earnest, and Bartlet and McGarry look on respectfully. While the president leads the group in the Pledge of Allegiance, the scene cuts to Bartlet's staff gathered to watch a fireworks display from the

White House lawn. The lighting is dark, with the staff members' faces illuminated only by the fireworks overhead and the sparklers that some carry. Here, the music is somber and reflective, punctuated only by the fading echoes of fireworks bursting above. The camera then cuts to Bartlet watching the same fireworks on the Truman Balcony, alone, notably not among his staff. The camera moves in closer to Bartlet, deep in thought as the fireworks reflect off the glass behind him, leaving viewers with a romantic image of the president of the United States on the Fourth of July.

Conclusion: Ideological Repercussions

TWW's contribution to the abiding mythos surrounding the Declaration of Independence—and, by extension, America's founding—originates in the show's multimodal rhetorical strategies. Through a combination of soaring oratory, stirring scores, and poignant visuals, *TWW* reverently frames the Declaration, continuing to hallow the document's position at the foundation of US American collective identity. While not the first artifact in US American popular culture to invoke the Declaration, *TWW*'s infusion of authentic US American history within its created fiction further produces a subtly powerful rhetoric simultaneously steeped in myth, identity, and affect. Although its mythic rhetoric is, at times, quiet, *TWW*'s presentation of the Declaration is nevertheless ideological—and, therefore, demands additional critical unpacking.

As longtime fans of the show, dissecting the force of *TWW*'s ideological rhetoricity is challenging. On the one hand, we firmly believe in the power of crafting, maintaining, and communicating a national civil religion. Civil religion is an implicit, collective code of beliefs based on a society's generally shared religious principles that informs narratives about the purpose and practices of a society.[40] When promoted in good faith, a US American civil religion can advance progress and justice, creating a better society not through the glorification of a problematic past but through an honest and rigorous examination of our shared history. In many ways, *TWW* does indeed advance an American civil religion in good faith.

On the other hand, we recognize the underlying precarity of a US American civil religion advanced with even the best intentions. As Raymie McKerrow reminds us, "Absence is as important as presence" when critiquing rhetorics of power—and conspicuously absent in *TWW*'s mythic narration of the Declaration is any honest assessment of the document, its historical context, and the document's role in maintaining iniquitous ideologies in the two and a half centuries since its publication.[41] In other words, *TWW*'s sanctification of the Declaration ultimately obfuscates many historical realities, ranging from, among others, the slave-holding practices of several Founding Fathers to the intentional denial of suffrage to women. Even in President Bartlet's sincere attempt to inspire increased youth voting turnout at the townhall in Rosslyn, Virginia, his reverential treatment of the Declaration helps conceal the document's glaring contradictions. Within this act of concealment, then, *TWW* reifies the Declaration's usefulness as a tool for the preservation of the hegemonic status quo. "Decisions," Bartlet told his audience, analogously referencing the decision to declare independence from Great Britain in 1776, "are made by those who show up." Sadly, just as it was in 1776, too many of those wanting to "show up" and participate in the decision-making process are still prohibited from doing so today.

In closing this chapter, it is important to reiterate that the mythic currents coursing through *TWW*'s employment of the Declaration also flow to and from the reservoir containing elements of US America's larger founding mythology—primarily elements of US American exceptionalism. While the lasting consequence emanating from the Declaration's mythologization in *TWW* may be in its manifestation of a progressive civic religion, we want to emphasize the dangers lurking beneath the surface of this cultural reservoir holding US America's larger founding mythology. These dangers range from a general, pervading ignorance of US America's past to the deliberate misrepresentation of this shared past for nakedly ideological goals.

The greatest danger emanating from and through a mythologized Declaration of Independence, however, often materializes in what Patricia Davis and Richard Branscomb call a "violent culture of white supremacist paternalism in the United States."[42] Situating the violence enacted by right-wing terrorists on January 6, 2021, as an example of "reactive memory," Davis and Branscomb position the right's fixation on "1776"—as a "weaponized . . . metonym for a hyperpatriotic 'revolutionary spirit'" born from the Declaration's signing that year that inspires racist, antidemocratic violence today.[43] Ultimately, although *TWW* offers a vastly different and good-faith interpretation of America's founding document, our task as critical scholars is to remain dedicated to revealing the interconnectedness of cultural rhetorics today, in order to, hopefully, help maintain an engaged citizenry.

NOTES

1. Writers Guild of America (WGA), "101 Best Written TV Series," June 2, 2023, https://www.wga.org/writers-room/101-best-lists/101-best-written-tv-series/list.

2. Scholarship that considers and critiques the mythologized nature of America's founding abounds across several academic disciplines to such an extent that we cannot hope to do it justice in this short chapter. For a helpful overview of this multidisciplinary scholarship, we recommend Kahn, "American Cosmogony."

3. "Jefferson Lives," *The West Wing*, NBC (original broadcast), Max (stream), October 8, 2003, https://play.max.com/video/watch/1a73c43b-be22-404b-9ec0-23f27e0ee26e/8c76c7c8-154f-45f0-b1cb-9b478cf32063.

4. Brian Moylan, "Ten Years On from the *West Wing* Finale, the Show's Shadow Still Looms Large," *The Guardian*, June 22, 2016, https://www.theguardian.com/tv-and-radio/2016/jun/22/west-wing-netflix-friends-binge-watching-nostalgia.

5. Moylan, "Ten Years On."

6. Janine Gibson, "Why I'll Miss *The West Wing*," *The Guardian*, July 25, 2006, sec. Media, https://www.theguardian.com/media/organgrinder/2006/jul/25/whyillmissthewestwing.

7. Will Robinson, "An Episode-by-Episode '*West Wing*' Podcast from One of Its Stars Is Happening," *Entertainment Weekly*, March 15, 2016, https://ew.com/article/2016/03/15/west-wing-podcast-joshua-malina-hrishikesh-hirway/.

8. Moylan, "Ten Years On."

9. Reid Wilson, "Americans Think 'West Wing' Is Most Realistic Political TV Show: Poll." *The Hill* (blog), March 21, 2022. https://thehill.com/homenews/media/599073-americans-think-west-wing-is-most-realistic-political-tv-show-poll/.

10. Scott, "'The Last Hurrah,'" 35.

11. Parry-Giles and Parry-Giles, *Prime-Time Presidency*, 51.

12. Parry-Giles and Parry-Giles, "*The West Wing*'s Prime-Time Presidentiality," 210.

13. Ulrich, "Cicero Would Love This Show," 133.

14. Ulrich, "Cicero Would Love This Show," 131.

15. McCabe, *The West Wing*, 118.

16. Holbert et al., "*The West Wing*."

17. Richardson, "Dark Arts of Good People."

18. Littlefield et al., "Patriotism and a Free Press."

19. Shepherd, *Gender, Violence and Popular Culture*, 58.

20. Semmler, McKay-Semmler, and Robertson, "Gendered Issue Depictions," 256.

21. Parry-Giles and Parry-Giles, *Prime-Time Presidency*.

22. Ulrich, "Cicero Would Love This Show," 133–134.

23. Littlefield et al., "Patriotism and a Free Press," 46.

24. For a more nuanced understanding of the debate about the nature of mythic criticism, see vol. 41, no. 2, of *Communication Studies* (Summer 1990). This discussion begins with Rowland's call for a narrower scope in mythic criticism and proceeds with rebuttals from Solomon, Osborn, Brummett, and Rushing.

25. Rowland and Frank, "Mythic Rhetoric and Rectification," 42.

26. Dorsey and Harlow, "'We Want Americans Pure and Simple,'" 63.

27. Rushing, "Mythic Evolution"; Wernecke, "Mythologizing Madiba," 139; Lewis, "Telling America's Story"; Dickinson, Ott, and Aoki, "Memory and Myth at the Buffalo Bill Museum."

28. Rushing, "Rhetoric of the American Western Myth"; "*E.T.* as Rhetorical Transcendence"; "Mythic Evolution"; "Evolution of 'the New Frontier.'"

29. Slotkin, *Gunfighter Nation*, 6–10.

30. Slotkin, *Gunfighter Nation*, 5.

31. "What Kind of Day Has It Been?," *The West Wing*, NBC (original), Max (stream), May 17, 2000, https://play.max.com/video/watch/7a512a36-5002-4860-9eb1-ad2b327403d8/604aaee1-970a-4214-8aae-5ff1d7502cd6.

32. Edwards and Weiss, introduction to *The Rhetoric of American Exceptionalism*, 1.

33. Put another way, instead of marking the April 19, 1775, battle(s) of Lexington and Concord as the date of America's founding, Americans consider July 4, 1776, as their country's birthday.

34. Lucas, "Rhetorical Ancestry."

35. Parry-Giles and Parry-Giles, "*The West Wing*'s Prime-Time Presidentiality," 211.

36. Parry-Giles and Parry-Giles, "*The West Wing*'s Prime-Time Presidentiality," 211.

37. "The Real-Life Namesake of Martin Sheen's '*West Wing*' President," National Constitution Center, May 19, 2016, https://constitutioncenter.org/blog/the-real-life-namesake-of-the-west-wings-president.

38. Parry-Giles and Parry-Giles, "*The West Wing*'s Prime-Time Presidentiality," 223.

39. Amber Paranick, "Deaths of John Adams and Thomas Jefferson on July 4th," *Headlines and Heroes* (blog), Library of Congress, July 6, 2022, blogs.loc.gov/headlinesandheroes/2022/07/deaths-of-john-adams-and-thomas-jefferson-on-july-4th.

40. Littlefield et al., "Patriotism and a Free Press," 42.

41. McKerrow, "Critical Rhetoric," 107.

42. Davis and Branscomb, "Reactive Memories of 1776," 180.

43. Davis and Branscomb, "Reactive Memories of 1776," 179.

BIBLIOGRAPHY

Brummett, Barry. "How to Propose a Discourse—a Reply to Rowland." *Communication Studies* 41, no. 2 (June 1, 1990): 128–35. https://doi.org/10.1080/10510979009368296.

Davis, Patricia, and Richard Branscomb. "Reactive Memories of 1776." *Communication and Democracy* 57, no. 2 (July 3, 2023): 178–202. https://doi.org/10.1080/27671127.2023.2222794.

Dickinson, Greg, Brian L. Ott, and Eric Aoki. "Memory and Myth at the Buffalo Bill Museum." *Western Journal of Communication* 69, no. 2 (April 2005): 85–108. https://doi.org/10.1080/10570310500076684.

Dorsey, Leroy G., and Rachel M. Harlow. "'We Want Americans Pure and Simple': Theodore Roosevelt and the Myth of Americanism." *Rhetoric and Public Affairs* 6, no. 1 (2003): 55–78.

Edwards, Jason A., and David Weiss. Introduction to *The Rhetoric of American Exceptionalism: Critical Essays*, edited by Jason A. Edwards and David Weiss, 1–8. Jefferson, NC: McFarland, 2011.

Holbert, R. Lance, David A. Tschida, Maria Dixon, Kristin Cherry, Keli Steuber, and David Airne. "*The West Wing* and Depictions of the American Presidency: Expanding the Domains of Framing in Political Communication." *Communication Quarterly* 53, no. 4 (October 1, 2005): 505–22. https://doi.org/10.1080/01463370500102228.

Kahn, Verity Rebecca. "An American Cosmogony: The Mythical Dimension of the Declaration of Independence." PhD diss., University of Aberdeen, 2017. https://abdn.alma.exlibrisgroup.com.

Lewis, William F. "Telling America's Story: Narrative Form and the Reagan Presidency." *Quarterly Journal of Speech* 73, no. 3 (August 1987): 280–302.

Littlefield, Christina, Theresa de los Santos, Patrick G. Rear, and Savannah Janssen. "Patriotism and a Free Press: A Content Analysis of Civil Religion in Aaron Sorkin's *The West Wing* and *The Newsroom*." *Journal of Media and Religion* 17, no. 2 (April 3, 2018): 41–60. https://doi.org/10.1080/15348423.2018.1531624.

Lucas, Stephen E. "The Rhetorical Ancestry of the Declaration of Independence." *Rhetoric and Public Affairs* 1, no. 2 (1998): 143–84.

McCabe, Janet. *The West Wing.* Detroit: Wayne State University Press, 2013.

McKerrow, Raymie E. "Critical Rhetoric: Theory and Praxis." *Communication Monographs* 56, no. 2 (June 1, 1989): 91–111. https://doi.org/10.1080/036377589093 90253.

Osborn, Michael. "In Defense of Broad Mythic Criticism—a Reply to Rowland." *Communication Studies* 41, no. 2 (June 1, 1990): 121–27. https://doi.org/10.1080 /10510979009368295.

Parry-Giles, Trevor, and Shawn J. Parry-Giles. *The Prime-Time Presidency: The West Wing and U.S. Nationalism.* Urbana: University of Illinois Press, 2006.

———. "*The West Wing*'s Prime-Time Presidentiality: Mimesis and Catharsis in a Postmodern Romance." *Quarterly Journal of Speech* 88, no. 2 (May 2002): 209–27. https://doi.org/10.1080/00335630209384371.

Richardson, Kay. "The Dark Arts of Good People: How Popular Culture Negotiates 'Spin' in NBC's *The West Wing.*" *Journal of Sociolinguistics* 10, no. 1 (2006): 52–69. https://doi.org/10.1111/j.1360-6441.2006.00317.x.

Rowland, Robert C. "On a Limited Approach to Mythic Criticism—Rowland's Rejoinder." *Communication Studies* 41, no. 2 (June 1, 1990): 150–60. https://doi.org/10 .1080/10510979009368298.

———. "On Mythic Criticism." *Communication Studies* 41, no. 2 (June 1, 1990): 101–16. https://doi.org/10.1080/10510979009368293.

Rowland, Robert C., and David A. Frank. "Mythic Rhetoric and Rectification in the Israeli-Palestinian Conflict." *Communication Studies* 62, no. 1 (January 31, 2011): 41–57. https://doi.org/10.1080/10510974.2011.532428.

Rushing, Janice Hocker. "*E.T.* as Rhetorical Transcendence." *Quarterly Journal of Speech* 71, no. 2 (May 1, 1985): 188–203. https://doi.org/10.1080/00335638509383728.

———. "Evolution of 'The New Frontier' in *Alien* and *Aliens*: Patriarchal Co-optation of the Feminine Archetype." *Quarterly Journal of Speech* 75, no. 1 (February 1, 1989): 1–24. https://doi.org/10.1080/00335638909383859.

———. "Mythic Evolution of 'The New Frontier' in Mass Mediated Rhetoric." *Critical Studies in Mass Communication* 3, no. 3 (September 1986): 265.

———. "On Saving Mythic Criticism—a Reply to Rowland." *Communication Studies* 41, no. 2 (June 1, 1990): 136–49. https://doi.org/10.1080/10510979009368297.

———. "The Rhetoric of the American Western Myth." *Communication Monographs* 50, no. 1 (March 1, 1983): 14–32. https://doi.org/10.1080/03637758309390151.

Scott, Ian. "'The Last Hurrah': *The West Wing* and the Future of American Politics After 9/11." In *Politics and Politicians in Contemporary US Television: Washington as Fiction*, edited by Betty Kaklamanidou and Margaret Tally, 34–46. Routledge Advances in Television Studies 6. New York: Routledge, 2017.

Semmler, Shane M., Kelly McKay-Semmler, and Terry Robertson. "Gendered Issue Depictions in *Commander in Chief* versus *The West Wing.*" *Atlantic Journal of Communication* 21, no. 5 (November 1, 2013): 247–62. https://doi.org/10.1080/15 456870.2013.840304.

Shepherd, Laura J. *Gender, Violence, and Popular Culture: Telling Stories.* London: Routledge, 2012. https://doi.org/10.4324/9780203105030.

Slotkin, Richard. *Gunfighter Nation: The Myth of the Frontier in Twentieth Century America.* Norman: University of Oklahoma Press, 1998.

Solomon, Martha. "Responding to Rowland's Myth or in Defense of Pluralism—a Reply to Rowland." *Communication Studies* 41, no. 2 (June 1, 1990): 117–20. https://doi .org/10.1080/10510979009368294.

Ulrich, Anne. "'Cicero Would Love This Show': The Celebration of Rhetoric and Citizenship in *The West Wing*." In *Contemporary Rhetorical Citizenship*, edited by Christian Kock and Lisa S. Villadsen, 131–46. Leiden: Leiden University Press, 2014.

Wernecke, Christopher J. "Mythologizing Madiba: Myth, Resistance, and the Globalized Post-presidency in Barack Obama's Nelson Mandela Lecture Series Address." *Howard Journal of Communications* 34, no. 2 (March 15, 2023): 132–50. https://doi.org/10.1080/10646175.2022.2101163.

13

PROXIMATE DELIBERATION AND THE 1776 MOMENT: THE PROUD BOYS' AND OATH KEEPERS' USE OF THE DECLARATION OF INDEPENDENCE

Leslie A. Hahner

On January 6, 2021, Donald J. Trump held a political rally that aimed to interrupt the peaceful transfer of power from his presidency to the next. The day was a large, riotous protest, with speakers, music, and displays of political symbolism, including a makeshift noose for Mike Pence. At 1:06 in the afternoon, Trump urged the crowd, "And we fight. We fight like hell. And if you don't fight like hell, you're not going to have a country anymore." He continued: "So we're going to, we're going to walk down Pennsylvania Avenue. I love Pennsylvania Avenue. And we're going to the Capitol, and we're going to try and give . . . them the kind of pride and boldness that they need to take back our country."[1] After these words from President Trump, the crowd walked to the Capitol and in the next few hours held Congress and the country hostage.

Trump encouraged the crowd to walk to the Capitol. He said it himself. But the president had assistance. Members of the Proud Boys and Oath Keepers, paramilitary terrorist organizations, whipped the crowd into a frenzy through their control and agitation techniques. As the protestors walked toward the Capitol, members of the Proud Boys acted as yell leaders. Proud Boys members marched among the protestors and urged the crowd forward into the building. Proud Boys organizers used a call-and-response system to work the crowd into a frenzy. The Oath Keepers similarly used their own arsenal and force to facilitate violence at the Capitol. In a host of ways, the Proud Boys and Oath Keepers used strategic actions to galvanize and propel the crowd toward violence.[2] The Proud Boys took their cues from a manual owned by

Enrique Tarrio, a nine-page pdf document that mapped the attack on the Capitol, titled *1776 Returns*. It offers explicit instructions that were used by the Proud Boys on January 6, 2021. Legal discovery on this document suggests that Tarrio received the document on December 30, 2020, from cryptocurrency investors in Florida.[3] Tarrio thus possessed a copy leading into the organization's frantic planning between December 19 and January 6.[4] Just after President Trump's December 19 statement to the Proud Boys, to "stand back and stand by," Tarrio had formed two internal militia groups within the Proud Boys: the so-called Ministry of Self-Defense and Boots on the Ground. Tarrio tasked these two groups with planning the attack on the Capitol and coordinating with other militias.[5]

1776 Returns laid out plans for the occupation of federal buildings and a mandate to deliver the presidency to Donald Trump. Readers were given a five-point plan to infiltrate, execute, distract, occupy, and sit in.[6] The document comprises two parts: "Storm the Winter Palace," which offered instructions for members of the Proud Boys and Oath Keepers, together with the "Patriot Plan," which was to be distributed to onlookers. Both documents supply explicit, if very brief, instructions to audiences. Together, these documents encouraged a rebellious crowd to become an active engine against this country's democracy. *1776 Returns* told folks on the ground to "Read Directions Carefully," as this document presented a unified and organized set of actions that rabble rousers could follow. The document urged readers to organize the "masses to rush the buildings," to distract law enforcement by pulling fire alarms around the city, to target specific legislator's offices, and to wear medical masks to disguise faces.[7] The Proud Boys planned to commit seditious conspiracy on January 6, 2021. *1776 Returns* is key to that violent commitment.

The document traffics in a radical understanding of what the year 1776 means. It also indexes the enunciative force of the Declaration of Independence. Throughout the weeks leading up to January 6, 2021, the year 1776 and several other symbols and ideas from the Revolutionary Era became the battle cry of militia members hoping to overthrow the national government. *1776 Returns* is loaded with revolutionary-era symbols and slogans that show the insurrectionists' commitment to revolutionary violence; it situates these historical symbols as fragments, textual references with powerful messages regarding what the founders insisted upon and what patriots should do for Donald Trump.

This chapter analyzes the bits and pieces of the Declaration of Independence and the Revolutionary Era as deployed in *1776 Returns* to warrant insurrectionary behavior at the Capitol on January 6, 2021. It shows that the use of these fragments by reactionary actors is one of proximate deliberation. Fragments from the Declaration of Independence and Constitution circulated in the public talk of political leaders and across social media sites, as well as in the planning and execution of the insurrection. Across myriad sites, these fragments seemingly bolster anti-state actions. In the insular communities of the reactionary Right, the mere skeletal inference of these historical documents became convincing; codes, symbols, and taglines substituted for significant deliberation. These actors were on the move within days. In circulation and repetition, the proximate influence of these fragments shaped reactionary views.

These revolutionary symbols and fragments serve as a warrant for anti-state action by proxy—that is, they stand in for deliberation. In some ways, it is deceitful to use the word "deliberation," given that this document displays the military-intelligence acumen of feral squirrels. Within *1776 Returns*, proximate deliberation refers to the repetition and placement of key words and figures in a proximate manner that compels action. By weaving these rhetorical fragments together, *1776 Returns* employs these symbols or fragments as bearers of truth to galvanize fantastical, conspiratorial communities. These pieces of rhetorical discourse sanctioned and guided insurrectionists to storm the Capitol and to hunt down congressional representatives. In *1776 Returns*, the relationship between these symbols and the posture of assumed success pushes proximate deliberation to its violent conclusion.

Though the Declaration of Independence is clearly a revolutionary document, the fragments selected and circulated surrounding the insurrection of January 6, 2021, show how the "moment" of the Declaration of 1776 creates a powerful a proxy for deliberation. They enunciate the specific ways in which the US government should be destroyed and replaced by a new world order. The creation of the *1776 Returns* brings these fragments together with a specific force. No longer just tweets or references, the document shows how the Proud Boys weaponized fragments from the Declaration of Independence and other founding documents. Their weaponization suggests that the Proud Boys and other insurrectionists may have followed Trump's demands to "stand back and stand by" on Twitter. The traveling bits of the document ultimately replaced deliberation itself on the part of the audience, manifesting a viewpoint that says a "separate and equal station" is theirs for the taking. This chapter demonstrates how rhetorical circulation presents itself as deliberation and, by proxy, mandates a populist reaction to the sovereignty of the state. The rhetorical power of *1776 Returns* exemplifies the ways in which reactionary groups read public discourse and respond with specific forms of violence; hence, understanding how fragments appear in this guidebook for insurrection helps clarify and explain how such extremists are motivated to act.

The 1776 Moment

The adoption of the Declaration of Independence in 1776 has forever marked the year's revolutionary status in the nation's self-understanding. The common refrain, for the United States of America, is that we are a nation of the free because of those Revolutionary War heroes who secured the nation's freedom. The year is used as an anthem in patriotic holidays and rituals and regularly lauded as a collective spirit to embody.

During the Trump administration and following the events of January 6, 1776 was used as a rallying cry to justify an attack on the nation itself. Presidential commissions, legislators, and insurrectionists used it to justify their symbolic and material violence. These actors operated in a proximate approach to one another, meaning that each rhetorical agent called to the others for violence in the same manner, namely, through the repetition of circulated slogans, symbols, and common references. These slogans emerge from a wealth of projects that center on the Revolutionary War, the Declaration of Independence, and the year 1776.

In late 2020, then President Trump created his 1776 Commission. As more fully analyzed in chapter 14 in this volume, the 1776 Commission's charge was to generate "patriotic education" to counter critical national histories including those of Howard Zinn and the *1619 Project* championed by Nikole Hannah-Jones.[8] The use of the year 1776 signaled that the education provided by the commission was to be tailored toward a rosy understanding of national history. Rather than teach the actual history of the nation-state, the 1776 commission propagandized US history through jingoism. Slogans, falsehoods, and symbolism appeared prominently in Trump's patriotic education; the gilding afforded the era of the US American Revolution was buffed to a most brilliant shine.

In April 2022, Marjorie Taylor-Greene (R-GA) fought against being disqualified as a congressional representative. At the time, it appeared that Taylor-Greene had declared support for the insurrection and those actors who were storming the Capitol. She was charged with blurting out a "code word" used by Trump and other anti-state actors.[9] During the hearings,

Taylor-Greene maintained that her commentary on the insurrection did not indicate her deep involvement with reactionary groups but rather that she was experiencing a "1776 moment," in which her support for the lie that Trump had won the 2020 presidential election simply *referenced* revolution and not any particular document or actions.

In the lead-up to January 6, 2021, it appeared that the Declaration had taken on renewed authority for a coming revolution. The word "1776" pulsed on the lips of political representatives and anti-state public figures, while the spirit of 1776 inspired protestors and insurrectionists at the Capitol. In these ways, "1776" indexes the Declaration of Independence, but as wielded by reactionary actors such symbols push for the populist, legal authority to, as written in the Constitution, "dissolve the political bands" of the state and "declare . . . their separation."

Reactionary Actors and We, the People

To organize for the insurrection on January 6, reactionary militias and public figures regularly employed pieces of the Declaration of Independence to warrant anti-state actions. Protestors proclaimed that they were saving the country from a corrupt election. Insurrectionists stormed the Capitol to hurt legislators and prevent the peaceful transfer of power.

The Proud Boys significantly contributed to the planning and execution of the attack on the US Capitol in January of 2021. Tarrio coordinated with the Oath Keepers in executing the attack—an anomaly, given that the two groups rarely worked together. Experts have conjectured that the document found on Tarrio is an abbreviated plan, not the full plan,[10] although we cannot know if it is the full plan or not. Nevertheless, even in this form, it is clear that for the Proud Boys the goal was to occupy federal buildings with as many people as possible. The document offers a basic set of coded instructions on using occupation to prevent the peaceful transfer of power.

The Proud Boys, and the reactionary Right more generally, regularly use phrases from the foundational documents of the nation. They are also known for mixing and blending phrases from the Declaration of Independence and the Constitution,[11] which is useful for their anti-state purposes. These actors aim to marshal the revolutionary ethos of founding documents while shedding historical context. Using fragments, bits, or soundbites from the Declaration of Independence and the Constitution serves to turn patriotism into jingoism and jingoism into terrorism.[12] Their tactic aims to move audience members from a vague anti-government sentiment to a more specific ambition: occupation of the federal government to thwart the peaceful transfer of power.

The importance of *1776 Returns* to the attack on and occupation of the Capitol cannot be overstated. This is a historically significant document that provides an outline of plans to attack the Capitol, take over federal buildings, and ultimately assume control of the country. According to a former federal prosecutor, Patrick Cotter, "This is like getting the plans of the Japanese to bomb Pearl Harbor on Dec. 5, 1941. . . . From a legal perspective, the real important legal issue is not the Capitol. The real important issue is an attempt to commit sedition."[13] The document, alongside corroborating testimony and video, was used to convict many members of the Proud Boys of seditious conspiracy.

1776 Returns is also rhetorically important insofar as it offers incremental, albeit truncated, instructions on how to persuade less radicalized protestors to join the insurrection. Throughout the document, the Proud Boys are told how to use tactics of persuasion to move people into federal buildings, with the goal of using control and agitation techniques to enlarge the presence and magnify the demands of the reactionary Right. For this reason, analyzing the rhetorical tactics of this document is essential.

1776 Returns, much like the actions used on the ground, engages in a work of proximate deliberation. Relying heavily on patriotic symbolism, specifically from the Revolutionary Era and the Declaration of Independence, it contains a set of rhetorical proxy moves intended to help usher the Proud Boys and Oath Keepers, and later people on the ground, into acts of sedition. To implement these proxy moves, the document makes use of a number of rhetorical fragments.

Rhetorical fragments are intertextual pieces of discourse for the audience to compile. Michael Calvin McGee suggested in 1990 that the circulation of these fragments functions ideologically as audiences compose rhetorical texts that seem finished. For McGee, dense rhetorical fragments become resources used by audiences to create meaning.[14] Audience members create meaning by assembling the bits and fragments they encounter into beliefs and actions. As it relates to the fragments of the Declaration used in *1776 Returns*, the meaning-making assemblage became a proximate form of deliberation for reactionary actors. Rhetorical fragments from the Declaration and the Revolutionary Era are interwoven throughout this document.

In *1776 Returns*, the use of the pronoun "we" and references to the phrase "We, the People" shape a collective out of disparate groups of people. The phrase "We, the People" is especially salient for those who revere the United

States' founding documents. In the Constitution, "We, the People" is a flourish with the power to stitch collectives together, to say that the people of this nation are materially significant, even more important than the whims of King George III. According to rhetorical critic Maurice Charland, narrative stories can found a new people: narratives about French Quebec reshaped its citizens' ideological view of the region.[15] *1776 Returns* lays the foundation for an opposition to the state that is loyal to a revolutionary ethos, what the founding fathers may have wanted had they been supporters of Donald. J. Trump.

The use of "We, the People" in *1776 Returns* draws a Trumpian revolutionary people together. Recruitment for the Proud Boys skyrocketed as the Big Lie spread across media networks in December 2020.[16] The symbolic power wielded in *1776 Returns* relies on the rabid belief in the Big Lie as a founding event for this new people. The phrase "We, the People" is sprinkled throughout *1776 Returns*, whose second half begins with the phrase "We, the People" transposed from the Constitution. Different from the Constitution, however, the Proud Boys reading *1776 Returns* are not the revolutionary figures who secured independence from England; instead they are individuals who are convinced that the 2020 election was fraudulent. The Proud Boys took radical action to ensure that their false belief would spread to other people. The use of the phrase "We, the People" in this document is not a founding like all others—it intends violence to overturn the democratic process.

One of the most potent rhetorical assertions of this document is to create an acting collective. The groups who terrorized the country on January 6 did not typically operate in tandem, let alone in coordination. A key feature of the reactionary Right is that its groups and individuals are rarely aligned.[17] Reactionary actors fight among themselves and are often ideologically distinct from one another. The Proud Boys are a notoriously finnicky group that may commit to and then quickly change political positions.[18] Yet *1776 Returns* possesses a rhetorical fiction that proved useful to events on January 6, the same sleight of hand seen in the founding documents of the nation: the first rhetorical fragment organizing this document is "We, the People."

In one location, the document references the people's house to describe federal buildings: "We need [as] many people as possible inside these buildings. These are OUR buildings, they are just renting space. We must show our politicians We the People are in charge."[19] Here, the phrase "We the People" solicits those reading the document *1776 Returns* to become part of the group addressed. These individuals are "patriots" who will remind politicians that they are not in charge. The phrases "we own" or "we are in charge" are sprinkled throughout this short document. The United States is positioned as the enemy of the "we" called to act against the state's electoral process.

The collective pronoun "we" creates a populist appeal among disparate actors. The phrase includes all those who seek to declare the 2020 election fraudulent. The document helps generate the rhetorical fiction of a unified set of anti-state actors.[20] It creates a symbolic but nevertheless palpable force of will that appears ready and able to resist the processes of the state. Conspiratorial actions often require that origin myths be wielded. As made evident by the use of collective, patriotic pronouns, in *1776 Returns* persistent collective utterances stand in for that origin myth and are repeated to supply the veracity of fact (often sans evidence). The Proud Boys are not a large group, certainly not large enough to execute an occupation on their own, as evidenced by their unusual cooperation with the Oath Keepers. But this document amplifies their rhetorical power as historical agents. The Proud Boys stand in for "We, the People" because they are willing to return "our buildings," to let the people run their own state.

The phrase asserts a populist force of will where splintered ideologies exist. The primary goal articulated in the document is to "occupy federal buildings and communicate our demands." The landscape of reactionary violence is broad and filled with conspiratorial demands that can never be met. For example, some groups on the ground on January 6 believe that the state is run by a deep network of pedophiles. Others believe that the state is composed of dark figures in human-meat costumes. And still others think that Donald Trump won the election despite the massive number of votes by which he lost. It would be nearly impossible to generate common ground among a group of such conspiracy-fueled, rogue individuals. The use of the phrase "We, the People" in this document papers over these differences to assert that there is a common will.

Additionally, copies of the second half of the document, the so-called Patriot Plan, were to be distributed to individuals at the Capitol. The distribution of this document was purposeful, with the opening lines reading "You are the revolution." The move from "We, the People" to "You . . . the revolution" is a charged rhetorical moment for the reader. The use of a historical declaration with a modern directive marks the events of the day as history in the making. Individuals who identify themselves as part of "the people" now understand their tasks as a very specific calling: to take action against the state.

Storm the Winter Palace

1776 Returns exhibits a set of coded practices that were well known to members of the reactionary Right who arrived that day. These references, symbols, and codes had already traveled across strong reactionary digital networks. That is, while Enrique Tarrio was the sole person caught with this document, it is clear that the plans and general strategy for January 6 and the specific references found in the document had already circulated online. Homeland Security investigations discovered that this event was "planned in plain sight": that much of the rhetorical fragments and symbols used in *1776 Returns* were not confined to this document.[21] The two sections of the document offer instructions for two groups: the Proud Boy / Oath Keeper organizers and those on the ground on January 6, 2021.

The first part of the *1776 Returns*, "Storm the Winter Palace," was likely created as a set of instructions for the Proud Boys and Oath Keepers, as well as other assorted militia members, who worked ground control. The second half of the document, "Patriot Plan," was a time-stamped list of instructions and buildings to target, intended to be distributed on the ground. Both sections offered very brief instructions to readers and skeletal references.

The title of the first section is a coded term referring to the Russian Revolution of 1917; it addresses the work of managing the people's commitment to revolution. Years into the Bolshevik Revolution, in 1920, artists created a mass spectacle outside the Tsarist Winter Palace. The event was one of ritual theater, featuring dancers, actors, and circus performers with tanks and cars. The images portrayed a symbolist utopia, with workers organizing to overthrow the state and battling their Tsarist oppressors, resulting in the victory of the October Revolution.[22] Here, the phrase "Storm the Winter Palace" indexes the need for the Proud Boys and Oath Keepers to arrange the collective imagination and force of people on the ground.

The title of the first five pages of *1776 Returns* also functions as a shortcut to action. Rather than introducing a deliberation on the appropriate course of action in the face of claims of ongoing corruption, the phrase asserts that the reader's spectacular performance at the Capitol will inspire others in the country. This fantasy suggests that by performing well on January 6, those taking action will rescue the country by securing the presidency for Donald Trump. "Storm the Winter Palace" is largely an abbreviated script for why the mass spectacle of January 6 was essential: it promulgates the lie that the 2020 election was stolen. Its directions, then, urge members of the Proud Boys to help correct this putative injustice.

To take the Winter Palace, *1776 Returns* proposes a set of tactics used to move people *en masse*. Donovan Ochs originally theorized the rhetoric of agitation and control through the concept of dissent.[23] According to Ochs, oppressed groups gather together to name and communicate dissent to the powers that be. As such, dissent is critical to a functional republic. In *1776 Returns*, collective agitation is voiced not as dissent but as a necessary revolution that is a foregone conclusion. By assuming that the election was stolen and by managing throngs of people in specific ways, the Proud Boys applied a mode of agitation and control that attempted to sweep everyday citizens into a large show of force. Such plans encouraged readers following the time-stamped plan for "execution day."

1776 Returns defined several different roles for members of the Proud Boys and other assorted insurrectionists to adopt. The first role was the "lead," that is, the person who would set up a fake tour of selected federal buildings to capture reconnaissance about the interior and locate key personnel. If the lead was caught, a second-in-command was to then make an appointment to tour the buildings and report back. Leads were similarly tasked with showing up on the morning of January 6 to walk near or into these buildings in suits, without any tactical gear. The planning document rhetorically positioned Proud Boys members as militia-like in the way they were to lead participants into federal buildings and use occupation to control sites.

Another part of the document offered instructions on how to move people toward the federal buildings. A "hypeman" was to lead the shouting of slogans and keep the energy of the crowd at a low boil. If that energy diminished, the hypeman was also tasked with collecting stray sheep and moving them back into the march toward to the Capitol. The hypeman also had a sidekick, the "recruiter," who would assemble the "patriots" outside the federal buildings and urge protestors toward occupation and sedition. In the document, patriots were encouraged to let people into the buildings and to cause trouble to distract law enforcement.

The Proud Boys explicitly used a hypeman to guide the crowd of protestors away from the White House. On January 6, protestors began the morning at the White House, listening to speeches, music, and enjoying the day. After President Trump's speech at 1:06 p.m., the crowd was pulled toward the Capitol. Without doubt, the president directly encouraged the crowd to walk down to the Capitol and "take our country back." Slogans such as this, combined with the Winter Palace imagery of *1776 Returns*, provided a set of marching orders to this would-be military. There is little room for interpretation when such conspiracy-based actions compel urgent action. The proximate use of multiple coded phrases and symbols set the Proud Boys and Oath Keepers in motion.

Video pertaining to January 6 shown in congressional hearings shows how effectively tactics on the ground generated crowd response.[24] After

Trump has concluded his speech, the Proud Boys' hypeman is seen leading the crowd down Pennsylvania Avenue, while a recruiter is seen responding to the hypeman's chants from the back of the crowd and urging people forward. Thus, the hypeman and recruiter—with limited manpower among throngs of people—successfully drove the march down Pennsylvania Avenue, effectively moving the crowd closer to the occupation of the Capitol. These roles were designed to use lean participant numbers in a manner that aggrandized the unified presence of insurrectionists.

As soon as the protestors arrived at the Capitol, the aim of the Proud Boys was to have fifty-person (minimum) teams target the buildings to be occupied. Several buildings were listed as prize locations: the Russell, Dirksen, and Hart Senate buildings, as well as the Cannon, Longworth, and Rayburn House buildings. The Supreme Court was also on a list to be targeted.[25] Their plans were downsized on January 6, however, to focus on impeding the due process of electoral business. The Senate chambers were occupied, and police officers defended the House. Pipe bombs were discovered at both the Republican and Democratic National Committees, while Molotov cocktails were reported in a nearby vehicle. These weapons show the danger of the event, while the spectacle of the event illustrates the capacity for small, reactionary groups to shape collective action swiftly.

Once "patriots" occupied the Capitol, the Proud Boys, Oath Keepers, and other assorted insurrectionists made it a point to seek out particular legislators. Video and audio taken inside the buildings shows insurrectionists calling the names of Mike Pence, Nancy Pelosi, and many other legislators.[26] Their words and actions once near or inside the offices of legislators make it clear that harming these individuals was their goal—that is, while the spectacle of storming the Winter Palace was the focus of *1776 Returns*, the Capitol insurrectionists took to heart the orders of slogans and symbols with an especially violent show of force.

Occupation and the Bundy Legacy

The word "occupy" and the belief that the occupation of federal buildings will guarantee the success of the Proud Boys and Oath Keepers are especially cryptic, but the term is popular in the reactionary sphere. This belief that the occupation of federal buildings would proceed successfully is based on faith in Cliven Bundy and the Bundy family's continued success at skirting the law. In 1993, the Cliven Bundy family began occupying the Malheur National Wildlife Refuge in Oregon. Over the next few decades, the family continued to graze cattle on land closed by the Bureau of Land Management (BLM). This longstanding conflict ultimately led to an armed conflict in 2014, often known as the Battle of Bunkerville, which erupted between Bundy family members, Oath Keepers, and other anti-state terrorist organizations on one side against the BLM and law enforcement on the other.[27] Despite the high risk of this moment, it inaugurated a persistent faith in reactionary circles that such a tactic could be used elsewhere.[28] The people asserting their rights in the armed 2014 conflict cited the authority of historical documents, relying on the transcendent action of the Constitution, specifically the postal clause of article 1, section 8, clause 7, which specifies federal powers for post offices and routes.[29] This clause is interpreted, in a popular misreading by so-called Sovereign Citizens and similar groups, to say that the federal government is limited to ten square miles of land and therefore that the remaining land belongs to the people.[30] Of course, the Bundy family, as well as the thousands of individuals who have used this strategy, disavow the possibility that there is a law or justification that predates the Constitution and therefore warrants their abandoning any and all claims to ownership in favor of Indigenous peoples' inalienable protections. In reactionary circles, the tactic of occupation is sacrosanct, seen as emerging from the Declaration as well as other founding documents.

The rhetorical work of the Bundy occupation gave a mythic cast to some of the fragments in *1776 Returns*. The continual demand that occupation is necessary for patriots suggests that there is a heroic character to the fight against the state. Throughout this document, language positions the Proud Boys, Oath Keepers, and other insurrectionists as patriots who are *actually* true to the Constitution and Declaration of Independence. In effect, readers of this document are encouraged to become more loyal to some imagined originalism. I use the word "originalism" (lowercase) on purpose, as this fragment is not meaningfully connected to the concept of constitutional originalism as taken directly from the Constitution. Instead, the document asserts that insurrectionists are patriots in regard to some imagined former nation that has fallen into disrepair. Its authors adopt a zero-trust attitude toward all arms of the government, asserting that the need for insurrection has already been decided, and that the Proud Boys, Oath Keepers, and so on are the perfect agents to effect the dissolution of the state.

To be sure, *1776 Returns* is delusional in regard to the scale of the operation proposed—that is, the occupation of many federal buildings for weeks. It was a naïve goal, at best. The Proud Boys and Oath Keepers combined did not have the numbers to carry out such a coup in the days between December 16,

2020, and January 6, 2021. But beyond that impossible horizon, in reality, the insurrectionists *did* successfully occupy the Capitol for hours.

Once inside a federal building, the insurrectionists were supposed to propose a list of demands that are given in the document, the first of which was to hold a new election to cancel the results of the 2020 election. The Proud Boys had already invested in the Big Lie, wherein Trump and his compatriots continued to contest the legitimacy of the election by spreading falsehoods.[31] Members of the Proud Boys, whom Trump had ordered to "Stand back and stand by," were at the ready to deliver the nation to Donald Trump.

1776 Returns, even in its abbreviated state, makes clear that this new election would be conducted on paper ballots, exclude all mail-in and absentee ballots, allow only in-person voting using a photo ID card in all states, and have the National Guard patrol voting locations. This highly regulated election was clearly designed to deliver the presidency to Trump.

The presumption of success that is proffered in *1776 Returns* is irrational. The document operates as a rhetorical delivery system for a series of fragments that were circulating around the election. The codes found within this document reveal an indebtedness to a set of reactionary beliefs about the Revolutionary Era. Those codes—populist foundations in "We, the People," revolutionary appeals in "Storm the Winter Palace," and hopeful investments to "Occupy" federal buildings—all appear in *1776 Returns*. Given that the document was given to Tarrio on December 30 by a source in Florida, it seems clear that the document was both a product of and a contribution to the revolutionary fragments in circulation during this period.

Conclusion

Significantly, the symbolic resources marshalled in *1776 Returns* did not offer arguments or reasons why such actions were strategic, or how, exactly, to accomplish such aims. It seems improbable that this document was the only planning document used by the Proud Boys and/or Oath Keepers, yet its rhetorical significance is vast. The document is key to explaining how a series of fragments and symbols wielded by paramilitary groups produced violent effects among their own ranks as well as among protestors. Although the insurrectionists were unsuccessful, their plans were on a much deadlier scale than what occurred. Nevertheless, four individuals died from the events at the Capitol, including three Trump supporters as well as Brian Sicknick, a United States Capitol Police officer and decorated military veteran. Several other law enforcement personnel were so shaken by the event that their own lives were shattered. Hundreds were injured during the events of that day. Even if these actors did not reach their goals, they nearly prevented the peaceful transfer of power.

The Proud Boys, Oath Keepers, and other assorted insurrectionists planned for the violent overthrow of the United States government. While their success was impeded in a number of ways, it is important to keep in mind that President Trump did not call for the National Guard or other federal troops to descend on the Capitol for a number of hours. Whether or not he supported the work of the Proud Boys and other insurrectionists, he certainly facilitated the violent events of that day: if those troops had been summoned to the Capitol, it is likely that much less harm would have been done. Some have asserted that Trump's refusal to summon the federal troops is evidence of his complicity with the rioters.[32]

The importance of *1776 Returns* to the reactionary violence of January 6, 2021, is monumental. It reveals how the Proud Boys defined themselves in opposition to the United States and demonstrates that a seditious conspiracy took place among the Proud Boys. These groups created a plan to take over government buildings and convert democratic power into militia rule. This document and several other forms of testimony, which proved that the Proud Boys had engaged in conspiratorial planning to impede the election and aimed to attack legislators, were essential to making the case that the Proud Boys were not rogue actors but had made a concerted effort to act against the state.

In May 2023, four prominent members of the Proud Boys, who had acted in seditious conspiracy—Dominic Pezzola, Zachary Rehl, Ethan Nordean, and Joseph Biggs—were convicted of seditious conspiracy and conspiracy to obstruct an official proceeding.[33] Charles Donohoe and Enrique Tarrio were also charged with seditious conspiracy and conspiracy to obstruct a proceeding. Donohoe pleaded guilty in April to two counts of conspiracy to obstruct an official proceeding and assaulting a federal officer; Tarrio was sentenced to twenty-two years in federal prison for his activities.

1776 Returns is an important historical document, but its greater significance lies in its rhetorical capacities. This document played a role in organizing the historic events of January 6, 2021. Yet despite that, the document is almost embarrassing in its limited success. Comprising a series of slogans, code words, and symbols, it holds little in the way of explanation or even justification; it is more of an outline than a how-to. Nevertheless, this document provided a guide for the Proud Boys to overtake the Capitol. It provided a set of proxy moves that stood in for and replaced deliberation. Individuals and groups acted according to the commands and fragments they found and assembled from this document and elsewhere.

On the ground, the Proud Boys and Oath Keepers did not generally attempt to make persuasive arguments to convince protestors to become insurrectionists; instead, they used slogans, hype, and other rhetorical symbols, thus asserting their own symbolic power. By using a hypeman and recruiter, and by adopting the vantage point of revolutionary heroes, these individuals and groups acted on those slogans and fragments that had saturated their worlds. Brought together in *1776 Returns*, those symbols and fragments operated in proximity to foment seditious and violent behavior.

NOTES

1. Brian Naylor, "Read Trump's Jan. 6 Speech, a Key Part of Impeachment Trial," NPR, February 10, 2021, https://www.npr.org/2021/02/10/966396848/read-trumps-jan-6-speech-a key-part-of-impeachment-trial.
2. "Watch: Jan. 6 Committee Shows New Footage of Capitol Attack," *PBS NewsHour*, June 9, 2022, https://www.pbs.org/newshour/politics/watch-jan-6-committee-shows-new-footage-of-capitol-attack.
3. *Anderson v. Griswold and Trump*, Civil Action No. 2023CV32577, District Court, Denver, CO (2023), https://www.justsecurity.org/wp-content/uploads/2023/09/Anderson-v-Griswold-and-Trump.pdf.
4. Defendant Zachary Rehl's Motion to Reopen Detention Hearing, Ex. 1, "1776 Returns," *United States v. Nordean, et al.*, No. 21-cr-175, ECF No. 401-1 (D.D.C. June 15, 2022), https://s3.documentcloud.org/documents/22060615/1776-returns.pdf.
5. *Anderson v. Griswold and Trump*.
6. Def. Zachary Rehl, "1776 Returns."
7. Def. Zachary Rehl, "1776 Returns."
8. "The 1776 Report," President's Advisory 1776 Commission, January 2021, https://trumpwhitehouse.archives.gov/wp-content/uploads/2021/01/The-Presidents-Advisory-1776-Commission-Final-Report.pdf.
9. *Rowan v. Raffensperger and Greene*, Civil Action No. 2022C364778, Superior Court, Fulton County, GA, https://www.justsecurity.org/wp-content/uploads/2023/04/greene-response-to-petition-for-judicial-review.pdf.
10. Will Carless, "'Devastating Piece of Evidence': Filing Reveals a Proud Boys Plan to Storm Buildings Jan. 6," *USA Today*, June 16, 2022, https://www.usatoday.com/story/news/politics/2022/06/15/1776-returns-proud-boys-enrique-tarrio-zachary-rehl/7640565001/.
11. Kriner and Lewis, "Pride and Prejudice."
12. For more on fragments and sound bites, please see Stuckey, "Forum."
13. Carless, "Devastating Piece."
14. McGee, "Text, Context, and Fragmentation."
15. Charland, "Constitutive Rhetoric."
16. Kriner and Lewis, "Pride and Prejudice."
17. Woods and Hahner, *Make America Meme Again*, 22–40.

18. Kriner and Lewis, "Pride and Prejudice."

19. Victoria Dugger, Laura Wainman, and Jordan Fischer, "Proud Boys Had Plan to Occupy House Buildings Where Jan. 5 Tour Took Place, Court Filing Says," WUSA9, June 16, 2022, https://www.wusa9.com/article/news/national/capitol-riots/proud-boys-1776-returns-plan-revealed-in-court-occupy-federal-government-buildings-demand-new-election-jan-20-2020-capitol-riot-jan-6/65-4413c027-4abc-463d-9d39-1acba4e58eae.

20. Mercieca, *Founding Fictions*, 17.

21. Ryan Nobles and Ryan J. Reilly, "'Planned in Plain Sight': Senate Report Finds Intel Agencies Failed in the Lead-Up to Jan. 6," NBC News, June 27, 2023, https://www.nbcnews.com/news/amp/rcna91166.

22. Golub, *Theatre as Action*, 22.

23. Bowers et al., *Rhetoric of Agitation and Control*, 44.

24. Ryan J. Reilly, "Court Document in Proud Boys Case Laid Out Plan to Occupy Capitol Buildings on Jan. 6," NBC News, June 15, 2022, https://www.nbcnews.com/news/amp/rca33755.

25. Reilly, "Court Document."

26. Def. Zachary Rehl, "1776 Returns."

27. Christie Turner, "Rancher vs. BLM: A 20-Year Standoff Ends with Tense Roundup," *High Country News*, April 11, 2014, https://www.hcn.org/blogs/goat/in-nevada-delicate-20-year-standoff-with-blm-ends-in-a-tense-roundup.

28. Southern Poverty Law Center (SPLC), "War in the West: The Bundy Ranch Standoff and the American Radical Right," July 10, 2014, https://splcenter.org/2014709/war-west-bundy-ranch-standoff-and-american-radical-right.

29. This clause states that Congress is granted the power to "establish Post Offices and post Roads" and "To make all Laws which shall be necessary and proper" to conduct postal business.

30. SPLC, "War in the West."

31. Zachary B. Wolf, "The 5 Key Elements of Trump's Big Lie and How It Came to Be," CNN News, May 19, 2021, https://amp.cnn.com/cnn/2021/05/19/politics/donald-trump-big-lie-explainer/index.html.

32. Josh Kelety, "Trump Did Not Sign an Order to Deploy 20,000 Troops on Jan. 6," Associated Press, October 18, 2022.

33. "Jury Convicts Four Leaders of the Proud Boys of Seditious Conspiracy Related to US Capitol Breach," Justice Department, May 4, 2023, https://www.justice.gov/opa/pr/jury-convicts-four-leaders-proud-boys-seditious-conspiracy-related-us-capitol-breach.

BIBLIOGRAPHY

Bowers, John W., Donovan Ochs, Richard P. Jensen, and David P. Schulz. *The Rhetoric of Agitation and Control*. 3rd ed. Waveland, IL: Waveland Press, 2009.

Golub, Lars. *Theatre as Action: Soviet Russian Avant-Garde Aesthetics*. Translated by Charles Rougle. New Directions in Theatre. London: Macmillan, 1993.

Kriner, Matthew, and Jon Lewis. "Pride and Prejudice: The Violent Evolution of the Proud Boys." *Combatting Terrorism Center Sentinel* 14, no. 6 (July/August 2021). https://ctc.westpoint.edu/pride-prejudice-the-violent-evolution-of-the-proud-boys.

McGee, Michael Calvin. "Text, Context, and Fragmentation in Contemporary Culture." *Western Journal of Speech Communication* 44, no. 3 (1990): 274–89.

Mercieca, Jennifer R. *Founding Fictions.* Tuscaloosa: University of Alabama Press, 2012.

Stuckey, Mary E., ed. "Forum on Rhetorical Circulation." *Rhetoric and Public Affairs* 15, no. 4 (2012): 609–94.

Woods, Heather Suzanne, and Leslie A. Hahner. *Make America Meme Again: The Rhetoric of the Alt-Right.* New York: Peter Lang, 2019.

14

FROM CULTURAL ARTIFACT TO CULTURE WAR: THE DECLARATION OF INDEPENDENCE AND THE FIGHT FOR CONTROL OF THE US CIVICS CLASSROOM

Mark Hlavacik

When Thomas Jefferson put quill to paper at Philadelphia's 700 Market St. in June of 1776, he and his revolutionary compatriots were certain they had been getting a raw deal. Ruled from afar by an arrogant Parliament and indifferent king, the British colonies in North America were living under an "absolute tyranny" that deprived their inhabitants of "inalienable rights," which the founders of a new nation were called to take action to secure. The Declaration was the public justification for their revolution, a document that by both its words and example created a standard for civic participation in the new country it introduced to the world. The composition and publication of the Declaration of Independence is the kind of high-minded civic act US Americans are routinely encouraged to aspire to in form, principle, style, and spirit. And so, many have.

Although reading the Declaration itself can be an inspiring exercise, transmitting its civic lesson about the nature of political action in a country that dares to call itself democratic entails much more than merely reading. The Declaration and what it stands for must be taught to those who call the United States their home and who wish to feel at home in its political culture. But like the founders, many US Americans feel that they and their fellow citizens have been getting a raw deal, not at the hands of a callous, European king but from the system of public education set up to teach the Declaration and all the other facets of civic participation in the United States.

Among the innumerable expressions of this disappointment from the past half century of public life in the United States, 1983's report *A Nation at Risk* stands out for the intensity of its rhetoric and the reaction it aroused. Much like the Declaration of Independence, *A Nation at Risk* was a justificatory call to action, and its Declaration-inspired energy is palpable as it laments how "if an unfriendly foreign power had attempted to impose on America the mediocre educational performance that exists today, we," the people of these United States, "might well have viewed it as an act of war."[1] The *Nation at Risk* report was the work of a blue-ribbon panel commissioned by the Reagan administration and overseen by Secretary of Education Terrell Bell. Its brash condemnations of the US public school system caused a sensation that permanently raised the temperature of the debate over public education, especially where social studies and civic education take center stage.[2]

But, of course, no foreign power had imposed a system of public education on the United States. Instead, "we have allowed this to happen to ourselves" admitted the authors of *A Nation at Risk*, by "committing an act of unthinking, unilateral educational disarmament." Although the report replaced the Declaration's struggle against an external enemy with an internal test of the collective will, it retained the Declaration's existential stakes. The "educational foundations of our society are presently being eroded by a rising tide of mediocrity that threatens our very future as a Nation and a people," warned the commission as they called upon their fellow citizens to renew their commitment to the success of their public schools.[3]

Since 1983, reports containing similarly urgent rhetoric about the dire state of education in the United States have kept coming and coming. And aside from borrowing the Declaration's high-minded rhetorical style and civic spirit, these reports also frequently include references to the Declaration itself. Therefore, this chapter follows the life of the Declaration within the pages of the headline-grabbing reports on education that have followed in the wake of *A Nation at Risk*'s popular success. Looking across reports from the early 1990s to the early 2020s, I note how the invocation of the Declaration has shifted over time, from those that characterize it as a cultural artifact and use it to call US Americans together to those that take issue with how others have interpreted the Declaration and turn the act of interpreting it into yet another point of division in a deepening culture war. Where allusions to the Declaration once offered evidence of what could be preserved through the embrace of an internal struggle within every US American to the cause of a high-quality civic education, such references are increasingly used to dramatize an internal struggle of a different kind—not within every US American but between them.

The Declaration remains at the center of these conflicts as an inspiration for both their content and their rhetoric. On the one hand, the Declaration's enduring relevance is a testament to the tremendous influence of a document that has been at the center of US political culture throughout the nation's history. But on the other hand, invocations of the Declaration in fights over school reform demonstrate how the Declaration's durability as a civic commonplace does not issue from the stability of its meaning but instead from its profound flexibility.

The Declaration as a Cultural Artifact within a Civic Education Jeremiad

By blaming themselves along with the nation, the authors of *A Nation at Risk* adapted the American jeremiad (a sermonic speech of blame with roots in the Old Testament) into a powerful template for civic discussions of educational failure. Like the prophet for which they are named, jeremiads condemn a society for neglecting a sacred responsibility and foretell some divine punishment as an impending consequence. In the New World, this form of speech was pioneered by the Puritans, who used it to urge the renewal of a covenant between European settlers and their Christian God. In much the same way as the prophet Jeremiah blamed the misfortunes of Israel on his fellow Israelites for breaking their covenant with God—usually by worshipping false deities—American preachers practicing the jeremiad condemn the entire nation—or before the American Revolution, the European settlers of a particular colony—for neglecting their covenant with God, who had commanded them to complete an errand in the wilderness that would make the Christian society they created in the New World a shining example for the Old World. These North American preachers innovated on the original speech form by also promising that if the covenant was fulfilled, a utopian future would follow, although in his prophesies Jeremiah offered no such path to salvation.[4]

Across the humanities and social sciences, scholars have often recognized the American jeremiad at work in US civic culture, where God is replaced by founding concepts such as democracy and freedom and the broken covenant has a negative effect on the United States' reputation among the nations of the world. By looking to civic life, public address scholars have found the American jeremiad a steadfast genre of civic speech used by civic leaders to galvanize support for reform or to marshal a public response in times of crisis.[5] Media scholars uncover the jeremiad lurking where fiction is turned to political ends, such as in the cause of environmentalism.[6] Scholars of African American political thought have also described and debated a Black tradition of public argument taking the form of the jeremiad.[7] Although far less often, education scholars have also found the jeremiad animating public discussions of key reforms. In particular, Kristen Olson Lanier uses the form to account for the persuasive success of *A Nation at Risk*, where the report famously turned the murky issue of flagging test scores into a matter of national survival.[8]

In their effort to recapture some of the popular success of *A Nation at Risk*, subsequent reports on US education have frequently returned to the jeremiad form, lamenting some failure of the educational system and calling on the US American people to rectify the problem through support for yet another program of reform. Frequently, jeremianic appeals are made openly, as with the 1997 report *A Nation of Spectators*, which called for schools to lead the way in a national program of "civic renewal." According to the report, such a renewal would require "the constitutional faith we share," which was "set forth in the Declaration of Independence." Like the "rebellious signers of the Declaration of Independence," who "risked everything," *A Nation of Spectators* calls upon readers "to strengthen the institutions that help form the knowledge, skills, and virtues citizens need for active engagement in civic life; to remove the impediments to civic engagement wherever they exist; and to multiply the arenas for meaningful and effective civic action."[9] Here, in 1997 as in 1983, the Declaration was invoked as part of an appeal to unify the US American people in their pursuit of better schools.

This rally-around-the-Declaration appeal remained popular into the 2000s, as reports continued to characterize the Declaration as a precious cultural artifact containing still-relevant civic wisdom in addition to historical significance. In 2003, for example, *The Civic Mission of the Schools* called for schools to place "an emphasis on the ideas and principles that are essential to constitutional democracy, such as those found in the Declaration of Independence."[10] According to *The Civic Mission of the Schools*, the Declaration was supposed to be educational content on which all US Americans could agree. Likewise, a 2011 report on the role of the schools in delivering effective civic education, titled *Guardian of Democracy*, spelled out this line of reasoning in detail:

> America's commitment to civic equality is as old as the nation itself; it began with the declaration that "All men are created equal" and was made real over the centuries by extensions of the franchise to nonlandowners, African Americans, women, and eighteen-year-olds. Yet true

> civic equality demands that all citizens have the knowledge and skills to make positive changes in their communities and in the nation at large. Only if transmitted through our public schools—which educate more citizens in a more sustained way than any other institutions—can all students, regardless of background, exercise their full potential as citizens.[11]

For the *Guardian of Democracy* report, teaching the Declaration is both a unifying practice and a way to support progress on difficult social issues, such as those that stem from institutionalized forms of classism, racism, sexism, and ageism.

Guardian of Democracy also gave voice to a conception of the Declaration as itself a covenant like the one Puritan preachers such as John Winthrop and Samuel Danforth invoked to call upon their fellow European settlers in North America to adhere more stringently to their brand of Protestant Christianity.[12] According to the report, "America as a new nation was not created out of devotion to a motherland, a royal family, or a national religion. Americans are instead defined by our fidelity to certain ideals, expressed in the Declaration of Independence."[13] Teaching the Declaration is thus depicted as a way of bringing US Americans together, not just to engage in the collective activity of appreciating their shared, civic inheritance embodied in the Declaration but also to bring them together ideologically to recognize their shared moral and philosophical commitments. Presented in the form of a jeremiad, these reports then urged their readers to see the Declaration as a binding proclamation of their civic duties, both what US Americans owe their fellow citizens and what their fellow citizens owe them.

So long as the public argument over civic education assumes the form of a jeremiad, it characterizes the Declaration as the textual embodiment of the nation's civic covenant. As a result, not only is the Declaration presented as a cultural artifact that every US American ought to study, but it is presumed to reflect a vision of the nation and its political culture, which are worthy of admiration and emulation. The desire to fulfill the promise of Declaration is thereby grafted onto civic education as an important part of its content and purpose. Much in the way it has been used in the broader political culture of the United States, the Declaration is offered as a rhetorical commonplace to which any United States citizen can lay claim as a justification for their own ideas about education or invoke as part of an argument about what they believe they should be able to expect from others. Treating the Declaration as a covenant that secures the nation's identity and accomplishments also reinforces the importance of civic education as the collective means by which the covenant is secured. This justificatory role for the Declaration is effective so long as there is widespread, popular agreement about its legitimacy as a foundational cultural artifact, but as recent reports on civic education demonstrate, that is no longer the case.

The Declaration as a Cultural War within a Civic Education Philippic

Aside from unleashing a multi-decade torrent of bureaucratic literature about the condition of US public education, *A Nation at Risk* also helped to tip the public discussion of K–12 schooling in the United States into an era of accountability.[14] Starting in the 1980s, increasing attention in the civic discussion of US school was paid to various tests such as the Scholastic Aptitude Test (SAT) and the Organization for Economic Co-operation and Development's Program for International Student Assessment (PISA). Concerns about declining SAT scores and PISA results that were not keeping pace with northern Europe and eastern Asia led policymakers to pursue accountability schemes as a way to strengthen the academic rigor of US schools. This effort reached its zenith with the passage of the No Child Left Behind Act in 2002, a law that made the federal funding of school districts dependent on their ability to demonstrate progress on standardized tests administered by each state.[15]

No Child Left Behind's ambitious goals for improving test scores proved hard to achieve, and the upheaval its testing regime visited on many schools proved unpopular. So, by the early 2010s, the law was already being denounced by former supporters such as education professor Diana Ravitch.[16] In December 2015, President Barack Obama signed a replacement into law that eliminated No Child Left Behind's requirement that states administer standardized tests.[17] This new law, the Every Student Succeed Act, had the intended effect of returning policymaking power to the states, but it also had the unintended effect of unmooring the civic discussion of education policy from the effort to improve academic achievement through accountability. In the absence of what once seemed like an interminable debate over accountability, culture wars blossomed. And they have been reflected not just in the reports on education during the late 2010s and early 2020s but specifically in how those reports characterize the Declaration of Independence.

Although it was not a report per se and it addressed more than just education, the *1619 Project* waded into the national conversation about the condition of US schooling with a well-publicized critique of the schools made by a group of experts, much like the authors of *A Nation at Risk, A Nation of Spectators,* and other reports. Published by the *New York Times Magazine* in August of 2019 to mark the four-hundredth anniversary of the first arrival of enslaved Africans at Jamestown, the *1619 Project* broke new ground for the civic discussion of education. First, the project explicitly challenged the practice of regarding July 4, 1776, as the United States' birthday. "The United States," wrote Nikole Hannah-Jones, the *1619 Project*'s originator, "is a nation founded on both an ideal and a lie." This is because the "Declaration of Independence, signed on July 4, 1776, proclaims that 'all men are created equal' and 'endowed by their Creator with certain unalienable rights.' But the white men who drafted those words did not believe them to be true for the hundreds of thousands of black people in their midst."[18] Because the founders believed in their own racial superiority, Jones and the other contributors to the *1619 Project* argue that white supremacy was an unacknowledged founding principle of the United States. The core idea of the project, according to Jake Silverstein, editor of the *New York Times Magazine,* was "to reframe American history by considering what it would mean to regard 1619 as our nation's birth year."[19] In this retelling of the nation's origin myth, the arrival of enslaved Africans in the British colonies is considered to be the nation's moment of conception because of the momentous economic and social impacts slavery would have on the nation-to-be, impacts that included the development of the white supremacist ideology that would make the sentiments of the Declaration hypocritical.

For the authors of the *1619 Project,* the Declaration of Independence is not a cultural artifact that can, or should, be universally endorsed by all US Americans. In her lead essay for the project, Jones argues that the Declaration was part of an attempt by the founders to evade the nation's and their own responsibility for slavery.[20] In an essay included in the broadside portion of the *1619 Project,* Nikita Stewart argues that many of the problems with the quality of civic education in the United States stem from the broader history of white supremacy that the *1619 Project* condemns. As an educational solution, Stewart cosigns a call to center lessons about the history and legacy of enslavement in the social studies curriculum made in greater detail by the Southern Poverty Law Center's *Teaching Hard History* report.[21] For *Teaching Hard History,* the Southern Poverty Law Center surveyed 1,700 social studies teachers to get a sense of how they taught slavery and found "a lack of deep coverage of the subject even among teachers expressing high degrees of confidence" in their ability to teach it.[22] The report noted that, while social studies educators "teach about the American enslavement of Africans as an exclusively southern institution," the historical reality is that "slavery existed in all colonies, and in all states when the Declaration of Independence was signed."[23]

The US American jeremiad is absent from both the *1619 Project* and *Teaching Hard History*. They do not cite the Declaration of Independence as the textual manifestation of a sacrosanct, civic covenant, and while they do ask their readers to envision a better, civic future for the United States, they do not characterize it as a renewal. Instead, they argue that the United States must break from its white supremacist past, which they denounce. Rather than jeremiads, the *1619 Project* and *Teaching Hard History* are philippics (bitter attacks or denunciations). They condemn those educators and educational practices, both past and present, that have sidelined the history of Black oppression in the United States, contending that the effort to sweep this uncomfortable history under the rug has been harmful for both the nation and its people.

The term "philippic" originally referred to a series of three condemnatory speeches the Athenian politician Demosthenes delivered against King Philip II of Macedon.[24] It is also closely associated with the ancient Roman senator Cicero, who delivered fourteen speeches attacking the character of Marc Antony, hardening the conflict between the senate and the Caesarians, and eventually convincing the Roman Senate to declare Antony an enemy of the state and wage war against him.[25] Unlike jeremiads, philippics do not condemn the person or group that gives them or the society they represent. Instead, philippics condemn someone else as the cause of the problem. Additionally, philippics do not offer a prophetic vision of a utopian future for the community to which they are addressed but are political speeches that ask their society to take some collective action against a person or group that is said to be responsible for a problem that has reached a point of crisis.

For the authors of the *1619 Project* and *Teaching Hard History*, the crisis is white supremacy. Educators and the educational institutions that either promote white supremacy or by their failure to act allow it to persist are sources of a problem requiring collective action to address. Unlike *A Nation at Risk*, *A Nation of Spectators*, or *Guardians of Democracy*, these appeals for education reform do not call upon US Americans to rally around a common understanding of the Declaration as a model of ideal civic action in a democratic society. Instead, the *1619 Project* and *Teaching Hard History* ask their readers not just to see the Declaration in a darker light, as an attempt to elide the United States' founding legacy of racial oppression, but also to see the previously popular call to rally around the Declaration as itself a harmful act that obfuscated the nation's repressive history and asked those harmed by that obfuscation to pleasantly acquiesce to it.

In 2021, the National Academy of Education published a report titled *Education for Civic Reasoning and Discourse.* In a portion of the report about representations of Indigenous peoples in civic education, Professor Megan Bang told the story of her high school son, who is a citizen of the Walpole Island Ojibwe. In a Chicago classroom with a "Blackhawks" hockey flag hanging from the wall, he was going to learn about the Declaration with his classmates. But aside from distilling Lockean political philosophy into memorable assertions such as that "all men are created equal," the Declaration also includes a list of grievances against King George III. In one of those grievances, the Declaration accused the British king of having "excited domestic insurrections amongst us, and . . . endeavoured to bring on the inhabitants of our frontiers, the merciless Indian Savages, whose known rule of warfare, is an undistinguished destruction of all ages, sexes and conditions."[26] So, Professor Bang bought her son a shirt with the phrase "Merciless Indian Savage" emblazoned across the chest and suggested that he call attention to the Declaration's hypocrisy by wearing it to school.[27] The point of her story, and no doubt part of the reason for its inclusion in yet another report on civic education, was to highlight the harm that can be done to minoritized students when they are encouraged to claim the Declaration as their own despite its hypocritical denial of their equal humanity.

This turn in the public discussion of civic education from appealing through jeremiads to appealing through philippics is not confined to those who critique the Declaration. In September 2020, after a summer of civic unrest unleashed by the police killing of George Floyd, President Donald Trump announced the creation of the 1776 Commission to "promote patriotic education." The commission was to "encourage our educators to teach our children about the miracle of American history and make plans to honor the 250th anniversary of our founding."[28] The commission was led by the president of Hillsdale College, Larry P. Arnn, and delivered its report in January 2021 during the chaotic final days of the Trump presidency.

The *1776 Report* includes a four-page section on "The Meaning of the Declaration," in which it asserts in direct contrast with the *1619 Project* that the United States "has a definite birthday: July 4th 1776" and that the United States "declares from the moment of its founding not merely the principles on which its new government will be based; it asserts those principles to be true and universal."[29] Unlike the *1619 Project, Teaching Hard History,* and

Education for Civic Reasoning and Discourse, the *1776 Report* presents the Declaration as a document that all US Americans *should* adopt without reservation as their own. However, even as the *1776 Report* holds on to a conception of the universality of the Declaration similar to the education reports of the 1980s, 1990s, 2000s, and early 2010s, it still slips into the philippic form.

Rather than white supremacy, the *1776 Report* addresses what it considers a crisis of declining patriotism resulting from a mistaken rejection of the principles set forth in the Declaration of Independence. In a section titled "Challenges to America's Principles," the *1776 Report* distinguishes between what it characterizes as positive sources of reform, such as "abolition, women's suffrage, anti-Communism, the Civil Rights Movement, and the Pro-Life Movement," and "movements that reject the fundamental truths of the Declaration of Independence and seek to destroy our constitutional order."[30] These "problematic" movements include slavery, progressivism, fascism, communism, and racism and identity politics, all of which the *1776 Report* labels as dangerous challenges to the Declaration.[31]

Jeremiads call the people of a nation together to accept their shared responsibility for a problem and to meet it with a collective act of renewal, whereas philippics blame a particular person or group for the arrival of a crisis and implore the nation to respond by acting against the offender(s). Confusingly, the *1776 Report* borrows the rhetoric of a renewal from the earlier reports as it makes a case against specific groups; indeed, the last section of the report is titled "The Task of National Renewal." In it, the *1776 Report* states: "All the good things we see around us . . . rest on the bedrock of our founding principles. Yet today our country is in danger of throwing this inheritance away."[32] As the *1776 Report* describes what it would mean to rescue the nation's inheritance, it uses its conception of the Declaration and its founding principles to identify wrongdoers, such as teachers and professors, whose left-leaning ideological biases make them responsible for imperiling the republic.

To save civic education, the *1776 Report* advises that "states and school districts should reject any curriculum that promotes one-sided partisan opinions, activist propaganda, or factional ideologies that demean America's heritage, dishonor our heroes, or deny our principles." It continues: "Any time teachers or administrators promote political agendas in the classroom, they abuse their platform and dishonor every family who trusts them with their children's education and moral development."[33] In this case, the pejorative terminology "political agenda" is defined as any form of instruction that interprets the Declaration—its history, meaning, or philosophical commitments—differently than the 1776 Commission. Unlike the authors of *A*

Nation at Risk, who lament how "we," all US Americans including the commission who authored the report, have let the schools reach a point of crisis, the *1776 Report* distinguishes between good and bad educators. Rather than asking every US American to recommit themselves to the yet-unachieved vision of the Declaration, the *1776 Report* asks its readers to view educators with certain political leanings—such as progressive or anti-racist—as traducers of "America's Principles." The goal of the report is not to realize Winthrop's shining city on a hill but to wrest control of the schools from ideological foes by declaring them un-American.

The *1776 Report*'s discussion of post-secondary education is even more strident: "Universities in the United States are often today hotbeds of anti-Americanism, libel, and censorship that combine to generate in students and in the broader culture at the very least disdain and at worst outright hatred for this country."[34] According to the report, "The choice before us now is clear. Will we choose the truths of the Declaration? Or will we fall prey to the false theories that have led too many nations to tyranny?"[35] Rather than renewal being an act of internal reflection that achieves its outward expression by bringing US Americans together, the *1776 Report* envisions an internal struggle between US Americans with irreconcilable ideological differences. "When we appreciate America for what she truly is, we know that our Declaration is worth preserving, our Constitution worth defending, our fellow citizens worth loving, and our country worth fighting for."[36] This fight that the report imagines is between groups of US Americans. On one side, the report aligns itself with traditionalists and the president who commissioned their work; on the other side, it places teachers, academics, activists, and presumably anyone whose interpretation of the Declaration leads them to engage in a more liberal politics. From a cultural artifact that calls US Americans together to ask who they have been, who they are now, and who they ought to strive to become, the *1776 Report* reimagines the Declaration as the basis for a litmus test. Those who do not interpret the Declaration as the 1776 Commission does do not just harbor opposing political views; they hate the United States and are thus responsible for its social, political, and educational ills.

Conclusion

As part of a jeremiad, references to the Declaration in the public discussion of civic education before the late 2010s were the basis for a unifying appeal that attempted to call US Americans together regardless of their political affiliations. However, this jeremianic appeal failed to acknowledge the extent to which the writers of the Declaration did not have all US Americans—especially Blacks, Indigenous peoples, women, and people of color—in mind when they made their supposedly universal pronouncements about equality and liberty. The educational jeremiad also assumed that all US Americans share certain political and philosophical commitments that they evidently do not. In a time of unabashed culture war in which US Americans openly contest the meaning of foundational texts such as the Declaration, the jeremiad loses its rhetorical effectiveness, as it relies upon a sense of unity that is manifestly absent from political life in the United States. In place of the jeremiad, philippics make more political sense.

Philippics are divisive. They marshal support against an opponent. Since the late 2010s, the debate about how the social studies should be taught in the United States has been divided between two sides whose larger, ideological commitments can be expressed in the form of two incompatible understandings of the Declaration of Independence. On one side, critics see a hypocritical document that is at once inhumane to minoritized US Americans and inhumanely foisted on them as a sacred, founding text they must embrace to be fully US American. For them, the philippic appeal is a way to motivate collective action by casting white supremacy and its defenders as the enemy. On the other side, the Declaration of Independence is a supremely important expression of US American political identity, and those who question its place at the center of the US American political mythos risk unleashing forms of oppression and tyranny it long ago put to rest. For them, the philippic appeal does the similarly partisan work of rousing opposition against a host of ideological enemies, from leftists to anti-racists.

For civic education, the shift from the American jeremiad to the philippic has had both costs and benefits. The jeremiad attempted to enforce an unrealistic unity on the social studies curriculum: since all educational enterprises are inherently political, there must always be room for many approaches to the same subject matter. Civic education is doubtless better off with a conflict between competing narratives than a single, unquestioned master narrative. That said, however, the jeremiad was particularly good at reinforcing the importance of civic education by portraying it as a matter of existential importance for the United States, whereas the philippic treats it as yet another partisan football. If the content of civic education is no more than a reflection of which political party currently has the upper hand in government, then it has no stable meaning nor hope of serving a unifying function for the nation.

Finally, by following invocations of the Declaration of Independence across this shift in the discussion of social studies education from jeremiad to philippic, the Declaration itself is revealed to serve just as readily as a basis for appeals for division as a basis for unity. For as important as the Declaration has been in forging the political culture of the United States, even it can be subsumed within a culture war and reduced to a device for manufacturing partisan leverage. Rather than teaching the Declaration as the highest expression of democratic principles the world has yet known or as the most marvelously effective evasion of a nation's responsibility for the crimes of slavery and genocide, perhaps the most honest form of civic education starts by simply acknowledging that the Declaration of Independence is legitimately a site of continuing contestation. It is important but not sacred. It is imperfect and arguably dishonest but worthy of study and qualified admiration. Perhaps the greatest drawback to talking moderately about the Declaration and its place in US civic education is that such talk makes for an ineffectual kind of rhetoric—neither jeremiad nor philippic—that has precious little hope of winning a culture war. But if the Declaration of Independence offers any universal lesson, it is that some stands are worth taking regardless of how long the odds are against them.

NOTES

1. *A Nation at Risk*, 5.

2. Tyack and Cuban, *Tinkering Toward Utopia*, 78; Anya Kamenetz, "What 'A Nation at Risk' Got Wrong, and Right, About U.S. Schools," *National Public Radio*, April 29, 2018, https://www.npr.org/sections/ed/2018/04/29/604986823/what-a-nation-at-risk-got-wrong-and-right-about-u-s-schools.

3. *A Nation at Risk*, 5.

4. See Bercovitch, *American Jeremiad*.

5. See Ritter, "American Political Rhetoric"; Johannesen, "Jeremiad of Jenkin Lloyd Jones"; Johannesen, "Ronald Reagan's Economic Jeremiad"; J. Murphy, "'A Time of Shame and Sorrow'"; Buehler, "Permanence and Change"; Jones and Rowland, "Covenant-Affirming Jeremiad"; A. Murphy, "Two American Jeremiads"; Henry, "'Slaves to a Debt'"; Dunmire, "Democratic Peace as Global Errand"; Gilmore et al., "Exceptional 'We' or Exceptional 'Me'?"; Hickel and Murphy, "Making America Exceptional Again."

6. See Owen, "Memory, War, American Identity"; Wolfe, "Ecological Jeremiad"; Singer, "Neoliberal Style."

7. See Howard-Pitney, *African American Jeremiad*; Wilson, "Political Paradoxes."

8. Lanier, "'Hearken to the Sound of the Trumpet.'" Lanier is not the only education scholar to recognize the role of the jeremiad in the civic discussion of education; see also Greene, "Jeremiad and Curriculum"; Hlavacik, *Assigning Blame*.

9. *A Nation of Spectators*, 12.

10. *Civic Mission of the Schools*, 21.

11. *Guardian of Democracy*, 13.

12. See A. Murphy, *Prodigal Nation.*

13. *Guardian of Democracy*, 10.

14. See Graham, *Schooling America*; Mehta, *Allure of Order*; Hlavacik and Schneider, "Echo of Reform Rhetoric."

15. See McGuinn, *No Child Left Behind.*

16. See Ravitch, *Death and Life*; Ravitch, *Reign of Error.*

17. Barack Obama, "Remarks by the President at Every Student Succeeds Signing Ceremony," White House: Office of the Press Secretary, December 10, 2015, https://www.whitehouse.gov/the-press-office/2015/12/10/remarks-president-every-student-succeeds-act-signing-ceremony.

18. Nikole Hannah-Jones, "Democracy," *New York Times Magazine*, August 18, 2019, 16.

19. Jake Silverstein, "Editor's Note," *New York Times Magazine*, August 18, 2019.

20. Hannah-Jones, "Democracy," 18.

21. Nikita Stewart, "Why Can't We Teach This?," *New York Times Magazine*, August 18, 2019, 3.

22. *Teaching Hard History*, 40.

23. *Teaching Hard History*, 10.

24. See Wooten, *Commentary on Demosthenes' Philippic I.*

25. Kennedy, *Art of Rhetoric*, 269–74.

26. See for yourself: "The Declaration of Independence: A Transcript," *National Archives*, https://www.archives.gov/founding-docs/declaration-transcript; accessed September 19, 2023.

27. Bang and Brayboy, "Indigenous Peoples and Civics Education," 178–79.

28. Donald J. Trump, "Remarks at the White House Conference on American History," edited by Gerhard Peters and John T. Woolley, *American Presidency Project Online*, September 17, 2020, https://www.presidency.ucsb.edu/node/343859.

29. *1776 Report*, 2.

30. *1776 Report*, 10.

31. *1776 Report*, 10–16.

32. *1776 Report*, 16.

33. *1776 Report*, 17.

34. *1776 Report*, 18.

35. *1776 Report*, 16.

36. *1776 Report*, 20.

BIBLIOGRAPHY

Bang, Megan, and Bryan McKinley Jones Brayboy. "Indigenous Peoples and Civics Education in the 21st Century." In *Education for Civic Reasoning and Discourse*, edited by Carol D. Lee, Gregory White, and Diane Dong, 165–89. Washington, DC: National Academy of Education, 2021.

Bercovitch, Sacvan. *The American Jeremiad.* Madison: University of Wisconsin Press, 1978.

Buehler, Daniel O. "Permanence and Change in Theodore Roosevelt's Conservation Jeremiad." *Western Journal of Communication* 62, no. 4 (1998): 439–58.

Civic Mission of the Schools. New York: Carnegie Corporation, 2003.

Dunmire, Patricia L. "Democratic Peace as Global Errand: America's Post–Cold War Foreign Policy Jeremiad." *Journal of Language and Politics* 16, no. 2 (2017): 176–94.

Gilmore, Jason, Charles M. Rowling, Jason A. Edwards, and Nicole T. Allen. "Exceptional 'We' or Exceptional 'Me'? Donald Trump, American Exceptionalism, and the Remaking of the Modern Jeremiad." *Presidential Studies Quarterly* 50, no. 3 (2020): 539–67.

Graham, Patricia Albjerg. *Schooling America: How the Public Schools Meet the Nation's Changing Needs.* New York: Oxford University Press, 2005.

Greene, Maxine. "Jeremiad and Curriculum: The Haunting of the Secondary School." *Curriculum Inquiry* 15, no. 3 (1985): 333–45.

Guardian of Democracy: The Civic Mission of Schools. Philadelphia: Leonore Annenberg Institute for Civics of the Annenberg Public Policy Center at the University of Pennsylvania and the Campaign for the Civic Mission of Schools, 2011.

Henry, Katherine. "'Slaves to a Debt': Race, Shame, and the Anti-Obama Jeremiad." *Quarterly Journal of Speech* 100, no. 3 (2014): 303–22.

Hickel, Flavio R., Jr. and Andrew R. Murphy. "Making America Exceptional Again: Donald Trump's Traditionalist Jeremiad, Civil Religion, and the Politics of Resentment." *Politics and Religion* (2021): 1–23. https://doi.org/10.1017/S1755048321000249.

Hlavacik, Mark. *Assigning Blame: The Rhetoric of Education Reform.* Cambridge, MA: Harvard Education Press, 2016.

Hlavacik, Mark, and Jack Schneider. "The Echo of Reform Rhetoric: Arguments About National and Local School Failure in the News, 1984–2016." *American Journal of Education* 127, no. 4 (2021): 627–55.

Howard-Pitney, David. *The African American Jeremiad: Appeals for Justice in America.* Philadelphia: Temple University Press, 2005.

Johannesen, Richard L. "The Jeremiad of Jenkin Lloyd Jones." *Communication Monographs* 52, no. 2 (1985): 156–72.

———. "Ronald Reagan's Economic Jeremiad." *Central States Speech Journal* 37, no. 2 (1986): 79–89.

Jones, John M., and Robert C. Rowland. "A Covenant-Affirming Jeremiad: The Post-presidential Ideological Appeals of Ronald Wilson Reagan." *Communication Studies* 56, no. 2 (2005): 157–74.

Kennedy, George A. *The Art of Rhetoric in the Roman World, 300 B.C.–A.D. 300.* Eugene, OR: Wipf and Stock, 2008.

Lanier, Kristen Olson. "'Hearken to the Sound of the Trumpet': 'A Nation at Risk' as American Jeremiad." Paper presented at the Annual Meeting of the American Education Research Association, New Orleans, LA, April 24–28, 2000.

McGuinn, Patrick J. *No Child Left Behind and the Transformation of Federal Education Policy, 1965–2005.* Lawrence: University Press of Kansas, 2006.

Mehta, Jal. *The Allure of Order: High Hopes, Dashed Expectations, and the Troubled Quest to Remake American Schooling.* New York: Oxford University Press, 2013.

Murphy, Andrew R. *Prodigal Nation: Moral Decline and Divine Punishment from New England to 9/11.* New York: Oxford University Press, 2011.

———. "Two American Jeremiads: Traditionalist and Progressive Stories of American Nationhood." *Politics and Religion* 1, no. 1 (2008): 85–112.

Murphy, John F. "'A Time of Shame and Sorrow': Robert F. Kennedy and the American Jeremiad." *Quarterly Journal of Speech* 76, no. 4 (1990): 401–14.

A Nation at Risk: The Imperative for Educational Reform. Washington DC: Government Printing Office, 1983.

A Nation of Spectators: How Civic Disengagement Weakens America and What We Can Do About It. College Park, MD: National Commission on Civic Renewal, 1997.

Owen, A. Susan. "Memory, War, American Identity: *Saving Private Ryan* as Cinematic Jeremiad." *Critical Studies in Mediated Communication* 19, no. 3 (2002): 249–82.

Ravitch, Diane. *The Death and Life of the Great American School System: How Testing and Choice Are Undermining Education*. New York: Basic Books, 2011.

———. *Reign of Error: The Hoax of the Privatization Movement and the Danger to America's Public Schools*. New York: Vintage, 2013.

Ritter, Kurt W. "American Political Rhetoric and the Jeremiad Tradition: Presidential Nomination Acceptance Addresses, 1960–1976." *Communication Studies* 31, no. 3 (1980): 153–71.

The 1776 Report. Washington, DC: President's Advisory 1776 Commission, 2021.

Singer, Ross. "Neoliberal Style, the American Re-generation, and Ecological Jeremiad in Thomas Friedman's 'Code Green.'" *Environmental Communication* 4, no. 2 (2010): 135–51.

Teaching Hard History. Montgomery, AL: Southern Poverty Law Center, 2018. https://www.learningforjustice.org/frameworks/teaching-hard-history/american-slavery.

Tyack, David, and Larry Cuban. *Tinkering Toward Utopia: A Century of Public School Reform*. Cambridge, MA: Harvard University Press, 1997.

Wilson, Kirt H. "Political Paradoxes and the Black Jeremiad: Frederick Douglass's Immanent Theory of Rhetorical Protest." *Howard Journal of Communication* 29, no. 3 (2018): 243–57.

Wolfe, Dylan. "The Ecological Jeremiad, the American Myth, and the Vivid Force of Color in Dr. Seuss's *The Lorax*." *Environmental Communication* 2, no. 1 (2008): 3–24.

Wooten, Cecil W. *A Commentary on Demosthenes' Philippic I: With Rhetorical Analyses of Philippics II and III*. New York: Oxford University Press, 2008.

15

BORROWING TROUBLE? THE DECLARATION'S THRESHOLD OF SUFFERING AND CARE

Brandon Inabinet

The Declaration of Independence, like Twisted Sister, tells us that "we're not gonna take it anymore," and the "it" is expansive. This end of toleration spans not just the couple of dozen listed slights against King George III. The text goes further to imagine the breaking of a universal standard, of Anglo-American "natural rights." And further, as explored in this analysis, the text indicts the lack of compassion for colonists' suffering. Boundaries of acceptable suffering are a key aspect of revolutionary political texts. These thresholds can be real, but quite often they may be borrowed from other marginalized or maligned groups. Heightening attention to these areas of the text will help judge further texts beyond the Declaration of Independence's announced philosophy (social contract theory and rights allocated to the deserving), toward articulations of justice that would deliver fuller equity and belonging.

In the Declaration, for example, the argument that there is a right to "alter or abolish" government is also an argument that there are limits beyond which governments cannot justifiably go. This is the threshold. When it comes to how different groups manage relationships with each other, it's quite possible for both sides to understand themselves as oppressed and marginalized, a fact that makes reconciliation and justice tricky. In this case and many others, mutual feelings of victimhood make further violence and war inevitable.

This chapter takes on this specific big question. In the first section I focus on how rebellious colonists justified their own suffering through the literary theft of others' pain—namely, enslaved African Americans and colonized

Native Americans. This part takes the form of a traditional rhetorical criticism and names the areas of evaluation—artistry, bodies, controversy, discursive conditions, and ethics. I continue the discussion of ethics and consider how the universal values in the text—those of being created equal, entitled to inalienable rights, and consenting to be governed—created space for these same borrowed thresholds of suffering to be borrowed back and shared widely. White colonists stole territorial sovereignty away from Native American people, then reimagined their own plight through the metaphor of a hostile imperial force dividing natural alliances. Bodies of women and the enslaved African diaspora were completely at the mercy of tyrant-owners and then imagined as the white male colonists' plight.

I then discuss the reversal of this discourse of (borrowed) harm. The authors of the Declaration make promises of mutuality, interdependence, and practical care, all of which demonstrate a foothold for better governance. The founders would have read works of rhetoric from antiquity and from the Scottish Enlightenment, such as Adam Smith's *Theory of Moral Sentiments*. They would be aware of fellow feeling and the activation of sympathy as a core of politics. Nations with secular origins must be built on the ability to mutually care for citizens one has never personally met; the Declaration of Independence covertly announces this criterion. I conclude with a few thoughts on how the Declaration of Independence can be reread as a text for reparative and transformative justice rather than only as a punitive declaration of war. This opens opportunities for new interpretation and new politics from the document—a text that remains key to building human capabilities and a just peace.

Suffering and Breaking with the Past

Every act of speaking and writing is a "reconstitution," James Boyd White explains, "not a wholly new and idiosyncratic way of thinking" but a "way to give new meaning, and sometimes new form, to the terms, structures, and methods of the language [we have] inherited."[1] Not only are we changing the symbols and tools of language as we use them, we also change ourselves, with new identities, new relationships with others, and new structures and possibilities for action. The Declaration of Independence makes these insights on reconstituting culture and language obvious, especially for US citizens who want the text to work in these ways. The document gave new birth to a language of individual and collective freedom, created citizens of a new political order, and liberated the world from tyranny through its performative recitation in other countries' independence movements around the globe.[2]

These are not controversial statements, even if together they are loaded with a profound naïveté regarding power. White's elevation of texts to revolutions of thought and culture is dramatically challenged by more recent contextual scholarship. In her 1997 book *American Scripture*, for example, Pauline Maier documents hundreds of local versions of such declarative statements that circulated, helping to show that no single text transformed the world overnight on July 4, 1776.[3] Similarly, David Armitage's *The Declaration of Independence: A Global History* demonstrates that many domestic social movements (such as the abolition of slavery and the Seneca Falls Convention for women's suffrage) and international independence movements (from Venezuela to Vietnam to Eastern Europe) quoted the document. Examples of direct quotation of the Declaration of Independence include Flanders (from Austria) in 1790, Haiti in 1804, Venezuela in 1811, Texas in 1836, Liberia in 1847, Ireland in 1919, and Vietnam in 1945. Many did so not because of its epic intellectual ripples alone but also because so many groups needed to ally themselves with capitalism and the American empire.[4]

The struggle to understand the Declaration of Independence in the last fifty years has been based in this tug-of-war between revolution and incrementalism. Let me divide these prior readings into the kinds of analysis they offer—analyses that elevate artistry, bodies, controversy, and discursive conditions. If the timescale is short and the capacity for independent action is strong, we will likely ask a question about text-based action, or "agency." What language and what artistry came together through the author(s) to make this document powerful to its audiences? Rhetoricians might label this "Question A," for Aristotle, artistry, and agency. Herbert Wichelns and Michael Leff helped develop this form of analysis from neoclassical roots. In particular, did the language of the text work to unify rebelling colonies? Stephen Lucas's analysis says yes.[5] Did it convince the French to ally with the new nation and lend their navy to stop British supply ships? No, not immediately at least. King Louis XVI of France took eighteen months to agree to an alliance, and the first French ships and soldiers did not enter the war until June 1778.

If the timescale is longer but human capacity is constrained, we likely ask about bodies. Whose identity was created, and by extension, whose identity was marginalized, silenced, or defined negatively (i.e., who was not "created equal")? Rhetoricians might label this "Question B," for the question of bodies. This question draws from Kenneth Burke's redefinition of rhetoric as an art of identification together with scholarship on the second and third persona by Edwin Black and Phil Wander. In regard to the Declaration, did the text work because the colonial elite galvanized white male colonizers through their negative identifications of Loyalists, African Americans, and Native Americans? The best answers regarding the Declaration can be found in Heidi Tarver's "The Creation of American National Identity," Jeffrey Ostler's *Surviving Genocide*, and Robert Parkinson's *Thirteen Clocks*. In particular, Parkinson claims that thirteen very different colonies, with varying experiences and ratios of Loyalists, would never have unified if not for the deployment of racialized rhetoric.[6]

If the timescale is long and human action is less constrained, we likely ask about controversy. What were the intellectual resources and the effects on ideology? How then do we track the text in traditions of thought and action? Rhetoricians might identify this as "Question C," for controversy, with Ernest Wrage's theorization of texts as indexes of intellectual ideas and ideologies, refined again in Thomas Goodnight's consideration of "controversy" as the unit of argumentative analysis. In particular, did the text work because it brought John Locke's theory of natural rights and a secular social contract into mainstream public philosophy? Bernard Bailyn and Gordon Wood's classic historical analyses make the case for the text popularizing liberalism, explored further below.[7]

And if the timescale is short and human action is highly constrained, we likely ask about discourse, or discursive constraints. What cultural conditions, especially in circulation of media, politics, and economics, made possible the moment of publication, and what reciprocal effect did the text have on those conditions? Rhetoricians might label this "Question D," for discourse, from Michael Calvin McGee's work, based on a theory of discourse found in Michel Foucault. This question makes rhetoric about the underlying institutional structures and ideologies rather than the agency of words and texts. In particular, did the Declaration of Independence circulate because of the wealth and power of the delegates and their patronage of the newspapers, and did it intervene to improve an unjust situation? In addition to gleaning this information from many of the works already referenced, we might pay special attention to the answers provided by scholars following Charles Beard's rethinking of the founders as elites. Works such as *Revolutionary Summer*, "Newspapers for Free," and *The Tyranny of Printers* all point to press circulation and subscriptions as the key to revolutionary success sponsored by this elite class of revolutionaries.[8]

Inspired by the Declaration of Independence's own break with the past, we can reread the above questions with attention to one final "Question E," for a trauma-informed ethics of care. We are after the questions of reparative and transformative justice that undergird the text. Who and what was harmed? Who and what suffers relative to the other bodies, controversies, and discourses? And how would this be remedied? Once again, like the questions above, the Declaration of Independence stands out as a perfect revolutionary text for answering this question of ethics. But this will be the first analysis to do so.

The author(s) frame the document around suffering and oppression and their opposites of safety and happiness. They share prudence as a regulating ideal to judge where along this spectrum the colonies exist. In particular, Jefferson wrote:

> Prudence, indeed, will dictate that Governments long established should not be changed for light and transient causes; and accordingly all experience hath shewn, that mankind are more disposed to **suffer**, while evils are **sufferable**, than to right themselves by abolishing the forms to which they are accustomed. But when a long train of **abuses and usurpations**, pursuing invariably the same Object evinces a design to reduce them under **absolute Despotism**, it is their right, it is their duty, to throw off such Government, and to provide new Guards for their future security.—Such has been the patient **sufferance** of these Colonies. (emphasis added)

The text attests to its own threshold value for prudence. People should suffer harm, to an extent, without taking revolutionary action against the systems that oppress them. This Western norm of prudential reform and compromise, rather than utopian-pitched revolution, is what Hannah Arendt thought so crucial to the entire US American Revolution.[9] In contrasting the US case to the unending bloodshed and unlimited scope of the French Revolution (and later in the Bolshevik Revolution, the Cultural Revolution of China, and so forth), Arendt, in the tradition of Cicero, approved of prudential political reform. She admired the high threshold rationale that gave meaning to goal-oriented, incremental newness in public life, rather than unleashed bloodshed chasing utopia.

To get here, though, and to achieve this prudence as a technical artistry within the text, we end up sacrificing bodies. Arendt misses the issue that essential to this "reformist" mentality was a low tolerance for high taxes but an incredibly high tolerance for the suffering of others. This "imagined marginality" used metaphors of suffering witnessed firsthand, especially on the Southern plantation in the punitive exploitation, torture, and rape of enslaved persons.[10] Without these firsthand experiences of harm, it is doubtful the accusations of a threshold having been crossed by a tyrant would have activated a collective response.

Suffusing the revolutionaries' discourse were themes of enslavement: complete powerlessness and lack of basic human dignity in the face of despotism, forced subjugation without recourse to the rule of law, begging and pleading for mercy not to a reasoned public but instead to one man's wrath over his inferior subjects, and forcing some of these subjects to enforce violence against other subjects. Through all these grievances, listed in the documents and chanted across the nation as the watchwords of the battle against the Crown, the disloyal colonists "borrowed trouble" from the enslaved and used their firsthand witness of crimes to activate their rejection of British control.

They borrowed the metaphors and examples of suffering not only from the enslaved but also from Native Americans. The white colonists complained of a lack of equality in controlling their own land and bodies, doing so in reference to the "Laws of Nature." Like the hypocrisy of using terms of enslavement to metaphorize their suffering under the Crown, the hypocrisy of using the term "Savages" is strong as well. Benjamin Franklin and other signers documented their indebtedness to Native culture for democratic practices. Native nations and confederations were political models for the founders, and many had been allies in hardship and war, hardly the "merciless Indian Savages" to which the text reduces them.[11]

The famously heinous last grievance of the Declaration reads, "He has excited domestic insurrections amongst us, and has endeavoured to bring on the inhabitants of our frontiers, the merciless Indian Savages, whose known rule of warfare, is an undistinguished destruction of all ages, sexes and conditions." "Domestic insurrections" refers to the order by Lord Dunmore (the colonial governor of Virginia) that freed enslaved persons if they fought for the British army. We know that in the final drafting of the Declaration of Independence, Jefferson had included an indictment that King George had failed to end the slave trade (see chapter 9 for the full quotation); paired with the broader language of freedom and inalienable rights, this would have made the document an easy foothold for anti-slavery agitation. The delegates to Congress deleted this grievance against the slave trade, yet kept the allusion to domestic insurrection—the ongoing newspaper rhetoric against Dunmore and his alliance with African Americans.

Making no attempt to code their racism this time, the language of genocidal Natives allied with the British is a reversal and projection by the colonists of their own abuse of Natives and Native alliances to fight colonizing wars. The grievance captured the spirit of the newspapers' us/them identification strategies, pitting the imagined marginalization of white colonists (both elite individuals involved in the slave trade and backcountry commoners expanding their landholdings into Native territory) against an alliance of British, African, and Indigenous forces.

It is important to mention at this point that just as in any war, suffering was widespread by 1776 and would continue to be so for seven more years. Fighters in the American Revolution were indeed being massacred, subject to poor governance, attacked by Native American nations, and undermined by enslaved "domestics." "Imagined marginality" does not mean that the claim of suffering is false or even that it must be of lesser magnitude than that of the groups and individuals accused and maligned. Rather, it suggests that the force of identification and persuasion relies on the borrowed images of suffering of others and circulates among those who see themselves as resistive and delegitimized in comparison to other social groups.

John Adams wrote, two years earlier in 1774, "I appeal to all experience, and to universal history, if it has ever been in the power of popular leaders uninvested with other authority than what is conferred by the popular suffrage, to persuade a large people, for any length of time together, to think themselves wronged, injured, and oppressed, unless they really were, and saw and felt it to be so."[12] To those of us living in the twenty-first century, Adams sounds silly, as world events have consistently shown that perpetrators of genocide and insurrection in free countries are often fueled by little more than propaganda of dominant groups' victimhood. Acknowledging the truth of even occasional or relatively slight harms experienced by the perpetrators is important to the reparative process. Even so, the rhetorics of imagined marginality, of "borrowing trouble" in texts, takes such claims of victimhood beyond the observable and into the realm of the imagined.

The founders were likely unaware of the hypocrisy of borrowing trouble or enacting this imagined marginality. The more the controversy relied upon high-minded liberalism, the more the perceived logic that an enlightened republic must be the antithesis of slavery. Take, for example, the most famous pamphleteer of the 1760s, John Dickinson, former Pennsylvania slaveholder. His simplification and clarification of this common argument was as follows (capitalization and italics come from the original pamphlet): "*Those* who are *taxed* without their own consent, expressed by themselves or their representatives, are *slaves. We are taxed* without our own consent, expressed by ourselves or our representatives. *We* are therefore SLAVES."[13]

Governments were constituted, said John Locke's *Two Treatises of Government*, by people combatting a capricious world of suffering and injustice.[14] Locke held that slavery could only be legitimated in modern (liberal) societies by the just war theory: that is, one completely owns one's own body in the same way that one owns other property; through war or similar conquest, therefore, one can give up one's body to avoid death. C. B. Macpherson argues that this "possessive individualism" is the underlying flaw of liberalism.[15] Everything, under liberalism, gets reduced to economic terms, even freedom and existence.

The white colonizers, on the other hand, were men of *prudence* who had never given away those rights. Rather, secular authority could be established by people with a correct threshold for such suffering, a threshold seasoned by status, elite education, and property holding—in short, by their economic standards of education and living: a modern, secular meritocracy that "happened" to be populated by European landowners. The more one read of the metaphorical British chains and oppression, the more one could avoid associating the signifier with the real experience. Thus, the fear of being reduced to "abject slavery" was the powerful, galvanizing force that made the Declaration of Independence possible.[16]

And yet what can also be said is that the revolutionaries lacked a full context of suffering. Discursively, they had created a system of media that circulated their pleas of despair but not those of Native Americans or enslaved persons of African descent. They had created an economy that relied on the dispossession of land and exploitation of labor but whose currency never reflected those debts. They enjoyed a political structure in which only persons of a certain identity could participate. The signatories could privatize their tyrannical power as household matters that avoided political scrutiny.

Historians have disagreed on whether the American Revolution was a "tax backlash in intellectual clothing." Gordon Wood sides with other historians such as Bernard Bailyn who say that, if anything, the ideological changes and public narratives of liberalism, more than economic unfairness, created the motive for war. In doing so, Wood notes the overwrought rhetoric demonizing King George III. His putative identity as a monstrous tyrant hardly reflected the reality: it was Parliament in fact that was largely responsible for the taxes and pressures the colonists faced.[17] The stigmatizing of British policy as tyranny and slavery had little basis in objective reality, "at least prior to the Intolerable Acts, but ceaseless repetition of the charge kept emotions at fever pitch."[18] This had the effect, says Arthur Schlesinger, that what at first was argued as being just poor local governance was elevated to poor British oversight of their (rightful) colony and finally to total subjugation. In other words, the United States "backed into" a universal discourse of sovereignty as it applied to themselves rather than its being an original position from which events unfolded; and yet that same philosophical system had also created the conditions for imagining a better, "freer" life from the beginning: European wars and conquest had held up the mirror to the ruthless, heinous acts visited on unsuspecting human subjects.

Beyond the specifics of the American Revolution and its causes, there are at least two underlying tendencies for publics to misrecognize the quantities and relative value of their own suffering.[19] First, public media circulation lacked controls that would ensure equal access to others' suffering. Colonists only received news framed and financed by the white male elites of their own colonies, united in a national printing press network in the late 1700s.[20] Colonial newspapers publicized stories to make colonists afraid of British-sponsored slave "insurrections" and Native "massacres." The threat of these neighbors whose voices had been silenced made for strong sales at a time when news and pamphlets were not easy to produce.

Second, a mass psychological effect of imagined marginality took hold, wherein, unlike repression and forgetting in cases of individual trauma, groups may re-narrate former suffering in a tragic-heroic frame.[21] Groups may heal their suffering by imagining the past as a meaningful and romantic reality from which their current existence may only be superficially derived. For the founders, the treatment of the colonists by the British after the French and Indian War came to be narrated as a series of moves to concentrate all authority within Britain and force all suffering onto the colonists. These narrated sufferings up to 1763 engendered a world that no longer resembled one of legal order and meaningful authority; instead, it reflected the world experienced by the enslaved African diaspora and the Native American dispossessed—a world of random violence and sneering disrespect from the colonizing forces.

Throughout this essay but especially here, I should note that the analysis is informed by theories of collective trauma. I have tried to avoid appropriating the language of trauma, given that my purpose is to describe the circulating texts and not diagnose a medical phenomenon. Collective trauma scholarship also tends to use genocide as its case study, whereas the dynamics I have described are operative in nearly all discourse that deals with legitimation crises and resistance against imagined dominant powers, which is nearly all politicized discourse. For any particular members of a collective, suffering may range from horrific torture to merely sharing stories of past wrongdoing. While scholars of rhetoric can appreciate what I am calling "imagined marginality" as a social phenomenon, it is helpful to avoid a conflation of it with diagnosed trauma, whether individual or collective.

In summary, the Declaration of Independence can be read as a basis for politics in a new way. Rather than as a clarion call for liberty in the modern world or as a text that merely motivates violent retribution, we can read for borrowed suffering and imagined marginality. The US founders' artistry, bodies, controversy, and discursive conditions all worked together to touch on something deep in human experience: the ethics of oppression and its psychological effects. Now let's turn toward the inverse of suffering, to see how healing can be read into the text.

A Declaration of Interdependence

What if the document had never been called the "Declaration of Independence"? The wording of the resolution (by Richard Henry Lee of Virginia) in the Second Continental Congress and in Jefferson's text was to declare "free and independent states," with the noun "independence" never mentioned. The resolution also called for "confederation," which would lead to the "united colonies" as the "united States of America" (capitalization as in the original). At the end of the document, the authors added "we mutually pledge to each other . . ." Even though the paragraph begins in the form of a resolution by the Congress, acting as "Representatives," the middle of the paragraph focuses on the united colonies themselves and their interrelationship with the representatives in breaking from the British state. By the end of the paragraph, the mutuality of fortunes, lives, and honors is not so clearly limited to the representatives but is also associated with the colonies and colonists. In other words, it is worth contemplating, obviously in its context and even through these linguistic clues, how the document is more a recognition of interdependence (as "free and independent states") than of independence.

Locke's theories of liberalism force an individual basis on natural rights, especially of "possessive individualism," according to which one can negotiate one's body and rights as if they are economic entities within the market.

Putting too much emphasis on Locke has meant that we read the document as a legal-contractual negotiation. But we know that Jefferson and the other founders were just as likely to derive their thinking from Cicero's *De officiis*, Rousseau's *The Social Contract*, and Adam Smith's *Theory of Moral Sentiments*. In these works, political action and the authority of the law are based in duties to others—duties derived from fellow-feeling or, in language stressing Smith, the narrative of the plight of others. Whether humans experience that plight firsthand, watch it unfold, or receive it through a storyteller, strong emotions are unleashed that produce righteous anger and sympathy with others.

We should remember, too, that this is how the founders and generations of white men afterward read the document. The language of universal equality and rights meant to these men that sympathetic figures had equal responsibilities to ensure rights to one another. It did not activate in them, as discussed regarding hypocrisies of identity above, an individualist notion that a Native American person, a woman, or an enslaved person had equal birthright, equal status under the law, or equal needs or desires for freedom and well-being. Their desire to protect life, liberty, and the pursuit of happiness reflects their relational care for one another as men of "prudence" rather than an objective, equal, and universal mandate.[22] Moral judgments are derived from relationships and empathy, not vice versa.

Care does not negate autonomy, though. In other words, while we should rebuke the founders for the limits of their sympathies, an ethics of care does not undermine liberal individualism and universal rights as a legal possibility. It simply reminds us that in all times and all places, human beings are likely political equals to those with whom they can sympathize in suffering. Universal rights and values can be socially constructed (and assigned to Providence, God, or other forces beyond our control to ensure their legitimacy) but come out of a position of care and are executed in narratives of care.

Further, to the extent that Jefferson and the Second Continental Congress's Declaration was so impactful and exceptional among the hundreds of others generated at the time, it likely provided a collective catharsis for the colonists. Frantz Fanon says that collective catharsis comes for a colonized people, who need violence (at least symbolic and often physical) and a collective "win" to undo the traumas of inferiority wrought by colonizers.[23] As a people who suffered together and imagined their marginality by borrowing the suffering of others, a statement of shared harm and desired liberation would have alleviated the psychic and emotional stresses of the collective. Further, it would have created resilience for the seven years of war and twelve years of poor governance to come under the Articles of Confederation. Rather than viewing this effect as born out of Enlightenment hope for a universal emancipation, we are better off viewing the Declaration of Independence as a testament of suffering and a threshold crossed, leading to resilience and mutuality.

A New Nation, Conceived in Care

Care is universal. It is our shared universal fabric, on which particles and plants and animals and humans act.[24] A network of mutuality, woven into a single garment of destiny, as Martin Luther King Jr. called it. Animating that fabric is practical judgment, born of signifiers inducing symbol use. Particles, energy flows, emotions, narratives, and memories—some within us, most beyond us—ask us to read and respond to them for the protection of relationships.[25] It constitutes a zone that is historically given and socially prescribed, always stretching and moving in different directions around us. By navigating it well, we hope to keep and even extend that zone of care. By navigating it poorly, we induce harm both individually and systematically that reduces and eventually obliterates this basic existence of care.

Despite this potential for radical good or evil, the norm of existence is material indifference toward the care of others. The particles and cells may or may not cause infection. My vote or yours, as one of several hundred million, exists in a bundle of policies and priorities with unknowable backlashes and impacts. And yet, at some particular moment, continuing harm to the zone of care becomes unsustainable. The individual or system breaks apart or dies trying to retake control of its autonomous zone of care. A revolution occurs. The fever comes. The minority power becomes the dominant one.

This threshold idea is deeply important, yet it has rarely been considered so in the study of circulated texts. The Declaration of Independence calls us to change the way we approach reading documents of rebellion and revolution. What happened in 1775 and 1776 fits the pattern described above. Hundreds of local individuals and bodies began coming up with various declarations of independence. White colonists, especially elite merchants, were experiencing harm to their zone of care from a world of indifference as well as harm they had hoped to leave behind and read theories about a chance for secular, inclusive governance based in popular support. In countering mercantile taxes, the colonists created outrage that highlighted and increased the precarity of life. The Indigenous peoples? . . . ready to take back their land, in alliance with an oppressor. The enslaved "domestics"? . . . insurrectionists ready to overthrow their "rightful" masters. The royal office holders? . . . ruthless lackeys. And the king? . . . a convenient scapegoat for all of this. Only when we get beyond the immediate rhetorical situation can we see something of real and enduring value for the human condition. Lloyd Bitzer famously appealed to Sophistic *kairos* and used the organic "ripeness" metaphor to describe this phenomenon of a right timing that transcends chronological awareness.[26] But the Declaration of Independence shines a light on a different form of timing, of rhetorical thresholds of pain and borrowed pain as the substrate on which political discourse operates. The circulation of the Declaration of Independence and its co-optation is a reflection of this underlying dynamic that grounds political life.

I am motivated to read this way not only by the 1776 document and its self-evident racial hypocrisy but also by its having been channeled directly by over half the nations and government bodies on the planet, as well as by its substantial impact on Black, Indigenous, and women's movements within the United States. Not only "official" declarations but all persuasion presents a track record and road map for detecting individuals' and groups' threshold values. We already read texts with an understanding of artistry, bodies, controversies, and discursive conditions. The Declaration of Independence calls us to also foreground an ethics of care, a threshold of suffering and tolerance and an invitation to create bonds of sympathy. In this text and so many others, we can discern when humans experience and borrow trouble; when their zone of care is infringed; when they generate something that locates and generates resilience and interdependence. All of these are acts of persuasion and identification—acts of rhetoric that determine our shared lifeworld and human capacity.

People are always vulnerable, and communication is often misdirected owing to real and perceived slights. Caring relationships involve the recognition of others' experiences and testimonies as valid sources of knowledge. They indicate a threshold beyond which punitive retribution will be necessary. These grounds for truth are more likely to yield results in the field of human action and are more likely to square with the "Laws of Nature and of Nature's God," however we define those. Certainly, the misdirection, projection, and amplification of grievances against King George III (when many were caused by colonists themselves) show how "universal reason" did little to solidify the grounds of argument.

Justice frameworks that extend from care ethics, like reparational and transformative justice, encourage actions that rebuild lives within supportive communities and avoid causing further harm. As a first step, both forms of justice require acknowledgment of harms in a meaningful way that all parties can deem true. From there, reparational justice focuses on victim-aggressor communication and repair. Meanwhile, transformative justice moves toward fixing the systems of power that created inequity in the first place, with a goal of *nunca más* (never again) causing suffering. Like so many ethical frameworks, they have tended to be forensic rhetorics and look back at past crime to determine present and future decision-making. The rhetorical threshold values proposed here would implicate significant texts in this process. If groups are circulating their suffering and their imagined marginality, then we have a new tool to understand their perception of harm and their perception of the use value of that harm relative to their audiences.

As Iris Marion Young argues, what we need is an enabling theory of justice.[27] "Justice," she writes, should not just refer to distribution, such as how much financial damage and taxation the colonists faced or how much their privacy and livelihoods had been invaded and controlled. It should instead, as she says, create the "institutional conditions necessary for the development and exercise of individual capacities and collective communication and cooperation."[28] In other words, when applied to the Declaration of Independence, we would look beyond the harm that legitimated the need to unite in violent rebellion and look instead to the capacities it gave and continues to give for mutual uplift and interdependence.

As we have seen, the footholds for such an analysis are there in the text. Even within the limited rhetorical situation of wartime, rebelling colonists such as James Otis, Benjamin Rush, and Lemuel Haynes subverted the threshold of *prudence* to include nonwhite persons.[29] And, of course, further down the road as the text was cited and enlisted for new causes, the same would be said for women, new locales and regions, and marginalized diasporas globally. In short, the "me-first" standard of suffering would be the unintentional opening by which institutions of inclusion, belonging, and resilience could take hold. The aggrieved founders opened a grievance politics that leads to mutuality, interdependence, and resilience. An understanding of the text that takes in all five properties—artistry, bodies, controversy, discursive conditions, and ethics of care—helps us see better what the text has to offer.

Conclusion

As we have seen in this analysis, the crossed thresholds of the Declaration of Independence were useful fictions for the creation of certain essential rights and their assignment to God or Providence as universal rights and obligations. Edmund Burke made this clear at the time, saying that in "Virginia and the Carolinas they have a vast multitude of slaves. Where this is the case in any part of the world, those who are free, are by far the most proud and jealous of their freedom."[30] Similarly, Samuel Johnson mocked what we are here calling imagined marginality:

> It has been, of late, a very general practice to talk of slavery among those who are setting at defiance every power that keeps the world in order. If the learned author of the Reflections on Learning [Thomas Baker] has rightly observed, that no man ever could give law to language, it will be vain to prohibit the use of the word slavery; but I could wish it more discreetly uttered: it is driven, at one time, too hard into our ears by the loud hurricane of Pennsylvanian eloquence, and, at another, glides too cold into our hearts by the soft conveyance of a female patriot, bewailing the miseries of her friends and fellow-citizens. . . . How is it that we hear the loudest yelps for liberty among the drivers of negroes?[31]

The Declaration's authors lacked a compelling basis for reparative or transformative justice, instead leveraging slights of suffering and reduced sovereignty in violent response. Thresholds of suffering and imagined marginality hold a key to opening the document for better understanding: they acknowledge borrowing trouble as a stealing and projection of what colonists had done to Native Americans and to enslaved persons, and then, once acknowledged, they open beyond that theft an invitation to interdependence, mutuality, and care. With an investment in relationships and universal regard for vulnerability, we may be able to build cultures of listening and healing and justice out of all our unnecessary pain.

NOTES

1. White, *When Words Lose Their Meaning.*
2. Schlesinger, *Prelude to Independence.*
3. Maier, *American Scripture.*
4. Armitage, *Declaration of Independence.*
5. Lucas, "Justifying America."
6. Tarver, "Creation of American National Identity"; Ostler, *Surviving Genocide*; Parkinson, *Thirteen Clocks.*
7. Bailyn, *Ideological Origins*; Wood, *Radicalism.*
8. Ellis, *Revolutionary Summer*; Steffen, "Newspapers for Free"; Pasley, "*Tyranny of Printers.*"

9. Arendt, *On Revolution.*
10. Inabinet and Moss, "Complicit in Victimage."
11. Grinde and Johansen, "Sauce for the Goose."
12. Adams, "Novanglus," 229.
13. Dickinson, *Letters,* 38.
14. Welchman, "Locke on Slavery and Inalienable Rights."
15. Macpherson, *Political Theory of Possessive Individualism.*
16. Okoye, "Chattel Slavery."
17. Wood, *Radicalism,* 9.
18. Schlesinger, *Prelude to Independence,* 34.
19. Noor et al., "When Suffering Begets Suffering."
20. Pasley, "*Tyranny of Printers.*"
21. Hirschberger, "Collective Trauma."
22. Andersen and Chen, "Relational Self"; Maibom, *Handbook.*
23. Fanon, *Black Skin, White Masks.*
24. Held, *Ethics of Care*; Pettersen, "Ethics of Care."
25. Bennett, *Vibrant Matter*; Coole and Frost, *New Materialisms.*
26. Bitzer, "Rhetorical Situation."
27. Young, *Justice and the Politics of Difference.*
28. Young, *Justice and the Politics of Difference,* 39.
29. Haynes and Royster, "Liberty Further Extended."
30. Burke, *Works,* 99.
31. Johnson, "Taxation No Tyranny," 144.

BIBLIOGRAPHY

Adams, John. "Novanglus." In *The Papers of John Adams,* vol. 2, edited by Robert J. Taylor, Mary-Jo Kline, and Gregg L. Lint, 217–354. Cambridge, MA: The Belknap Press of Harvard University Press, 1977.

Andersen, Susan M., and Serena Chen. "The Relational Self: An Interpersonal Social-Cognitive Theory." *Psychological Review* 109, no. 4 (2002): 619–45.

Arendt, Hannah. *On Revolution.* New York: Viking Press, 1963.

Armitage, David. *The Declaration of Independence: A Global History.* Cambridge: Cambridge University Press, 2008.

Bennett, Jane. *Vibrant Matter: A Political Ecology of Things.* Durham, NC: Duke University Press, 2010.

Bernard, Bailyn. *The Ideological Origins of the American Revolution.* Cambridge, MA: Belknap Press of Harvard University Press, 1992.

Bitzer, Lloyd F. "The Rhetorical Situation." *Philosophy and Rhetoric* 1, no. 1 (1968): 1–14.

Burke, Edmund. *The Works of the Right Honourable Edmund Burke.* Vol. 2. London: John C. Nimmo, 1857.

Coole, Diana, and Samantha Frost, eds. *New Materialisms: Ontology, Agency, and Politics.* Durham, NC: Duke University Press, 2010.

Dickinson, John. *Letters from a Farmer in Pennsylvania to the Inhabitants of the British Colonies.* Philadelphia, 1768.

Ellis, Joseph J. *Revolutionary Summer: The Birth of American Independence.* New York: Alfred A. Knopf, 2013.

Fanon, Frantz. *Black Skin, White Masks.* Translated by C. L. Markmann. Chippenham, UK: Grove Press, 1952.

Grinde, Donald A., Jr., and Bruce E. Johansen. "Sauce for the Goose: Demand and Definitions for 'Proof' Regarding the Iroquois and Democracy." *William and Mary Quarterly* 53, no. 3 (July 1996): 621–36.

Haynes, Lemuel, and Paul Royster, eds. "Liberty Further Extended: Or Free Thoughts on the Illegality of Slave-Keeping; Wherein Those Arguments That Are Used in Its Vindication Are Plainly Confuted. Together with an Humble Address to Such as Are Concerned in the Practice." *Electronic Texts in American Studies* 94 (1776). Available at https://digitalcommons.unl.edu/etas/94; accessed September 30, 2023.

Held, Virginia. *The Ethics of Care: Personal, Political, and Global.* Oxford: Oxford University Press, 2005.

Hirschberger, Gilad. "Collective Trauma and the Social Construction of Meaning." *Frontiers in Psychology* 9, no. 1441 (August 2018): 1–14.

Inabinet, Brandon, and Christina L. Moss. "Complicit in Victimage: Imagined Marginality in Southern Communication Criticism." *Rhetoric Review* 38, no. 2 (2019): 160–72.

Johnson, Samuel. "Taxation No Tyranny: An Answer to the Resolutions and Address of the American Congress (April 4, 1775)." In *The Works of Samuel Johnson*, 93–144. Troy, NY: Pafraets, 1913.

Lucas, Stephen. "Justifying America: The Declaration of Independence as a Rhetorical Document." In *American Rhetoric: Context and Criticism,* edited by Thomas W. Benson, 67–130. Carbondale: Southern Illinois University Press, 1989.

Macpherson, C. B. *The Political Theory of Possessive Individualism: From Hobbes to Locke.* Oxford: Oxford University Press, 1962.

Maibom, Heidi, ed. *Handbook of Philosophy of Empathy.* London: Routledge, 2017.

Maier, Pauline. *American Scripture: Making the Declaration of Independence.* New York: Alfred A. Knopf, 1997.

Noor, Masi, Nurit Shnabel, Samer Halabi, and Arie Nadler, "When Suffering Begets Suffering: The Psychology of Competitive Victimhood Between Adversarial Groups in Violent Conflicts." *Personality and Social Psychology Review* 16, no. 4 (2012): 351–74.

Okoye, F. Nwabueze. "Chattel Slavery as the Nightmare of the American Revolutionaries." *William and Mary Quarterly* 37, no. 1 (January 1980): 3–28.

Ostler, Jeffrey. *Surviving Genocide: Native Nations and the United States from the American Revolution to Bleeding Kansas.* New Haven, CT: Yale University Press, 2019.

Parkinson, Robert G. *Thirteen Clocks: How Race United the Colonies and Made the Declaration of Independence.* Chapel Hill: University of North Carolina Press, 2021.

Pasley, Jeffrey L. *"The Tyranny of Printers": Newspaper Politics in the Early American Republic.* Charlottesville: University Press of Virginia, 2001.

Pettersen, Tove. "The Ethics of Care: Normative Structures and Empirical Implications." *Health Care Analysis: Journal of Health Philosophy and Policy* 19, no. 1 (2011): 51–64.

Schlesinger, Arthur M. *Prelude to Independence: The Newspaper War on Britain, 1764–1776.* Westport, CT: Greenwood Press, 1958.

Steffen, Charles G. "Newspapers for Free: The Economies of Newspaper Circulation in the Early Republic." *Journal of the Early Republic* 23, no. 3 (Fall 2003): 381–419.

Tarver, Heidi. "The Creation of American National Identity: 1774–1796." *Berkeley Journal of Sociology* 37 (1992): 55–99.

Welchman, Jennifer. "Locke on Slavery and Inalienable Rights." *Canadian Journal of Philosophy* 25, no. 1 (1995): 67–81.

White, James Boyd. *When Words Lose Their Meaning: Constitutions and Reconstitutions of Language, Character, and Community*. Chicago: University of Chicago Press, 1984.

Wood, Gordon S. *The Radicalism of the American Revolution*. New York: Vintage Books, 1991.

Young, Iris Marion. *Justice and the Politics of Difference*. Princeton, NJ: Princeton University Press, 1990.

CONTRIBUTORS

Noor Ghazal Aswad is Assistant Professor in the Department of Communication Studies, University of Alabama. Her research and scholarly activities span several interdisciplinary areas, including rhetorical theory, political rhetoric, immigration, postcolonialism, and environmental communication. Her most recent work examines transnational grassroots social movements in the Middle East and meaning-making mechanisms for solidarity with those in liberatory struggles. Her published work has appeared in several well-regarded journals, such as *Quarterly Journal of Speech, Environmental Communication, Presidential Studies Quarterly, Critical Studies in Media Communication*, and *Rhetoric and Public Affairs*, among others.

Jason Edward Black is Professor of Rhetoric, Culture, and Social Change at the University of North Carolina at Charlotte, where he focuses mainly on Indigenous decoloniality. A Fulbright Canada alum (transnational Indigenous chair), Black is the coauthor of *Mascot Nation: The Controversy over Native American Representations in Sports* (University of Illinois Press, 2018) and the author of *American Indians and the Rhetoric of Removal and Allotment* (University Press of Mississippi, 2015). He is also coeditor of *Decolonizing Native American Rhetoric* (Peter Lang, 2018), and numerous books and articles on Indigenous, LGBTQIA, and Black resistances.

Stephen Howard Browne is Liberal Arts Professor of Rhetoric and Professor of Communication Arts and Sciences Emeritus at Pennsylvania State University. He specializes in the rhetorical culture of the early republic and is the author, most recently, of *The First Inauguration: George Washington and the Invention of the Republic* (Pennsylvania State University Press, 2020).

Ann E. Burnette is a Minnie Stevens Piper Professor and Regents' Teacher in the Department of Communication Studies at Texas State University. Her research on presidential rhetoric, political campaign rhetoric, and freedom of expression issues can be found in a number of journals and edited volumes, including the *Journal of Contemporary Rhetoric, Communication and Democracy, The George W. Bush Presidency* (vol. 3), and *Public Communication in the Time of COVID-19*. In addition to teaching graduate and undergraduate courses in political communication, persuasion, American public address, and rhetorical criticism, Dr. Burnette is also a past president of the Southern States Communication Association.

Leslie A. Hahner is Professor of Communication at Baylor University. Her work explores how the circulation of aesthetic values and visual forms shapes public culture. She is an award-winning author of two books and dozens of essays on visual rhetoric and public culture. She is a renowned expert on the reactionary right, having written an expert statement for the House of Representatives' January 6th Committee and presented on this topic for various intelligence groups. You can find her discussing her research on *BBC World News*; in the *Chicago Tribune*, the *Houston Chronicle*, and *The Atlantic*; and on various other media outlets.

Stephen J. Heidt is a Lecturer in Communication Studies at California State University Northridge. His research focuses on the intersections between the presidency and American foreign policy. He is the author of *Resowing the Seeds of War: Presidential Peace Rhetoric Since 1945* (Michigan State University Press, 2021) and has published in *Rhetoric and Public Affairs*, *Western Journal of Communication*, *Southern Communication Journal*, and more.

Mark Hlavacik is Associate Professor of Communication Studies at the University of North Texas, where he studies controversies over education and education over controversies. He is the author of *Assigning Blame: The Rhetoric of Education Reform* (Harvard Education Press, 2016) and articles in academic journals in the disciplines of communication and education. His current work on controversies over education includes a book about controversial social studies curricula from the 1970s to the present. His current work on education over controversies includes a research conference funded by the American Education Research Association to develop critical approaches to inquiry-based social studies instruction.

Davis W. Houck is Fannie Lou Hamer Professor of Rhetorical Studies at Florida State University. His most recent book is *Black Bodies in the River: Searching for Freedom Summer*, published in 2022 by the University Press of Mississippi. His documentary work includes *Fannie Lou Hamer's America*, which won the 2022 International Documentary Association's "Best TV Feature Documentary" award.

Brandon Inabinet is Professor of Communication Studies at Furman University. His publications in *Southern Communication Journal*, *Rhetoric and Public Affairs*, and *Rhetoric Society Quarterly* include analyses of eighteenth- and nineteenth-century American political texts and controversies. This historical scholarship links to efforts to create reparative frameworks for past injustices, including his book *Reconstructing Southern Rhetoric* (coauthored with Christina L. Moss) and chairing the Task Force on Slavery and Justice at Furman University, with its report "Seeking Abraham." Inabinet serves on the steering committee of Universities Studying Slavery.

Rebecca Oliver is a Lecturer at Auburn University. She studies rhetoric and political discourse at the intersection of ideology and is concerned with asking how ideology is communicated and constructed within discourse about identities. Specifically, she focuses on how political figures construct identities for themselves and their constituencies using scapegoating and constitutive rhetoric in war discourse.

Jelte Olthof is Assistant Professor in the American Studies Department at the University of Groningen. His research focuses on US political, legal, and environmental rhetoric from the founding to the present. His publications include *Profiles in Power: Personality, Persona and the U.S. President* (edited with Maarten Zwiers; Brill, 2020) and "More Than the Penman: John Dickinson as Orator" (forthcoming). He is currently working with Mark Thompson on a digital humanities project called H-Gear: Historiographing the Era of the American Revolution, which studies the political discourse of the founding era.

Mary E. Stuckey is Edwin Erle Sparks Professor of Communication Arts & Sciences at Pennsylvania State University. She specializes in political and presidential rhetoric, political communication, and American Indian politics. She is the author, editor, or coeditor of seventeen books and author or coauthor of roughly a hundred essays and book chapters. She has served as editor of the *Southern Communication Journal*, as editor of the *Quarterly Journal of Speech*, and as interim editor of *Rhetoric and Public Affairs*.

MaryAnn Trasciatti is Professor of Rhetoric and Director of Labor Studies at Hofstra University. She is coeditor (with Edvige Giunta) of *Talking to the Girls: Intimate and Political Essays on the Triangle Shirtwaist Factory Fire* and (with Robert Forrant) *Where Are the Workers? Labor's Stories at Museums and Historical Sites*. She is finishing a book on the civil liberties activism of Irish American radical labor organizer Elizabeth Gurley Flynn.

Scott J. Varda is Associate Professor of Communication at Baylor University. His work analyzes political rhetoric and emphasizes questions of race, class, gender, social movements, misinformation, and extremism. He publishes in a wide variety of communication journals and has authored expert testimony for congressional hearings concerning the Sovereign Citizen Movement. Among his current projects are books on the Moorish Science Temple of America, as well as a book (coauthored with Leslie A. Hahner) on media representations and rape culture.

Christopher J. Wernecke is Assistant Professor in the Department of Communication Studies at the University of North Carolina Wilmington. In addition to Dr. Wernecke's research interests in political rhetoric, history, and popular culture that motivated his and Dr. Burnette's contribution to this volume, his research interests also include health and medicine rhetorics. Inspired by his own experience as a young cancer patient, Dr. Wernecke's dissertation, "Rhetorics of Cancer in America," reveals and critiques the constitutive consequences of American cancer rhetoric across discursive and nondiscursive modalities. His research can also be found in *Critical Studies in Media Communication*, *Communication and Democracy*, the *Howard Journal of Communications*, the *Journal of Contemporary Rhetoric*, the *Western Journal of Communication*, and the *Southern Communication Journal*.

Amy (Anna M.) Young is Professor of Communication at Pacific Lutheran University. Her work examines how experts use rhetorical style to reach wider, typically non-expert publics in order to solve pressing social problems. Her work has been published in *Quarterly Journal of Speech*, *Communication and Critical/Cultural Studies*, *Rhetoric Society Quarterly*, and *Women's Studies in Communication*. Her book *Prophets, Pundits amd Gurus: Rhetorical Styles and Public Engagement* traces a series of public intellectuals in different fields to understand how they are able to connect with non-expert publics to advance political and social engagement.

INDEX

Other books in the series:

Karen Tracy, *Challenges of Ordinary Democracy: A Case Study in Deliberation and Dissent* / Volume 1

Samuel McCormick, *Letters to Power: Public Advocacy Without Public Intellectuals* / Volume 2

Christian Kock and Lisa S. Villadsen, eds., *Rhetorical Citizenship and Public Deliberation* / Volume 3

Jay P. Childers, *The Evolving Citizen: American Youth and the Changing Norms of Democratic Engagement* / Volume 4

Dave Tell, *Confessional Crises and Cultural Politics in Twentieth-Century America* / Volume 5

David Boromisza-Habashi, *Speaking Hatefully: Culture, Communication, and Political Action in Hungary* / Volume 6

Arabella Lyon, *Deliberative Acts: Democracy, Rhetoric, and Rights* / Volume 7

Lyn Carson, John Gastil, Janette Hartz-Karp, and Ron Lubensky, eds., *The Australian Citizens' Parliament and the Future of Deliberative Democracy* / Volume 8

Christa J. Olson, *Constitutive Visions: Indigeneity and Commonplaces of National Identity in Republican Ecuador* / Volume 9

Damien Smith Pfister, *Networked Media, Networked Rhetorics: Attention and Deliberation in the Early Blogosphere* / Volume 10

Katherine Elizabeth Mack, *From Apartheid to Democracy: Deliberating Truth and Reconciliation in South Africa* / Volume 11

Mary E. Stuckey, *Voting Deliberatively: FDR and the 1936 Presidential Campaign* / Volume 12

Robert Asen, *Democracy, Deliberation, and Education* / Volume 13

Shawn J. Parry-Giles and David S. Kaufer, *Memories of Lincoln and the Splintering of American Political Thought* / Volume 14

J. Michael Hogan, Jessica A. Kurr, Michael J. Bergmaier, and Jeremy D. Johnson, eds., *Speech and Debate as Civic Education* / Volume 15

Angela G. Ray and Paul Stob, eds., *Thinking Together: Lecturing, Learning, and Difference in the Long Nineteenth Century* / Volume 16

Sharon E. Jarvis and Soo-Hye Han, *Votes That Count and Voters Who Don't: How Journalists Sideline Electoral Participation (Without Even Knowing It)* / Volume 17

Belinda Stillion Southard, *How to Belong: Women's Agency in a Transnational World* / Volume 18

Melanie Loehwing, *Homeless Advocacy and the Rhetorical Construction of the Civic Home* / Volume 19

Kristy Maddux, *Practicing Citizenship: Women's Rhetoric at the 1893 Chicago World's Fair* / Volume 20

Craig Rood, *After Gun Violence: Deliberation and Memory in an Age of Political Gridlock* / Volume 21

Nathan Crick, *Dewey for a New Age of Fascism: Teaching Democratic Habits* / Volume 22

William Keith and Robert Danisch, *Beyond Civility: The Competing Obligations of Citizenship* / Volume 23

Lisa A. Flores, *Deportable and Disposable: Public Rhetoric and the Making of the "Illegal" Immigrant* / Volume 24

Adriana Angel, Michael L. Butterworth, and Nancy R. Gómez, eds., *Rhetorics of Democracy in the Americas* / Volume 25

Robert Asen, *School Choice and the Betrayal of Democracy: How Market-Based Education Reform Fails Our Communities* / Volume 26

Stephanie R. Larson, *What It Feels Like: Visceral Rhetoric and the Politics of Rape Culture* / Volume 27

Billie Murray, *Combating Hate: A Framework for Direct Action* / Volume 28

David A. Frank and Franics J. Mootz III, eds., *The Rhetoric of Judging Well: The Conflicted Legacy of Justice Anthony M. Kennedy* / Volume 29

Kristian Bjørkdahl, ed., *The Problematic Public: Lippman, Dewey, and Democracy in the Twenty-First Century* / Volume 30

Ekaterina V. Haskins, *Remembering the War, Forgetting the Terror: Appeals to Family Memory in Putin's Russia* / Volume 31

Carolyn D. Commer, *Championing a Public Good: A Call to Advocate for Higher Education* / Volume 32

Derek G. Handley, *Struggle for the City: Citizenship and Resistance in the Black Freedom Movement* / Volume 33

José G. Izaguirre III, *Becoming La Raza: Negotiating Race in the Chican@ Movement(s)* / Volume 34

Mónica Brito Vieira, *Democracy and the Politics of Silence* / Volume 35